Understanding the Women
of Mozart's Operas

Understanding the Women of Mozart's Operas

Kristi Brown-Montesano

UNIVERSITY OF CALIFORNIA PRESS
Berkeley · Los Angeles · London
OCM 65204973

University of California Press, one of the most
distinguished university presses in the United States,
enriches lives around the world by advancing
scholarship in the humanities, social sciences, and
natural sciences. Its activities are supported by the UC
Press Foundation and by philanthropic contributions
from individuals and institutions. For more
information, visit www.ucpress.edu.

University of California Press
Berkeley and Los Angeles, California

University of California Press, Ltd.
London, England

Library of Congress Cataloging-in-Publication Data

Brown-Montesano, Kristi, 1963–.
    Understanding the women of Mozart's operas /
Kristi Brown-Montesano.
        p.   cm.
    Includes bibliographical references and index.
    ISBN-13 978-0-520-24802-1 (cloth : alk. paper)
    ISBN-10 0-520-24802-3 (cloth : alk. paper)
    1. Mozart, Wolfgang Amadeus, 1756-1791.
Operas.   2. Operas—Characters.   3. Women in
opera.   I. Title.
    ML410.M9B8195   2007
    782.1092—dc22   2006009348

Manufactured in the United States of America

15   14   13   12   11   10   09   08   07   06
10   9   8   7   6   5   4   3   2   1

This book is printed on New Leaf EcoBook 50, a
100% recycled fiber of which 50% is de-inked post-
consumer waste, processed chlorine-free. EcoBook 50
is acid-free and meets the minimum requirements of
ANSI/ASTM D5634–01 (Permanence of Paper).

To B.
"un uom d'ottimo core"

And to S., C., and G.
"schön, hold, und weise"

Contents

Acknowledgments

My fascination with the female characters of Mozart's operas has followed me through several life stages, beginning with my days as a graduate student at U.C. Berkeley. I am indebted to my many mentors and contemporaries there and also at U.C. Davis and UCLA, including Wendy Allanbrook, Andrew Dell'Antonio, Greg Dubinsky, Joseph Kerman, Peter Mercer-Taylor, Mitchell Morris, David Nutter, Judith Peraino, Christopher and Alessa Reynolds, Stephen Rumph, David Schneider, Robynn Stilwell, Richard Taruskin, James Turner, and Maria Luisa Vilar-Payà, who influenced my fundamental approach and offered numerous insights. I am especially beholden to Daniel Heartz—whose encouragement and astonishing knowledge of everything Mozart sent me off in the right direction—and to Elisabeth Le Guin, whose illuminating comments on a late version of the manuscript clarified the "big picture" issues and galvanized my final revisions.

The nitty-gritty of process of turning a manuscript into a published book surely would have stalled without the amazing skill and intuition of acquisitions editor Mary Francis, who knew just when it was time to talk me down from panic or nudge me along to the next step. I was also fortunate to have the excellent direction of production editor Kate Warne and the marvelous copyediting skills of Sharron Wood, to whom I am truly grateful.

Throughout my work on this project I have been supported and energized by a miraculously faithful, perceptive, and kind group of friends and family members, several of whom have followed this project since it was merely a notion in my head. My love and gratitude goes to Ken and Marlene Brown, Barbara Estes, Robert Fink, Maurizio Motolese, John and Linda Oery, Marcelyn Voorhees, Robert Voorhees[†], and, especially, Michael Zwiebach and Kimberly Fox, the godfather and godmother of what we have jokingly referred to as my "fourth child." I also want to express my appreciation to my colleagues and students at the Colburn Conservatory and School of Performing Arts, who rooted for me all the way, forgiving an increasing emotional and mental instability as I approached the finish line.

Finally, to my husband, Bruno Montesano, and my children, Caterina, Stefano, and Giovanni: it would be impossible to thank you enough for all that you have given to me. *Voi siete la casa del mio cuore, il posto dove capisco il significato della mia vita.*

Overture

What is your book about? Most authors, I imagine, have to face this difficult question repeatedly during the long process of writing a manuscript. In my case, the stock answer was "It's a critical study of the female characters of the Mozart–Da Ponte operas and *The Magic Flute.*" Frequently, this response satisfied questioners' curiosity (or frightened them away), but on other occasions it led to dialogue or even to a passionate debate. The subject of that debate often depended on who was doing the asking. I have been lucky enough to share ideas with opera fans, occasional listeners, singers, directors, producers, students, and musicologists. All of them had concerns that reflected their particular relationship to opera, with varying degrees of emphasis on performance, listening and viewing, and scholarship. These exchanges not only helped me to refine my ideas, but they also illuminated an amazingly diverse audience. It is my hope that the essays in this book will stimulate further dialogue *with* and *between* this broad group of readers, which consists of anyone who is seriously interested in Mozart's operas. The chapter on Donna Elvira, for instance, has something to say to

- the soprano who is studying the role
- the director who is staging *Don Giovanni*
- the opera-goer who has already seen the work numerous times

- the educator who is teaching a music/humanities course
- the student of women's studies who is also a new listener

as well as the expert musicologist. Taken together, the chapters offer a big-picture view of Mozart's representations of women and a variety of sociocultural issues. The chapters are also, however, written to stand alone, allowing readers to follow their interests.

Of course, the issue of audience—*who* I am writing for—raises another vital question: "*why* am I writing this book?" In a very basic sense, my book is about stating the obvious, looking squarely at the issues that arise when an old and revered work of art exists in a contemporary world. Two "case studies" will serve to illustrate what I mean. The first ("Professor X versus the Opera Company") compares two different perspectives on the "right" way to present a well-loved opera to an audience. The second ("Out of the Mouths of Babes") underlines the critical concerns raised by a small child's response to her first operatic experience. Both stories illustrate some part of what I see as the most pressing issues with respect to Mozart's canonical stage works for today's opera lovers—including audiences, performers, scholars, critics, administrators, and directors—and for anyone who is interested in the conjunction of art, education, and culture.

PROFESSOR X VERSUS THE OPERA COMPANY

The first tale concerns an acquaintance of mine—a musicologist and university professor—who was asked to write program notes for a production of *Die Zauberflöte*. The major opera company in charge of the production had given Professor X the green light to write about political content, such as the work's association with the ideology and practices of eighteenth-century Freemasonry. Knowing that his colleagues at the university had written provocative notes on cultural and political issues for this same organization, Professor X decided to address obvious challenges that *Die Zauberflöte* presents to contemporary audiences, including its misogynistic and racist content, the "uncomfortable mix of pretentiously serious subject matter and clownish, hackneyed stage business," and the opera's "curiously exclusionary account of enlightenment political ideals." Professor X also wanted to consider the relevance of such a treasured work to our culture, refuting the idea that the music somehow transcended this discourse:

If we hold on to *The Magic Flute* because of its almost impossibly ingratiating music, we should not be blind to how insistently that music lends its persuasive power to all manner of objectionable situations and attitudes, virtually compelling us to be charmed into an accepting alignment with them. The democratic ideals of *The Magic Flute* are [for instance] configured along rather undemocratically hierarchical lines: noble white males might succeed despite their obvious inadequacies, but second-order beings (well-behaved women and commoners) are redeemed only through their association with successful noble white males, while those on the bottom rung (blacks and ambitious women) will inevitably betray whatever privileges they have been accorded. . . . Moreover—and this is the crux of the matter—the intimate ways in which the music of *The Magic Flute* invests in this hierarchy are precisely why we want to return again and again to the opera, warts and all.

In response, the opera company cordially, but emphatically, rejected this version of the notes, asking Professor X to make them more positive. It is worth quoting some of their e-mailed comments:

Para 2: we don't want to begin the article on a negative tone . . . speaking of "voiced objections." Again, this is a work that many opera-goers love & know well, and they have invested a lot in coming to the opera. We want to ensure that they enjoy every aspect of their experience. If we can start the article off with what is positive or exciting or complex about the opera without getting into race or stereotypes, that would be good.

Para 5: again—if we can frame the opera in a more positive light . . . take out mention of "this flawed package, problematic political allegory, pretentiousness, and overabundant dissonances." It doesn't really make sense in a program book to speak against a work we have decided to produce.

Para 6: if it can just be reworked to take out mention of problematic politics.

Para 7: if we can finish with something more neutral or even uplifting, leaving out mention of injustices and imperfections. People are also interested in feeling like their view of Mozart's "perfection" is justified.

Though Professor X attempted a revision, he and the opera company never could settle on a version acceptable to both parties. It is easy to understand why. Bound by principles of effective marketing and "customer service" (essential to the business of opera production), the company wanted to ensure that its patrons enjoyed their evening, undisturbed by polemics. Professor X was more interested in a serious engagement with all aspects of this great work. From his viewpoint, the work contains hot-button elements that intelligent opera-goers cannot miss, so why not deal with them? Baffled by the opera company's resistance, he observed, "It would be hard to imagine a major production of Shakespeare's *Merchant of Venice* that did not devote some of its program to a discussion of Shylock and attempt to relate Shakespeare's stereotypical Jewish moneylender to anti-Semitism in both Shakespeare's time and our own."

Is It Okay to "Read" an Opera?

Any artist or institution involved in opera production certainly has a tough time of it these days. Funds are always an issue, ticket prices must remain high to support costly productions, and the genre itself is regularly knocked as a cultural joke or, increasingly, ignored altogether. In an attempt to keep up with the times, current opera marketing materials play up the sex, violence, and other mature content of the genre— but only up to a point. The goal is to sell tickets, not to problematize a work's status as transcendent and edifying "high art." Opera audiences have been exposed to a lot of gimmicky "updated" productions in recent decades; at the same time, however, they have been kept remarkably sheltered from the kind of genuinely critical discussions that have surrounded opera from its infancy and which are a regular part of discourses on theater, popular music, television, and film. With the steady aging (and concomitant conservative tastes) of the opera-going public, the opera company's cautious approach is understandable but not necessarily in the best long-term interests of either the artwork or its audience. Unflaggingly positive program notes may go down easily, but who says that an audience needs or wants this kind of blind optimism all the time? In reality, the opera company's ultra-protective attitude risks making a work like *The Magic Flute*—at least in production and reception— dramatically *static,* something that Mozart would surely have disliked. Conflict and ambiguity abound in his operas and are a big part of why we continue to be fascinated by them as *performed* art works, not just musical museum pieces.

Scholarly reception, too, exhibits its own brand of apprehensive protectiveness toward canonic operas, for reasons that are related to but slightly different from the ones put forth by the opera company. In the preface to *In Search of Opera,* Carolyn Abbate elegantly describes the anxieties surrounding the debate about ontological distinctions between the musical "work" and its "production." She observes that opera "in a curious way needs a defense against performance (including staging) and not just against bad performances, because in defending opera against performance, we defend it against the sense that something is being lost to us," adding that the possibility that an opera might "acquire alternative histories constituted by . . . adaptations and stagings . . . is a threat that many scholars regard with horror."[1] The uneasiness surrounding the tangled relationship between the work and its performance logically extends to the critical literature, which promotes "alternate histories" insofar as it influences performed interpretation and audience appreciation.

In the Cambridge Opera Handbook on *Die Zauberflöte*, for instance, Peter Branscombe admonishes us to be careful not to ruin the experience of the "genuine" work with what he judges to be external and irrelevant cultural baggage. Bemoaning the license that many productions take with *Die Zauberflöte*, he hopes that we, like him, deem that "the most faithful, least obtrusive reading gives the greatest pleasure."[2] Branscombe plays down the issue of slavery and the way that women are "disadvantaged and looked down upon," protesting that "it is unhelpful to judge these matters in our own times," for Sarastro's world represents "not a paradise on earth but a still-developing society."[3] He emphasizes *Die Zauberflöte*'s lasting popularity, explaining that although the opera has "always been a controversial work" and the "object of heated scholarly debate and critical comment," the "ordinary opera-goer does not find it difficult to come to terms with."[4]

Branscombe demonstrates a two-front defense strategy that is common in the reception literature on Mozart's *Die Zauberflöte* and other controversial works. He stresses that 1) these works represent a *historic* context and should be understood primarily in these terms; and 2) at the same time, they are *ageless* masterpieces that merit our highest esteem and continued patronage. Bruce Alan Brown's Cambridge Opera Handbook on *Così fan tutte* presents another good example of this reasoning. Brown states that a "degree of familiarity with eighteenth-century culture in general" is important to fully understanding the opera, adding that "the times in which such a work as *Così* might be created are long past." In the conclusion of his analysis, however, he claims that the opera "fascinates and teaches in direct proportion to its complexity, ambiguity, and *timelessness*."[5] Clearly, there is some truth to both of these statements. However, when the historic/ageless dichotomy is wielded as a defensive axiom—the final answer to sticky issues of reception—further discussion is difficult if not impossible. For instance, if we suggest that *Così fan tutte* presents outmoded (and offensive) ideas, we are reminded that it is from a "time long past"; if we then question its continued cultural relevance, we are directed to its timeless beauty and edifying final moral. A little ethical gravity à la Branscombe helps to succeed in this critical balancing act: it is potentially *harmful* to judge the work with reference to "our own time."

Is It Okay to Question Mozart?

As the opera company's comments to Professor X suggested, some of their defensiveness was related to the opera's composer, the beloved Mozart. In an opinion piece published in the *New York Times* in 1990, "Why Mozart Has Become an Icon for Today," Richard Taruskin comments on various critical approaches to identifying the "real" Mozart and the meaning of his works, particularly during the period leading up to the 1991 bicentennial of his death.[6] Among other things, he discusses the revival of "Romantic Mozart worship" in the prose of Charles Rosen, as well as the modern trend of demystification, evident in writings as divergent as Wolfgang Hildesheimer's revisionist biography and Susan McClary's pioneering feminist analyses. Counterbalancing these "interpretive" treatments were the "historical" studies, of which Taruskin cites Neal Zaslaw's *Mozart's Symphonies: Context, Performance, Practice, Reception* as an example. Zaslaw's rigorous scholarship rejected in their entirety the misguided assessments of present-day criticism of Mozart's symphonies, claiming that the authentic significance of Mozart's works could only be recovered with careful consideration and analysis of their original context.

A long-time skeptic of "authenticity" in performance practice as promoted by the so-called early-music movement, Taruskin proposes that such traditions are as much a matter of modern taste as historical tradition. He also questions the critical validity of a "historically authentic meaning" of a piece of music, since "it rests on the implicit assumption, still regnant in the musical academy, that the meaning of an artwork is complete at the time of creation, and that the passage of time entails nothing but loss of meaning. Tradition, in this view, is only noise and distortion, a cosmic game of 'telephone'."[7] Taruskin offers an alternative view in which contexts "are not simply lost but changed," and suggests that this change of context "adds as much meaning as it may take away." He uses Mozart's *Don Giovanni* as an example:

> For us today, *Don Giovanni*, say, is not just the opera Mozart and da Ponte knew, bearing only the meanings it had for them and for the audience that

greeted it in Prague two centuries ago. *Don Giovanni* is also something
E. T. A. Hoffmann has known and construed, and Kierkegaard, and
Charles Rosen, and Peter Sellars. Its meaning for us is mediated by all that
has been thought and said about it since opening night, and is therefore in-
comparably richer than it was in 1787. Reconstruction of the original
meaning, assuming it could be recaptured pure, should add its valuable
mite to the pile, but cannot replace it. For that, were it possible, would be
an impoverishment.[8]

Don Giovanni is more than an artifact that exists in our time; it is an
accumulation, a *continuing history.* This idea becomes even more vertiginous if we admit that reception in all its forms—performances, writings,
lectures—potentially affects a work's identity and cultural value. This
open exchange is frightening, but the alternative is a kind of censorship,
filtering out controversy in order to "protect" the work. Many scholars
and music lovers—like the opera company in the tale of Professor X—
worry too much about how *Die Zauberflöte* and other favorites will survive if left unshielded in an age of litigation and political correctness.
Avoiding debate goes against much of the spirit of opera, which, at its
best, has always been both entertaining and provocative. This is no less
true at a time when most of our operatic repertoire is not contemporary.
Even at its premiere, for instance, *Die Zauberflöte* was a socio-political-
philosophical manifesto costumed as a fairytale. The opera has not
changed, but perspective has. Today, just as in the past, performers and
audiences must deal with the fact that the opera casts a black slave, a
widow, and three unattached women as the "bad guys" and celebrates
their demise for reasons that are not as persuasive today as they may have
been in the late eighteenth century. This does not require scrapping the
opera, however, or reducing it to an example of "political incorrectness."
We must deal, though, with disjunctions between the past and the present if we want to have an honest, culturally relevant appreciation for the
whole work, including its not-so-pretty elements. Abbate neatly sums up
the critical challenge of reconciling the work and its accumulated meanings, that is, the need to "embrace and acknowledge the perils of interpretation, while remaining aware of two historical contexts," namely
"that of the music, and that of my own interpretive claims."[9]

Breaking with Convention without Breaking the Work

Analyzing Peter Sellars's (in)famous staging of *Così fan tutte,* Mary
Hunter engages with this same basic idea, weighing the effects of this

convergence between a particular "interpretive claim" and the original notated object. She cites the philosophical theories of Roman Ingarden, who theorizes the musical work as both "schema" (i.e., the score) and the "intersubjective, dominant aesthetic object" that is "the equivalent . . . of the . . . opinions of the musical public in a given country at a given time."[10] Hunter proposes that it is precisely this "commonly understood but historically variable *Così*—the range of meanings that Sellars's contemporaries and elders have attached to this text—against which Sellars performs."[11] His production abandons many of the "historical" components of the opera, which some scholars might argue are essential to proper understanding. Although the result is not wholly successful, Sellars's postmodern vision clearly marks the difference between historical traditions and contemporary culture, inspiring a new understanding of both. His psychological treatment of Despina, for example, made Hunter more conscious of the ways in which eighteenth-century opera buffa conventions run contrary to late-twentieth-century thought on representation, raising "fascinating questions about the historical and sociopolitical responsibilities and obligations of performance and about the relations between those obligations."[12]

Together with Gretchen Wheelock and Wye Jamison Allanbrook, Hunter revisits the issue of performance responsibility in "Staging Mozart's Women." The authors focus specifically on two arias—Konstanze's "Martern aller Arten" and Zerlina's "Batti, batti"—but the questions they raise in the introductory remarks are generally applicable to the arias and characters explored in this book:

> Both arias explore or express something about the nature of female power in the late eighteenth century, and what they have to say raises interesting questions for staging. Is it a salutary discomfort they may induce? Should producers and singers "do something" about it, and if so what? How does the act of performance endorse, undercut, or relate in any way to the dramatic and social content of the work? And ultimately, what is the responsibility of those who put on Mozart's opera to take and "perform" a position on their values? Can a performance resist? Should a performance endorse? How separate should the actual performer be from the performance of a (distasteful) role?[13]

These crucial questions reach beyond the strict definition of "staging," implicating the fields of criticism and education. In a sense, the three essays in "Staging Mozart's Women" are not only thoughtful proposals for performance of these two arias, but also abbreviated performances themselves. In the final analysis, anyone who studies and writes about a work shares the responsibility that Hunter assigns to actual production. The class lecture, newspaper column, pre-concert presentation, program note, and musicological essay or book—all of these things potentially influence singers, directors, spectators, and students and thus help to shape the rapport between artwork and audience. The ethical burden of this influence is considerable, which brings me to my second story.

OUT OF THE MOUTHS OF BABES

In her vanguard study *Opera, or the Undoing of Women,* Catherine Clément urges us to pay attention to the words and stories of opera, to reckon with the whole experience. She admits that opera attracts her independent of the words, but adds that when she knows "the words, the passions, what is at stake, then opera wraps me totally in a world of fantastic clarity, of matchless life. The music is then revealed in all its richness. There are two irreconcilable options, two irreconcilable ways of living—and living opera: understanding it or not; enjoying the effects of all the actual implications or being satisfied with what is not known."[14] She proposes that, in opera, "the forgetting of words, the forgetting of women, have the same deep roots. Reading the texts, more than listening at the mercy of an adored voice, I found to my fear and horror, words that kill, words that told every time of a woman's undoing." At the close of the introduction, she suggests that she is addressing her essay, at least in part, to her son, Michel; he is also the book's co-dedicatee, together with Claude Lévi-Strauss. Michel has not yet been to the opera, but Clément believes that someday he will, and so she offers him guidance. "He is a young man," she writes. "This is for him so that, when the time comes, he will love differently; so that the music and the words will be clear to him; so that his pleasure will be all the greater because he can understand the opera's story and history, and that of past centuries."[15]

Clément's desire to share opera—her passion—with her son, to guide him into the world of opera and help him understand its complex beauty and dangerous undercurrents, resonates strongly with me. My own daughter Caterina had her first experience with opera when she was only four years old. The event was not planned. I had just begun to watch Bergman's film version of *Die Zauberflöte* for a project when Caterina sat next to me, eyes glued to the television. To help her understand, I identified the characters as they entered, giving the most basic preschool version of the subtitles. She watched fairly quietly, with only a few intermittent comments. Suddenly, during the finale, she turned to me and asked a simply amazing question: "Is the Queen a good lady or a bad lady?"

Sarastro said the Queen of the Night was bad, but Caterina was not sure. Neither was I. Looking at her puzzled face, I realized that even if I read her the entire libretto, she would not necessarily be satisfied. More questions followed. "Why did the man take the princess from her mamma?" "Why did they send the Queen away instead of making friends with her?" Obviously, a preschooler cannot comprehend the subtleties of sexual and social politics, but Caterina's misgivings are not just toddler naiveté. I share them and would venture to guess that many audience members do as well, at least until they are told that such concerns are irrelevant.

I do not want for my children or my students to merely "enjoy every aspect of their [operatic] experience," as the above-mentioned opera company would have them do. Naturally, I want them to take pleasure in the gorgeous voices, the fusion of music and drama, and the stagecraft and artistry. However, I do not want to protect them from the uncomfortable, because there is gratification in thinking seriously about these aspects, pleasure in seeing the whole work, both its perfect lines and crooked fractures, and allowing yourself to be enthralled at one moment and to resist the next. It is not a matter of critical petulance, some ideological need to go against the grain. It is a preference to be fully aware of both the historical and the current reality of a work, and also the *responsibility* involved in "reading" it.

Striking the Ethical Balance

This is precisely what Wayne Booth describes as the primary aim of what might be called "ethical" or "evaluative" criticism: not suppression or wholesale rejection of canonical works, but "any effort to show how the virtues of narratives relate to the virtues of selves and societies, or how the ethos of any story affects or is affected by the ethos—the collection of virtues—of any given reader."[16] Booth's speculation on the idea of ethical criticism was motivated by his own discomfort with an African-American colleague's refusal to teach *Huckleberry Finn*. Booth himself found much to be praised in Twain's work, but he was unable to dismiss his colleague's sincere, intelligent objection. Exploring the idea of "an ethics of fiction," Booth defines it in terms of what the sincere reader owes to the work of art, to him- or herself, and to other readers. He asks, "If I am to give myself generously, must I not also accept the responsibility to enter into serious dialogue with the author about how his or her values join or conflict with mine? To decline the gambit, to remain passive in the face of the author's strongest passions and deepest convictions is surely condescending, insulting, and finally irresponsible."[17]

Booth makes "a plea for engagement with the political questions that naturally spring from any serious thinking about the ethical powers of fictions."[18] Although he is mostly concerned with fictional works of literature, he also refers specifically to two of Mozart's operas—*Don Giovanni* and *Così fan tutte*—as examples of musical narratives that require this kind of conscionable critical assessment, the only way to preserve a healthy and mutually beneficial communion between the reader/audience and the work. Like Professor X, Booth draws a parallel with *The Merchant of Venice*, contending that if "there is anything questionable about Shakespeare's wonderful story of the cruel, miserly, revengeful Jew, or Mozart's ravishingly beautiful musical narrative, in *Così fan tutte*, of how two silly lovers manipulate, humiliate, and finally subdue two silly, fickle women, the answer is not to be found in isolation from our picture of what human life should or might be, or how it should be portrayed, or of what kinds of artistic experiences are worth having."[19]

Evaluating whether the Queen of the Night is a good lady or a bad lady—and the many other questions that arise with Mozart's representation of woman—I have kept before me Booth's challenge: to "honor an author's offering for what it is, in its full 'otherness' from me, *and* take an active critical stance against what seem to me its errors or excesses," pursuing an "ethics of self-culture in narrative, an ethics that entails both surrender and refusal."[20] Two related subcategories of Booth's umbrella of ethical criticism—feminist and reader-response criticism—have strongly influenced my own analyses of Mozart's female characters. Both stress the vital importance of evaluative reading, which, among other things, is dedicated to investigating and revealing the sociopolitical responsibilities of scholarship. In fact, when I started this study, I was primarily motivated by variations of what Sydney Janet Kaplan identifies as the two "origins" of feminist literary criticism, one that begins with the "recognition of our love for women writers," and another that is driven by "the urge to reveal the diverse ways women have been oppressed, misinterpreted and trivialized by the dominant patriarchal tradition, and to show how these are reflected in the images of women in the works of male authors."[21] Fundamentally, I wanted to "honor"—to use Booth's term—these characters by considering each as the primary *subject* of an analysis, not just as an element in a general

study of Mozart's operas or even of a specific opera. For my close readings I have considered a variety of elements that have contributed to the
accumulated meaning of these characters, including the music, libretto,
literary sources, historical factors, and reception history.

The literature on the operas was a major stimulus, insofar as it captures attitudes about characters that are frequently adopted in production. I perused scholarly texts, but also more popular writings, ones that
are commonly carried in opera gift shops and arts sections of general
bookstores. During my research I found numerous passages in the critical literature on Mozart's operas that "misinterpreted and trivialized"
the female characters to varying degrees, from simple inaccuracies (like
the mistaken claim that the Queen of the Night and Sarastro are an estranged couple) to glibly misogynistic fantasies like William Mann's "diagnosis" of Donna Anna as an old-school Freudian, "frigid and hysterical . . . victim of noble birth and puritanical upbringing," who "bursts
repeatedly into florid patter about her anger and the rascal's perfidy, so
much so that we others may believe her somewhat deranged."[22] I was
especially interested in the ways in which writers have perpetuated or,
more rarely, refuted inherited attitudes about the operas and the roles.
Not surprisingly, I discovered that critics tend not only to castigate or
praise particular characters, but also to castigate or praise them in particular ways.

MOZART'S MEN: THE HERO COMPLEX

Most of the misogynistic readings and many of the neutral ones as well
reflect a bias in favor of a male protagonist, especially Don Giovanni
(antimoralistic, convention-defying sensual man), Sarastro, (humanity-
loving, enlightened patriarch), and, to a lesser extent, Don Alfonso (rational pedagogue à la Rousseau). The reception literature of *Don Giovanni,* for example, has helped to create a mythic hero out of the
eponymous rake—originally an ambiguous figure at best. A cultural figure since at least the seventeenth century, Don Juan attained an enduring aesthetic appeal with Mozart's opera, which provoked rhapsodic
responses from literary notables like E. T. A. Hoffmann, Goethe, Kierkegaard, Shaw, and others. Too often, however, Mozart's willful, seductive, and violent protagonist has been rarified by idealization and
projection, credited with virtues—unflagging bravery, triumphant self-
determination, revolutionary resistance to oppressive societal power,
and sensual idealism—that are, at best, equivocally represented in the

opera, and are sometimes flatly contradicted. The Don has also served as the libidinous and eternally resourceful poster boy for centuries of restless (male) envy and self-indulgence masquerading as autonomy, transcendent vision, and unyielding personal power. .

Even interpreters who claim to avoid the subjective pitfalls of earlier reception traditions around Mozart's Don cannot resist a degree of reverential hype. Frits Noske—whose interpretation of the opera is allegedly "based on a study of historical data and on a close reading of the full score" and for which "anachronisms stemming from nineteenth- and early twentieth-century interpretations have been totally discarded"— nevertheless promotes Don Giovanni as "a man who is far superior to his fellowmen."[23] Noske sees the fundamental theme of the drama as "the Individual against Society" and describes Don Giovanni's activity as reflecting his quest for power against the existing social order and prescriptions. To this end, Don Giovanni attacks the most vulnerable point of the social system, "the relation between the sexes," conquering as many women as he can, though "this does not make him a sexomaniac." Noske argues that although Don Giovanni feels attracted to women, "his essential goal is power, or perhaps rather the consciousness of power." All of this makes him "an existentialist hero *avant la lettre;* he is a man who tries for total freedom to justify his existence, freedom that can only be realized by obtaining total power."[24]

In other words, Don Giovanni must take power away from the women he seduces or rapes in order to attain his own "liberty"—a slippery term, etymologically related to that less gallant concept, *libertine.* Indeed, the process of aestheticization focused on the figure of Don Giovanni has all but expunged the opera's original main title, the one that Mozart himself entered into his catalogue of works: *Il dissoluto punito,* or "the dissolute punished."[25] At the same time, the female characters of *Don Giovanni* have been interpreted primarily in terms of their relationship to the lionized Don: friend or foe, validation or obstacle. In the end, any woman who resists is suspect. In the words of Kierkegaard's fictional Mr. A, "a foolish girl it would be who would not choose to be unhappy for the sake of having once been happy with Don Juan."[26]

MOZART'S WOMEN: ANTI-(HERO)INES AND SISTERHOOD

Naturally, the premise that a main male protagonist—particularly Don Giovanni, Don Alfonso, or Sarastro—is fundamentally "positive" tends to skew critical interpretations of the other characters. Among the female

roles in Mozart's operas, Donna Anna, the Queen of the Night, and Despina have probably suffered the nastiest critical responses arising from
this bias, but even the popular women such as Pamina and Zerlina end
up being treated more as objects than subjects. I have chosen instead to
make each female character the central point, consciously considering
her as the "star" of the analysis and, within reason, the opera. Inspired
by the work of Clément, Abbate, Hunter, Allanbrook, Wheelock, and
McClary, among many others, I have attended to the characters' dramatic and musical components with equal seriousness. What might be
called the "feminist dimension" of my study is represented by two key
inquiries. First, I carefully investigate common assumptions about each
character's relationship to a critically favored "hero," exposing how
male-centered readings consistently oversimplify both the drama and the
character. In some cases I strongly refute prevailing interpretations; often
these have roots in sources other than the opera, including long-held social biases about women. Second, I focus on the alliances between the
women—bonds forged and bonds broken—primarily within each opera,
but also theoretical associations between characters of different operas.

To this end, the book is organized in two "acts." The first part,
"(Anti-)Heroines and Women on the Edge," deals with *Don Giovanni*
and *Die Zauberflöte*, which introduce us to two of Mozart's most complex and most maligned characters. Both Donna Anna and the Queen
of the Night (along with the Three Ladies) defy Enlightenment era and,
to some extent, contemporary ideas about appropriate female responses
to issues of power, sentiment, and revenge. The chapters on Donna
Elvira, Pamina, and Zerlina explore possible reasons as to why these
characters have been more favorably appreciated by critics and audiences and how their greater popularity may be tied to long-held definitions of a proper "heroine," addressing the issues of female isolation,
emotional dependency and fragility, and compliance. These two operas
also present very different scenarios regarding female alliances. Galvanized by Donna Elvira, potential female rivals come together against
their betrayer in *Don Giovanni*; in *Die Zauberflöte* the sacrosanct
mother-daughter attachment is ruptured.

The second part of the book, "Sisterly Alliances and Sisters Subverted," continues the investigation into female unity and disunity, with
a more precise focus on sisterly bonds, both social and biological. These
chapters consider how the relative stability or frailty of sisterhood affects the female characters and the final outcomes in *Le nozze di Figaro*
and *Così fan tutte*. As with *Don Giovanni* and *Die Zauberflöte*, there is

an oppositional pull between these two operas: in *Figaro* female friendships are forged and strengthened, saving the day, while in *Così* all bonds are suspect and easily forgotten. Accordingly, I have paired the Countess Almaviva and Susanna, as well as Fiordiligi and Dorabella, within single chapters; the individual chapters on Marcellina and Despina also deal with how these characters fit into and sway the dynamic of female unity.

Other themes that run through this book are reflected in the titles of each chapter. The servant Despina and peasant Zerlina, both acting within and against the constraints of their low social status, highlight the issue of class. The Queen of the Night and Donna Anna are different types of female avengers. Elvira, too, fits into this category, though her fundamental identity is the abandoned woman. Pamina represents the ideal woman in the Masonic-influenced utopia of *Die Zauberflöte,* but she also stands apart from other women; a good wife and daughter, she is elevated primarily because of her allegiance to patriarchal authority (father and husband) and a male community. The chapters on Marcellina and the Three Ladies examine Enlightenment definitions of femininity and how these characters illuminate the boundaries between social approval and social alienation, boundaries to which women of the eighteenth century were particularly vulnerable. Together these essays celebrate a dazzling spectrum of woman, who in Mozart's works is sometimes undone, but rarely promises to stay that way.

(Anti-)Heroines and Women on the Edge

CHAPTER I

Feminine Vengeance I: The Assailed/Assailant

Donna Anna

That's when things got out of control / She didn't want to, he had his way / She said, "Let's go" / He said, "No way!" / Come on babe, it's your lucky day. / Shut your mouth, we're gonna do it my way.

Sublime, "Date Rape"

"Don't hope, unless you kill me, that I will ever let you escape" (1.1): with these words, Donna Anna responds to Giovanni's criminal trespass, vowing that she will bring him into custody or else die in the effort.[1] Though many of the characters chase after Giovanni at one moment or another during the course of the opera and eventually band together, Donna Anna is the first to articulate the idea of this pursuit. And while Donna Elvira sings about cutting out Giovanni's heart, it is Anna whose desire for vindication remains constant throughout the opera. Recounting to Don Ottavio the violent details of Don Giovanni's nocturnal visit to her room, Anna encapsulates perfectly her function in the drama: "I boldly follow him right into the street to stop him, and, assailed, I become assailant" (1.13). Donna Anna's haunted and haunting presence throughout the opera challenges spectators, performers, and scholars

I

alike. Her dual role—as both grieving victim and clarion-voiced agent of retribution—is one of many factors that keep *Don Giovanni* from fitting comfortably into the comic-opera category. From the violence and on-stage homicide of the *introduzione* to the final images of death and eternal damnation, this opera challenges the pleasure-oriented conventions of late-eighteenth-century opera buffa. And, in fact, *Don Giovanni*—the second Mozart–Da Ponte collaboration—boasts a dual heritage: it relies upon both the traditions of late-eighteenth-century opera buffa and the Don Juan story itself, a morality tale that was already more than 150 years old by the time Da Ponte and Mozart fashioned their own version. The figure of Donna Anna, too, is firmly rooted in this Don Juan tradition, and represents one of the legend's earliest heroines. Likewise, in Mozart's operas, she is a heroic component. Doubly injured by Don Giovanni's aggression, Donna Anna grips us with her seriousness; from the opening *introduzione,* she implores us to witness her tragic circumstances. Unlike so many other blue-blooded ladies of opera buffa, however, Anna is not frozen in *seria* stasis in the middle of comic flurry. Rather, from her first appearance she staggers and bolts into emotional extremes that are fully justified by the tragic events of her life. Ravished and robbed of her father, Donna Anna injects fresh psychological possibilities into a formula-ridden genre.

It is puzzling, then, that many critics have reduced her, for the most part, to some form of the "hero's enemy"—the repressed hypocrite, vengeful harpy, or humorless ice princess. In most cases this critical hostility stems from two distinct but related biases about what is appropriately "feminine" in opera (and perhaps also in the real world). First, there is the issue of Donna Anna's demand for retribution, which, however justified, sets her apart from the sentimentally selfless and endlessly lenient feminine ideal so prevalent in the operatic canon. Second, Mozart and Da Ponte do not fully expose Anna's amorous "soft" side, even in her exchanges with her betrothed, Don Ottavio, leading commentators to generate theories about her "real" feelings about Don Giovanni. Before introducing the main proponents of the ironic, hidden-passion reading of Anna's character, it would be useful to consider Donna Anna's literary predecessors in earlier versions of the Don Juan story, some of which evidently influenced Da Ponte's libretto. I have selected a few of the most important sources, each of which paints not only the Donna Anna character type, but also her relationship with the most famous lothario in history in a different shade.

DONNA ANNA BEFORE DA PONTE:
(EN)COUNTERING DON GIOVANNI

In Tirso de Molina's *El burlador de Sevilla y convidado de piedra* (1616?)—generally recognized as the original Don Juan story—there are two characters who might be seen as Donna Anna's earliest ancestors. The first, Duchess Isabela, is betrothed to Duke Octavio. The play opens with her bidding a discreet goodnight to a man she believes to be her fiancé. Perhaps nervous about having risked an amorous premarital tryst—a venturesome activity for a young noblewoman in seventeenth-century Spain—Isabela seeks assurance:

> *Isabela.* Will you honor me with truths, promises and offerings, gifts and compliments, good will and friendship?
> *D. Juan.* Yes, my dear.
> *Isabela.* I wish to have a light.
> *D. Juan.* But why?
> *Isabela.* So that my soul may confirm what it is about to enjoy.
> *D. Juan.* I will put out the light [if you bring one].[2]

Isabela realizes that she has been deceived, that she has not been romancing with the Duke. Though she initially cries out for help, her protests are abruptly silenced by the King's voice. Isabela knows that she has lost her honor, an unpardonable, even if unintentional, fault. Panic stifles her initial reaction—the desire to have her seducer punished—and she considers instead how to save her reputation at the Neapolitan court and, most importantly, her engagement to Duke Octavio. Isabela knows that if she loses these things, she might as well lose her life. She accepts as a matter of course that she will be found culpable and that a harsh judgment will be rendered: "How can I look at the King?"[3] Indeed the King angrily censures Isabela, making it clear that her actions have personally affronted him and blemished his reputation. Indifferent to her distress, he turns his back on her, as he would on a criminal: "It is just and right to punish an offense committed behind my back by turning my back on the one who is guilty."[4] To avert personal disaster, Isabela accuses the innocent Octavio of being her accomplice in the illicit lovemaking, since her only hope lies in making her actions appear more legitimate. She is resourceful in her misfortune, using calculated reason to avoid social ostracism, the isolated austerity of convent life, or death by suicide, so commonly the dishonored woman's fate. There is not the slightest ambiguity about Isabela's situation. Tirso makes it very clear that Don Juan has been successful, that Isabela—believing herself with the Duke—was a willing partner. Justice and retribution are of little concern to her: the pragmatic Isabela seeks only to protect what promises to be an auspicious and lucrative alliance with Duke Octavio.

Much closer to the Mozart–Da Ponte Donna Anna, both in name and character, is Doña Ana, the daughter of Don Gonzalo. She, too, is visited by Don Juan, now cleverly disguised as her beloved cousin, the Marquis. We know that Doña Ana's affection for the Marquis is genuine, for she requested a secret encounter with him in a letter, which Don Juan conveniently intercepts and uses to his advantage. From offstage, we hear her cries:

> D. Ana. Liar! You are not the Marquis, but have deceived me!
> D. Juan. I tell you I am he.
> D. Ana. Cruel enemy, you lie, you lie!
>   [Enter Don Gonzalo *with his sword drawn*]
> D. Gonz. It is the voice of Doña Ana that I hear.
> D. Ana. Will no one slay this traitor, murderer of my honor?
> D. Gonz. Is such insolence possible? Her honor dead, she cries "Woe is me," and her tongue tolls this for all to hear!
> D. Ana. Kill him.[5]

Two details are especially notable in this passage. First, Doña Ana reacts far more violently to the insult to her honor than Isabela. Second, her bold and truthful public accusation—in contrast to Isabela's deceit—shocks her father, who is, initially at least, more distressed about Ana's "insolent" outcry than Don Juan's deception. Not only has his noble daughter been molested, but she is *telling everyone about it*. Doña Ana's indignation overrides modesty and social dictates. Still, Don Gonzalo's horror of public exposure demonstrates further the precarious position of any woman touched by sexual scandal, whether she was complicit or forced. Tirso makes a point, in fact, of keeping Ana above seventeenth-century Spanish reproach by having Don Juan admit to Don Gonzalo himself that she was untouched, for "she saw through my deceptions in time."[6] Skeptical commentators may reject this confession and conclude that the deed was done. Assuming that the Don spoke the truth, however, Doña Ana's reaction is even more intriguing, for it shows that Don Juan's *attempt* to seduce her was enough to warrant the harshest penalty. Moreover, we should remember that Doña Ana does not need nor want a Don Juan. Her love for the Marquis is in its first bloom: her attraction to him lacks neither erotic appeal, nor the added incentive of material promise—two of Don Juan's main lures. In this prototype for the Don Juan story, and for Donna Anna's story as well, we meet an Ana who is capable of both affection and sensual feeling, but who is also a formidable and proud opponent against the man who would assault her virtue.

As the Don Juan legend developed over the next two centuries, the relationship between Donna Anna and Don Giovanni prototypes frequently assumed central dramatic importance. Though Tirso's Doña Ana never appears onstage, her fearless denunciation of Don Juan—who, unbeknownst to her, was once to have been her bridegroom in a politically arranged marriage—accelerates his damnation. In a slightly later version of the Don Juan story—Dorimond's *Le festin de Pierre ou Le fils criminel* (1658?)—the Doña Ana character (named Amarille) is more fully realized, a remarkably vigorous personality whose disdainful account of Don Juan's illicit visit to her room anticipates that of Mozart's Anna: "He tried to force me, but I was able to break the course of both his words and his treacheries" (2.3). Considering Amarille's "forceful and robust" temperament, Charles Russell remarks that "it is almost as if the legend, with an instinctive life of its own, were now beginning to realize that the heart of the drama lay in a deadly contest of personalities and wills between Donna Anna, pillar of public virtue, though privately not without hidden faults and hypocrisies, and Don Juan, scourge of public virtue, though privately not without a certain melting fascination. All extraneous matters were being cast away."[7] Highlighting the libertine's weakness for the Donna Anna character type, Alonso de Córdova y Maldonado's three-act play *La venganza en el sepulcro*, written in the last third of the seventeenth century, dramatizes Don Juan's return to Seville after fifteen years of debauchery. At age thirty, he is finally ready to settle into tranquil domesticity. Approaching his hometown, he sees Doña Ana and immediately falls in love with her. The play centers on his attempts to marry her, though her father—not to mention her fiancé—is against the union. For her part, this Doña Ana remains faithful to her father and betrothed, but she also reveals a fascination with Don Juan, weeping when she hears of his death. Other playwrights developed this theme of mutual attraction, which was taken to rather incongruous extremes in Gioacchino Albertini's 1783 opera produced in Warsaw, *Don Juan, albo libertyn ukarany* (Don Juan, or the libertine punished), in which Donna Anna and Don Juan are portrayed as doomed lovers.

Clearly, then, there was nothing new about a Donna Anna / Don Giovanni attraction at the end of the eighteenth century, though there was no standard formula for their relationship either. Only one point of consistency stands out: even the most pride-bound Anna, if she feels some flicker of amorous interest in Don Juan, reflects this unmistakably in her words and actions. This is no less true in one of the most celebrated eighteenth-century Don Juan plays, *Don Giovanni Tenorio* (1736), by acclaimed playwright Carlo Goldoni. His Donna Anna is not only enamored of Don Giovanni, but she also makes no secret of her aversion to her betrothed, Don Ottavio, who feels the same way about her. The pair never has a scene alone: all of their dialogue is formal and almost indirect. (In their first scene together [3.2], one can almost imagine the patriarchal chaperon Don Alfonso jabbing Don Ottavio in the ribs as he commands him to "say something nice to your new fiancée.")[8] Goldoni clearly spelled out the antipathy between the noble lovers and their respective attractions to others. Don Ottavio addresses his warmest comments to the Elvira-like Donna Isabella, while Donna Anna immediately recognizes the power of Don Giovanni's sensual charm. She speaks about her desire for Don Giovanni with the same conflicted intensity that marks the recitatives and arias of Da Ponte's Donna Elvira. For all of her aristocratic correctness, the Donna Anna of *Don Giovanni Tenorio* is a romantic. She acknowledges that filial duty and the promise of future power and riches (Ottavio will probably inherit the throne) should be enough to win her affection, but she cannot deny her heart's passionate nature. Thus, in her first scene, Donna Anna counters Don Alfonso's definition of conjugal love—an arranged affair, which first ignites from the affection for one's parents and honor—with a far more personal vision:

> I have heard tell of this love, and it seems to me,
> If I am not mistaken, it is that spirit
> That links two hearts in sweet affection.
> For a pleasing face, for the gentle
> Features of a knight, I have heard it said
> That a young woman can feel love;
> I did not learn, however, that an unknown,
> Perhaps hateful object would have the power
> To light an amorous flame in one's breast. (1.1)

Strong-willed and ardent, Goldoni's Anna is far more outspoken and demonstrative than her operatic descendant; nevertheless, she shares with Da Ponte's Donna Anna a self-possession and conviction that, in the end, resists everyone who tries to control her, even Don Giovanni.

Though there are few exact parallels between these two characters, two soliloquies in Goldoni's play might reasonably be read as reflecting the private thoughts of the later operatic Donna Anna, who is unable to dispel the vision of her slain father from her mind. The first appears just after Donna Anna's encounter with Don Giovanni Tenorio. Left alone with the young nobleman, the lady is initially entranced by his handsome face and noble bearing, but she defies him when he grows too aggressive, and finally cries out for help when he draws his sword to kill her. Her father, the Commendatore, comes to her rescue, but he is murdered by the libertine. Left alone, Donna Anna is confused and self-damning:

> If I was less strong,
> What would have become of me? Sacred honesty,
> How many enemies you have! In how many guises,
> How many insidious forms they appear to you! Oh dear father,
> You willed that I be left near the traitor;
> You pushed. . . . But no, I was the incautious woman.
> At the first wicked words, at the first
> Flattering glances, I should have,
> Fleeing, taken myself away. (4.5)

Finally Goldoni's Donna Anna responds to the world with words that might easily correspond to the trembling allusions and tearful outbursts of the operatic Donna Anna; she privately rebukes those around her who presume to understand her pain and who glibly urge her to go on with her life:

> How effortlessly do those who do not feel pain
> Advise the afflicted to be pacified.
> No one could understand better than me
> How much I lost in my dead father. (4.9)

Goldoni's Anna expresses one of the basic truths about all of the Donna Anna characters of the Don Juan tradition: they suffer from a grief that *isolates* them from even their closest companions. This isolation—beginning with Tirso's offstage Doña Ana—is more than the social separateness that generally characterizes *seria* characters in comedies: this is a psychological isolation as well. Donna Anna's circumstances seem to demand some degree of reclusion, and playwrights and librettists have always had to grapple with the problem of how much Donna Anna should be seen or heard at all. Sometimes the solutions hearken back to almost Tirso-like invisibility. This is true, for example, of Giovanni Bertati's libretto for the one-act opera *Don Giovanni ossia il convitato di pietra* (Don Giovanni or the stone guest), which premiered in Venice on 5 February 1787 with music by Giuseppe Gazzaniga and which was the direct source for the Mozart–Da Ponte *Don Giovanni*.[9] Though Bertati's Donna Anna makes a dramatic entrance, she removes herself from the action after scene 3, retiring without ceremony to the seclusion of a convent.

Mozart and Da Ponte rejected Bertati's expedient but uninspired solution, creating instead what Heartz describes as arguably "the greatest *seria* role in all Mozart." Bertati only sketches the bare bones of passion and reserve, the strong sense of purpose and the emotional devastation that stamp Da Ponte's Donna Anna. Bertati, for example, confines Anna's dismay at seeing her father's corpse to three sentences; for the corresponding scene in his libretto, Da Ponte gives his Anna a dozen short utterances, the bewildered, gasping speech of a person in shock.

From Bertati's libretto, scene 3:

> D. Anna. Ah! the pallor of death is already painted on his face . . .
> His heart no longer beats . . .
> Ah, my father is dead!
> [falls into the Duke's arms]

From Da Ponte's libretto, act 1, scene 3:

> D. Anna. Ah! the assassin murdered him; that blood . . .
> that wound . . . that face . . .
> tinged and covered with the colors of death . . .
> He no longer breathes . . . his limbs are cold . . .
> My father . . . dear father . . . beloved father . . .
> I am fainting . . . I am dying . . .

Da Ponte echoes the main ideas and even some of the words of Bertati's libretto, but he projects Anna's anguish with far more color and energy. The punctuation he uses, especially the numerous ellipses, indicates an emphasis on the aesthetic of *sensibilité* rather than comedic conventions. As Stefano Castelvecchi explains, "The experience of *sensibilité* seems to have a fragmentary and incomplete quality, reflected in the tendency to fragmentation and incompleteness within sentimental texts. The person overwhelmed by emotion is often incapable of continuous discourse; the amount of the unspoken (interrupted speech, silence, bodily signs) unveils the communicative limits of verbal and rational language."[10] Mozart carefully marks the emotional progression leading to her swoon (Ex. 1) with a series of striking musical progressions—diminished-seventh chords, chromatic voice leading, and unusual chord

EXAMPLE 1. *Don Giovanni,* No. 2, Recitative, "Ma qual mai s'offre, oh Dei!"

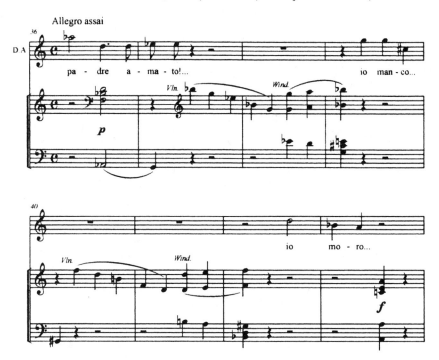

changes—culminating in the reeling harmonic sequence at "io manco
. . . io moro."[11] Mozart and Da Ponte elaborate on Anna's whirling emotions in the duet that follows: awakening from unconsciousness, she
drifts confusedly from horror and outrage to overwhelming sorrow. By
contrast, Bertati's Donna Anna abruptly turns from her woeful encounter with her father's corpse and begins to describe—with remarkable self-possession and calm attention to detail—the events preceding
the old gentleman's slaying. Bertati's version does not beg the question as
to whether the seducer was successful. When this Donna Anna explains
that she defended herself, causing the fiend to flee, the Duke immediately
assures her that he will vindicate both daughter and father. The Duke also
offers his betrothed the comfort of a "husband's love," but this sensible
Donna Anna makes it clear that there will be no talk of marriage until
the criminal is found and punished.

The Mozart–Da Ponte Donna Anna strives at times to adhere to these
stiff-backed conventions of the noble *seria* heroine but is not able to
sustain it. Even her loftiest professions of anger and grief quiver with

fragility, as she tries to check a growing wave of hysteria. She does not invite us to feel the voyeuristic pity that Donna Elvira arouses. Rather, her sorrow and shame—for like all Donna Anna types, she partially blames herself for the scandal and murder—cause her to turn inward, making her less accessible to us. Yet she does not conveniently disappear from the stage after her first scene: she is a reminder that this opera has high stakes. Mozart and Da Ponte keep their Donna Anna in the spotlight; her cries for vindication reach all the way to the afterworld, driving the work to its apocalyptic finale. Elvira forgives, Zerlina forgets, but Anna does neither. Ultimately she is unable, mostly because of her gender, to be the actual agent of revenge, but she definitely invokes and sustains the concepts of justice and retribution. Ultimately her unswerving opposition to Don Giovanni—the man who assaulted her and killed her father—may account for a great deal of anti–Donna Anna critical reception. She fails to follow the well-worn path of so many favorite operatic heroines, both comic and tragic. She neither pines for nor pardons the "hero," Don Giovanni. She says nothing about his charm, boldness, or diabolic vigor. Before she recognizes him as her father's killer, he is simply a neighbor and a friend about whom she makes no remarkable comment: after her realization, he is the villain who took away her father and her peace. Even Don Giovanni himself sees the threat that Donna Anna poses to him. Alarmed at the thought of losing his anonymity, the fleeing libertine mutters, "Questa furia disperata / mi vuol far precipitar," which might be translated as "This desperate Fury wants to make me do something rash," or, more seriously still, "wants to bring about my downfall." In fact, Donna Anna fills an essential dramatic purpose: she is a tangible symbol of Don Giovanni's criminal behavior, a unforgettable connection between *Il Dissoluto* and that other eponymous character in the Don Juan tradition, the Stone Guest.

E. T. A. HOFFMANN AND BEYOND: ROMANCING RAPE

From the nineteenth century right up to the present, a formidable list of musicians, poets, playwrights, critics, philosophers, and scholars have put their own stamp on Donna Anna, filling in the spaces that Da Ponte and Mozart left blank and, in doing do, ignoring many details they made explicit. The Romantics were interested in updating Donna Anna (and Don Giovanni, for that matter) to reflect their own tastes in heroines and heroes. Probably the most famous "adaptation" of the story is E. T. A. Hoffmann's "fantasy piece" on Don Juan, through which he

hoped to make the subject of the libretto more worthy of Mozart's in-
genious music.[12] In Hoffmann's tale, Anna really does nurture a secret
passion for her seducer, but she also represents the redeeming antidote
to Giovanni's infernal actions:

> Donna Anna, so highly favored by Nature, is thus set in opposition to Don
> Juan. Just as Don Juan was originally a wonderfully powerful, magnificent
> man, so is she a divine woman, over whose pure spirit the Devil has no
> power. All the craftiness of Hell could corrupt only her mortal part.—Once
> Satan has completed her ruin, Hell will be unable to delay the avenging
> forces from their task, which even Heaven has ordained.[13]

Hoffmann's Donna Anna is a passionate angel that has been ravaged
by a demonic force ("the heat of a superhuman sensuality, glowing like
Hell-fire, coursed through her and made all her resistance futile"), but
whose soul remains pure. She is tormented by the infamy of the fatal encounter. And, of course, like all good Romantic heroines, she is doomed
to die from the aftereffects of her "unholy passion":

> As [Don Juan] tried to escape after the deed was done [seducing her], the
> thought of her ruin wound around her with racking agony like a horrible,
> venomous, death-spraying monster. Her father's demise at Don Juan's
> hand, her connection with the cold, unmanly, ordinary Don Ottavio, whom
> she once thought to love—even the raging love that, in the moment of high-
> est pleasure blazed up to consume her innermost spirit, now burns with the
> ardor of annihilating hatred. Only Don Juan's undoing can procure peace
> for her frightened soul from its fatal torments; but this very peace will sig-
> nal her own earthly demise.[14]

The spirit of Hoffmann's tale continues to loom large in modern productions of *Don Giovanni* and in commentary on the opera, though the
value of its influence is open to debate, especially as regards the character of Donna Anna. Since the mid-twentieth century, critics and scholars
have frequently asserted Donna Anna's shameful secret passion as fact,
but they have replaced the poet's earnest sympathy for her plight with a
disparaging cynicism. On the other hand, the hero worship that is so
evident in Hoffmann's portrayal of Don Giovanni continues to thrive.
As critical reception attributed more and more positive qualities to
Don Giovanni—vitality, sexual prowess, charisma, independent thinking, endless potential, nonconformity, determination, and courage—it
also began to view Donna Anna in increasingly antithetical—that is,
negative—terms. Not surprisingly, many of these modern interpretations are scant on actual analysis of Donna Anna's words, actions, and
music, amounting to dismissive and sometimes shockingly misogynistic

invention. In the early part of the twentieth century, Edward Dent set the tone for this kind of reading:

> Anna has been made a tragic figure by later interpreters, but it may be doubted whether she is really anything more than self-absorbed and aloof. . . . [She] treats even Don Ottavio in so distant a manner that we cannot expect her to reveal her true self in a duet or trio. She seems to have been brought up from childhood always to conceal her real feelings and never acknowledge to herself any motive but duty and family pride. If she had been Italian and not Spanish, she might have been Fiordiligi in *Così fan Tutte,* and there seems every probability that she will eventually become first lady-in-waiting to the Queen of the Night. She is in fact a thoroughly unpleasant lady.[15]

And in 1977—in what might be called fictional slander—William Mann augments Dent's complaints in a downright nasty attack:

> Anna is an upper-class Spanish lady who has etiquette where her feelings and brains should reside. Duty and honor are her watchword [sic]. Towards all her fellow-creatures she presents a coldly correct personality. If she loves her father it is because the Bible told her so. Her censorious anger against others is a juvenile trait. All men, to her, are beasts, *and it would be beneficial to her personal growing-up if she had been pleasantly raped by Don Juan.* . . . Her upbringing has made her afraid of other people, and she has given most of her sincere outgoing emotion to lapdogs or possibly horses.[16]

A final example testifies to how this critical animosity toward Anna has persisted right up to the politically sensitive present. In his 1991 study *Così? Sexual Politics in Mozart's Operas,* Charles Ford manages to camouflage the same brand of hoary chauvinism with a slick, progressive-sounding book title:

> We never feel that we know Anna's true feelings. . . . [She] is known only as her silhouette within a cameo of rejection, and this, her cardboard one-dimensionality, induces a curiosity concerning what seems to be an emotional secrecy. The implication that Anna is secretly in love with the man who violated her cannot be avoided. . . . Within the Enlightenment's conception of femininity, the complicity of every rape victim must always be in doubt, for no woman can *naturally* resist the sexual intentions of a man, for she is nothing more than an object of his desire. Anna's "un-natural" resistance towards Ottavio seems to demand explanation by way of her "natural" lack of resistance towards Giovanni, which adds to his greater glory as a damned, sexual hero. This is why critics feel compelled to establish Anna's sexual complicity; and why William Mann suggests that she deserves to be pleasantly raped.[17]

By citing Mann, Ford demonstrates how ancient prejudices—especially the privileging of the masculine perspective—persist in the critical literature, including his own writings. His conclusion that "Anna's whole fictive being is exhausted in the suspicion that she is guilty of 'contributory negligence' " and his remark that "implications" about her secretly being in love with him "cannot be avoided" clearly indicate his own interpretive biases.[18]

Admittedly, these passages—especially Mann's outrageous description—are extreme in their offensive language and lack of scholarly argument, but a general pessimism about Donna Anna turns up in rigorous critical analyses as well. Wye Allanbrook, for instance, evaluates Donna Anna's musical language with evident skepticism:

> Anna's *opera seria* indignation betrays her immediately upon entrance . . . and so does the ambiguity of her first words to her seducer, "Non sperar, se non m'uccidi, / Ch'io ti lasci fuggir mai!" It would be merely insensitive to accuse Donna Anna of real ambivalence toward her enemy in her present fury; yet later, when she persists in directing all her ardor toward the pursuit of her seducer rather than toward marriage with her affianced lover, these words will afford a second meaning.[19]

Allanbrook's reading is based on a fairly hard-line position—*seria* cannot be taken at face value in the context of opera buffa—and ignores the particular dramaturgical qualities of this hybrid work, an opera buffa on Don Juan, which mixes comedy and tragedy in its own manner. Traditionally, as we have seen, Donna Anna's primary function is to counter Don Juan; whether she loves him or not is of secondary importance. Her demand for justice is expected and validated, and, to this end, a serious musical style is completely appropriate.

(UN)FEMININE RAGE AND RETRIBUTION

So why has Donna Anna become such a lightning rod for "bad press" and unsympathetic representations in productions? There are, naturally, historical factors. Revenge has long been considered a man's business, and the Age of Enlightenment was no different in this regard. Mary Hunter explains that eighteenth-century notions about women made it "increasingly difficult to represent women out of control" and explains that rage arias, which often allude to vengeance, exhibit an "intensity of passion that is ill-suited to both the aesthetic and to the gender ideology of opera buffa," which generally attempts "to control and rationalize the potentially dangerous power of fury"[20] Examining versions of the Don Juan story from the eighteenth century, Charles Russell identified a related dramatic trend, nothing that "in the eighteenth century, it was wrong for a Donna Anna to assert herself too boldly, wrong for a Don Giovanni to be deeply disturbed by self-doubts. Those were erratic male and female patterns of behavior unbecoming to the spirit of the legend; they did not fit and were not retained, at least until reexamined and revised in light of new, nineteenth-century sensibilities."[21] It is true that many Donna Anna characters in the Don Juan story tradition exhibit some moment of expected feminine softness. Tirso avoided the problem by giving his Doña Ana only the briefest (though unequivocal) plea for vengeance before taking her out of the action altogether; Bertati and Gazzaniga adopted a similar solution. Goldoni's Donna Anna expresses her outrage at Don Giovanni's trespasses, but she also responds with an almost involuntary pity to his pleas for forgiveness. Her amorous, "womanly" heart is explicitly implicated in her reaction, for which she begs the pardon of her father's ghost: "Shade of my father which wanders about me, forgive my weakness of heart. I am a woman at last . . ." (5.5).

Mozart and Da Ponte gave their Donna Anna a vulnerable side as well—seen best in her swooning grief for her father and in "Non mi dir," her profession of love to Don Ottavio—but this does not include pity for Don Giovanni, which, in any case, is amply provided by Donna Elvira. Still, the act of forgiveness holds a special place in Mozart's operas, where revenge usually serves as an unattractive foil to the more perfect gesture of clemency: the juxtaposition of the Queen of the Night's "Der Hölle Rache" and Sarastro's "In diesen heil'gen Hallen" in *Die Zauberflöte* is a clear example.[22] The related category of anger is tricky, too, in the context of opera buffa. As Hunter points out, "pure" rage arias (which often speak of revenge) are "a clear and frequent category of opera seria," but they are generally transformed within the opera buffa repertoire, so that "the arias that express rage can often be assimilated into other aria types. Noble rage shades into expressions of pride, nobility, haughtiness, or a demand for sympathy, while the rage expressed by comic characters turns into sputtering *buffa* displays."[23] Mozart used *seria*-derived musical idioms to convey very different meanings (and degrees of seriousness) depending on the dramatic situation, and his treatment of the theme of vengeance is no different. Looking at some examples of "revenge" music in other Mozart operas may help us to evaluate the particular dramatic context and musical language of Donna

Anna's rage-revenge numbers, specifically the duet section of No. 2, "Fuggi, crudele," and the aria No. 10, "Or sai chi l'onore."

At one end of the spectrum, there are the two rage-revenge arias in *Le nozze di Figaro:* Dr. Bartolo's puffed-up *buffa* aria "La vendetta," and Count Almaviva's bravura number "Vedrò mentre io." Both the Count and Bartolo want revenge against Figaro, who at one time or another has duped each of them. Both Bartolo's and Almaviva's arias aspire to the exalted alla breve mode, but neither of them is effective as a true rage aria. Musically, Bartolo manages only a tone of pretentious bluster, while the Count is far more convincingly indignant in his recitative than in the aria itself, which is a little too lyrically self-pitying until the last section. Nor does the drama rouse much sympathy for their complaints. Bartolo, the scheming troll aspiring to the ranks of the powerful, has always played the tyrant in his limited arena of control, while the duplicitous, womanizing Almaviva exemplifies the self-indulgent arrogance of class privilege. Both the nobleman and the doctor believe they have been injured, but their own overbearing actions are to be blamed. Their threats of vengeance thus become just another unattractive feature of their abuse of power.

In other cases the distinction between hypocritical vindictiveness and righteous anger is not so straightforward. In two of Mozart's most famous rage arias—Elettra's aria "Tutto nel cor vi sento" in *Idomeneo* (1.6.4) and, ten years later, the Queen of the Night's "Der Hölle Rache"—the character's resentment is understandable, but not entirely honorable or without innocent victims. Both of these arias are in D minor; they also share a common tempo indication (allegro assai) and meter (common time). Furthermore, both arias allude to the darker side of vengeance, the madness that can distort a legitimate affliction. The Queen of the Night and Elettra are both driven to rage by the perceived betrayal of a loved one who holds the key to their ambitions and happiness. With Pamina's submission to Sarastro and the Initiates, the Queen of the Night's permanent expulsion from "humanity" grows more certain. In the case of Elettra, her vengeful passions grow out of unrequited love and a genuine anxiety about her ultimate fate. As is typical of rage arias, the language suggests a potential for violence:

Tutte nel core vi sento,	I feel you all in my heart,
Furie del crudo Averno	furies of cruel Avernus,
Lunge a sì gran tormento,	keep love, mercy, pity
Amor, mercè, pietà.	far from such a great torment.
Chi mi rubò quel core,	She [Ilia] who stole that heart,

Quel, che tradito ha il mio,	that one which betrayed mine [Idamante],
Provin' dal mio furore	may they feel my fury,
Vendetta, e crudeltà.	vengeance, and cruelty.[24]

Elettra never actually harms Idamante or her rival Ilia. She hopes to exploit Idomeneo's decision to send Idamante away with her (and, consequently, away from Ilia), but she manages only to increase her own unhappiness. In the end, deprived of her heart's desire, she longs for death. Elettra's music speaks more of an internal battle, a self-destructive emotional unhinging, than a concrete plan of revenge. The only thing she shares with the Count and the Queen of the Night is pride of rank: more than once she stresses the difference between herself and the "slave," Ilia. Nevertheless, the anguished sentiments of this aria are fundamentally personal, not a matter of station. Expressing Elettra's crazed passion, the music combines common rage/revenge elements, such as conspicuous dynamic alternations, *sforzandi,* and tremolos, with harmonic peculiarities that betoken the princess's eventual descent into despair. Once past the triadic, almost martial, introductory line and mythic references ("Tutto nel cor vi sento / furie del crudo Averno"), Elettra suddenly grows doubtful and checks herself, seeking refuge in an aimless chromatic line that finally disintegrates into sobs, the result of her "gran tormento" (mm. 31–37). Her rage derails the return of the primary material: expecting the tonic D minor to be reestablished, we hear instead C minor (at m. 77). Elettra is (harmonically) lost in frenetic emotions. Even after the harmony stabilizes, her tempestuous feelings are captured by the two pairs of horns with their squally fanfare on the final "provin' dal mio furore, vendetta e crudeltà."

How does Donna Anna's appeal for retribution compare with that of Elettra or the Queen of the Night? Why does she end up singing in the *lieto fine* while they are excluded from any kind of happy ending? The difference might lie in part in the "righteousness" of Donna Anna's accusation. The Queen has been injured, but she also injures others: more than the struggle for her daughter, her desire for power over Sarastro drives her actions. Elettra has been abandoned, in a sense, by the object of her affections, yet she focuses most of her punitive energy on her innocent rival, Ilia. Donna Anna, however, blames only Don Giovanni, who openly brags about his transgressions. There is nothing exaggerated about her allegation against him: at the very least, Don Giovanni violated her privacy, attempting an illicit and deceitful seduction, and then killed her father. As Maynard Solomon points out, "the cardinal crimes in the

Da Ponte operas and *Die Zauberflöte* are those aimed against virtue, in the first place seduction and rape. Indeed the threat of sexual violation is central to all of Mozart's opera buffas and singspiels from *Zaide* to *Die Zauberflöte*. . . . The threat of seduction or rape provides a backdrop of menace in these operas, which is quite at odds with their comic surface."[25] He identifies the main themes of Mozart's operas as "the critique of power, the protest against injustice, and the safeguarding of innocence" in front of which the composer's "main question is, 'How do we make things right?' "[26] In general, Mozart's operas have more faith in forgiveness than in retribution, but the Don Juan legacy presents a special problem. The story relies heavily on the ending, the spectacular downfall of a remorselessly dissolute aristocrat: everyone waits for the "bad guy" to meet a theatrically satisfying end. From his origins through the eighteenth century, Don Juan had usually been punished. Mozart and Da Ponte did not stray from the narrative convention, emphasizing the fact that Don Giovanni rejects and despises forgiveness and remorse. Conversely, Mozart, who so often celebrates the act of forgiveness, humanizes Donna Anna's vindictive feelings through a compelling musical language, endowing her righteous anger with its own positive dramatic value while never letting it deteriorate into bloodthirsty madness.

The key of D (both minor and major modes) is central to this opera. It is the key of the overture, with its slow, eerie D-minor introduction that returns in the scene of Don Giovanni's cataclysmic fall, and it is also the key of Donna Anna's revenge numbers. (In contrast, the Queen's "Der Hölle Rache" stands in jarring dissonance to the E-flat tonality of *Die Zauberflöte*.) Donna Anna's first call for revenge occurs shortly after she sees the corpse of her father and realizes that he has been murdered while defending her honor. It is an intense and terrible moment of drama, one that Da Ponte and Mozart knew would inspire the sympathy of the audience, especially since the fatal stabbing occurs onstage, with the hemorrhaging body of the Commendatore in plain view. Wracked by the anguish of both her own encounter with Don Giovanni and its bloody consequences, Donna Anna makes a tearful plea to Don Ottavio to avenge the night's ghastly events. Her desperation is of the utmost importance to understanding the entire third scene. During the recitative where she urges Ottavio to hurry to her father's aid, she is still the *furia disperata* in frenetic shock, hoping to capture the intruder. When she sees her father lying on the ground, blood surrounding his body, she slowly begins to collapse. The vigorous energy of her struggle with Don Giovanni dissipates. The forceful alla breve of her first entrance—with the martial dotted rhythms and strident, patterlike outbursts of "come una furia disperata"—is temporarily silenced. For, despite her bravest efforts, the villain has escaped and her father is dead. Her sung reaction—with its gasping phrases and disorienting series of diminished chords—is devastating, a masterly depiction of assailed sensibility. The *recitativo obbligato* passage that precedes "Fuggi, crudele" totally contradicts the allegation that Donna Anna lacks sincerity or vulnerability, being "as high in its pathos as the preceding [dialogue between Leporello and Don Giovanni] was low in its comedy."[27]

Donna Anna swoons, then, recovering her senses to some extent, she launches—*disperatamente,* as indicated by the stage directions—into the duet. Her words suggest delirium: she has either taken Don Ottavio for her attacker or else lashed out at him in blind anguish.[28] As with the "io manco . . . io moro" passage discussed above, the emotional confusion and broken speech that characterize Donna Anna's music in the first part of the duet, before she demands revenge, are consistent with the expressive conventions of *sensibilité.* At the same time, however, Donna Anna reassumes the exalted alla breve style, reminding us of her *seria* origins.[29] The alla breve is also the language of her family, so to speak. In the context of the opera, we could say that she "inherits" this style from her father; the Commendatore utilizes the same idiom during the trio following his fatal injury and again during the supper scene. In response to Donna Anna's outburst—with its mixture of expressive idioms—the imperturbable Don Ottavio gently commands his beloved to listen and to look at him; at the same time, his music smoothly shifts the harmony away from D minor toward more tranquil F major. Still shaken, Anna returns to the fragmented phrasing of the preceding recitative. Recognizing her beloved ("mio bene"), she asks his pardon, her melodic phrase coming to rest briefly on F major as well (m. 88). When she asks for her father, however, the harmony begins to slip downward once more. Don Ottavio hesitates, attempting to avoid another collapse; he urges her to "forget these bitter memories," his music gently insisting on F-major consolation. Remembering now what happened, Anna turns to thoughts of vengeance, signified by the descending, staccato motive in the bass at measure 124.[30] Overcome with emotion and a sense of helplessness, Anna begs Ottavio to avenge the bloodshed "if he can." Ottavio swears on their love to do so, and the two lovers, united by this pledge, return to D minor and the alla breve tempo for "Che giuramento, oh Dei."

Ratner describes this duet as consisting of a double presentation of three affects: 1) Anna's sorrow and despair; 2) Ottavio's consolation;

and 3) their resolution for vengeance. Yet, for the most part, these affects can best be heard in the preceding accompanied recitative and in
the moments of the duet where Anna demands that Ottavio swear revenge and Ottavio obliges her (see mm. 125–33 and mm. 155–67).
Strikingly, in the passages of the duet where they sing together, Anna
and Ottavio do not elaborate on their rage or on possible punitive actions. Instead, their united hearts and minds agitated with "a hundred
different emotions," they reflect on what a "terrible moment" it is that
incites "such an oath." The accompaniment well illustrates their trepidation with a pulsating dominant pedal and *piano* dynamics that suddenly explode with *sforzandi;* the two lovers are breathless as they
gasp out the words "fra cento affetti e cento," rising shrilly on the final
word, suggesting something between urgency and dread. This is not
ruthless, cold resolve, but rather a relatively conflicted, self-conscious
"vengeance" that is essentially a demand for justice. Only after Donna
Anna recognizes Don Giovanni as her assailant does her will harden
into the unflinching directive of "Or sai chi l'onore."

Another revenge duet—that of Vitellia and Sesto in the opening scene
of *La clemenza di Tito*—offers a useful comparison. Like Elettra, Vitellia resents a would-be suitor, in this case Emperor Tito, for choosing another bride; like the Queen of the Night, she has a royal title and believes
that her rightful claim to power has been usurped. Complicating matters further, Vitellia is betrothed to Sesto, for whom she apparently feels
nothing. Enslaved by his passion, on the other hand, Sesto suffers Vitellia's thoughtlessness with a mixture of self-pity and self-sacrifice. When
the ireful princess concocts a plan to redress the snub to her pride, she
enlists Sesto as her aide, bullying him into submission by threatening to
release him "from every promise" (1.1). In the end, he agrees to do what
Vitellia asks:

Sesto. Come ti piace imponi:	Command as you please:
Regola i moti miei.	rule my every movement.
Il mio destin tu sei;	You are my destiny;
Tutto farò per te.	I will do everything for you.
Vitel. Prima che il sol tramonti,	Before the sun sets,
Estinto io vò l'indegno.	I want the unworthy man dead.
Sai ch'egli usurpa un regno,	You know that he usurps a kingdom,
Che in sorte il ciel mi diè.	which heaven destined to me.
Sesto. Già il tuo furor m'accende.	Already your fury ignites me.
Vitel. Ebben, che più s'attende?	Well, what more do you await?

Sesto.	Un dolce sguardo almeno	Let one sweet glance at least be
	Sia premio alla mia fè!	the prize for my faith!
a2.	Fan mille affetti insieme	A thousand emotions together
	Battaglia in me spietata.	battle relentlessly within me.
	Un'alma lacerata	There is not a soul
	Più della mia non v'è.	more torn than mine.

Musically, this duet resembles "Che giuramento, oh Dei" in several ways. Both sections, the opening Andante and the Allegro that joins the two characters, are alla breve. The piece is set in the seemingly more benign key of F major, but it hints at D minor at the transition between the two sections. Both duets end with a section using detached syllabic settings to reflect the wave of tumultuous emotions with which the characters are overcome (see, for instance, mm. 37–42 in "Come ti piace imponi" and mm. 147–50 in "Che giuramento, oh Dei"). In *Tito*, however, we find a more convincing example of the steely, imperious femininity and malleable, lovesick (read "weaker") masculinity that so many writers attribute to Donna Anna and Don Ottavio.[31]

Donna Anna reveals a far more sensitive personality than does Vitellia. Her anguish both tempers and feeds her fury, trapping her in a cycle of fragility and indignation. The *introduzione* vividly presents the violent events and personal agony that impel Donna Anna and Don Ottavio to their pact of retribution. Vitellia, on the other hand, has already formed her plan by the time we first meet her in *Tito*. She is true *seria* royalty, whose "injury" is as much political as it is personal. Only when she fears that death may be waiting for her does Vitellia reconsider her murderous designs. Additionally, though Vitellia and Sesto comment in a general way about their warring emotions, Donna Anna and Don Ottavio specifically connect this idea to their awareness of the ugly nature of revenge: what a "barbarous" oath they have been compelled to make. It is this very sense of conscience that Vitellia lacks and Sesto disregards until, much later in the opera, fear and guilt lead them to regret their actions.

"BUT DONNA ANNA, WHAT DID SHE ASK FOR?"

The theme of retribution returns dramatically in Donna Anna's first aria, No. 10, "Or sai chi l'onore." On the surface, this aria might seem a mere showpiece for the singer in an old-fashioned alla breve meter and style; after inciting Ottavio to vengeance once again, Anna makes an opera seria–style exit. But the dramatic importance and musical weight of "Or sai chi l'onore" must be considered in context, as the culmination of a crucial scene of *discovery*. Dressed in mourning, Donna Anna and Don Ottavio encounter Don Giovanni and ask him for help in their difficult situation. Giovanni plays the cavalier with Donna Anna, offering his consolation with fabricated tenderness. At that moment, Donna Elvira rushes in and warns Anna of the treacherous nature of "quel barbaro." Listening to Elvira plead her case in the quartet "Non ti fidar, o misera" (1.12), both Donna Anna and Don Ottavio are struck by Donna Elvira's "noble" and "majestic" characteristics. Seeing that the couple show an interest in the poor woman's complaints, a nervous Don Giovanni bids Elvira to be quiet lest she bring criticism on herself. Elvira snaps back furiously that she is not concerned about this, but desires only "to reveal to everyone your guilt and my state." While neither Anna nor Ottavio can hear clearly what Elvira is saying to Giovanni, both of them notice Giovanni's change of color at the distraught young woman's words. Their suspicions are aroused and gain substance throughout the quartet. Sensing their misgivings, Giovanni makes a hasty exit, but not before offering assistance to "bellissima Donn' Anna": "If I can serve you, I await you at my home."

He should have remained silent: the lascivious twist of his voice identifies him unmistakably to Donna Anna as her attacker. She shares this terrible revelation with Don Ottavio in the extended accompanied recitative that introduces "Or sai chi l'onore": "Don Ottavio . . . I am dying! This recitative, one of Mozart's most dramatic, is organized into three main sections: 1) the identification of Don Giovanni as the Commendatore's killer (Allegro assai, mm. 1–23); 2) the detailed description of what happened in Donna Anna's room (Andante, mm. 24–53, with a brief recall of the *Primo Tempo*); and 3) the conclusion of Donna Anna's account, focusing on her escape and her father's death (*Primo Tempo*, mm. 54–69), leading directly *(attacco subito)* to the aria. In the introductory Allegro assai of the recitative, the music staggers into C minor—the same key, incidentally, of the passage in which Donna Anna saw her father's dead body. A lurching double-dotted motive in the strings signals Anna's alarm, the suffocating swell of adrenaline that comes with an appalling revelation (mm. 3–4ff.). She cries out to Ottavio to help her, her voice rising in barely suppressed panic, "Oh Dei, oh Dei!" She names Don Giovanni as her father's murderer, a forceful cadence in C minor punctuating her shocking disclosure.

After the initial recitative, Donna Anna regains her fragile composure and relates the previous night's devastating events. Her speech is slower and more regulated now, though she brings in the unusual key of E-flat minor.[32] The harmony descends (in thirds) through various other minor keys: her mistaken belief that the cloaked figure she beheld was Ottavio (E-flat minor), her terrified realization that it was a stranger (B minor), and his attempts at physical intimacy (G minor). When Donna Anna mentions her scream for help, the music suddenly bolts into the original allegro tempo and anxious, double-dotted motive. The passage is similar to the earlier one in which she identified Giovanni as the assassin, and it seems likewise to be heading to another decisive cadence, now emphasizing the key G minor, which Mozart often used for anguish or distress. But her forlorn "non viene alcun" ("no one came") leads only to a new diminished chord, and the tempo returns to andante. As she describes her fear of being overpowered ("che già mi credo vinta"), the harmony slips another third to E minor. The urgent leaps in the violin parts (mm. 49–51) simulate Anna's vigorous fight—"torcermi, e piegarmi" ("twisting and bending myself")—to break from Don Giovanni's grasp.

Hearing of her successful escape, Don Ottavio (characteristically) tries to see the happier side, heading off Donna Anna's A minor with a relieved deceptive cadence toward his preferred key of F major ("Ohime, respiro"). His musical sigh of relief has often been seen as ridiculously sunny and gullible. Alfred Einstein's reading is typical in this regard. He concludes that Don Ottavio's response has a "tragicomic flavor" for "every understanding listener," since it was generally understood in the eighteenth century that Don Giovanni has "reached the summit of his desires" with Donna Anna, and that she discovers the "terrible truth of her betrayal" just after the quartet.[33] In this way Einstein harnesses Don Ottavio's relief to a scenario that owes more to Hoffmann than Da Ponte. But the recitative is focused on Donna Anna, and there is nothing silly about her narrative or about the "horror of the infamous attack" in her bedroom. What she has described to Don Ottavio, after all, is not seduction, not a betrayal, but an attempted rape: "with one hand he tries to stifle my voice, and with the other he clutches me tightly, so much that I think I am already overcome."

There are numerous libertines in the Don Juan literary tradition who cross (or are willing to cross) the line between seduction and force, and Da Ponte's Don Giovanni is no different: after all, Zerlina's screams in the finale to act 1 are not ecstatic, but fearful. Both in the Mozart–Da Ponte opera and in the Bertati-Gazzaniga Don Giovanni, the Leporello character insinuates that his master would willfully steal what was not offered freely. In the Bertati libretto, the servant Pasquariello offers sardonic congratulations to Giovanni: "Bravo! Two heroic deeds. Donna Anna violated, and to her father a thrust of the sword" (1.2). Echoing Pasquariello, Leporello also implies that Don Giovanni's "seductions" could be heavy-handed: "Bravo: Two pretty feats! *Force* the daughter, and kill the father" (1.2).[34] To Don Giovanni's retort that the Commendatore "asked for it," Leporello snidely responds, "But Donna Anna, what did she ask for?" For whatever reasons, Don Giovanni is uncomfortable with this remark. Rather than gloat over his good fortune (as he does when he later recounts his success at seducing Leporello's girlfriend), he brusquely orders his servant to shut his mouth unless he "wants something as well." Whether Don Giovanni forced Donna Anna or had to flee before he could enjoy her, Leporello's sarcasm rankles. The debacle was not to the libertine's credit. Don Giovanni himself remarks on his poor luck just before he meets up with Donna Anna and Don Ottavio (and just after Elvira has broken up his tryst with Zerlina): "It seems to me that the devil is amusing himself by opposing my pleasant dealings; they are all going badly" (1.11). For a man who generally does not want more of an entrée that he has already tasted, Giovanni seems more than amenable to a meeting with the lovely Donna Anna at his house, perhaps hoping for a second chance. And so, as Solomon concludes, "despite imaginary efforts by commentators to convert Don Giovanni's failures into offstage conquests, it is fairly unambiguous that he is literally thwarted in carrying out five attempted seductions."[35]

Considering what might have happened, Don Ottavio takes Anna at her word and, understandably, breathes again with relief, though this hardly breaks the tension. Transfixed by her grim memories, Donna Anna continues with her story, for her escape did not end the night's outrages. The allegro tempo and double-dotted motive return and the harmony continues to linger in the minor mode as she recalls her renewed cries for assistance and her attempts to impede and unmask Don Giovanni. When her father appeared on the scene he, too, wanted to know Don Giovanni's identity, but, unlike his daughter, he was silenced forever. In this way, Donna Anna laments, the "iniquitous man added to his crime." Her aria "Or sai chi l'onore" follows immediately, an impressive alla breve rage aria cast in a modified da capo form: the D-major "A" section sets forth Anna's confident accusation and righteous anger, while the "B" section (in D minor) conjures up the pathetic mood associated with the Commendatore's gaping wound and spilled blood. In both of these sections, Anna urges Ottavio to vindicate her slain father:

Or sai chi l'onore	Now you know who
Rapire a me volse	wanted to steal my honor,[36]
Chi fu il traditore	who the betrayer was
Che il padre mi tolse;	that took my father from me,
Vendetta ti chiedo,	I ask you for vengeance,
La chiede il tuo cor.	you heart asks for it.
Rammenta la piaga	Remember the wounding
Del misero seno,	of that poor breast,
Rimira di sangue	behold again the ground
Coperto il terreno	covered in blood
Se l'ira in te langue,	if righteous anger
D'un giusto furor.	languishes in your heart.

"Or sai chi l'onore" shares fundamental characteristics with the earlier revenge duet, namely the key of D (now the major mode) and the alla breve style. Allanbrook describes the aria as "the prototypical march of the *opera seria* heroine." She views the musical style of the aria as both its greatest strength and, in the context of *Don Giovanni*, its greatest liability, remarking that the suppleness of comedy "subtly undercuts the monolithic intensity of the heroic style." Accordingly, Donna Anna, whose "emotions and gestures are as noble—and as monochromatic— as the affections of the most queenly of *seria* demigoddesses," loses a dramatic edge in what Allanbrook believes is fundamentally a *buffa* context.[37] But this is *Don Giovanni*, not *Le nozze di Figaro*, where the most serious injury we see is Cherubino's scratch or Figaro's feigned sprained ankle. The Countess may shed tears in her room, but *Don Giovanni* presents a veritable parade of weeping or screaming women. It is true that opera seria style is commonly parodied in eighteenth-century opera buffa, but, as Hunter notes, "the high style is used both seriously and for parodistic purposes," so that "musical context rather than content almost always determines the tone of the moment."[38]

Donna Anna is a singularly affecting *seria*-in-*buffa* heroine, a synthesis of *Empfindung* and exalted styles. As in the case of her previous *seria* moments ("Fuggi, crudele" and "Che giuramento, oh Dei" in the duet No. 2), "Or sai chi l'onore" comes after a substantial, sensibility-laden preparation: overwhelmed by emotion, Donna Anna impulsively adopts the controlled language of her noble station, imitating her father's commanding rhetoric, at least for the opening section. Nevertheless, Mozart sustains, or even intensifies, the same dramatic tension between indignation and horrified grief of the recitative. The shuddering

EXAMPLE 2. *Don Giovanni*, No. 10, "Or sai chi l'onore," early sketch of opening melody from autograph score

EXAMPLE 3. *Don Giovanni*, No. 10, "Or sai chi l'onore," revised final version of opening melody

accompaniment, the gasping effect of the melodic repetitions, and the hint of D minor (mm. 116–18) provides a contrast to the broad gestures of the main material and invests the return of the "vendetta" material with new urgency. Interestingly, Mozart was not satisfied with his original idea for the opening melody (Ex. 2) and revised it in the autograph score. The new melody not only corresponds better to the text accentuation, but it also makes more striking use of the registral plunge and echo of dissonance between the top and final notes of each phrase (Ex. 3). The result is an edgy imperiousness that alternates with the pathetic passages, in which Donna Anna implores Ottavio to remember the Commendatore's gory wounds.

CAUGHT BETWEEN "PADRE E SPOSO": DONNA ANNA AND LOVE

A proponent of the "unholy passion" hypothesis, Charles Ford concludes that "Or sai chi l'onore" does nothing "to resolve the violent passions of the recitative which were induced by Anna's identification of Giovanni."[39] Intent on finding hints of Anna's hidden love, Ford overlooks the resolution that "Or sai chi l'onore" provides, a resolution that is both dramatic (Anna has identified the perpetrator and can now call for revenge against him) and musical (the return to the opera's keynote). The rhetorical-musical tone of "Or sai chi l'onore" appeals to Don Ottavio—and the audience—in two ways. First, it is a simply riveting aria. Donna Anna's charge to Don Ottavio rings with the kind of "presentational power" that Hunter identifies in *seria* statements of nobility, which command respect even when set off by the distancing effect of comedy.[40] More importantly, perhaps, "Or sai chi l'onore"—a perfect example of a rhetorical aria—is an effective appeal for sympathy: Donna Anna speaks to Don Ottavio in the manner most likely to make him take action. The trembling umbrage of the opening section and the plaintive chromaticism of those gruesome, sanguinary images are meant to move Don Ottavio and remind us that, despite the comedic undertone, serious wrong has been done.

It is interesting, then, that while Donna Anna directs *all* of her important musical numbers to Don Ottavio, a great deal of critical reception has focused primarily on her failure to embrace his optimism and her unwillingness to think about their nuptial plans. Ford, for example, insists that "the only intention for which Anna is given musical credit is her rejection of Ottavio."[41] As an example, he indicates the noble lovers' exchange in the second-act sextet No. 19, "Sola, sola in buio loco." Following the amusing interaction between Elvira and Leporello (disguised as his master), which begins the septet, Don Ottavio enters with Donna Anna (m. 28), interrupting the B-flat tonality with the sudden brightness of D major, complete with trumpets and drums. They are dressed in mourning: perhaps they have returned from the burial of the Commendatore. Ottavio urges Anna to wipe her eyes and ease her suffering, so as not to distress the ghost of her father with her grieving. With its chromatic ascent to a brilliant high G, Ottavio's melody— which, coincidentally or not, is strikingly similar to the first theme of the overture Allegro—is both heroic and poignant.[42] But Anna cannot dispel her anguish so easily, in so short a time: it seems to her that grief will follow her to the grave. She begs him, "Grant to my pain this meager solace; only death, my treasure, will end my tears."[43]

It is true that Donna Anna shuns Ottavio's bright D-major tonality, shifting abruptly to D minor—with a motivic reference to "Fuggi, crudele"—returning briefly to the original key of B-flat major, and finally cadencing in C minor.[44] Analyzing this dialogue in the context of the sextet, Allanbrook remarks, "in the meditative twilight of the 'bujo loco' E flat is the tonic and D the unstable degree," so that "Ottavio's and Anna's public tableau of wooing and withstanding is the mode which strikes a false note." Of course, from a global harmonic perspective, it is poor Elvira's favorite key of E-flat major that stands at odds with the opera's keynote of D.[45] There is certainly a harmonic friction between the tonality of the sextet and the D-major entrance of the noble couple, but it is specifically Don Ottavio who "strikes the false note"; Donna Anna instead moves the harmony back into the sextet's tonal framework, moving quickly to dominant B-flat major before settling on the relative minor, C. She is refusing something, but is it Don Ottavio himself or his ebullient consolation? Not even well-meant gestures of love can dispel profound sorrow in a matter of hours: like her counterpart in Goldoni's play, this Donna Anna cannot be cajoled out of her grief. However, she tries to speak to Don Ottavio in a way that he will understand and accept. Still, Donna Anna's constant deferment of marriage—even in the conventional *lieto fine*—disappoints time-honored opera buffa expectations. In terms of Don Juan literature, however, it is Don Ottavio—and his courteous insistence on an *amoroso* cure-all—that is out of step. Very few of the earlier Don Juan plays and operas feature Donna Anna making wedding plans, even when she is plainly in love with someone; many times she does not even appear in the final scenes of the opera to witness or hear about the seducer's demise. Her place in the tradition is that of catalyst, her sorrow the most unwavering reminder we have of the damage caused by Don Giovanni's amoral indulgence of his sexual appetite.

The obvious exception is her final aria, No. 23, "Non mi dir, bell'idol mio," which offers a glimpse of Donna Anna's amorous side and the happiness she enjoyed before her father's murder. During the simple recitative that begins the scene (2.12), Ottavio finally loses patience with his fiancée. This is a revealingly human moment, important in its implications, but one that critics generally gloss over: "Is it that you would like to increase my sorrows with new delays? Cruel one!" Now it is Don Ottavio who turns to D minor; his miserable cry of "Crudele!" is punctuated by an emphatic dotted motive and restless diminished-seventh harmonies (the section marked *Risoluto*) that recall the tense accompanied recitative introducing "Or sai chi l'onore." His reproach triggers a response, Donna Anna's accompanied recitative for No. 23. Alarmed at Ottavio's accusation, Anna realizes—as intimated by the sudden appearance (mm. 3–5) of what will be the main melody of the aria's slow section—that he needs reassurance. Grieving, she has forgotten *his* need for the same compassion he so generously offers to her. She explains to him how difficult it is for her to put off their souls' desire; her melody embraces his preferred key, F major, as the strings play another fragment of the "Non mi dir" melody (mm. 7–9).

But the world—the now-painful demands of filial love, family honor, and justice—imposes itself once more: "Ma il mondo, oh Dio." Allanbrook dismisses these exclamations as vague, "unconvincing excuses mostly to do with respectability," but the return at this point to a rheto-

EXAMPLE 4. *Don Giovanni*, No. 23, Recitative, "Crudele! Ah no, mio bene!"

ric of *sensibilité*—and emotional turmoil—is unmistakable. The text explicitly confirms this: "non sedur la constanza / del sensibil mio core!" ("do not tempt the constancy of my sensitive heart!"). Even as she reaches out to her lover, Donna Anna cannot forget what she owes her slain father. The harmonic ambiguity at measure 10 underlines the dramatic conflict (Ex. 4). Besides the dissonant crunch between Donna Anna's melodic F and the diminished-seventh chord of the accompaniment ("oh Dio!"), the melodic sequence in the first violin makes a startling harmonic downshift, seemingly from D minor (Donna Anna's revenge key) to B-flat major; later, this same melodic motive will conspicuously reappear in the aria accompaniment, precisely at the moment when Donna Anna speaks of her love for Don Ottavio (Ex. 5). Donna Anna is caught, musically and dramatically, between the conflicting demands of her father's unavenged murder and Don Ottavio's romantic devotion. The recitative ends on D minor, but Anna's desire for happiness with Ottavio radiates warmly in the last vocal phrase. The caressing Neapolitan harmony at measure 13, an ethereal vocal line that extends itself gracefully to its upper boundaries, introduces Donna Anna *amorosa*: "Rest assured that love speaks to me for you." Finally we hear the gentle melody of the Larghetto in its entirety, its slow tempo and long-breathed beauty unmatched in the opera. She abandons her usual D (-minor inflected) tonality, favoring the happier key of B-flat major. Clarinets, an essential instrument in Donna Elvira's music, make their first appearance in Donna Anna's solo music, their rich sonority replacing the sharper resonance of the oboes that accompanied "Or sai chi l'onore."[46] Though her words still reflect some reserve, her music

EXAMPLE 5. *Don Giovanni,* No. 23, Rondo, "Non mi dir, bell'idol mio"; mm. 28–30

caresses Don Ottavio with refreshing—nonaggressive, nonsatirical—familiarity:

Non mi dir, bell'idol mio	Do not tell me, my beloved idol,
Che son io crudel con te	that I am cruel to you.
Tu ben sai quant'io t'amai,	You know well how much I loved you,
Tu conosci la mia fè.	you know my faithfulness.
Calma, calma il tuo tormento,	Calm, calm your torment,
Se di duol non vuoi ch'io mora!	if you do not wish that I die of sorrow
Forse, un giorno il cielo ancora	Perhaps one day Heaven will again
Sentirà pietà di me.	feel pity for me.

She speaks of a relationship to which we have not been privy: "You know well how much I loved you; you know my faithfulness." There have been several instances in the opera where Anna's words and actions have hinted at her affection for Don Ottavio. She runs to him when her father needs help, and she confides in him after the murder. When Ottavio and Anna, along with Elvira, enter Don Giovanni's house in act 1, scene 19, she expresses her concern that Ottavio, her "caro sposo," might be in danger. Now, in the Larghetto of "Non mi dir," Donna Anna addresses Don Ottavio with uncharacteristic calm, reassuring him of her devotedness and begging his patience. Only when she refers to her own unhappiness at seeing Don Ottavio's doubts ("se di duol non vuoi ch'io mora") does Anna slip into the unpredictable harmonic progressions, minor-key inflections, and chromatic writing of grief. At measures 42–47, for instance, the melody is fairly quiescent, but the syncopation of the upper strings and grumbling flourishes of the violas and bassoons evince an underlying distress. Donna Anna's struggle to reconcile her feelings becomes even more obvious with the abbreviated repeat of the initial material. The violin sequence that first punctuated Donna Anna's exclamation of "Ma il mondo, oh Dio" in the recitative and later ornamented her expressions of love ("tu ben sai quant'io t'amai") in the aria now reappears, extended, with a different text (mm. 55–57): "Calma, calma, il tuo tormento." Twice it reaffirms the tonic key, F major, but by the third iteration ("se di duol non vuoi ch'io mora") it begins to sink again, tracing the tonic minor (C–A-flat–F) as Donna Anna begs for her lover's leniency (Ex. 6).

The ensuing Allegro moderato features more *seria*-style vocalizing: lengthy coloratura passages, leaps of an octave or more, and an expansive range. Yet there are noticeably odd details that work against this default musical idiom that Donna Anna assumes when she is beyond the limits of her emotional threshold. The frail-sounding, predominantly treble sonority of the orchestral prelude and Donna Anna's first phrase hover without a stabilizing anchor, the resolute strength of purpose that she demonstrated in her rage aria. The melodic line and harmonic progression are also quirky: the sudden descent to the subdominant B-flat major (mm. 66–68, 74–76) following the half cadence of the first phrase sounds almost like the sort of harmonic "error" that Mozart used to depict Elettra's emotional disorientation. (The vocal part in measures 75–76 is especially striking, picking up a tritone below where it left off.) Even the coloratura passage, with its repeated high tones, demonstrates a shaky balance between exultant hopefulness and hysteria. Certainly measures 101–4 express how close to the surface Anna's "torments" lie: she stammers ("forse . . . il cielo . . . un giorno . . ."), her sequence of appoggiaturas collapses in alternation with that of the orchestra, and the tonic minor appears briefly before the cadence. The last two measures of the vocal section offer a poignant, earnest finish; the final melodic gesture, intensified with a sudden crescendo, and the parallel fall of the woodwinds' thirds and sixths (mm. 111–12) recall the end of Zerlina's endearing aria "Vedrai carino."

There are many musical markers of intimacy, conflict, and feeling in the *scena* of "Non mi dir," including the warmer orchestration (more sensual, with the addition of the clarinets) and tonality (F major, a conciliatory gesture for Don Ottavio), as well as the overt references to Donna Anna's love for Don Ottavio. Nevertheless, critics have regularly bashed the aria as an example of musical (and sexual) frigidity. Dent concludes that "the scene has no reason whatsoever for its existence, ex-

EXAMPLE 6. *Don Giovanni*, No. 23, Rondo, "Non mi dir, bell'idol mio"; mm. 55–59

cept to give Donna Anna the opportunity of singing a set aria." He concedes that "Non mi dir" is "certainly beautiful," but adds that it is also "singularly cold and unemotional."[47] Allanbrook, too, hears a fundamental lack of warmth and envisions Donna Anna as unattractive, even repellent, at this moment: "On Anna's face is frozen an ambiguous grimace. The victim turned huntress, the 'assaulted turned assailant,' as she describes herself, pursues her prey in an access either of righteous anger or of unholy passion. It will always be a question whether her outstretched hand is a sign of menace or of desire. If desire, its urgings are buried too deeply within her for her to admit them even to herself. Certainly she thrusts Ottavio away both often and instinctively. 'Non mi dir,' her last aria, and a singer's showpiece, is a chilling affair."[48] Allanbrook's almost exclusive focus on the alla breve section of the aria helps to sustain the concept of an emotionally static *seria* "voice" at odds with the comic framework, and even with the other characters. But the extended accompanied recitatives and *amoroso* Larghetto are essential components of the role. If Anna expresses her feelings of outrage with the imperious control of a *seria* queen, she does so only after having succumbed to her own version of *sensibilité*, marked by a convulsive, changeable musical and textual rhetoric. Her weeping, fainting, moments of disorientation, and cries of horror are crucial to a comprehensive understanding of her temperament.

"Non mi dir" does *not*, however, make Donna Anna into one of Mozart's arguably more beloved sentimental heroines such as Donna Elvira and the Countess Almaviva. Generally, the appeal of an operatic heroine depends greatly on her efforts to maintain, even to the point of self-destruction, an explicit emotional connection with a male character, usually a lover or a husband. It is precisely this *apparent* forgetting of self, the steadfast attachment to love and the beloved, that makes these heroines so admirable to opera lovers. Thus, citing the correspondences between "Non mi dir" and the Countess's "Dove sono," Allanbrook explains her preference for the latter aria. In the slow section of "Dove sono," the Countess languishes in self-pity, but she transforms this emotion into hope and resolve in the more florid, expansive Allegro section, so that the coloratura becomes "an integral part of her passionate $\frac{4}{4}$ march affect." The Countess assuages her pain by reaffirming her constancy: she will help convince the Count of his love through the strength of hers. Donna Anna expresses love, reassurance, and, finally, hope in "Non mi dir," but, Allanbrook concludes, she cannot "get out of herself"; her coloratura is thus seen as "mere icy ornament."[49] The comparison is not entirely fair, since the dramatic circumstances are so different. Donna Anna is not lamenting a husband's philandering or a lover's indifference: that would be Donna Elvira's role. Instead, Donna Anna is a casualty of Don Giovanni's violence, dramatizing the conflict between two loyalties. Her responsibility to her father comes first: he died defending her honor, and she must do the same if necessary. Until she has obtained justice for the Commendatore, she cannot give her hand and heart fully to Don Ottavio.

In many ways, this conflict between *padre* and *sposo* defines Donna Anna and sets her apart. In both opera buffa and opera seria, romantic love generally takes precedence over filial love should a conflict between the two arise. In Mozart's serious opera *Idomeneo*, for instance, the Trojan princess Ilia mourns her father and brothers cut down in the war by Idomeneo, king of Crete; her anger and hatred, however, must contend with her growing love for the Cretan prince, Idamantes. The strength of her amorous feelings is apparent from the outset; her emotional transfer is complete early in the second act. She gives herself over to her love for Idamantes, and even accepts Idomeneo as her new father: "Now I no longer remember anxieties, troubles. Now Heaven has granted me joy and contentment, compensation for my losses" (2.2). Resolution does not come so easily to Donna Anna. Her struggle with the demands of two different loves, two different men—three, if you count her would-be seducer—extends beyond the last finale. Her refusal to forget everything that has happened and to join Don Ottavio in an expeditious happy ending has provoked charges of inflexibility, emotional coldness, ulterior motives, and even narcissism. It is possible, however, that critics find Donna Anna's "unnatural" behavior disturbing because it is also, paradoxically, the most realistic in the opera. Her drama reads against opera's favorite truism: love heals all—and quickly. Comparing Donna Anna's painstaking progress toward happiness with Ilia's more rapturous transformation, we must ask which comes closer to human experience. Far from being a plaster demigoddess, Donna Anna is, in many ways, one of Mozart's most flesh-and-blood creations.

CHAPTER 2

Sisterhood and Seduction I: Abandonment and Rescue

Donna Elvira

Marianne's abilities were, in many respects, quite equal to
Elinor's. She was sensible and clever; but eager in every thing;
her sorrows, her joys, could have no moderation. She was
generous, amiable, interesting: she was every thing but
prudent.

Jane Austen, *Sense and Sensibility*

"If abandonment brings out the worst in women, their enslavement to
men or their passion," remarks Lawrence Lipking, "it also brings out the
worst in common attitudes toward women . . . reduc[ing] them to a few
types or caricatures: the poor lost soul or the avenging virago."[1] Not surprisingly, Lipking had Donna Elvira in mind when he wrote these words.
Excessive sensibility and an imprudent nature ensnare her in a cycle of
humiliation, whether she wants to kiss Giovanni or kill him. Explaining
the significance of this arresting *mezzo-carattere* role in the context of
what might be categorized a black comedy, many interpreters—who are
as ambivalent about Elvira's emotional immoderation as her creators
were—fall back on the "common attitudes" that Lipking describes.
Hence, when Elvira indicts Don Giovanni, she is a crazed and ridiculous
harasser, but she is pitiable and commendably "human" as his adoring

protector. On the whole, Donna Elvira satisfies conventional expectations about operatic women in a way that Donna Anna does not: in a phrase, she "goes soft." Seduced and betrayed by Don Giovanni, Donna Elvira launches a vigorous campaign against his treachery in act 1, but her rancor eventually dissolves into pity and renewed adoration. In general, critical reception (including productions) implies that this makes her a more "feminine" heroine than Donna Anna. But sympathy is not necessarily the same thing as admiration. We may appreciate Donna Elvira's earnest heart—apparent even in her relationships with the other characters—but not all love is laudable. In the end, Donna Elvira is more the lead character in a cautionary tale than a model for emulation. She is exactly the kind of "undone" woman that opera celebrates and destroys. In fact, throughout the opera Elvira pleads with us—as she does with most of the characters—to listen carefully to her warning, to take her *seriously*.

We first encounter her roaming the dark, unfamiliar streets of a Spanish city, looking for the "husband" who has forsaken her:

Ah chi mi dice mai	Ah who will ever tell me
Quel barbaro dov'è	Where that barbarous man is,
Che per mio scorno amai	Who, to my shame, I loved,
Che mi manco di fè?	Who was faithless to me?
Ah se ritrovo l'empio,	Ah if I ever find the wicked man,
E a me non torna ancor,	And he still does not come back to me,
Vo' farne orrendo scempio,	I want to slaughter him horribly,
Gli vo' cavare il cor.	I want to tear out his heart.

Donna Elvira's outrageous threats of physical violence carry none of the horrible gravity of the Commendatore's murder in the opera's *introduzione*. The music of this aria—replete with rapid shifts in dynamics, successive wide leaps, and an extensive melodic range, with *sforzandi* and tremolos—certainly conveys Elvira's spitting anger. Almost immediately, however, Don Giovanni and Leporello interject from the sidelines, detracting from the aria's tone of righteous fury. Elvira does not hear them, but we do. In the recitative that precedes "Ah chi mi dice mai," the libidinous master and his servant engage in an unsavory dialogue—Giovanni effectively introduces Elvira when his nose picks up the "scent of a woman"—so that Donna Elvira is already more object than subject, the focus of Giovanni's obvious arousal and Leporello's wry asides. Giovanni calls to the young lady in his most tender lilt, but when she turns to face him, his ardor is doused by cold disappointment. He has *already* had the pleasure, thank you. Leporello can hardly contain his amusement at his master's mistake: it was Giovanni himself who jilted this *"pove-rina."* Looking into her seducer's face, Elvira now sees only indifference and irritation. A master of escape, Don Giovanni abruptly dismisses himself, leaving the catalogue-keeping Leporello to enlighten Elvira about the sobering reality: she is only one of the more than two thousand women that Don Giovanni has seduced.

ELVIRA AS PROTECTOR: RESCUE, RHETORIC, AND REASON

For many, this scene is unequivocally comical. The men's dialogue, Dent says, lets us know at once that "we are not going to be allowed to take Elvira seriously for a moment."[2] No doubt Leporello's assessment (act 1, scene 5, following her first impassioned recounting of Don Giovanni's crimes toward her) reinforces for the audience the image of Elvira as emotions run amok, the satirical product-producer of her own romance novel: "Pare un libro stampato" ("She seems a printed book").[3] Similarly, Donna Elvira enters the opera with a distinct disadvantage in the struggle to bring Don Giovanni to justice through her own testimony. She is a stranger in town, and her situation is scandalous. Who will believe her when she denounces a well-respected local gentleman? What kind of justice can she hope to attain? The strategy that Donna Elvira chooses stands out both in the tradition of opera buffa and in the Don Juan literature. For the rest of act 1, Donna Elvira places herself between Don Giovanni and the other women that he tries to seduce, not as the typical jealous rival, but as a *rescuer,* the female defender of feminine virtue. After the disgrace of the catalogue aria, Donna Elvira pursues Giovanni, catching him in the act of a little "innocent amor" with the peasant girl Zerlina (1.10). She wields her outrage shrewdly, aiming both to save the girl and to punish Don Giovanni by taking away the object of his momentary obsession. After chastising the libertine in recitative, Donna Elvira turns away from him completely, addressing the aria to a bewildered Zerlina:

Ah fuggi il traditor	Ah, run away from this traitor,
Non lo lasciar più dir:	Do not let him say more to you:
Il labbro è mentitor,	His lips are lying,
Fallace il ciglio.	His eyes deceitful.
Da' miei tormenti impara	Learn from my torments
A creder a quel cor,	How that heart is to be believed
E nasca il tuo timor	And let your fear be born
Dal mio periglio.	From my peril.

Elvira's candor with this potential rival—a stranger of inferior social class—is striking. Typically, this scenario would feature a furious tirade directed at the traitorous lover, a pitiful lament in the sentimental style, or, as we find in numerous operas, a catfight between the two women. In the Bertati-Gazzaniga *Don Giovanni,* for example, Donna Elvira and the peasant girl Maturina exchange a series of insults with one another. Bertati further emphasized their consciousness of station by having Donna Elvira use the familiar "tu" with Maturina, while the latter is careful to address the noble woman with the formal "Lei," even when gibing her. The Mozart–Da Ponte Elvira, on the other hand—menacing as she tries to sound in "Ah chi mi dice mai"—is fundamentally fair-minded and altruistic. She is willing to reveal her own shameful circumstances, exposing herself to further mortification. There is a nobility of purpose that transcends the stock denunciation of "Ah fuggi il traditor." Unable to act directly *against* Giovanni (except in the form of public denouncement), Elvira assuages her hurt by acting *for* others: "Stop, scoundrel: Heaven has caused me to hear your treacheries; I am in time to save this poor innocent from your barbarous clutches."

Caught with his breeches down, as it were, Don Giovanni tries to reassure his young prize, telling her that Donna Elvira is delusional. Undeterred, Elvira plunges ahead. Though the accented, wide leaps of the violins and the jagged vocal line reflect her turbulent passions, the aria serves as an admonishment, garnered from experience. The relatively old-school musical style—relentless dotted rhythms and angular melodic fragments worked out in a patently Handelian fashion, complete with emphatic hemiola cadences—heightens the authoritative tone. Her testimony grows even more insistent in the musical return (the aria is in ternary form): she repeats the word "fuggi" three times (mm. 23–25) rising to G above the staff, the highest vocal pitch of the aria to this point. Her melody later leaps up an octave to this same pitch (more striking in that it is the dissonant pitch of the dominant-seventh chord) at the word "mentitor" (m. 34), then extends the range, both vocal and affective, with the closing melismatic outbursts on "fallace." Whatever the peculiarities of its rhetorical manner, "Ah fuggi il traditor" is undeniably effective: Donna Elvira exits with a silent Zerlina in hand, leaving Don Giovanni unsatisfied.

She does not have to wait long for another confrontation with Don Giovanni and another rescue attempt, this time of Donna Anna. A change of scene shows Don Giovanni meeting up with Donna Anna and Don Ottavio, who take him into their confidence (1.11), asking him, as a gentleman, for his aid. Don Giovanni assumes his most sympathetic guise, his ingratiating words to Donna Anna seemingly full of concern: "But you, lovely Donna Anna, why are you crying so? Who was the cruel one who dared to disturb the calm of your life?" Once again, Donna Elvira appears (1.12) just in time to witness this new perfidy. This time, however, she hardly acknowledges the seducer. Instead, in the quartet No. 9, "Non ti fidar, o misera," she immediately appeals to Donna Anna, cautioning her as she did Zerlina: "Do not trust that roguish heart, unhappy lady! That cruel man already betrayed me; he wants to betray you as well." Once again, Elvira's musical style suits the circumstances and intended listener. Instead of the agitated, forceful allegro she used to alarm the infatuated Zerlina in "Ah fuggi il traditor," she begins the quartet with a composed and dignified Andante. Her melody—which features the noble alla breve rhythm that Anna favors—communicates both her sincerity and her sorrow. (Hermann Abert aptly describes this melody as "the mournful voice of all womanhood trampled underfoot by Don Giovanni.")[4] Elvira appeals to tearful Donna Anna not as a chaperone (as with Zerlina), but as a gentle ally and defender. Her candor and quiet urgency provoke a spontaneous empathy from Anna and her fiancé. They remark on her "noble aspect" and "sweet majesty," how her sorrowful countenance and tears fill them with pity.

Their sympathy and esteem for his accuser unsettles Don Giovanni. He tries a favorite ploy, casually remarking that Donna Elvira is crazy: "la povera ragazza è pazza." His music, however, betrays a distinct nervousness beneath his sham courtesies as he tries to undermine Donna Elvira's petition. His position is undeniably precarious. The baffled couple remains unconvinced by his muttered chromatic insinuations; moreover, he utterly fails to suppress Donna Elvira, whose plea becomes more emphatic with each musical gesture. At first she only asks that Donna Anna and Don Ottavio hear her out; her request is set to a twice-stated ascending arpeggio, a development of her original, stately melody (mm. 28–31). Noticing the couple's uncertainty, however, she grows anxious: the second violin quickens the rhythmic pulse with a sixteenth-note fluctuation (mm. 34–36), just as the vocal line loses its melodic grace. Finally, when Donna Anna, Don Ottavio, and Don Giovanni sing together (m. 36) about the troubling feelings stirring in their souls—united in words and music, though not perspective—Donna Elvira unleashes her frustration in a barrage of sixteenth notes, clambering up to the B-flat that marks the top of her range: "Indignation, rage, spite,

EXAMPLE 7. *Don Giovanni*, No. 9, "Non ti fidar, o misera"

torment agitate my soul." Musically, she resists Don Giovanni's attempt to close the argument with his lies: her melodic line accentuates the dominant pedal tone with octave vacillations and insistent repetitions on a high F (the highest note of the phrase and also the dominant pitch), and also weakens the finalizing effect of the cadence in tonic B-flat major with the *forte* "No!" on the mediant tone D (Ex. 7). Determined, Donna Elvira presses forward with a literally breathless melodic line, compelling Donna Anna and Don Ottavio to continue their deliberation, until all four voices cadence—not in the tonic, but the dominant key.

Don Giovanni's control of the situation falters even more in the harmonically unstable section that follows (mm. 50–69), as Don Ottavio and Donna Anna each begin to make their own inquiry. Don Ottavio, the gentleman, expresses his desire to "get to the bottom" of things; Anna, moved by Elvira's fervent entreaties, observes that the sorrowful woman's countenance and speech do not suggest insanity: "Non ha l'aria di pazzia il suo volto, il suo parlar." There is a momentary impasse. Don Ottavio presses Giovanni—who is eager to escape from the scene but does not want to arouse further suspicion—but the conniver insists that Donna Elvira is out of her mind. Donna Anna questions Donna Elvira, who again calls Don Giovanni a faithless deceiver. Fearing that her betrayer might be temporarily "acquitted," Donna Elvira takes up again her vehement octave fluctuations on F. Three times she cries "mentitore!" ("liar!"), the enraged response to Don Giovanni's patronizing "Infelice!" ("Unhappy woman!").

Many productions make Donna Elvira look and sound like an out-of-control hysteric at this point, but the dramatic result argues against this interpretation. Something about her demeanor and frantic exclamations must be cogently persuasive, for now Donna Anna and Don Ottavio "begin to have doubts" about Don Giovanni, their voices united in a turn to the tonic minor. The profligate aristocrat senses the danger: if his word as a gentleman cannot override Donna Elvira's pathetic appeals, if he is *doubted*, he will have lost one of his most reliable sources of immunity. He will be forced to choose between fight and flight, both of which will result in unfavorable consequences for him. Alarmed at this turn of events, Don Giovanni tries a new strategy. Breaking into a *buffa*-style patter, Don Giovanni pulls Donna Elvira aside and tries to bully her into keeping quiet for the sake of discretion. He could not have chosen a worse means of intimidation. Donna Elvira knows very well that her relationship to well-born society has already been forever damaged by her illicit affair with Giovanni, so she has little to lose. Observing Giovanni's chagrin, she seizes what may be her only chance for vindication. The music firmly returns to the tonic key of B-flat major (reinforced by the conspicuous tonic pedal in the strings and winds) as Donna Elvira speaks loudly enough for everyone to hear, "Do not hope [for my silence], wicked man, I have lost all prudence! I want to reveal your guilt and my condition to everyone." Anna and Ottavio now regard Giovanni with obvious suspicion, noting his change of color and nervous speech.

For the moment, Donna Elvira is triumphant. In fact, the scenes of "Ah fuggi il traditor" and the quartet "Non ti fidar" are the only times in the opera when Donna Elvira gains the advantage over her seducer. Caught off guard, Don Giovanni relies in both instances on a standard defensive strategy: he accuses Donna Elvira of being "pazza," a madwoman, counting on female jealousy and society's suspicion of unchecked emotion to justify his accusation. This strategy is successful in numerous Don Juan tales, but not with this particular Donna Elvira. Not only is she credible enough to pry Zerlina out of Don Giovanni's embrace, but, more significantly, she is able to win the favor of Donna Anna and Don Ottavio over one of their friends and neighbors. As

Donna Anna concludes, the "noble" and "majestic" Donna Elvira does not look or act like a crazy person.

ELVIRA'S "MADNESS"

There is, however, one kind of "madness" that afflicts Donna Elvira, and that is what is sometimes called "lover's folly," the inability (or unwillingness) to recognize anything false in the beloved. The original Elvira-type character—Elvire in Molière's *Dom Juan ou le festin de pierre*—admits herself that she suffers from this malady. Meeting Dom Juan for the first time since his disappearance, Elvire confesses that she ignored sense in favor of illusory love. Her clear-eyed diagnosis demonstrates how lover's folly confuses an otherwise reasonable mind, preying on innocent sensibility and desire:

> Yes, I well see that you were not expecting me; and you are indeed surprised, but quite differently than I hoped you to be; and the manner in which you show it fully convinces me of that which I refused to believe. I marvel at my simplicity and the weakness of my heart to doubt a betrayal, which all appearances confirmed for me. I confess that I was good enough, or rather foolish enough, to want to deceive myself, and to make efforts to refute my eyes and judgment. I sought reasons to excuse to my tenderness the remissness of friendship it perceived in you; and I deliberately forged for myself a hundred legitimate motives for such a hasty departure in order to justify you of the crime of which my reason accused you. My just suspicions advised me many times each day: I rejected the voice that made you a criminal in my eyes, and I listened with pleasure to a thousand ridiculous chimeras that fashioned you innocent to my heart. But in the end, your manner of reception no longer allows me to doubt, and the look with which you received me teaches me many more things than I would be pleased to know. (1.3)

Both Elvire and Donna Elvira hope against hope that wholehearted devotion will win Don Giovanni over again. In a sense, the Countess Almaviva suffers from a comparable affliction. We are meant to sympathize with these ingenuous women, especially when they are made to face harsh reality in the end. This is why Donna Elvira gains the compassion of every character in the opera except for Don Giovanni. It is puzzling, then, that many critical interpretations support the libertine's derisive viewpoint rather than the opera's generally empathetic position. Her high emotions and lack of restraint—particularly in act 1—are linked to a fundamental lack of reason, just as Don Giovanni would like them to be. In her analysis of "Ah chi mi dice mai," for example, Allanbrook describes the music in terms that strongly reinforce the idea of Elvira as "pazza." The "framing gesture of the orchestra propels Elvira; she seems not to be mistress of her own movements," while "the triadic string flourishes are only the most perfunctory filler, making the approach of the marcher jerky and spasmodic." She adds that "in relation to the beginning of the orchestra's repetition of the ritornello," itself "overornate and exaggerated," Elvira's "first vocal entry is askew—one measure late— giving the impression at least of distraction, if not dementia."[5]

"Distraction" is exactly the right word for the situation of an irate lover, and no one can deny that Don Giovanni has driven Elvira to it. "Dementia," however, invalidates Elvira's reaction: her emotions are disconnected from reality. It is striking how often commentators describe Donna Elvira's music in act 1—and particularly "Ah fuggi il traditor"—in terms of insanity:

> The very promptness with which Donna Elvira reappears makes her entrance all the more comical, and the quartet, in spite of the momentary seriousness of Anna and Ottavio, still maintains the *buffo* style. . . . [Elvira] may well seem mad to [Anna and Ottavio], with her wild outburst [mm. 44–49] that mixes the styles of "patter" and *coloratura* so strangely. . . . Further on such little dignity as she had breaks down completely.[6]

> The enigmatic Elvira occupies the ambivalent middle ground in temperament, just as she does in purely musical terms. But when she adopts the graver tones of Anna and Ottavio, the ironic intention is again clear, as in the aria 'Ah, fuggi il traditor.' Here is a woman who has already succumbed to the temptation (and a promise of marriage from Don Giovanni), denying the *same pleasure* to another, and she does so with formal archaic severity. The words show an exaggerated, histrionic hostility, quite inappropriate for the simple task of cautioning a peasant maid. The tone of the outburst is a product of Elvira's passion and not the circumstances in which she finds Zerlina. Indeed, the unwavering nature of her passion turns Elvira into a butt for the comic business of the opera.[7]

> The *stile antico* [of "Ah fuggi il traditor"] is not affected merely out of a desire for rhythmic urgency; surely it is intended as a musical expression of personal eccentricity. . . . High-strung and high-minded, [Elvira] pursues the "barbaro" Giovanni with the same fanatical ardor she will later turn to doing Christian penance. She is a woman of great passion and not a little madness. . . . It is a measure of the bleak perspective of *Don Giovanni* that such high excesses are rendered as near-comic idiosyncrasies by the stiff-gaited rhythms of an antique style.[8]

Even Lipking, who chides critics for perpetuating clichés about the abandoned woman figure, falls into the trap. He, too, misreads the scene of "Non ti fidar," imagining reactions from Donna Anna, Don Ottavio, and even Zerlina that are completely at odds with the libretto:

> Indeed, Elvira's infatuation may be thought to amount not merely to weakness but madness. . . . Is she quite sane? Don Giovanni has some success in persuading the company that her accusations of him prove she is out of her mind; and from his point of view that diagnosis must look correct, since only a madwoman would make such a fuss about so insignificant an affair as the usual seduction and betrayal. We know better, of course. Yet Elvira's obsession, her extremity, her rapid shifts of mood—all perfectly realized not only by what she sings but by orchestral punctuation and italics—do indicate that she is on the edge of madness.[9]

This preoccupation with "madness" says as much about the favor (bias?) Don Juan still enjoys as it does about the role of Donna Elvira. Unusual or sensational as her rhetorical-musical language may be, she nevertheless has wits enough to track down Don Giovanni and thwart his further deceptions. Elvira remains a galvanizing presence in the act I finale, accompanying Donna Anna and Don Ottavio to Don Giovanni's ball, where they hope to reveal his villainy to the public. One can easily believe that she devised the strategy of entering the house, camouflaged, in festive masks. In any case, it is obvious that the noble couple has taken her into their confidence, an indisputable sign of their trust in her. Donna Elvira exhorts her "cari amici," her dear friends, to be brave. Don Ottavio agrees, urging Donna Anna to dismiss her worries and fears, for "our friend speaks well." It is no longer Donna Anna who drives the impulse of revenge; on the contrary, she is almost weak with dread, frightened for them all. Rather, it is Elvira who reintroduces the key of D minor with a melody reminiscent of Donna Anna's "Fuggi, crudele" (mm. 173–82). When the three conspirators join together in prayerful entreaty before entering Don Giovanni's house, Elvira specifically asks for heaven to "avenge her betrayed love," while Donna Anna and Don Ottavio beg only for divine protection of their heart's zeal. Later, when Zerlina screams for help, Elvira leads the others in the indictment, "We know everything." With these words, *la pazza* attains vindication, if not peace of mind.

PITY AND EROS: THE ABANDONED WOMAN'S APPEAL

At the end of the first act, it seems that Don Giovanni must at last face justice. Perhaps this is why Donna Elvira succumbs to romantic nostalgia in her first appearance in act 2. The scene of the trio "Ah taci, in-giusto core" (No. 15) highlights her struggle between punitive indigna-tion and infatuated compassion. The A-major tonality and $\frac{6}{8}$ meter re-call Giovanni's seduction of Zerlina in "Là ci darem la mano," but now the blushing heat of desire belongs to Elvira. The orchestral introduc-tion, all fluttering pulsations, truly sounds like the music of her heart, which yearns once more for Don Giovanni:

Ah taci, ingiusto core,	Ah be silent, unjust heart
Non palpitarmi in seno;	do not throb within my breast;
È un empio, è un	He is an ungodly man, he is a
traditore,	betrayer
È colpa aver pietà.	it is wrong to have pity.

The melody begins simply, but it is increasingly embellished as Elvira feels herself overwhelmed by amorous feelings. At the final words, her resistance is portrayed musically; after the orchestra's alluring chro-matic insinuation (m. 12) we hear the ringing force of her high A on the word "colpa": it is *wrong* to pity him.

In opera buffa, feminine *pietà*—often quite distinct from disinterested charity—is both desirable and dangerous, since it relies on the vulnera-bility of pliant, "womanly" sensibilities. The lenient Countess Almaviva, for instance, pardons the Count's violent treatment of her in the closet scene (2.9), then complains to her maid, "Ah Susanna, how softhearted I am! Who can believe in a woman's fury ever again?" Susanna replies, "With men, my lady, no matter how much you twist and turn, you al-ways end up in that same place." In *Così fan tutte*, pity serves as an im-portant levering tool for impelling Fiordiligi and Dorabella into the illicit embrace of their Albanian suitors. Pity—imbued by erotic feeling—is op-eratic womanhood's strength and weakness: it is not always rewarded well, and it sometimes leads to crushing disgrace. This is certainly re-flected in "Ah taci, ingiusto core," which—much in the same way as "Ah chi mi dice mai"—makes Donna Elvira and her sensitive emotions the target of merciless comedy. Hearing Elvira's voice, Leporello and Don Giovanni arrive on the scene, upsetting the intimate mood of her lyric balcony confession. The orchestra, Leporello, and Don Giovanni churn out the same musical motive eight times without pause, a moment of static banality as Giovanni figures out what to do. Finally, the seducer comes up with a cruel diversion, inverting the yearning orchestral chro-matic ascent of Elvira's final phrase with an insidious chromatic descent. He appropriates Elvira's melody (now in dominant E major) as a camouflage, the perfect mask of longing and love. She answers him disparagingly, but Giovanni implores her to have pity, enticing her with a gracefully embellished melody (mm. 28–32): "Yes, my life, it is I, and I beg for your forgiveness." Now Elvira takes up the men's "cogitating" motive; Leporello remarks on her confusion and waning resolve, reckoning correctly that "the madwoman will believe him again."[10]

Sensing her uncertainty, Giovanni launches into a "serenade." The key shift to C major within an A major number is striking; Mozart will use this harmonic (and dramatic) device again in the final seduction duet between Ferrando and Fiordiligi. It is an alluring tune—Abert thinks it might be Giovanni's most seductive—and Giovanni will soon recycle it for courting Elvira's maid.[11] Indeed, Elvira's reaction suggests that it is not altogether fresh: perhaps she has heard it before. "No, I don't believe you," she cries again and again, her anger evinced by the angular melodic line, as well as the tremolos and *sforzandi* of the accompaniment (mm. 46–49). But Giovanni is just warming up. He threatens to kill himself in a threefold repetition of falling sevenths, his declaration made, according to the stage direction, "in transports and almost crying." Settling back to the original tonic A major, the consummate wooer begs Elvira to come to him, completing his appeal with an impassioned—and manipulative—cadential sweep.

Elvira yields. For her, the rest of the trio becomes a prayer, one that would seem to retract her petition in the masker's trio with Donna Anna and Don Ottavio in act 1. At that time, she begged for celestial vengeance; now she asks for protection for her credulous, "unfair" heart. Touched by her vulnerability, Leporello sheds his cynicism and toady's glee, joining Elvira in her invocation. Her entreaty means nothing to the self-interested and callous Giovanni: "I hope she falls for this quickly! What a lovely little coup this is; a more fruitful talent than mine cannot be found." Naturally, he gets his wish. In the final cadential passage of the trio (mm. 76–83), the orchestra brings back the sensuous, ascending chromatic gesture that Elvira had resisted at the beginning of the trio. This time, the vocal leap to the high A segues not into a dutifully regulated, descending arpeggio but rather a gracefully swooning scale as Elvira gives in to love. Don Giovanni immediately takes off for an amorous adventure elsewhere, leaving Leporello, dressed in his master's clothes, as his surrogate. The servant's ephemeral moral objections fade away as he warms to the role of phony *gentiluomo*.

Eternally gullible and invariably abused by Don Giovanni, Elvira frequently brings out the Leporello in the audience, eliciting jeers and then guilty sympathy. Discussing "Ah taci, ingiusto core," Lipking aptly captures this "Leporellian" perspective:

> Even when most serious she is vulnerable to ridicule, as in the extraordinary trio early in Act Two, where her troubled, budding hope for reconciliation harmonizes with Giovanni's self-congratulations at deceiving her and Leporello's amazement at her credulity. The beauty of what we hear is almost (but not quite) enough to cover the embarrassment we feel at watching Elvira's foolishness exposed. Delicate and delicious as the scene may be, it also indulges in a smile at the sex-starved heroine's expense . . .

> . . . Caught up in the action, each of us (whatever our moral disapproval) is in complicity with the facile, amusing stratagems of Don Giovanni. In this respect Leporello is our surrogate. He makes wry faces but goes along with his master, and while condemning the libertine code he also enjoys it. Yet Donna Elvira will not let him or us get away with it. She shames us for giving into the entertainment, and warns us that when we go home we shall be alone with ourselves. Therefore we laugh at her; there is safety in numbers. Nevertheless, in the long run truth is on her side. Most of us know little about being heroes, about exercising power without conscience, debauching multitudes, and forcing the devil himself to take an interest in our doings. But most of us do know something about feeling lost and lonely. Donna Elvira speaks for those private feelings.[12]

Her erotic surrender stirs desire as well as compassion in the onstage *and* offstage Leporello. Identified from the beginning as the perfumed essence of *donna abbandonata,* Donna Elvira serves as the opera's ripe object of voyeuristic pleasure:

> The woman forgets herself, the man's attention is pricked. Not even Kierkegaard, in his visionary portrait of Elvira in *Either/Or,* can help noticing her throbbing bosom and streaming hair; "her nun's veil was torn and floated out behind her, her thin white gown would have betrayed much to a profane glance, had not the passion in her countenance turned the attention of even the most depraved of men upon itself." That has the authentic note of a male response to an abandoned woman: a deep respect for her suffering that still manages to leave room for some speculative glances behind the torn veil. Like Giovanni and his followers in the audience, Kierkegaard wants nothing more than to console her torment.[13]

This artless but profound sensuality—so different from Zerlina's knowingly manipulative coquetry—carries forward to the great sextet No. 19, "Sola, sola in buio loco." Elvira is now alone with Leporello—still playing Don Giovanni—in the darkness of Donna Anna's interior courtyard. She is almost feverish with anticipation, eager for the kisses and caresses of her *caro sposo.* Her voice trembles and she speaks of death, but there is a sexual undertone to her words as well:

Sola, sola in buio loco,	Alone, alone in this dark place,
Palpitar il cor mi sento,	I feel my heart throbbing,
E m'assale un tal spavento	and such a fear assails me
Che mi sembra di morir.	that I seem to be dying.

Initially, the music highlights Elvira's fear: the dramatic seventh leap downward of the vocal line and the simultaneous *sforzando* on the word "loco," the palpitating heart rhythms of the bass line, the gasping vocal melody at "palpitar il cor mi sento," and the shuddering violins that set off the line "un tal spavento." But in the repetition of the final phrase of text (mm. 10–12) there is a voluptuousness that recalls the final trio of "Ah taci, ingiusto core," the "chromatic surge" that frequently signifies eroticism in the music of Mozart and his contemporaries. As Heartz explains, the orchestra reveals "Elvira's inner thoughts. . . . [T]hey are on a certain kind of death—the kind that poets since time immemorial have used as a metaphor for the sexual act. The perceptive listeners among Mozart's audience must have relished this point."[14] It is not that Elvira is afraid of the dark; rather, the obscure shadows further stimulate her already overwrought sensibilities. Even Leporello cannot long bear the intensity of her passions: he gives up his chance to play the super-lover and frantically searches in the dusk for a way out of the garden. The abandoned Donna Elvira—sultry with longing—is more appealing to him from the voyeur's seat, where distance can temper his sense of guilt and fear.

When Donna Anna, Don Ottavio, Zerlina, and Masetto discover Donna Elvira alone with the disguised Leporello, she pleads to them for mercy for her "husband." None of the other characters comment on her change of heart vis-à-vis the dissolute Don Giovanni, but they adamantly refuse her request for clemency. (Don Ottavio actually moves to kill the pretend Giovanni.) The scene confirms Donna Elvira's separation from the fellowship of victims that she herself brought together. Even after she discovers Leporello's ruse, she carries on with her lonely mission to redeem a man who despises redemption. For the remainder of the opera, the defiant rescuer of women becomes the voice of helpless devotion to Don Giovanni.

THE DILEMMA OF THEN AND NOW:
THE WOMAN WHO LOVES TOO MUCH

Many critics, directors, and interpreters present the Donna Elvira *della pietà* of "Ah taci, ingiusto core" as far more sympathetic than her scrappy, prosecutorial counterpart in act 1. In part, the reason is musical: the dulcet and ethereal trio is certainly one of the most gorgeous musical numbers of the opera, very distinct from Elvira's earlier nettled exclamations. But inherited presumptions about what makes a character more "genuine" and, concomitantly, more agreeable also exert considerable influence. Donna Elvira's confessional accessibility and "selflessness" in act 2—even when self-destructive—transforms her into a more conventional and, for many, more acceptable opera heroine.

Two examples serve to illustrate this critical-interpretive perception. Analyzing "Ah chi mi dice mai," Allanbrook complains that "it is the final and most ruinous indignity to render another human being's passions impotent by one's amusement," but then justifies the joke in the case of Donna Elvira by adding "with Enlightenment emancipation we too give a little smirk at the fulminations of *la belle Dévote.*"[15] The Elvira of the balcony scene, on the other hand, deserves our commiseration. "She is the only person in the opera whose inner conflicts we are allowed to witness, and in the process she becomes less of a caricature."[16] Allanbrook elaborates further in a comparison of Donna Anna's "Non mi dir" and Donna Elvira's second-act music. "Both women speak of pietà," she remarks, "but Anna invokes it in cool and distant self-interest, while Elvira is describing feelings stirred in her heart *both by and for another.*"[17] Coming from a different angle, Charles Ford reaches the same conclusion, but he also clearly reveals its fundamental and historical gender bias: "Elvira's reactionary, resentful and moralistic music is unlikely to arouse our sympathy," he claims, but he also maintains that "her contributions to the second act trio and sextet, in which she begins to admit to her uncontrollable love for Giovanni, comprise far more idiosyncratic music, in recognition of her Enlightenment-feminine yielding to her "natural" sexual dependency."[18]

Putting aside for now the possibility that there might be more appreciation today for Elvira as avenging rescuer, it is true that Donna Elvira is gentler, more loving, and more vulnerable to Don Giovanni in "Ah taci, ingiusto core" and that such a representation of femininity was much valued in Mozart's time. And yet it does her no good. In "Ah chi mi dice mai," it could be argued that irony impinges on Don Giovanni and Donna Elvira equally. Instead, the balcony scene turns solely on Elvira's abasement: if it arouses our sympathy, it should also prick our conscience. Even the decidedly nonfeminist Edward Dent, writing in the first half of the twentieth century, could not survey Donna Elvira without a deliberate critical filter. He admits that "if we give her a moment's

serious consideration, she is as tragic a personality as Gluck's Armida or
Verdi's Amelia, but by the exigencies of that very character which Da
Ponte has given her she is forced to conform to the general *opera buffa*
standard set by Don Giovanni himself throughout the opera, and which
is an absolute necessity, because a really serious treatment of the whole
story would have been too utterly repulsive for stage presentation."
Dent implies that the spectator is also forced into an opera buffa standard, concluding that "it is only by accepting a generally frivolous
standpoint to the whole opera that we can tolerate the dialogue between
her and Don Giovanni, or the scene with Leporello that follows, culminating in the famous catalogue aria.[19] He endorses the same strategy in
dealing with the "repulsive" dramatic situation of "Ah taci, ingiusto
core," which "is endurable only if one takes a completely frivolous view
of the whole play and even then one feels that it would be more appropriate to a puppet-play than to one in which real human beings appear."[20] Considering the trio, Spike Hughes takes a similar line, forcibly
"keeping it light," though he also wags a finger at the opera's creators:
"The purely sensuous beauty of this trio can have a most unbalancing
effect. The dramatic situation itself does not deserve music of such an
absorbing and overwhelming character, for the dramatic situation, after
all, is flippant, comic, and not to be taken seriously unless we wish to
charge both Da Ponte and Mozart with an almost unforgivable lapse of
taste."[21]

Predictably, neither Dent nor Hughes (nor many other critics, for that
matter) steps up to answer the heretical question implied in their writings: could it be that golden boys Mozart and Da Ponte managed to "out-
Giovanni" the libertine himself, manipulating us with words and music
into enjoying a sadistic display of power over a helpless woman? Traditionally, the crucial function of the Elvira-type character is 1) to dramatize the plight of the higher-born woman who truly loves Don Giovanni
but is abandoned by him, and 2) to elaborate on the theme of heaven's
revenge by denouncing and/or pleading with him to repent. She does not
need to be seduced again, though she may express herself along the lines
of "Ah taci, ingiusto core." None of the most famous Don Juan stories—
for example, the plays by Tirso, Molière, Goldoni, and Shadwell—has a
scene comparable to the balcony seduction. Only Mozart and Da Ponte
milk Donna Elvira's mortification for its comic potential. Fundamentally,
the scene is an act of revenge, Don Giovanni's payback for Donna Elvira's
meddling, but there is a trace of authorial endorsement of the punishment as well: Da Ponte and Mozart carry Elvira's disgrace forward to the

very end of the opera. Even after the balcony scene and the embarrassing disclosure of the sextet, it would have been entirely plausible to restore some of the "noble aspect" and "sweet majesty" that Donna Anna and Don Ottavio saw in her. Da Ponte would have had to look no further than Molière, who first introduced Elvire to the stage. The French playwright allows his dishonored woman the chance to reclaim her dignity. Renouncing her infatuation and her anger, his poised Elvire bravely confronts her self-delusion and chooses a new course:

> It is no longer that Donna Elvira who made vows against you, and whose irritated soul hurled nothing but threats and breathed only revenge. Heaven has banished from my soul all of the unworthy ardors I felt for you, all those tumultuous transports of a guilty attachment, all those shameful passions of an earthly and vulgar love; and it has left for you in my heart a flame purged of all commerce of the senses, a tenderness completely sacred, a love detached from everything, which does not act for itself, but concerns itself with your interest only. . . . It is that perfect and pure love that brings me here for your good, to impart to you a warning from heaven, and to endeavor to make you retreat from the precipice into which you are running. Yes, Dom Juan, I know about all the dissoluteness of your life, and that same heaven which has touched my heart and made me examine the aberrations of my conduct inspired me to come to you and to tell you on its behalf that your offenses have exhausted its mercy, that its fearful wrath is ready to fall upon you, that it lies in your power to avoid this by an immediate repentance, and that perhaps you have not even a day longer to escape from the greatest of all misfortunes. For my part, I am attached to you no longer by any worldly affection. I am, thank Heavens, recovered from all of my foolish thoughts. My retreat is resolved upon, and I only desire life enough to atone for the fault I have committed, and to merit, through an austere penance, a pardon for the blindness into which the transports of a reprehensible passion plunged me. But in this retreat I should be extremely saddened that a person whom I had cherished so tenderly should have become a fatal example of Heaven's justice; and it will be an incredible joy to me if I can help you to avert the dreadful blow that threatens you. I beg you, Dom Juan, grant me as a last favor this sweet consolation, do not refuse me your salvation, which I tearfully request; and if you are not concerned for your own interest, be so then for my prayers at least, and spare me the cruel displeasure of seeing you condemned to eternal torments. (4.6.73–74)

There is no doubt that Elvire's conversion to altruism is genuine. Lured away from the convent, the young woman requires its sanctuary again to strengthen and purify her heart. Naturally, she reinforces her petition with reminders of all that she has suffered for his sake, yet she nevertheless maintains a stately self-composure to the end. Even Dom Juan is sensible to the change in her. There is nothing mocking about his address to her now; he even asks her to stay with him a while, admitting later to Sganarelle that her speech rekindled a momentary return of warmth for his former lover. Elvire dismisses his overture as "superfluous discourse" and solemnly leaves him to his fate.

Da Ponte and Mozart also devised a petition scene for the finale (2.14), but the continued degradation of Elvira sets it apart from Molière's version. Her final speech to Don Giovanni, ardent and sincere, begins very much like Elvire's, but the dignity of her purpose is almost immediately subverted by Giovanni's glib sarcasm:

D. Elv.	*[entra disperata]*	*[enters, desperate]*
	L'ultima prova	I want to perform
	Dell'amor mio	yet the ultimate test
	Voglio ancor fare con te.	of my love for you.
	Più non rammento	I no longer remember
	Gl'inganni tuoi,	your deceptions;
	Pietade io sento . . .	I feel compassion . . .
D. Gio.	*[sorgendo]*	*[rising]*
& Lepr.	Cos'è, cos'è?	What is it, what is it?
D. Elv.	*[s'inginocchia]*	*[she kneels]*
	Da te non chiede	This oppressed soul
	Quest'alma oppressa	does not ask of you
	Della sua fede	any reward
	Qualche mercè.	for her faithfulness.
D. Gio.	Mi maraviglio!	I am amazed!
	Cosa volete?	What do you want?
	Se non sorgete	If you do not rise,
	Non resto in piè!	I will not remain standing!
	[s'inginocchia]	*[he kneels]*
D. Elv.	Ah non deridere	Ah, do not mock
	gli affanni miei!	my sufferings!
Lepr.	Quasi da piangere	She almost makes
	Mi fa costei.	me cry.
D. Gio.	*[sorgendo fa sorgere*	*[rising, he helps*
	Donna Elvira]	*Donna Elvira to stand]*
	Io te deridere?	I mock you?
	[con affettata tenerezza]	*[with affected tenderness]*
	Cieli! perché?	Heavens! why?
	Che vuoi, mio bene?	What do you want, my dear?
D. Elv.	Che vita cangi.	That you change your life.
D. Gio.	Brava!	Excellent!
D. Elv.	Cor perfido!	Perfidious heart!
D. Gio.	Lascia ch'io mangi;	Let me eat;
	[torna a sedere a mangiare]	*[returns to sit and eat]*

	E, se ti piace,	and, if you like,
	Mangia con me.	eat with me.
D. Elv.	Restati, barbaro,	Remain in this foul
(a3)	Nel lezzo immondo,	stench, barbarous man,
	Esempio orribile,	horrible example
	D'iniquità.	of iniquity.
	[sorte]	[leaves]
Lepr.	(Se non si muove	(If he is not moved
(a3)	Del suo dolore,	by her sorrow,
	Di sasso ha il core,	he has a heart of stone,
	O cor non ha!)	or no heart at all!)
D. Gio.	Vivan le femmine,	Long live the ladies!
(a3)	Viva il buon vino,	Long live good wine!
	Sostegno e gloria	Sustenance and glory
	D'umanità!	of humanity!

Disrupting the pleasant wind band music that accompanies Giovanni's dining, Elvira's entrance changes the key (from D to B-flat major), the meter (duple to triple), and the tempo (moderato to allegro assai). The steady quarter-note rhythms and predominantly triadic movement of the almost wholly unornamented melody is vigorous but fairly controlled. Initially Elvira demonstrates forbearance, yet there is already an undercurrent of agitation in the music. The strings and bassoons shudder with *forte-piano* eighth notes between Elvira's phrases, which come in short, slightly separated bursts. She plunges ahead, businesslike, with her plea until she recalls Giovanni's "inganni," his deceptions. Here, Elvira falters slightly, silent for a few beats. Finally she closes her phrase with a half cadence that is notably warmer and more effusive than the opening: "pietade io sento" (Ex. 8). There is still a trace of *amore* in her *pietà*. The musical gesture connects effectively with her wavering "ingiusto cor" in the balcony scene. She drops to her knees for the next phrase, and her vocalizing becomes more expansive, leaping first a seventh and then an octave (mm. 223–30): "This oppressed soul does not ask of you any reward for her faithfulness." Giovanni kneels as well, stating ironically that he will not stay on his feet if she does not. Wounded, she implores, "Ah, do not mock my sufferings." Leporello acknowledges that her appeal has *almost* reduced to him to tears, but Giovanni only smirks and patronizes, the jaunty staccatos and trills of the music conveying his amusement. He lifts Elvira to her feet, asking—with feigned affection, as indicated by the stage directions—"I mock you?" Finally Giovanni asks Elvira what it is that she wants.

EXAMPLE 8. *Don Giovanni*, No. 24, Finale (act 2, scene 14), "L'ultima prova"; mm. 209–18

She answers him with the peculiar "pity" figure, pleading with Giovanni to change his life—"che vita cangi" (Ex. 9). This time, however, the figure is primed, both melodically and harmonically, by Giovanni's question, so that Elvira's response appears as a more elaborate variation. The accompaniment has changed as well, with a larkish figure in the violins. As in the balcony scene, the seducer has baited Elvira with her own musical language, and she has replied with credulous candor. However, this time the libertine is showing himself openly, as he truly is. His condescending "Brava!" demolishes any hope Donna Elvira had of being treated with respect and taken seriously. Her indignation ("Cor perfido!") swells on a long-held F, for which Leporello provides spontaneous, commiserating reinforcement (mm. 275–78). Tiring of the game (and completely unmoved by Elvira's concern), Giovanni brusquely commands her to let him finish eating. Walking toward the table, however, he issues a casual, innuendo-laden invitation to dine with him. It is just another insult. Don Giovanni feels none of the sentimental warmth

EXAMPLE 9. *Don Giovanni*, No. 24, Finale (act 2, scene 14), "L'ultima prova"; mm. 260–66

that stirred in the heart of Molière's Dom Juan. Likewise, Donna Elvira is unable to sustain Elvire's imperturbable dignity. Her anger always lies under the surface: love stirs pity and rage in equal portions, and Donna Elvira frequently has little authority over the direction that her supercharged feelings take. As Julian Rushton observes, Elvira's "vehemence and tenderness emerge from the depths of her love and shame, and alternate in any number long enough to accommodate both."[22] Elvira's music here audibly signals the interrelationship between these two emotions, anger and pity. She castigates the "horrible example of iniquity" (mm. 295–302) with her opening music, the same austere melody that she used to announce her mission of forgiveness (mm. 201–8). She does not punctuate her bitter condemnation with a full cadence; she still has plenty to say to the scoundrel. Don Giovanni, however, responds only with an ironic toast: "Vivan le femmine, viva il buon vino, sostegno e gloria d'umanità!" The music whirls giddily around the three characters as the master brushes off Elvira's fury and Leporello's disdain with ruthlessly sardonic cheer.

Unable to break away from her former lover's "superfluous discourse," Donna Elvira makes a final desperate attempt to censure him (mm. 322–32). As in the quartet of act 1, "Non ti fidar," her wrath reaches a climax in a barrage of declamatory octave leaps on the dominant F. This time, however, Elvira's tenacious hold on the relatively high pitch must compete with Don Giovanni's bold toast and his own elevated tessitura. In the quartet, Elvira's note resisted closure on the tonic by holding fast to the dominant key area. Now, Giovanni is the one who skillfully controls the cadential progression.[23] When he does decide to close the section (and the argument), he does so emphatically and with no effective resistance. Far from her brilliant triumph in the quartet, Elvira now flees, utterly defeated. Yet even this is not enough: Mozart and Da Ponte use her exit for one more gag. Hurrying out the door, Donna Elvira encounters the vivified statue outside and is forced to return into the house to seek escape in another direction. Da Ponte makes her final utterance in the scene a screamlike high A-flat, to which the men respond "Whatever cry is this?"

TRADITA E ABBANDONATA: ELVIRA'S WARNING

In the original version of *Don Giovanni* (Prague, 1787), Donna Elvira was limited in act 2 to this unrelenting disgrace, from the hoax of the balcony scene and sextet to the fruitless confrontation with Giovanni in the finale. For the 1788 Viennese production, Da Ponte and Mozart supplemented the role with the *seria*-inflected *scena* "In quali eccessi, o Numi / Mi tradì quell'alma ingrata" to please the celebrated soprano Catarina Cavalieri.[24] Notwithstanding its origins as a virtuoso showpiece, the *scena* also adds something gratifying and, frankly, redeeming to the role: it is the only time in the entire opera when Elvira is able to express herself fully *without* the distracting commentary of other characters. It is not that the *scena* significantly alters what we already know about Donna Elvira, but it does allow her to revisit and explore the conflicting passions introduced in "Ah taci, ingiusto core" in unassailable solitude:

In quali eccessi, o Numi, in quai misfatti	In what excesses, o gods, in what horrible,
Orribili, tremendi	tremendous misdeeds
È avvolto il sciagurato!	is the wretched man entangled!
Ah no, non puote tardar l'ira del cielo, . . .	Ah no, the wrath of heaven cannot be delayed . . .
La giustizia tardar! Sentir già parmi	nor justice postponed! I seem to hear already
La fatale saetta,	the fatal thunderbolt,
Che gli piomba sul capo . . . Aperto veggio	that crashes down upon his head! . . . I see
Il baratro mortal . . .	the mortal abyss open . . .
Misera Elvira,	Miserable Elvira,
Che contrasto d'affetti in sen ti nasce! . . .	what conflict of passions is born in your breast! . . .

| Perchè questi sospiri, e queste ambascie? | Why these sighs and these anguishes? |

The idiosyncratic orchestral figure that opens the recitative—with its restless phrasing and edgy dynamics—recalls the Donna Elvira of "Ah chi mi dice mai," but concern has once again displaced wrath from her heart. Envisioning the infernal doom that awaits Don Giovanni, she abandons her repertory of disparaging labels for him—"scellerato," "barbaro," and "mentitore"—and instead calls him a "sciagurato," an unfortunate man. As she describes the lethal thunderbolt and sees the fateful chasm open to swallow her betrayer, the orchestral figure rises from its original B-flat major to C minor and finally to D minor, the vengeance key. Yet Donna Elvira slowly backs away from both the tonality of revenge and the phantasmal abyss. The accompaniment figure softens and wavers over a descending bass line that alludes to the grieving key of C minor. Violins evoke Donna Elvira's heaving sighs as she ponders her enduring solicitude toward the ungrateful roué.

The aria that follows shares many of the musical features of Elvira's other numbers: the key of E-flat major, the prominence of the clarinets—which appear in almost all of Elvira's music, though they are used sparingly with the other roles—the florid, relatively extravagant vocal style, and a sometimes mechanical rhythmic vitality. Essentially, "Mi tradì" encapsulates the fundamental emotional vacillation from yearning to pity that has besieged Elvira from the moment Don Giovanni deserted her:

Mi tradì quell'alma ingrata,	That ungrateful soul betrayed me,
Infelice, oddio! mi fa.	he makes me, oh God, unhappy.
Ma tradita e abbandonata,	But betrayed and abandoned,
Provo ancor per lui pietà	still I try to have pity for him.
Quando sento il mio tormento,	When I feel my torment,
Di vendetta il cor favella:	My heart speaks of vengeance;
Ma se guardo il suo cimento,	but if I consider his danger,
Palpitando il cor mi va.	my heart begins to throb.
Mi tradì . . .	That ungrateful soul . . .

As we have seen, Donna Elvira's anger toward Giovanni and her inexorable love for him are not antithetical: the real conflict, instead, is between emotional connection with him (whether inspired by fury, desire, or pity) and emotional autonomy. Though the rondo is a commonplace *seria*-type aria form, it is hard not to hear the recurring ritornello as indicative, too, of Elvira's general inability to escape from her dependence on Giovanni. She fusses and protests, yet always returns to the same basic principle: "That ungrateful soul betrayed me, but still I love/pity him." Don Giovanni has become her purpose to the point that she is, as the saying goes, lost without him. Donna Elvira's disorientation is musically expressed by the restless harmonies of the middle section of the aria (mm. 91–117), where her familiar E-flat-major tonality shifts to gloomy E-flat minor, made murkier by the oscillations of the cellos and bassoons. At the word "vendetta," surging violins register a momentary rekindling (in G-flat major) of Elvira's ire (mm. 95–98), but the thought of Giovanni's perilous condition stifles her battle cry. The rondo melody wells up from the lower strings, as the bass line sinks chromatically to D and hints at a mediant G-minor harmony. We hear the irregular beats of Elvira's heart as she imagines her beloved's fate. The high strings and flute whip up Elvira's anxiety, so that she too takes up the frenetic gesture and spins it into a brief coloratura embellishment on the word "palpitando." But Mozart certainly intended more than a moment of vocal gymnastics with this phrase. The confused wandering of this melisma—which hovers briefly on Neapolitan-sounding A-flat major before soaring back toward G minor—does more to illustrate Elvira's terror (and her internal strife) than anything else in the aria (Ex. 10). Once again she sings the word "palpitando" in a gasping manner, her breath taken away by fear. She does not even finish the text, but seeks to escape from her unbearable premonitions by throwing herself into the steady movement and optimistic tone of the bright E-flat-major refrain.

Indeed, by the time Elvira approaches Don Giovanni for the last time at his home, she imagines that she has attained a saving detachment: she goes to him to prove that she has forgotten his treachery and cares only about his eternal fate. Sadly, we soon discover that Elvira's "transformation" in "Mi tradì" is only a transitory upswing of the pendulum: her charity cannot withstand Giovanni's taunting abuse in the finale, and her reflexive disgust and resentment return. Still, Rushton asserts that Elvira is at least partially victorious in act 2:

> Her adaptability makes her like Giovanni, his complementary opposite (as Leporello is his shadow): constant in love where he is changeable, changeable in intention where he is constant. The strength of her love is her undoing and her triumph, for while it lets her be fooled it also permits the moral victory of final renunciation. There is no practical result; her feelings overwhelm her, she is incoherent, and Giovanni is amused rather than moved. But this Elvira is more human than any of her prototypes.[25]

Rushton's spot-on perspicacity goes a bit mushy with this last sentence, a common pitfall experienced by many when discussing Elvira. She stirs

EXAMPLE 10. *Don Giovanni,* No. 21, "Mi tradì quell'alma ingrata"

our compassion and even our affection. We should remember, however, that this "more human" character also reinforces deleterious stereotypes and attitudes. Inasmuch as Elvira's love is fundamentally sustained by irrepressible, heedless sensibility—a complete surrender to feelings, even when they might destroy you—what kind of triumph is really possible? Donna Elvira's renunciation and forgiveness never truly materialize because they are contingent on Giovanni' response. True, she always loves him, but one has to wonder whether desperate constancy is all that commendable. The hyper–emotionally dependent Donna Elviras of today are now routinely directed to best-selling self-help books like

Smart Women / Foolish Choices. To err is human, of course, but sadly, Donna Elvira never learns from her mistakes.

The relationship between sentiment, security, and seduction has long been a pressing issue for women. Jane Austen, for instance, dedicated *Sense and Sensibility* to this theme and, though she communicates an enormous amount of affection for her feeling-dominated Marianne, she admonishes against tyrannical romanticism. In fact, the "romantic" Marianne learns from her sister Elinor the crucial importance of regulating passion with sense and responsible discretion. As Jane Miller notes, Austen "allows women to find men seductive," but also "emphatically requires of women that they take responsibility for their sexual behaviour." "Most importantly," adds Miller, "she asserts the possibility of a woman's morality and a woman's resistance, even as she perpetuates the tradition which made both so necessary and so difficult to represent."[26] This literary and philosophical tradition

> offered the libertine as a kind of libertarian, hero, free spirit, and individualist. That tradition focused on women only in so far as they were the generalized object of male desire, thus narrowly determining women's scope for choice and resistance within narratives of seduction and ignoring the account of events they might have given themselves, if asked. The same tradition bypasses women as readers of such narratives, though they are readers who might, after all, be in a position either to endorse or deny them, or even replace them with alternatives. If women readers are assumed or implied at all they must be presumed to switch allegiance effortlessly and often, from a man's view of it all to a receptive and womanly one.[27]

This definitely applies to "readers" of *Don Giovanni.* The opera encourages us to take a basically Leporellian, though arguably more intellectual, view of Donna Elvira, fluctuating between mordant amusement and passive pity. But Donna Elvira is not your typical sentimental victim/heroine: she is also one of Mozart's best representatives of "sisterhood." Defying Don Giovanni, Donna Elvira attempts to protect other women by revealing to them the true nature of this "gentleman." She also traverses the class barrier: both a peasant and a noblewoman benefit from her custodial camaraderie. Sadly, Elvira is unable—or, rather, not allowed—to develop a sustaining friendship after her triumphant collaboration with Donna Anna and Don Ottavio; in that vague time lapse between acts she does an about-face and follows her perfidious ex-lover almost into the abyss. Ultimately Elvira is left with trembling, empty hands. During the *lieto fine,* between the happy exchanges of the two pairs of lovers, Elvira—alone—sums up her future plans in two measures: "I will take myself to a retreat [convent] to finish my life." For those critics, like Kierkegaard's anonymous essayist, who hold that a moment of happiness with Don Giovanni more than compensates for the consequent void, Elvira's end may seem heroically eloquent. In the cold light of cloistered dawn, however, Elvira's lonely destiny flickers as a warning, not an ideal. Unlike Marianne in *Sense and Sensibility,* she has no sisterly companion to offer a counterbalancing influence or refuge, nor are we, as spectators, able to change her fate.

We are, however, able to reject and move beyond the hackneyed perspectives on the *donna abbandonata* that *Don Giovanni* encourages. For this to happen, neither Don Giovanni nor Leporello can provide our surrogate viewpoint. To realize the full potential of the role of Donna Elvira, the singer, spectator, critic, and director must acknowledge the gravity of her situation from the very first entrance: her only real choices are marriage to Don Giovanni or an ignominious retreat from society. In the historical dynamic of seduction that *Don Giovanni* represents, only women faced this high-risk roulette of consequences. To appreciate fully Donna Elvira's triumph and tragedy we must imagine her, then, not as the ex-lover of a mythic sexual hero, but as a sister, daughter, or friend that has been used and discarded by the man she loves. Elvira's story further reveals the cruel side to what is, on the surface, an amusing, masterfully composed entertainment. Pay thoughtful attention: that is all she asks.

CHAPTER 3

Class Survival

Zerlina

His Words, I must confess fir'd my Blood; all my Spirits flew
about my Heart, and put me into Disorder enough, which he
might easily have seen in my Face: He repeated it afterwards
several times, that he was in Love with me, and my Heart
spoke as plain as a Voice, that I lik'd it; nay, when ever he
said, I am in Love with you, my Blushes plainly reply'd,
wou'd you were Sir.

Moll Flanders

It is no surprise that among the women of *Don Giovanni* Zerlina is generally the critical favorite. Quite simply, she is easy to like. In contrast
to Donna Anna and Donna Elvira, the country girl seems almost always
to be smiling. She does not waste time on regret or worry, taking life as
it comes. Hers is arguably the happiest ending in the opera: Don Giovanni gives her some pleasure, but he is never able to do her lasting
harm. Her good fortune owes something to her rescuers, the women
who suffer most in the opera, but her own deft adaptability plays a part,
too. Like many of her opera buffa rustic cousins, she is the capricious,
sensible survivor of an already-forgotten danger who looks out for her
own pleasure. She takes a chance on the charming Giovanni, but later
recoils at his heavy-handed embrace, offering her best melodies with
no apparent regrets to her roughshod, devoted beau, Masetto. By and

large, peasant and servant girls fare poorly in the Don Juan tradition, quickly conquered and quickly forgotten. Zerlina, however, not only lands on her dainty feet, but she plays a central role in the drama: she is the only woman in the opera who *incontrovertibly* refuses Don Giovanni's sexual advances even after having once welcomed them.

However, Zerlina does not immediately reveal her significance. She is introduced as a typical *contadina* character in a familiar scene of bucolic revelry: she is a pretty girl in a crowd of pretty girls at a peasant wedding, remarkable to Don Giovanni primarily because she is the bride. Joachim Kaiser suggests that "Don Giovanni hits the nail on the head shrewdly when he does not just tell her that she is beautiful, but gives her clearly to understand that she is of a mettle above her station," that she is worthy of more than a country bumpkin.[1] But a quick perusal of earlier Don Juan stories reveals that this kind of class-conscious flattery is typical, particularly when he is seducing a woman of low birth. One of his favorite lures is what might call the "manine" strategy. Caressing calloused, work-worn fingers, Don Juan flatters the charming country girl or maidservant with ideas of her latent, "natural" nobility as testified by her soft, fragrant hands. She is worthy of a better life, which he, of course, can provide: lost in illusion/delusion, she almost always succumbs.

The idea that the appearance of a woman's hands determines her social standing—and Don Juan's exploitation of this idea—is evident even in the earliest Don Juan literature. In Tirso's *El burlador de Sevilla*, we meet Aminta at her wedding feast. Unlike Zerlina, who commands our interest from her first appearance (it is she who leads the chorus/duet "Giovinette che fate all'amore"), Aminta demurely redirects the attention she receives.[2] When the chorus sings of her beauty, she asks them to sing instead "to my sweet husband [who possesses] thousands of graces" (2.20.644–45). Self-effacing and temperate, she responds to her fiancé Batricio's elaborate compliments with neither coyness nor spirited repartee, but rather with an earnest profession of her attachment: "Thank you, Batricio; you are false and a flatterer; but if you let your light shine on me, I will be worthy to be your moon. You are the sun who makes me grow after waning, so that the dawn may sing your greeting in a subtle tone" (2.20.656–63). Her first encounter with Don Juan also confirms her integrity and her sober nature. Having maneuvered his way into the bridegroom's place at the nuptial table, Don Juan lavishes courtesies on the bride, remarking on her beauty and his good fortune. As with Batricio, Aminta answers by calling him a flatterer but offers no further comment. Don Juan then takes her hand, but she draws it away and hides it from his view. When he inquires as to the reason, Aminta answers tersely, "It is mine" (2.22.740).

Aminta claims her hand not so much for herself as for her husband: it is a symbol of her honor and her vow. Having rebuffed Don Juan's transparent gallantries, Aminta forces him to attempt a subtler ploy. She is far less predisposed than Zerlina to fall victim to the Don's advances; in fact, she criticizes the impudence of the nobility and proclaims hatred for Don Juan, who has imposed himself between her and Batricio and insults her fiancé. Don Juan knows all too well that he must create a rift between bridegroom and bride in order to further his plans. The dissimulating rake easily convinces Batricio of Aminta's infidelity, fabricating a story of their clandestine passion.[3] Entering Aminta's bedroom, Don Juan answers her protests with arguments of his noble intent, of his prestigious lineage, and, most importantly, of Batricio's renunciation (accomplished, predictably, through Don Juan's deceitful scheming) (3.2). He then appeals to Aminta's ability to judge his sincerity, for "women are the friends of truth" (3.8.233–34). Nonetheless, Aminta requires several promises before conceding her hand. And, naturally, Don Juan loses no time in claiming the treasure previously denied:

> *D. Juan.* Good, now give me your hand, and your will confirm with it.
> *Aminta.* What, you are not deceiving me?
> *D. Juan.* I will be the one deceived.
> *Aminta.* Then swear that you will fulfill your promise.
> *D. Juan.* I swear, my lady, on this hand, an inferno of cold snow, to fulfill my promise.

When Don Juan pledges to put jewels on those white fingers, Aminta gives in completely. She accepts his praises, taking his pledge of marriage as a fait accompli: "From now on, husband, my will bends to yours: I am yours" (3.8.297–99). It is difficult to judge how much Don Juan is stretching the truth with Aminta. It could be that her hands are indeed somewhat whiter or softer and her manners more polished than those of her peers, but we cannot be sure.[4]

In *Dom Juan, ou le festin de Pierre*, Molière shows us just how devious—and effective—the "manine" ploy can be when his Dom Juan encounters the pretty rustic, Charlotte (2.2).[5] Molière's provincial maiden displays the easy cheerfulness of a Zerlina, responds with girlish longing when her fiancé Pierrot speaks of courtly life, and then teases him with skittish admissions of affection. But Charlotte's uneducated wit is no match for Dom Juan's strategies and stylish language. His elegant phrases and overt admiration of her physical features completely enthrall her:

D. *Juan.*   What is your name?

Char.   Charlotte, at your service.

D. *Juan.*   Ah! what a lovely person, and such piercing eyes!

Char.   Sir, you make me ashamed.

D. *Juan.*   Ah, do not be ashamed to hear the truth about yourself. Sganarelle, what do you say about this? Can you imagine anything more agreeable? Turn a little, if you please. Ah, what a pretty shape! Raise your head a little, I beg you. Ah! what a delicate face! Open your eyes completely. Ah! how beautiful they are! Pray, let me see your teeth. Ah! how amorous they are, and those inviting lips! For my part, I am ravished, and have never beheld so charming a person.

Char.   Sir, you enjoy saying that, and I can't tell whether you are making fun of me.

D. *Juan.*   I, make fun of you? God forbid! I love you too much for that, and I am speaking from the bottom of my heart.

Char.   If that's so, I'm obliged to you.

D. *Juan.*   Not at all; you are not at all obliged to me for what I say, and owe it to your beauty alone.

Char.   Sir, these words are too well spoken for me, and I have not wit enough to respond to you.

D. *Juan.*   Sganarelle, look at her hands.

Char.   Fie! Sir, they're as black as I don't know what.

D. *Juan.*   Ha! what are you saying? They are the loveliest in the world; allow me to kiss them, I beg you.

Char.   Sir, you do me too much honor, and had I known a little while ago, I would not have failed to wash them with bran.

Charlotte's language marks her class status as clearly as her hands. In an earlier dialogue with her dejected suitor, Pierrot, she uses archaic words and expressions in a kind of peasant slang. She addresses Dom Juan with more "correct" speech, but she is overwhelmed by the aristocrat's poetic turns of phrase. His speech is almost like a foreign language to her: she grasps the message but cannot begin to respond. Unfazed, Dom Juan simplifies the exchange, focusing on a single detail: Charlotte's hands. By kissing them, Dom Juan offers the poor girl a stunning compliment, transforming her callused and stained hands into visions of pristine loveliness. She eagerly welcomes the illusion, thrilled by her new magnificence.

The "manine" scheme also appears in the Bertati-Gazzaniga opera *Don Giovanni*. When Don Giovanni first addresses the vivacious peasant Maturina (during prenuptial festivities for her and her bridegroom, Biagio), he takes her hand and exclaims, "How charming and graceful you are! What a delicate and soft little hand!" (1.12). After he has threatened her bridegroom, Biagio, into leaving them alone, Don Giovanni returns to this image and takes it a step further:

D. Gio. Now we two are alone here.
         [he takes her hand]
Matur. But Sir . . .
D. Gio. Ah, my joy!
         And you with those little eyes so lovely,
         with that rosy little mouth,
         will give this dear hand
         to a boorish peasant?
         No, my sweet, no. You deserve
         a far better life;
         and I already feel myself in love with you. (1.14)

More playful than Aminta, more articulate than Charlotte, Bertati's Maturina—an obvious predecessor to Zerlina—questions Don Giovanni's intentions, letting him know that she has heard about rakish noblemen and will trade her virginity only for a marriage vow. Yet she is easily satisfied in this respect, for she finds her seducer's earnest professions too alluring to doubt. And, like Aminta and Charlotte, she allows herself to enjoy the illusion of marriage before the bonds are official. In the end, Maturina loses her honor and her fiancé: though she turns up at the finale, rejoicing with the others after Giovanni's demise, we hear nothing more of her relationship with Biagio.

Zerlina's first encounter with Don Giovanni (1.8–10) largely follows this general pattern, but crucial differences make her eventual escape from the libertine and her reconciliation with Masetto more plausible. First, Mozart and Da Ponte establish a genuine if pragmatic affection between the betrothed lovers even in their first meeting with Don Giovanni. Unlike Maturina, who immediately distances herself from Biagio so as not to offend the intruding nobleman, Zerlina proudly announces to Giovanni that she is the bride of the wedding to be celebrated. And while Maturina never mentions her husband-to-be, Zerlina warmly praises Masetto to Giovanni, using a fond possessive: "Oh! My Masetto is a man of the very best heart" (1.8). Maturina's resistance is unmistakably contrived; after her fiancé's retreat, she feigns shame only as a means of having Pasquierello dismissed and thus enjoying privacy with Giovanni (even Pasquierello marks how forward she is). Although Zerlina bids Masetto to go ahead to the feast, she seems only to want to keep the peace while enjoying a harmless flirtation. Alone with the "signore" and genuinely uncertain about the situation, she refers often to Masetto. Don Giovanni begins his usual spiel, wooing the maid with visions of upward class mobility:

D. Gio. Alfin siam liberati, Zerlinetta gentil, da quel scioccone. Che ne dite, mio ben, so far pulito?	At last we are free, gentle little Zerlina, of that big fool. What do you say, my darling, did I not manage things well?
Zerl. Signore, è mio marito . . .	Sir, he is my husband . . .
D. Gio. Chi! colui? Vi par che un onest'uomo, Un nobil cavalier, com'io mi vanto, Possa soffrir, che quell visetto d'oro, Quell viso inzuccherato	Who! him? Think you that an honest man, a noble Cavalier, as I pride myself to be, could bear for that little face of gold, that sugar-sweetened face,
Da un bifolcaccio vil sia strapazzato?	to be abused by a coarse plowboy?
Zerl. Ma, signore, io gli diedi Parola di sposarlo.	But sir, I gave my word to marry him.
D. Gio. Tal parola Non vale un zero. Voi non siete fatta Per esser paesana; un'altra sorte Vi procuran quegli occhi bricconcelli, Quei labbretti sì belli, Quelle ditucce candide e odorose: Parmi toccar giuncata e fiutar rose.	Such vows are worth nothing; you are not made to be a peasant: another fate will be procured by those roguish eyes, those dainty lips so beautiful, those snow-white and perfumed little fingers: I seem to touch junket and smell roses.
Zerl. Ah! . . . non vorrei . . .	Ah . . . I would not want . . .
D. Gio. Che non voreste?	What would you not want?
Zerl. Alfine Ingannata restar[6] Io so che raro Colle donne voi altri cavalieri Siete onesti e sinceri.	To be deceived in the end; I know how rarely you cavaliers are honest and sincere with women.

D. Gio.	È un'impostura	It is a commoner's falsehood!
	Della gente plebea. La nobiltà	Honesty shines in the
	Ha dipinta negli occhi l'onestà.	eyes of the nobility. Come now,
	Orsù, non perdiam tempo;	let us not lose time:
	in questo istante	this very moment,
	Io ti voglio sposar.	I wish to marry you.
Zerl.	Voi!	You!
D. Gio.	Certo, io.	Certainly, I.
	Quel casinetto è mio: soli saremo,	That little house is mine:
	E là, gioiello mio, ci	We shall be alone, and there,
	sposeremo. (1.9)	my jewel, we shall marry.
		(1.9)

Here begins what is possibly the most familiar and beloved piece of music in all of Mozart's operas. Mozart allows us, in the *duettino* No. 7, "Là ci darem la mano," to experience fully the seductive art of Don Giovanni as he "instructs" a naturally gifted student.[7] Capitalizing on the shock value of his faux proposal—"I wish to marry you"—Giovanni forgoes the usual orchestral introduction and presses on immediately with the main melody, a tune so artless and gentle that it we, too, almost believe his words. Zerlina responds, thinking out loud with a mixture of curiosity and concern.

D. Gio.	Là ci darem la mano,	There we shall give each other
	Là mi dirai di	Our hands, there you will say
	sì;	to me, "I do."
	Vedi, non è lontano,	See, it is not far:
	Partiam, ben mio,	let us leave from here, my
	da qui.	love.
Zerl.	Vorrei, e non	I would like to and not like
	vorrei,	to . . .
	Mi trema un poco il cor;	My heart trembles a little . . .
	Felice, è ver, sarei,	It is true that I would be happy:
	Ma può burlarmi	but he could still be tricking
	ancor.	me.

At first, she seems to be acclimating herself to the supple rhythms of Giovanni's gallant speech. New to the game of courtly seduction, Zerlina initially echoes her mentor's simple eight-measure (4 + 4) period, adding only the simplest alteration; her text demands an initial upbeat and she highlights the word "cor" with a lovely appoggiatura. She learns quickly, however, and not only makes the style her own, but also adds a subtly ornamented cadential extension (mm. 16–18). This embellishment reveals Zerlina's conflict, for she is both attracted and suspicious. Her sensuous expansion of Don Giovanni's melody conveys an emotional—and corporal—yielding, yet Zerlina is unwilling to commit herself. In the next section, when the nobleman pressures her more urgently (mm. 19–29), Zerlina cuts him short. Expressing concern for Masetto, she does not match Don Giovanni's syllabic delivery but persists with the embellished melodic style of the extended cadence. Even the chromaticism of the phrase "presto non son più forte" ("soon I will no longer be able to resist"; mm. 24–28), with its thrice-stated motive, is more fretful than acquiescent.

Not to be put off, Giovanni grows ever more emphatic, his voice rising to D natural ("Vieni, vieni"); the *sforzando* accompaniment testifies further to his restless desire. He maneuvers the harmony back to the tonic and repeats the opening melody. The energy of the previous section swells, and the dialogue quickens. Zerlina seems more eager to respond to Don Giovanni now; her musical phrases come more closely upon his, reflecting, perhaps, a greater physical closeness as well. Her sustained high F-sharp ("Ma può burlarmi ancor" at mm. 38–39) marks her last attempt at resistance. From that point the vocal phrases overlap, caressing one another. The effect is exhilarating. We feel the warmth of hands and of cheeks: voices grow shaky as do, most probably, those enticing fingers. What began as an elegant, genteel love duet escalates into an intense prelude to lovemaking. Giovanni compels Zerlina's acceptance, singing "Io ti cangerò tua sorte" ("I will change your fate"). When she repeats the text "Presto non son più forte," the music droops with heavy eroticism (mm. 42–46): by the end of the phrase, even before she echoes Giovanni's "Andiam!" Zerlina is definitely no longer "forte."

The second part of the duet, an Allegro in $\frac{6}{8}$ over a drone bass, confirms Zerlina's surrender; the tension ebbs as the couple joins in parallel tenths: "Andiam, andiam mio bene, a ristorar le pene d'un innocente amor" ("Let us go, dear, to restore the pains of innocent love"). It is interesting to note that the music of this section shares many characteristics with the rustic chorus "Giovinette che fate all'amore" ("Young girls who play at love"), which introduced Zerlina and Masetto. The bagpipelike drones, plentiful thirds and sixths, simple harmonies, and $\frac{6}{8}$ meter are typical of such pieces depicting rural settings and festivities. The unpretentious, lilting melody and static harmony serve to reinforce the fantasy of arcadian simplicity, suggesting a shepherdess and her lover enjoying natural pleasures. The unpretentious style suits Zerlina well; for Giovanni it is an artful con job. Indeed, the slinky chromatic

string interlude at measures 56–57—a musical illustration of intertwin-
ing limbs or, perhaps, a fleeting slip of Giovanni's ingenuous mask, revealing the practiced predator beneath—casts a fleeting minor-mode
shadow on the bright A-major illusion of innocence.

A "NATURAL" WOMAN

In the end, Zerlina is rescued before she becomes a statistic on Don Giovanni's growing list. Donna Elvira arrives in time to warn her about the
consequences of an "innocente amor" with the libertine. Her suspicions
aroused once more, Zerlina listens to Elvira and, more significantly, *believes* her. Without a word of protest she follows Elvira out of Don Giovanni's house. Sensibly, she starts looking for Masetto and the security
that he offers. She finds her bridegroom, angry and embarrassed, among
the other local peasants (1.16). When Zerlina tries to talk with Masetto,
he brushes her off scornfully: "Treacherous girl! Do I have to put up
with the touch of an unfaithful hand?" But clever Zerlina refuses to
squabble about theoretical offenses; anything that *might* have happened
seems irrelevant to her now, for the circumstances have changed. When
Masetto lists for her his grievances—she was alone with a man, she
abandoned him on his wedding day—Zerlina censures him for being so
cruel, for believing her to be genuinely unfaithful. We know, of course,
that she and Don Giovanni walked to his house "embracing" ("abbrac-
ciati" according to the stage directions), yet Zerlina denies that he
touched even the tip of her little finger. Duped by the *cavaliere* and subsequently saved by Elvira, a wiser Zerlina must now fabricate her own
defense. Having experienced Giovanni's heady but hazardous seduction, Zerlina seems content with the less exotic love of Masetto. Besides,
she sees no reason why her aborted tryst with Don Giovanni should pro-
hibit her from reuniting with Masetto. If anything, Zerlina merely trans-
fers her erotic energy into a safer channel, seducing her outwitted fiancé
into reconciliation.

It is not surprising, then, to find the same basic structure and many
elements of "Là ci darem la mano" in Zerlina's kiss-and-make-up aria,
No. 12, "Batti, batti, o bel Masetto." Like the earlier duet, "Batti, batti"
is comprised of two sections, the first a lovely gavotte-like Andante
grazioso and the second a pastoral Allegro in $\frac{6}{8}$. Though Zerlina adopts
the elegant gavotte (in what Leonard Ratner describes as a "middle
style" not usually used by peasant characters) in her attempt to recapture Masetto's heart, she fashions it to meld better with the rustic
setting and Masetto's understanding. The pervasive mood of the aria

is tranquil, evoking the sounds—the twittering of birds, the babbling brook—of Don Giovanni's gardens. In the midst of sensuous nature, Zerlina offers herself coyly to whatever punitive violence Masetto wishes:

Batti, batti, o bel Masetto,	Beat, beat, oh handsomeMasetto,
La tua povera Zerlina:	your poor Zerlina:
Starò qui come agnellina	I will stay here like a little lamb
Le tue botte ad aspettar.	awaiting your blows.
Lascierò straziarmi il crine,	I will let you tear out my hair,
Lascierò cavarmi gli occhi,	I will let you gouge out my eyes,
E le care tue manine	and your dear little hands
Lieta poi saprò baciar.	I will then happily kiss.

Wye Jamison Allanbrook rightly describes the aria as "an arch parody of submission."[8] Singers and directors have certainly taken full advantage of the moment to showcase Zerlina's blithe sensualism: she appeals to Masetto semiprostrate, with breasts conspicuously visible and her eyes wide with mostly feigned contrition. In the recitative that precedes the aria she dramatically invites him to satisfy his jealous anger—"kill me, do anything you like to me"—but then stresses, with a striking full cadence, that there must be peace afterward. In essence, "Batti, batti" is a skillfully manipulative and irresistible pretense: Zerlina symbolically relinquishes power to Masetto, who is able, in turn, to be merciful and thus forgo an actual show of force. But Zerlina always maintains actual control, seducing her lover even as she "awaits his blows." There is nothing in the music, however, to suggest that Zerlina really fears violence at Masetto's hands. There is a smile behind the repetitive, almost singsong phrase in which she describes her lamblike defenselessness. The ensuing string trills and staccatos (mm. 16–18, 20–22) might even represent a suppressed giggle. Hurrying through a list of the various drastic ways in which Masetto might injure her, Zerlina lingers—again with melodic repetition—on the words "e le care tue manine lieta poi saprò baciar" ("and then I will know how to kiss your dear little hands"); she has appropriated Don Giovanni's act and turned the "manine" ploy on its head. Zerlina punctuates her words with little kisses, the meaning of which grows clearer with each dominant-seventh appoggiatura and orchestral *sforzando*: if Masetto is smart he will be rewarded with much more than kisses on *his* "care manine." Confident and thoroughly enjoying herself, Zerlina subtly ornaments the return. After the repeat of the A section (mm. 36–52), the gleeful trills and staccato articulations of the violins can hardly be contained. Reading

Masetto's face ("Ah, I see that you don't have the heart"), Zerlina sets aside the tragedienne's facade and offers him her genuine, lovely smile.

With Masetto's mute but visible compliance, Zerlina happily proceeds to the part of the aria that stylistically and psychologically suits her best:

Pace, pace, o vita mia;	Peace, peace, o my life;
In contenti ed allegria	we should pass night and day
Notte e dì vogliam passar.	in happiness and joy.

Cheerful and at ease with her captivated lover, Zerlina sings more naturally and more convincingly as well. The gavotte idiom of the initial Andante attested to her skill at imitation, but the melody of the Allegro shows Zerlina at her shining best. The triadic oscillations that seemed a little precious in the Andante are well suited to the Allegro, invigorating it with an energy that spills over into the coloratura flourishes on "passar" (mm. 66–76). The violoncello obbligato offers more than rhythmic vitality: its deep-toned and enthusiastic interaction with Zerlina's melody suggests that perhaps the voice of Masetto's heart has made this a duet after all. The roseate conclusion of "Batti, batti" does not entirely dispel the cloud of doubt. Zerlina is still getting away with something, since she did in fact choose to go with Don Giovanni. Masetto is mostly pacified, but at the same time he is fully aware that he is being sweet-talked. At the end of the duet he remarks sullenly, "Just look how this witch is able to seduce me! We men are really weak in the head!"

How are we to understand Zerlina and her shifting *amore*? One theory—as set forth and tested, for instance, by Don Alfonso and his young disciples in *Così fan tutte*—proposes that Zerlina cannot help it: she is compelled by her nature—*feminine* nature. Hence, Alfonso lectures, "Everyone accuses women, but I excuse them if they change lovers a thousand times a day; some call it a vice, and others a habit; and to me it seems a necessity of the [female] heart" (2.13.30). Voicing a popular view of women during the eighteenth century, Don Alfonso believes that women are tied to nature in such a way as to impede then from acting according to reasoned morality or a willed sense of fidelity. A literary predecessor of Zerlina, the peasant Elisa in Goldoni's *Don Giovanni Tenorio,* plainly demonstrates Don Alfonso's maxim. When we first meet her she is reflecting on the difference between past amorous diversions and her novel, mature love for Carino the shepherd:

It's about time that a constant flame alights in my breast.
Until now I've loved almost in jest, and now I want to change my ways.

Out of vanity I pretended to enjoy the affections of Titiro and Montan,
of Ergasto and Silvio, of Licisca and Megacle and of Fileno, and of
many others who were my lovers; Carino has a something—I don't know—
out of the ordinary that penetrates my heart.
His sweet, modest speech, his humble look, the honesty of his ways,
his sincere heart set him apart from the others,
and I reserve for him the best place in my breast.
I love him, and want to grant this glory to
his merits, to have made my heart constant and faithful. (2.2)

Soon after this ardent declaration Elisa stumbles upon an injured
Don Giovanni, and in due course Carino loses his preeminence in her
mind and heart to the nobleman who would undoubtedly be able to
provide a more luxurious setting for playing the constant lover. The
logic behind Elisa's choice overrides any sentimental attachment:
"Don't feel badly, Carino, if I betray you," she says to her absent lover,
"But you are not the first. More than her lover, a woman loves her fortune" (2.3). Even after the noble Isabella warns her about Don Giovanni's libertine behavior, Elisa continues to seek his attentions. Naturally, she also tries to keep Carino within reach should her plans fall
through. Twice Carino finds Elisa with Giovanni, and twice she fabri-
cates a story of her innocence. Later, she explains (in a soliloquy directed
to the audience) how such duplicity is accomplished through nature's
gift to females:

To the angry lover's rash oaths,
Jove does not listen, and they are scattered to the wind.
I trust in my charms. These weapons are
rarely unlucky. Nature has
provided such defenses for the creatures
of the earth and the sea. She gave to the tiger
rapacious claws, to the fierce lion its strength,
horns to the bull, feet to the runner,
teeth to the dog, and scales and gullet to the fish,
and feathers and beak to the flying fowl;
to man she gave wisdom, and to woman
soft charms, sweet glances, tears. (3.14)

In the end, Elisa captures neither beau, but she is not concerned. Bam-
boozled by Giovanni, she nevertheless returns gaily to the countryside
to dally with the local shepherds, claiming "I am a master of the art of
imprisoning their hearts" (5.9).

Elisa truly seems incapable of any lasting attachment. She accepts this
lapse as a part of her womanly nature and considers it not without its
advantages; so far, she has never lacked for ready sweethearts. She ex-

emplifies perfectly the concept of "natural" femininity, which, stimulated by untamed instincts, embraces pleasure without discretion. Even modern critics frequently depict Zerlina as a child of nature who, on the very day of her wedding, helplessly succumbs to Don Giovanni's courting. Hermann Abert, seemingly a great admirer of Zerlina, applies the philosophy to her with obvious enthusiasm: "She is simply an unspoiled peasant girl with a lively temperament, natural grace, and, above all, healthy instincts. These govern all her feelings and actions, which are therefore not capable of analysis on an ethical plane dealing with innocence or guilt; and it is this naively sensual impulse that makes her fall into Don Giovanni's trap and then return to Masetto. Mozart has freed this natural, subconscious instinct from all worldly codes and thus made it artistically viable, shaping events according to his higher ideas of realism and so silencing all reservations of either a moral or a dramaturgical kind."[9]

WHEN NATURE SAYS "NO"

On the surface, Abert's praise for Zerlina's "healthy instincts," unshackled from stiff-necked mores, reads a bit like a plug for women's sexual liberation. Paradoxically, however, this "freedom"—an impulsive response to unreasoned and uncontainable desires—implies a significant constraint, one that dovetails with Don Alfonso's philosophy: in a word, Zerlina cannot say "no," or at least she cannot really mean "no" when it comes to sex.[10] For better or worse, this contradiction has informed innumerable interpretations of the role, right up to the present day. For this reason, many scholars and stage directors treat the garden encounter between Zerlina and Don Giovanni ("Tra quest' arbori" from the finale of act 1) as a continuation of their aborted lovemaking. Considering the scene, Abert remarks:

> We find ourselves again in that seductive atmosphere familiar from the Duettino (No. 7). First there is the mysterious beauty of the dialogue between strings and flutes; the somewhat uncertain tone in which Zerlina begins does not hide the fact that she is already on the point of falling prey once again to Don Giovanni, and when he swiftly seizes her hand, accompanied by the whole orchestra, the old game is about to repeat itself. He begins by echoing all her phrases, but now he no longer needs to play the rustic lover, for Zerlina is already trembling with secret desire, and so he has only to emphasize her own bashfully stammered words. The situation is much more tense than in the Duettino, and almost explodes with longing when the voices come together to the accompaniment of a semiquaver figure in the woodwind that ripples constantly downwards.[11]

Is Zerlina really quivering with desire? Or could it be fear? Fixed on Zerlina as an emblem of unregulated desire, Abert sees the garden scene merely as an intensification of "Là ci darem la mano," driven by the same sexual energy that powered the earlier duet. However, the garden scene is a good example of how Mozart and Da Ponte use a parallel setup to accentuate difference. In the earlier scene Zerlina welcomed Don Giovanni's notice and encouraged Masetto to leave her alone with the *cavaliere*. Now, however, she blanches at the nobleman's voice and urges Masetto to leave with her. Masetto assumes it is because she wants to hide her guilt, but there is more to it than that. For all of her vivacity and natural inclination to the sensual, Zerlina is now *afraid* of Don Giovanni. When Masetto hides nearby so that, unseen, he can hear for himself whether his bride told the truth, Zerlina is genuinely concerned for his safety: "Ah, don't hide yourself, Masetto. If he finds you, poor boy! You don't know what he can do."

Initially the music of the garden encounter evokes the emotional lyricism of "Là ci darem la mano," but the mood and dialogue are undeniably changed:

Zerl.	Tra quest' arbori celata	Hidden between these trees
	Si può dar che non mi veda.	perhaps he won't see me.
	[vuol nascondersi]	*[she tries to hide]*
D. Gio.	Zerlinetta mia garbata,	My graceful little Zerlina,
	Ti ho già visto, non	I have already seen you, do
	scappar.	not run away.
	[La prende]	*[he catches hold of her]*
Zerl.	Ah! lasciatemi andar via . . .	Ah! let me go . . .
D. Gio.	No, no, resta, gioia mia!	No, no, stay, my joy!
Zerl.	Se pietade avete in core!	If you have pity in your heart!
D. Gio.	Sì, ben mio, son tutto amore . . .	Yes, my dear, I am all love . . .
	Vieni un poco in questo loco,	Come here for a moment,
	Fortunate io ti vo' far.	I want to make you happy.
Zerl.	(Ah! s'ei vede il sposo mio,	(Ah! If he sees my betrothed,
	So ben io quel che può far.)	I know well what he can do.)

As Don Giovanni draws nearer, Zerlina tries unsuccessfully to hide from him (1.18). He spots her and—in a mirror image of "Là ci darem"—echoes her legato phrase with ever-smiling coercion. When Zerlina tries to leave anyway, Giovanni abandons the melody and rushes forward—musically and physically—to detain her. As he grabs her there is an abrupt change in the accompaniment (mm. 101ff.): the amicable dialogue between strings and winds comes to an abrupt end,

EXAMPLE 11. *Don Giovanni*, No. 13, Finale (act 1, scene 18), "Tra quest' arbori"

replaced by the anxious immobility of pulsing violins and long-held notes (Ex. 11). Lovely as the music is, the language of seduction has been precariously altered, moving a step closer to rape. Describing this second encounter, Joseph Kerman notes that "Don Giovanni does not so much cajole Zerlina as push her . . . [and] a new plangency in the music indicates also that she now wants nothing to do with her seducer. Her chromatic appoggiaturas no longer sound pert, but painful; her tremulous semiquavers, if not frantic, are rushed and squeezed by comparison with 'Là ci darem.' "[12] The conflicting desires Zerlina expressed in their earlier duet have vanished; now she only begs, "Ah! lasciatemi andar via" ("Let me leave!"). Don Giovanni presses her, using the same basic proposal he did before—"Come with me awhile; I will make you happy"—but where she had once sighed "presto non so più forte," she now worries, "Ah, if he sees my husband, I know well what he can do."

The strain increases when Masetto suddenly comes out from his hiding place; the harmony descends from F major to D minor, the key of retribution and Don Giovanni's fate (mm. 121–22). Mozart highlights the moment for us: we hear an echo of one of the chromatic motives used to such haunting effect at the beginning of the overture. For the first and only time in the opera we sense that Masetto gains the advantage over the shrewd nobleman. The peasant's maneuver catches Don Giovanni completely off guard; the stage directions indicate that the aristocrat "starts with surprise." Recovering his equilibrium, Don Giovanni hastily slips out of D minor and conducts the harmony back to F major. He addresses Masetto graciously—"your Zerlina cannot be without you"—but the mocking chirps of the violins belie his sincerity. For his part, Masetto stays on guard, fully aware of the arrogance and potential violence behind the nobleman's courtesies. He echoes (un poco ironico) Don Giovanni's cadence, complete with decorative trill: "Capisco, sì, signore" ("Yes, sir, I understand").

Hearing the ballroom orchestra, Don Giovanni urges both Zerlina and Masetto to accompany him to the festivities. Again, some critics interpret Zerlina's quick acceptance of this invitation as proof that she still hopes for a romantic liaison with him, but this overlooks the demands of class privilege that she and Masetto must accommodate. The aristocratic Don has already shown that he does not easily accept denial, and certainly not from peasants living on his land. In fact, Masetto himself quickly seconds Zerlina's acceptance, as they exclaim together, "Yes, let all three of us go!" Predictably, the gesture of truce hardly lasts past their entrance into Don Giovanni's halls. The pretense of friendship unravels with the frenetic activity of the ball, as Don Giovanni resumes his caresses and flattery. But Zerlina gives him only a perfunctory response, her attention fixed on Masetto, who quickly becomes enraged. Leporello pulls Masetto into the dance, allowing Don Giovanni to pull Zerlina away from the rest of the revelers. This time she does not give her consent, but exclaims apprehensively, "Oh gods, I am betrayed!" Soon afterward we hear her off-stage screams for help. As everyone runs to rescue her, Zerlina continues to cry out, screaming "Scellerato!" ("Villain!"), just as Donna Anna did in the introduzione. Fittingly, after Zerlina's escape, these two women are united in the public denouncement of Don Giovanni.

Zerlina's declaration to Giovanni that "Tutto già si sa!" ("Everything is known now!") implicates more than the libertine's crimes; she also demonstrates that Giovanni can be rejected. This repudiation invests Zerlina's second aria to Masetto with far more poignancy than "Batti, batti." Discovering her *sposo* beaten and bruised by Don Giovanni (disguised as Leporello), Zerlina scolds him again for his jealous nature and temper, but also gently nurses his wounds. The melody of her aria "Vedrai carino" is undoubtedly one of Mozart's most ingratiating, displaying that mixture of elegance and playfulness that is utterly Zerlina. The text is sensual and teasing, full of the childish idioms and diminutives used in private by young lovers:

Vedrai, carino,	You will see, little dear,
Se sei buonino,	if you are good,
Che bel rimedio	what a lovely remedy
Ti voglio dar	I want to give to you.
È naturale,	It is natural,
Non dà disgusto,	not unpleasant
E lo speziale	and the druggist
Non lo sa far.	does not know how to make it.
È un certo balsamo[13]	It is a certain balm
Che porto addosso:	that I carry with me:
Dare te'l posso	I can give it to you
Se'l vuoi provar.	if you want to try it.
Saper vorresti	Would you like to know
Dove mi sta?	where I keep it?
[facendogli toccar il cor]	[bringing his hand to her heart]
Sentilo battere,	Feel it beat,
Toccami qua.	touch me here.

Like "Batti, batti," this aria weds suggestive words with demure, graceful music. Like "Là ci darem" and "Batti, batti," it consists of two contrasting sections, the second being more lively in rhythmic pulse and affect, if not actual tempo. The second part is also characterized by greater physical and emotional intimacy. The steady pulse of the bass line, palpitating woodwind "heartbeats," irregular phrasing, and ascending melodic sequences come together in an irresistibly voluptuous word painting: "Sentilo battere, toccami *qua*." Masetto must feel Zerlina's beating heart and thus the soft, curving breast that shields it. Their wedding bed awaits them. As the lovers depart together, the orchestra responds with a lush postlude combining material from both sections of the aria.

Maynard Solomon observes that in dealing with a universe in which "everywhere there are dislocations, fissures, tears, and weak spots," Mozart utilized music in the opera as a "talisman against corruption, fear, and death," as in Cherubino's ballad "Voi che sapete," the flute and chimes of *Die Zauberflöte,* and even Donna Anna's "Non mi dir."

Solomon claims that comedy also provided an "escape" for Mozart: "forget menace, forget the uncanny, forget philosophy and all excessively weighty questions."[14] "Vedrai carino" assuredly represents this kind of safe haven from the discords of the opera. Possibly this aria corresponds to Mozart's own experience of romantic love. In any case, "Vedrai carino" holds a very special place in the opera, representing the one time when love is at peace, unconcerned with and undisturbed by the rest of the world.

TAKING MATTERS INTO HER OWN LITTLE HANDS

Clever and resilient, Zerlina traverses the distressing events of the opera with humor (and honor) intact. The refinement and sweetness of her music are reason enough for her enduring popularity, but Zerlina also intrigues us because her natural grace is complemented by an overt and *happy* sensuality that few of Mozart's heroines can match. "For each of the situations in which she culpably or innocently finds herself she supplies an appropriate physical dimension," observes Kaiser, "She consciously brings her body into play."[15] Unquestionably Zerlina is one of the most alluring manifestations of the peasant- or servant-girl type in opera buffa, most of which accentuate her physical dimension to one degree or another. Discussing the typical *serva/contadina* aria type, Hunter stresses the fundamental self-consciousness of these arias, noting how "the melismas that often occur toward the end are normally quite short and not conspicuously virtuosic, but they may have given the singer an opportunity to show off her pretty throat and flirt with the on- and off-stage audiences." She identifies this "undercurrent of sexual experience or availability" as one of the "significant aspects of these arias," distinct from "romantic fulminations of the Dorabella sort" as well as the "sensitivity and apparent purity of the sentimental heroine." However, Hunter cautions against imagining "this aria type as the place where sexuality ran amok in opera buffa," for it was precisely the "clarity and tidiness of the serving girl's rhetoric" that controls "the potential dangers of staged licentiousness by diminishing and trivializing it."[16]

Mozart's music gives Zerlina a genuine edge on the usual *contadina* role: she is sexy, but there is elegance, too, in her provocative musical gestures. Indeed, her greatest triumph may be the seduction of all the spectators who have watched her cross the stage. Many of them believe she deserves better than Masetto. Allanbrook, for instance, argues, "Given the shortcomings of Masetto and the shadow of the Don, Zerlina's solution is not the luminous reunion of equals in an inviolable garden which Susanna effects, but a shaky and somewhat disturbing compromise made with the acceptance of lowered expectations and the knowledge of the ever present threat of the void. Wit and resilience are not rewarded with plenty in *Don Giovanni;* they are merely the equipment necessary if one is to survive."[17] But whose expectations exactly have been raised or lowered? There is no indication that Zerlina is unhappy with her life before Don Giovanni arrives on the scene. As for equality, it is true that Masetto is no Figaro, but neither is Zerlina, the country girl, commensurate with Susanna, the lady's maid. It is not just a matter of social class, but also of character. Susanna marries good sense to fidelity and uses both to help those she loves as well as for her own happiness. Zerlina's "wit and resilience" are basically self-serving, though she gladly makes up for any hurts she causes. Finally, it is no accident that Mozart directed both of her lovely arias to Masetto, not her aristocratic seducer. Don Giovanni may have been more exciting, but his kind of attention lasts only a moment, leaving one kind of heartache or another. Zerlina is the kind of woman who needs more than an illusory devotion from her beloved, and she thus she chooses reality—Masetto's rough-edged but enduring affection—over romantic illusion. And in doing so, she offers us, perhaps, a valuable lesson about where happiness actually lies.

For his part, Masetto shows more patience than many bridegrooms would be able to muster. Given the circumstances, his invidious ranting is far less ridiculous than Figaro's own jealous invective, "Aprite un po' quegl'occhi." While Masetto knows from experience that his bride can be capricious, Figaro has no such precedent, yet, like Alfonso, he manages to impugn all women. As for the verbal abuse Masetto launches at Zerlina, she hardly seems bothered. It is worth mentioning that Da Ponte gave Zerlina a rather coarse vocabulary and manners in a scene and duet with Leporello added for the Vienna premiere.[18] This interpolated scene (2.10a) not only shows a more aggressive Zerlina, but the duet skewers the *manine* theme. When Leporello tries to flatter Zerlina as his master did ("by these your two hands, white and tender, but this fresh skin, have mercy on me!"), she responds by dragging him around by the hair and menacing him with a razor blade. Calling the feckless manservant a "schiuma de' birbi" ("scum of rogues") and "mascalzone" ("scoundrel"), she terrorizes him with threats of dismemberment. She wants to take off his head and hair and extract his heart and eyes, bestowing upon him the "reward that comes to he who injures young women." Shouting to Masetto for assistance, she mutters when she receives no answer, "Where the devil has he gone?" By the duet's end, Zerlina makes it clear that she knows how to deal with rascals: still armed with her blade, she binds the trembling Leporello to a chair and exclaims, "Joy and delight glitter in my breast. This is the way one handles men."

Unlike other additions to the Viennese production ("Dalla sua pace" and "Mì tradì"), "Per queste tue manine" never caught on with audiences and is not commonly included in modern productions. True, the music is comparatively uninteresting compared to the rest of the already-packed second act. One wonders, however, if this omission also reflects a discomfort with a tough-talking, blade-wielding Zerlina. Whether performed or not, the duet should make us think twice about elevating Zerlina too high above her comfortable earthy plane, reimagining her, à la Giovanni, as smooth, high-minded, and worthy of a "better life." She may have taken pleasure thinking about the wealth, power, and leisure of the nobility, but Zerlina does not heave a sigh at the end of the opera. Rather, the *contadina* happily retires with her rustic bridegroom to their dinner and their bed, leaving others to worry about what might have been.

CHAPTER 4

Feminine Vengeance II: (Over)Powered Politics

The Queen of the Night

She looked for a recipe for the overthrow of a regime. She
found much on power, and damage, but little on strategy.

Gregory Maguire, Wicked

I scheme a lot, I know. I plot and plan: that's how a queen in
prison spends her time. But there's more to me than that. Can
I not say I love a son and be believed?

Eleanor of Aquitaine in A Lion in Winter

"She has no proper name," writes Jacques Chailley, but is a "lunar symbol of rebellion against that supremacy of the 'strong sex.'"[1] "She" is
the Queen of the Night, arguably the most famous iconographic symbol
of Mozart's operas, her star-encircled form appearing on legions of
books, recordings, posters, coffee cups, and clothing. Reviled for her
character and revered for her song, the Queen is also the most enigmatic
of all Mozart's creations, a dramatic puzzle that has never been—and
perhaps never can be—fully solved. She is often understood as everything her daughter, Pamina, is not: vengeful, scheming, defiant toward
male authority, proud, violent, and stubborn. As the cases of Donna
Anna and Donna Elvira have already shown, critical reception almost
invariably views these qualities as unattractive in a woman, even when
the story offers them some measure of validation. However, no other fe-

male character in Mozart's operas manifests these negative characteristics as thoroughly as the Queen—or is as severely punished.

On the other hand—and this is no small point—Mozart gives her the most awe-inspiring arias in the opera, pure musical exhilaration beyond the capacity of your run-of-the-mill antagonist. How, then, can we begin adequately to understand this *über*-antiheroine, this operatic fusion of wicked witch and queen mother? First, as when considering the female roles in *Don Giovanni,* we must begin on a level playing field to fairly assess the Queen of the Night. Mozart may well have intended Sarastro and his Initiates to represent Good with a capital G, but this does not necessarily make it so; we may not agree with the creator's viewpoint, or be convinced by his argument. Complicating the matter further, Emanuel Schikaneder's libretto is a mess of inconsistencies and disjunctions in characterization and plot, a problem frequently made worse in production via cuts and scene rearrangements. In the end, despite its beautiful music and grave moral platitudes, *Die Zauberflöte* fails to sustain the coherent message of universal brotherhood that so many critics have ascribed to it. With his own prejudices and power plays, Sarastro is no less contradictory than his adversary, and it is within this context of ambiguity—not a simplistic dualism—that the Queen and her claims against Sarastro are most fruitfully evaluated.

Of course, there is a strong symbolic component to the story. Whether one believes that *Die Zauberflöte* is based on a high-minded fairy tale, Masonic ideology and practice, or a mixture of various mythic and philosophical sources, its characters are essentially archetypal, dramatizing the relationship between power, sexual politics, and "enlightenment." Symbolic readings of the vividly titled Queen of the Night are especially common since this role, more than any other except that of Sarastro, invites allegorical interpretation. None of the literary works commonly identified as sources for the plot of *Die Zauberflöte* offers a clear precedent for her character: no direct parallel for the Queen of the Night is to be found, for instance, in either the various fables of Wieland's *Dschinnistan* (1786) or the "Masonic" literature such as Jean Terrasson's *Sethos* (German trans., 1777) or Ignaz von Born's *Über die Mysterien der Aegyptien* (1784).[2] In the libretto itself, most of the characters call her the "star-flaming Queen of the Night," though Pamina refers to her early in the opera as her "good, tender mother," and Sarastro dismisses her merely as a "proud woman." In the traditional critical literature she has traditionally been cast as "Unenlightenment," a nocturnal, female evil, a feminine principal with an unnatural drive to power.

Still, pinning down the Queen hermeneutically is not easy, especially because she presents two seemingly incompatible "faces" in her two arias. The first time we see her she is a bereft mother pining for her stolen daughter; when she reappears, she is a jealous matriarch who breaks off relations with this same cherished child, screaming threats of revenge. Her two arias exhibit such differences in sentiment and tone that many scholars in the past concluded that Schikaneder and Mozart must have changed their dramatic conception midway through the creation of the opera. Although this theory has been largely discredited in recent years, the problem of reconciling the two disparate images that the Queen presents remains central to any reading of her character. The most prevalent explanation for this apparent disjunction is that the Queen is inherently dishonest. Not surprisingly, this critical line argues that the Queen's most ruthless manifestation, the rage aria "Der Hölle Rache," is also her most genuine, her evilness providing a convenient counterbalance to a nearly beatified Sarastro, or at least a beatified Enlightenment à la Mozart.

Even Chailley, who reads the entire opera in terms of esoteric Masonic symbolism and displays a degree of empathy for the Queen, nevertheless contends that she is the anti-Sarastro, and therefore suspect: "Nowhere, in truth, is it said that the Queen of the Night represents Evil. Night is darkness, not wicked in itself. But it is the opposite of Day, and if the conflict becomes sharp, the creators well know where their sympathies lie. *Die Zauberflöte* is essentially a symbolic illustration of that conflict between two worlds, the Masculine and the Feminine, the conflict to be resolved, after the necessary purification, by the new, perfect union in the Mystery of the Couple."[3] Later, Chailley shows us more clearly where his own sympathies lie, falling back on the rubric of the two-faced Queen in this sardonic description of her act 1 aria:

> Unquestionably . . . the music of this aria ["Zum leiden"] leaves an impression of the Queen's complete insincerity. The description of her motherly sorrow is remarkably arid, impossible to confuse with the genuine sorrow of Pamina in No. 17. She is not sincere until she spits out her hatred against the *"Bösewicht"* (scoundrel) Sarastro, her enemy. The description of Pamina's terror during her abduction is extravagantly theatrical, and the intentional artificiality is brought out in a significant detail: "Help," the text says, "is all that she said." And the contrast between the theatrical cry *"Ach helft!"* and the neutral, strictly noncommittal *"war alles was sie sprach"* tells us a lot about her psychology. The impression left is comparable to that made during a rehearsal by a tragedienne interrupting a dramatic tirade to ask a stage-hand to bring her a chair.[4]

If Chailley vacillates between "objective" symbolism and sarcasm, other interpreters doggedly perpetuate and expand upon the blatant antifeminine rhetoric of the libretto. Robert Moberly, for example, views the Queen as wholly undeserving of pity on account of her criminally deceptive nature:

> In the present opera, the [characters] who are presented with sympathy include even Monostatos; but exclude the Queen. She has a plausible-seeming story, but her first aria should be sung in such a way that only a very innocent and earnest young person would fall for it. Tamino is therefore duly deceived. In Act One, Pamina trusts her. *13A* and *14* are therefore a shocking revelation of the Queen of the Night as she is, with all civilised pretences gone; a cold, brilliant, selfish bitch.[5]

Director Anthony Besch forgoes Moberly's crude labels but likewise expresses his animosity toward the Queen, whom he sees as nothing less than the feminine incarnation of the Great Liar:

> It is true that to different people she displays alternating aspects of her personality—with Tamino she is persuasive, cajoling and disarming, and with Pamina she is dogmatic, unyielding and vindictive—but these are all aspects of an unwavering megalomaniac personality. . . . When the Queen is cast like Lucifer into subterranean darkness, she will preserve her vindictive integrity in the bottomless pit.[6]

HERMENEUTIC FALLOUT: THE BINATE QUEEN

In her essay "Magic Flute, Nocturnal Sun," Carolyn Abbate concludes that both the "deception theory" (that the Queen reveals her true self only in act 2) and its discredited alternative (that the direction of the libretto was changed mid-creation) testify to the obvious fact that "the presence of two different Queens is hermeneutically radioactive, very, very hot." Moreover, she finds both of these theories "equally hollow," since the first "mirrors too readily the concept of 'Weibertücke,' the inherent deceptiveness of women, so often cited by Sarastro and the Priests of Wisdom," and the latter has "no factual basis." Abbate proposes instead a far more challenging theory, namely "that the Queen is as she appears: both the kind regent, and the monster ready to eat up its child."[7] Analyzing the Queen as both a symbolic and a musical representation, Abbate views her actions in the second act not as a revelation of concealed truth, but as a *parallel* truth, another part of the Queen's magical and chimerical nature: "There is no initial deceptiveness, no revelation of a hidden truth, but simply a great change. She is prone to metamorphosis, to mutation in body and mind: that is her symptom."[8] Comparing the story of *Die Zauberflöte* to an "appalling fairy tale"— Louis Chevalier de Mailley's "Le roi magicien" (The wizard king), first published in 1698—Abbate concludes that the Queen's transformation is neither intentional nor necessarily permanent, but rather a "condition" that occurs as the consequence of her nature and circumstances. Although the Queen is "demonized in terms that reflect deep cultural anxieties about female rule" within the dramatic fiction, "the historical bases for these anxieties are patent and were reflected in many contemporary allegorical readings of the plot." Abbate adds that the Queen's "habit of metamorphosis can be understood in this economy of anxiety as a transsexual symptom, the sign of her masculine aspirations."[9]

There is no doubt that the Queen of the Night bears the burden of two centuries of (masculine) cultural apprehension about what Abbate terms a "female king." W. H. Auden's "Metalogue to the Magic Flute," written in 1956 for the Mozart bicentenary, drolly analogizes this unease, casting Sarastro as an antiquated university professor "tolerated for his knowledge" and the Queen as "a highly paid and most efficient Dean (Who, as we all know, really runs the College)."[10] The controversy around the Queen stems not only from her "masculine" aspirations, but also, from a slightly different perspective, from the perennially suspicious pairing of motherhood and sovereignty. Too often critics accept the opera's dichotomies as axiomatic. Writing in 1964, Alfons Rosenberg theorizes about the Queen's character in terms of night goddesses and devouring mothers, including Isis, Nut, Demeter, and other symbols of both birth and death. He offers the kind of baldly reductive interpretation that frequently gets handed down in both critical studies and program notes:

> The mother is both her daughter's protector and, if she places her daughter's well-being over her own interests, her friend. When, however, gender envy and a will to authority predominate, then she becomes tyrant and enemy; then, she refuses to give her daughter up to freedom and tries to keep her in endless dependency. The relationship of the Queen of the Night corresponds to this latter tendency of desiring to hold on and abuse her daughter for her own purposes. Certainly every love relationship contains an element of authoritative will. Therefore love only becomes pure and healthy for the beloved—man, woman, son or daughter—if this will to authority is sacrificed. When one is not prepared to do this, as the Queen of the Night is not, then the features of the "devouring Mother" come out, pernicious and deadly. Because for the Mother, as for the "terrible goddess," an all-or-nothing principle applies: either complete possession or destruction of her own fruit.[11]

Focusing on mythic images, Rosenberg ignores the historical evidence, which has more commonly demonstrated the father's tyrannical enforcement of a "will to authority" in order to protect his rule and his interests. Rosenberg also follows an established critical tradition of justifying Sarastro's authoritative will as enlightened wisdom, portraying him as an ideal father whose benevolence culminates in the happy union of "children" at the opera's close. He, like so many other writers, leaves unexamined the question of whether Sarastro would have allowed any other outcome. Furthermore, he allows that the mother-daughter bond is, in general, a close one conditioned by a common heritage of gender-determined constraints, but he does not consider how these factors relate to the Queen's actions or significance, except as a figure set in opposition to men:

> The connection between mother and daughter is naturally closer than that between mother and son; for mother and daughter share the same fate, the same dependence on man, the same steps from girl to woman, the same sufferings and joys of their peculiar birthright. They both belong to the female-type, on the Nature side of Life; both have a true portion of intuition—a hidden, though not consciously formulated, wisdom—while the "Son," the male type, the Spirit side of Life, represents the obvious knowledge and the strength of world-changing action. The mother and daughter are on the same side of existence, while the father and son, who are challenging just as much as complementary, are set in opposition to them.[12]

This kind of essentialist-symbolic reading—all too common with *Die Zauberflöte*—merely reinforces the opera's day-versus-night propaganda, but here is the shocking truth: there is no such balanced dualism in the opera, for there is nothing even close to a parity of power. Sarastro is always in control; indeed, both he and the Queen of the Night attest to her relative powerlessness. All of the poetic discourse on birth and rebirth and on the dangers of the innately destructive, essence-devouring, supernatural Mother is strangely at odds with the actual Queen, who never wields the kind of power that Sarastro does, much less the potency of a truly "terrible goddess." She does not appear to have magical powers or military resources; after Pamina is taken, she does not raise an invading army, but pins her hopes on an almost total stranger—Tamino—merely because he is a man and therefore has a better chance of slipping into Sarastro's temples. In a sense, then, this Queen is defined by her *lack* of power. She is a sovereign (and a mother) backed into a corner—her marginal, mountainous province on the outskirts of civilization. Even after her only child and heir, Pamina, goes to the "other side," the Queen fights for the kingdom she has been denied.

In fact, the Queen's "shift" is easily understood as an unfortunate conflict between her identity as ruler and as mother. Nor is this rupture unusual for someone in her circumstances. History is full of male potentates and guardians who have placed the exigencies of power or kingdom above even the most beloved child. A king must be king before father: society has never seriously questioned the truth of this concept. But the terms "mother" and "monarch" have clashed in the cultural mindset of Western civilization for centuries.[13] Or, more specifically, it is believed that "mother love"—that mysterious quasi-instinctual emotion that is affirmed as immutable—cannot genuinely exist in a woman who places such a premium on her own personal power and the well-being of her realm: it is assumed that there is something "masculine," and therefore aberrant, about her. Her "mother love" appears changeable, and therefore counterfeit.

In Rose Subotnik's deconstructive analysis of the opera, the Queen of the Night is suspect precisely because she sees herself as a queen. Subotnik asserts that the Queen's awareness of rank is "unnatural" in an opera that allegedly celebrates "natural" selfhood and whose unifying theme is "social rank does not equal human worth." Considering the purported disjunction between the Queen's Larghetto and her Allegro moderato, Subotnik proposes, "the Queen's embryonic natural self (expressed through the recitative and Larghetto, and to an extent through the key of G minor) is too fragile to combat adversity on its own, and thus succumbs to the weaponry of established social rank. Or perhaps this natural self never existed at all; perhaps its evocation was merely a role assumed by the Queen to draw Tamino into an orbit devoted to her own self-serving power." Ultimately, Subotnik concludes that the Queen's "self" is either "stillborn, or it is false," and that, whatever the case, the Queen's willingness "to identify her 'true' self as this conventional monarch, safe in a social position of power and needing help from no one, makes it clear that she . . . has no individual, natural self of her own."[14]

Once again we find a justification, rather than a critique, of the libretto's troubling inconsistencies.[15] It is ironic that Subotnik makes such a to-do about the Queen's classist artificiality in an opera that concludes with a prince and princess, bonded together by a divinely robed master, elevated above the admiring throng. The question begs to be asked: in an opera where Initiates interact only superficially with peasants and women, where Sarastro declares gallantly that the prince is "just a man," yet choreographs a finale that reaffirms the usual social hierarchies, could it be that the Queen of the Night is one of the least phony representations? This idea turns common critical convention on its head: the Queen is not a hypocrite, but rather one authentic (though not necessarily pleasant) reflection in Sarastro's world of smoke and mirrors. She also raises the biggest challenge to the priestly Initiated Ones' profession of imperturbable benevolence.

It is impossible to know exactly what Mozart thought of the Queen, though tradition has it that he mentioned her on his deathbed, thrilling in her high notes and powerful curse as he lay in a delirium.[16] Mozart the Freemason may have placed the Queen on the negative side of a pseudo-Manichaean duality, but Mozart the dramatist and composer seems to have been more ambivalent. Perhaps reception has overstated the justness of the Queen's condemnation and Sarastro's elevation, or at least we may hope so. "I harbor a fantasy that Mozart didn't really believe in this authoritarian utopia," writes Maynard Solomon, "for I would like to think that he could not suppress his innate mistrust of institutionalized power. I would even like to think that the greatest absurdity about *Die Zauberflöte*'s patchwork of absurdities plagiarized and plundered from myth, Utopian fantasy, mystical tradition, and Masonic mummery is the subsequent appropriation of this bitterly satirical opera to the service of patriarchal imperatives that would have been very much to the liking of such rationalists as Don Alfonso, Sarastro, and Leopold Mozart."[17] One thing is clear: Mozart made his Queen musically unforgettable, a sonorous marvel. However, if we are able to hear her story together with her song—productions often cut most of her crucial dialogue—the result is even more powerful, marking the difference between fable and drama.

THE MOTHER-QUEEN'S "POWER"

Before we actually see the Queen of the Night or hear her voice, we are prepared for a fascinating, magical presence. Tamino mentions that his father spoke about this "mighty sovereign of the night," and the young prince is eager to know if Papageno "has ever been so lucky to see this goddess of the night." Exasperated by Tamino's lack of understanding and respect, Papageno warns that he will lock him up and hand him over to the Queen for dinner if he talks like that. The bird-man exclaims, "See? See the star-flaming Queen? What mortal can boast of having ever seen her? What human eye would be able to look through her black woven veil?" Papageno's awestruck reverence is offset by the more approachable description of the Three Ladies who explain to Tamino that their sovereign has been moved by her "maternal heart" to reward the prince with the honor and joy of her daughter's hand in marriage. Acting as the Queen's agents, the Three Ladies might also be assumed to reflect her mode of governance, a mixture of no-nonsense discipline and judicious mercy. In the Queen's name they punish Papageno's lying by placing a golden padlock on his lips, but they soon rescind the penalty at her command.

When the Queen of the Night finally appears to Tamino, she reveals her composite nature: she is a protective mother but also exhibits a ruler's proud spirit and formidable will. Her first entrance (1.6) is nothing short of spectacular: thunder roars, mountains move, and suddenly the Queen herself gazes down on the prince from a star-encrusted throne. The brief B-flat-major orchestral introduction, Allegro maestoso, signals the appearance of an expansive, glittering presence as the music ascends up through the orchestral registers. Though it heralds the arrivals of the nocturnal Queen, this ascending prelude might easily be perceived as "sunrise" music, similar to the beginning of Haydn's Symphony No. 7 in C, "Le Matin." Abbate puts a different spin on it, calling it a *creatio ex nihilo* opening.[18] Countering this ascent, the bassoons, violas, and second violins introduce a descending chromatic line, a magnificent unfolding in all directions. Though this chromatic inflection may denote a hidden perniciousness, as many have been quick to suggest, it might just as easily reflect her current misery, a groan escaping from behind a veil of resolute majesty. Or, perhaps, it alludes to the fearful awe she inspires in those who behold her; one can imagine Papageno and Tamino dropping slowly to their knees as she comes more clearly into view. The Queen herself recognizes the overwhelming effect she has on those around her. When she speaks to Tamino, "mein lieber Sohn," her tone is intimate and soothing:

O zittre nicht, mein lieber Sohn,	O do not tremble, my dear son!
Du bist unschuldig, weise, fromm—	You are innocent, wise, and pious.
Ein Jüngling so wie du, vermag am besten,	A youth, such as you, may best comfort
Das tiefbetrübte Mutterherz zu trösten.[19]	this mother's greatly oppressed heart.

This text is set entirely in obbligato recitative, one of the few times this style is used in the opera and the only time it is connected to an aria in the manner of an opera seria *scena*. Of course, this style sits naturally on the Queen of the Night, and functions as a sign of her royal position. To put Tamino at ease, the Queen maintains a tone of calm dignity, keeping her voice within the temperate middle range. She speaks calmly to the prince, taking time between phrases to return to this composed manner, yet the orchestration suggests there is a hidden turmoil. Every time the Queen pauses the lower strings, bassoons, and oboes fill in the space, each arpeggiated lift and dissonant fall sounding like a heavy sigh (mm. 12–14, 16–18), while the strings jitter in nervous syncopation. Perhaps the trembling youth, so "innocent, wise, and pious," reminds her painfully of her own treasured child, who quivered with fright at her abduction. When the Queen turns to Tamino for consolation, the music moves toward G minor, Mozart's favorite key for portraying grief and sadness. The sustained Neapolitan at measures 19–20 marks a moment of true emotional vulnerability for the Queen, and all of the parts sink with the heavy burden of her suffering "Mutterherz."

Notwithstanding its serious style, the G-minor aria (Larghetto) that follows is typical of the tight, compact formal structures in *Die Zauberflöte*. Within the space of forty measures, the figuration and orchestration of the accompaniment change eight times, capturing the agitated spirit of the Queen's emotional narrative:

Zum Leiden bin ich auserkoren,	I am destined to suffer,
Denn meine Tochter fehlet mir.	for my daughter is lost to me.
Durch sie ging all mein Glück verloren,	With her, all of my happiness was lost:
Ein Bösewicht entfloh mit ihr.	a villain fled with her.
Noch seh' ich ihr Zittern	I still see her trembling,
Mit bangem Erschüttern,	moved with fearful alarm,
Ihr ängstliches Beben,	her anxious shaking,
Ihr schüchternes Streben.	her timid struggling.
Ich mußte sie mir rauben sehen,	I was forced to see her taken from me.
"Ach helft!" war alles, was sie sprach—	"Ah help!" was all that she said;
Allein vergebens war ihr Flehen,	But her entreaty was in vain,
Denn meine Hilfe war zu schwach.	for my aid was too weak.

Initially the music is almost listless with melancholy. Although the preceding recitative firmly established G minor, there is no stable, root-position tonic chord (or dominant, for that matter) in the Larghetto until measure 25: "for my daughter is lost to me" (Ex. 12). The voice is barely supported by a thin string accompaniment, and each phrase ends with an appoggiatura sigh. Thinking forward to Pamina's G-minor

EXAMPLE 12. *Die Zauberflöte*, No. 4, Largo, "Zum Leiden bin ich auserkoren"

EXAMPLE 13. *Die Zauberflöte*, No. 17, "Ach ich fühl's, es ist verschwunden"

lament "Ach ich fühl's" (Ex. 13), it is easy to hear what Abbate calls their "acoustic geneology."[20] The vocal melodies of both arias initially descend from the fifth degree to the tonic, make a dramatic leap followed by a gently punctuating 6–5 appoggiatura, and fall again to a 4–3 appoggiatura over a dominant chord.

As the Queen ponders the enormity of her loss, however, her heartache mixes with indignation. Oboes and bassoons parallel her melody in eerie octaves (mm. 27–31), lacing it with sardonic trills, the hollowed-out sound of misery tinged with mocking ire ("With her, all of my happiness was lost"). Still controlling her anger, the Queen broadens her range, modulating to the relative major. She refers disdainfully to Pamina's captor—"a villain" ("ein Bösewicht")—and the orchestra responds, firmly in B-flat major, with a brief gesture of fanfare. Possibly Mozart intended this majestic flourish as a subtle retort to the Queen's disparaging epithet, signaling Sarastro's "true" character, but it also accords with the style and key of the Queen's recitative and the upcoming

Allegro section of the aria itself. In any case, the Queen's tearful reproach is mixed with regal contempt as she relates the details of her daughter's abduction. The vocal tessitura extends even higher, and the melodic style grows more angular (mm. 36–40). Strings double the Queen's melody, breaking it up into rapidly pulsing sixteenth notes, a musical illustration of Pamina's trembling or, perhaps, the Queen's. She continues to envision her terrified daughter; a doleful bassoon and viola line accompanied her chromatically descending melody. The dreary parallel octaves of the bassoons and oboes return, doubling the vocal line: "I was forced to see her taken from me." There is nothing false about the Queen's wrenching description of Pamina's cries for help, though it is obvious that she is now thinking as much about the abductor as the victim. Nor is there any hidden agenda: she wants her daughter back *and* she is seething about Sarastro's colossal nerve. The Queen's fervent reenactment of the abduction is an overt act, not a veiled feminine ploy. She makes no secret about the fact that she needs outside—and specifically *male*—assistance. Part of her frustration stems from exactly this point: she is unable to manage the mission on her own.

This dependence is exactly what Subotnik and others fail to recognize. The Queen of the Night does not have to feign weakness. Far from being a "conventional monarch, safe in a social position of power and needing help from no one," she is at a grave disadvantage throughout the drama, even as she lights up the sky with starry majesty. Her next words confirm this humiliating reality: "But her entreaty was in vain, for my help was too weak." At these last words the music returns to the rootless, forlorn sonority of the Larghetto's opening. The subdued strings and plaintive vocal line of the final eight measures hearken back to the sorrowful beginning. The anguished high A-flat of the vocal line (m. 59) strains against the G (V/iv) of the violins and cellos as the Queen moans about her impotence: the loss of Pamina is only the bitterest symbol of a more general dispossession. We will later learn about how her force was so devastatingly reduced, leaving her only a peripheral place in the regional power structure. But even in the Larghetto, the Queen of the Night, far from dissimulating, has revealed the mortifying truth. Pamina is not only a beloved daughter—and one of the few companions the Queen has in her remote nocturnal domain—but also a possession and a possible means of establishing her authority: "with her all of my happiness was lost." She is keenly aware of how power works; Sarastro is no less cognizant of Pamina's value as an ally and social currency, either as the heir-apparent of a starry kingdom or a sunlit prince's consort.

With the dazzling Allegro that follows, Mozart creates an unforgettable musical force, a mosaic of movement, energy, and spectacular sound packed into a comparatively small musical space:

Du wirst sie zu befreien gehen,	You will go to free her,
Du wirst der Tochter Retter sein!—ja!	you will be my daughter's rescuer—yes!
Und werd ich dich als Sieger sehen,	And when I behold you as conquerer,
So sei sie dann auf ewig dein.	then she will be yours forever.

The notoriously thorny coloratura passages and cliff-hanging range (soaring over two octaves to F above the staff) have sometimes been described as an audaciously exaggerated version of baroque opera seria style, but there is only a superficial correspondence. Sensational vocal gymnastics were quite popular in singspiel arias, particularly when there was a magical aspect to the drama.[21] In Mozart's other great singspiel, *Die Entführung aus dem Serail* (1782), Konstanze's arias—"Ach ich liebte" and "Martern aller Arten"—feature highly demanding coloratura passages and a vocal melody that stays above the staff for extended periods.[22] Even the soubrette role in *Die Entführung*, Blonde, must negotiate tricky vocal melismas and a range that extends two and a half octaves to high E. The Allegro section of the Queen of the Night's first aria fits this same template. Though only forty-three measures long, a third of this bravura section (mm. 79–92) is devoted to one brilliant passage of coloratura writing that finishes with a stratospheric F above high C on the word "*e*-wig." Gone are the emotional vacillations of the Larghetto; the Allegro expounds renewed confidence and an almost manic delight at the possibility of victory. The Queen of the Night is revealed in her full majesty, tremendous roulades gushing from her now smiling lips. She echoes Tamino's words from his portrait aria, "she will be yours *forever*," my dear son, her savior and champion; her virtuoso pledge rings like an ecstatic battle call.

We do not see the Queen of the Night again for many scenes, though we hear various contradictory opinions about her. Both Sarastro's slaves and Pamina describe the Queen as a "zärtliche," a word that connotes gentleness and affection. Sarastro's slaves envision Pamina (1.9) hurrying back to the castle of her "loving mother" ("ihrer zärtlichen Mutter"). Echoing this (1.13), Pamina worries about her "good, loving mother" ("gute, zärtliche Mutter") dying of grief from the loss of her daughter; she continues to feel an affectionate attachment for the Queen even after she has fallen in love with Tamino. Sarastro, on the other hand, doggedly opposes this positive maternal image, describing the Queen as insolent and a detrimental influence. In the course of the story, only Tamino's viewpoint about the Queen radically changes. Once he switches his allegiance to Sarastro, the erstwhile champion sneers at the Three Ladies when they appear during his trials. He pronounces that the Queen "is a woman, has a woman's mind," meaning her judgment cannot be trusted. We assume that the Three Ladies inform their mistress of the prince's repudiation, for the Queen herself ventures into hostile territory a couple of scenes later. Stealing into Sarastro's domain, she discovers her daughter struggling against the lust-filled Monostatos (2.8). The Queen commands the moor to withdraw: she has no time to deal with him, but must speak immediately to Pamina. The frightened girl falls into her mother's arms, crying to her "Mother! Mother! My mother!"

It is telling that productions and recordings of the opera habitually shorten or delete the dialogue between mother and daughter that follows. It is common to cut bluntly to the end of the dialogue, so that the Queen's only reply to her daughter's pathetic cry appears to be the terse "Kein wort!" ("Not a word!"). In part, this omission demonstrates one downside of the singspiel, which uses spoken dialogue, for audiences that don't speak German; lengthy *spoken* passages in a foreign language are not tolerated very well. (Everyone is far more careful about cutting something that Mozart actually *composed*.) But this cut is particularly regrettable, if not downright irresponsible in dramatic terms, for it deprives listeners of hearing the Queen's side of things. Her spoken words are the only explanation we have of her demotion from power, first by her dying husband and then by the Brotherhood. Without this dialogue, "Der Hölle Rache" appears as an unexpected, unprovoked, and vicious diatribe, a factor that has definitely shaped common perceptions about the Queen, making it easier to see her as the consummate fairy tale "bad lady." When the Queen is allowed to speak, however, her explanation suggests the same complex emotional friction that characterizes her first aria, a volatile fusion of mother love and desperate regency:

> *Queen.* You may thank the power by which you were wrenched from me that I may still call myself your mother.—Where is the youth whom I sent to you?
>
> *Pam.* Ah Mother, he has withdrawn forever from the world and humans.—He has dedicated himself to the Initiated Ones.
>
> *Queen.* The Initiated Ones?—Unfortunate daughter, now you are torn from me forever.—
>
> *Pam.* Torn?—O let us flee, dear Mother! Under your protection I will brave every danger.

Queen. Protection? Dear child, your mother can no longer protect you.—
My power went with your father to the grave.

Pam. My father—

Queen. Handed over of his own free will the sevenfold Sun-Circle to the
Initiated Ones; Sarastro wears this mighty Sun-Circle on his
breast.—When I discussed this with [your father], he spoke with a
wrinkled brow: "Wife! my last hour is here—all of the treasures
which I alone possessed are yours and your daughter's."—"The
all-consuming Sun-Circle"—I quickly interrupted him in mid-
speech—"Is appointed to the Initiates," he answered. "Sarastro
will manage it in a manly way, as I have hitherto. And now not a
word more; inquire not into affairs which are incomprehensible to
the womanly mind.—Your duty is, you and your daughter, to relinquish leadership to wise men."

Pam. Dear mother, to conclude from all this, the youth is also likely lost
to me forever.

Queen. Lost, if before the sun colors the earth, you do not persuade him
to flee through these subterranean vaults . . . —The first gleam of
day will decide whether he will be given wholly to you or to the
Initiated Ones.

Pam. Dear Mother, am I not allowed then to love the youth as an Initiated One as tenderly as I now do love him?—My father himself
was connected to these wise men; he often spoke of them with delight, praised their goodness—their understanding—their virtue.—
Sarastro is no less virtuous.—

Queen. What do I hear!—You, my daughter, could defend the infamous
cause of these barbarians?—To thus love a man, who, allied with
my mortal enemy, would with every moment prepare my fall?—So
you see this dagger?—It is honed for Sarastro.—You will kill him
and pass on to me the mighty Sun-Circle.

Pam. But dearest Mother!—

Queen. Not a word!

Enraged at Pamina's implied defection, the mother-queen turns on
her daughter. The orchestra bristles for a single measure before erupting
with a *sforzando,* and the Queen of the Night voices, in dark D minor,
her dreadful indignation:

Der Hölle Rache kocht in meinem Herzen,	Hell's vengeance boils in my heart,
Tod und Verzweiflung flammet um mich her!	death and despair blaze around me!
Fühlt nicht durch dich Sarastro Todesschmerzen	If by your hand Sarastro feels not death's pain
So bist du meine Tochter nimmermehr:	then you are no longer my daughter:

Verstoßen sei auf ewig, verlassen sei auf ewig,	Let all natural bonds be forever cast off,
Zertrümmert sei'n auf ewig alle Bande die Natur,	forever abandoned, forever destroyed
Wenn nicht durch dich Sarastro wird erblassen	if through you Sarastro does not die!
Hört, Rachegötter, hört!— der Mutter Schwur!	Hear, gods of vengeance, a mother's oath!

Mozart densely packs "Der Hölle Rache" with the musical elements common to his other "revenge" arias—agitated rhythms, pulsating bass lines, quickly shifting dynamics and *sforzandi*, tremolos, and angular melodies—overwhelming us with effects. The Queen's first phrases (mm. 2–10) exploit the chromatic possibilities of the minor mode, particularly at the words "death and despair blaze around me," where the vocal part surges to high B-flat before falling (via a Neapolitan triad) to C-sharp a diminished seventh below. She is not the first character to use this "death and despair" motive—a melodic descent of a diminished seventh (filled in by scale or arpeggio)—but it is almost always connected to her, directly or indirectly. The first instance of this motive occurs during Tamino's initial dialogue with the priest outside the temples in the first act finale, when the latter alludes to the "death and vengeance" that has inflamed the youth (1.15). A few scenes later, Sarastro counters Pamina's praise of her mother with two contrasting melodic gestures, one of which (mm. 429–30) seems to prefigure the Queen's melody and her corresponding fate (1.18). Lecturing Pamina, Sarastro insinuates that "death and despair" are the consequences of unyielding female audacity.[23]

Sarastro and the priests insinuate that death and despair is the Queen's nature as well as a punishment meted out to all who associate with her, but the Queen's own reference to death and despair in "Der Hölle Rache" seems less a threat than a shriek against fate. Like Vitellia, who envisions death approaching her, the Queen sings of her own doom. Panicked by her daughter's about-face, the Queen immediately gives Pamina an ultimatum: prove her devotion or be forever motherless. The words are harsh but candid—and not exclusively her own. In a sense, the Queen is only repeating what Sarastro has established: he will not let Pamina return to her mother as long as he is in command. He offers no conditions for a rapprochement. Cornered, the Queen turns to that expedient but unpredictable weapon of political warfare, assassination. A lofty, controlled musical style introduces the subject of Sarastro's murder; the initial ascending arpeggio and well-ordered sequences recall the B-flat-major Allegro of the Queen's first aria. The real thrust of the aria, however, is the message of dispossession. The Queen's plan (and resultant acquisition of the Sun-Circle) depends on Pamina's bond to her mother, so, after a passing reference to Sarastro's death pangs (mm. 11–16), the Queen threatens abandonment—"so bist du meine Tochter nimmermehr"—over the space of 31 measures. The aria's most notorious coloratura passage (mm. 24–32, repeated at mm. 35–43), with its emphatic repetitions and high-soaring arpeggios, aptly illustrates the daunting significance of "nevermore."

Strikingly, the next section (mm. 52–67) is stripped of vocal ornamentation. The Queen's declaration regarding the irreparable dissolution of the mother-daughter bond—"All natural bonds will be forever cast off, forever abandoned, forever destroyed"—uses the simplest melodic means, exploiting the cumulative rhetorical effect of repetition. Three times she sings a short phrase in dotted rhythms on a single note, F, punctuating each "ewig" with an octave fall (mm. 52–58). The orchestra, too, adopts this repetitive style. The strings and bassoons toss a constricted motive (made up of parallel thirds) between different octaves and dynamic levels in correspondence to the movement and inflection of the vocal part. The distinct change at "alle Bande der Natur" brings an uncanny nuance to the Queen's threat: the sudden quiet, the woodwind doubling (in three different octaves) of the vocal line, and the soft tremolos lace her words with the very sound of clenched-jaw fury. Keenly aware of her dependence, the mother continues to intimidate her daughter, her voice rising sequentially higher (mm. 61–67). She rises to her full height, as it were, unleashing a new barrage of vocal fulminations (mm. 68–79) on "Bande" before returning to a more declamatory style ("if through you Sarastro does not die"). The aria ends with what is essentially a brief accompanied recitative. The Queen of the Night invokes the gods of vengeance as witness to her dreadful vow, with the threefold repetition of a single word ("Hört!") on an arpeggiated chord. The orchestra's vigorous triplets call to mind again her earlier Allegro, but the majestic optimism of that number has warped now into bitter, blistering rage. The Queen sees herself utterly betrayed: by her husband, her young champion, and now her only child, who wants to join the Initiated Ones, the very ones who would see the Queen cast into the eternal darkness.

Pamina does not realize, of course, that the Queen's imperious tone camouflages her relative powerlessness. The dagger is pitifully ineffectual in the hands of her mother, who has no direct access to Sarastro.

The singer who takes on the role of the Queen, however, must never forget this fundamental incommensurability between the Queen's pride and her actual power. In a sense, this aria represents a fight for survival both in the story and on the stage. A single false note by the singer can ruin the impression of superhuman vocality; the Queen of the Night's "performance" for Pamina is likewise a musico-rhetorical strategy of illusory "shock and awe." This is the paradox of "Der Hölle Rache" and of the Queen, for her most terrifying exclamation is also her most vulnerable. In this aria, music resists dramatic pull, for even without the preceding dialogue and the Queen's exclamation, "Der Hölle Rache" argues for our sympathies, if only because we cannot help but cheer the singer/character that pulls it off.

Paradoxically, "Der Hölle Rache"—a desperate response to defeat—is the Queen's most powerful musical moment. When it is finished, however, so, too, is the Queen; her fate is set. In her last appearance, accompanied by her Three Ladies and Monostatos, she is sadly diminished. Gone are the vocal fireworks and her dramatic autonomy: she becomes part of the Three Ladies' aggregate, her melody often doubled by the First Lady. Moreover, the music that accompanies her surreptitious entrance has a distinctly satirical tone, more in line with Leporello's furtive night watch than a coup d'état. As they near the temples, the party announces its intention: "We will attack [the Initiates] there, to strike the bigots from the earth, with glowing fire and mighty sword!" (2.30). One cannot help but wonder at the bootlessness of this raid—four women and one man against the entire fraternity of Initiated Ones in their own domain—considering that the Queen herself could not offer protection to her daughter.[24] Indeed, the five malcontents are soon cast into "eternal night" by the rising, victorious sun, tumbling down a series of thirds to a hollow, barely audible low B.

THE "BAD SUBLIME"

Why, in Sarastro's allegedly hallowed halls of friendship and mercy, is this emphatic expulsion necessary? What makes the Queen so threatening to the Brotherhood when her powers are clearly limited? Perhaps one clue lies in the fact that the Queen manifests both the beautiful and the sublime, upsetting the sexual assumptions that informed these categories for Enlightenment thinkers. Philosophers such as Edmund Burke (1729–97), Immanuel Kant (1724–1804), and Jean-Jacques Rousseau (1712–78) addressed these complementary but distinct ideals with highly gendered language that reflected social ideology and convention. In *A Philosophical Enquiry into the Origins of Our Ideas of the Sublime and Beautiful*, published in 1757, Burke compares the two ideals, concluding that beauty is small, smooth, gradually varied, rounded or gently sloping, delicate, and light colored, while the sublime is vast, rugged, at right angles or sharply deviating, solid, dark colored, and gloomy. Beauty is lovable and compliant, but the sublime is admirable and commanding; "we submit to what we admire, but we love what submits to us," he concludes.[25] Kant's *Observations on the Feeling of the Beautiful and Sublime* contains many of these same oppositions: "The sublime must always be great; the beautiful can be small. The sublime must be simple; the beautiful can be adorned and ornamented. Sublime attributes stimulate esteem, but beautiful ones, love."[26] In the section "On the Distinction of the Beautiful and the Sublime in the Interrelations of the Two Sexes," Kant contends that women are chiefly known by "the mark of the beautiful," while "the sublime clearly stands out as the criterion" of men.[27] For both philosophers, the sublime is compatible with the terrible and the awesome. In nature it appears in jagged or wild landscapes, raging storms, and earthquakes. Among his categories that resonate with the concept of sublimity, Burke includes darkness, blackness, obscurity, and the night; Kant states simply, "Night is sublime; day is beautiful."[28]

The Queen of the Night lives in sublimity. Roaming into her realm, Tamino is overcome by a terrible serpent. Around him, as the stage directions indicate, is a rocky, mountainous landscape, with trees here and there and a round temple. These mountains divide with a thunderous roar, revealing the veiled Queen, the Isis of the mountains, who appears like a vision, glittering amidst transparent stars. However "beautiful" she might be physically, she brings the sublime into play from her first entrance. It is no wonder that Tamino can hardly believe his eyes, and Papageno trembles at the idea of actually facing this presence, which is both frightening and magnificent. Her music, too, merges the beautiful and the sublime. Initially, the Queen's maternal grief, tearful pleas for (masculine) aid, and sparkling adornment frame her as conventionally feminine. She is the lovely, star-lit mother of the beloved Pamina. However, her character expands to alarming dimensions in the Allegro of her first aria, then supernovas into terrible sublimity with "Der Hölle Rache." The coloratura of her arias is more vertiginous than decorous, her voice ascending and plummeting as sharply as the steep slopes of her mountains.

Abbate notes that one of the most striking things about the coloratura passages of "Der Hölle Rache" is that they consists only of arpeggios, with no conjunct melodic lines at all. With this aria, she says, "an unprecedented voice comes into being," and the human voice "metamorphoses into an impossible device, a wind instrument unknown in 1791, unknown ever since." Abbate concludes that the effect is anything but what Catherine Clément describes as a "losing song, femininity's song":

> This is not . . . simply a moment of passion, hysteria, rage, irrationality, babbling, essentially feminine noise, not a shriek, not a degradation, not the philosophical nightmare of *logos* dissolved into *melos,* nor any natural sound, not a losing song, not at all. Voice is suspended in a sonic overworld, as if it wanted to linger there for a few seconds, in itself serene but at the same time, to the listener, strange in a way that disarms the very fear that threatens one's astonishment: it is cold. This cannot possibly be sustained. Conventional operatic vocalism returns along with perceptible human speech, right before the end.[29]

The main issue for Abbate is the mechanical quality of the Queen's sound, the transformation from organic to metallic and back again. There is something inhuman about this voice, or, perhaps more accurately, superhuman. The effect of this sound on the listener also corresponds to the nature of the sublime experience: strange, disarming, threatening, astonishing.

Because the sublime aspect of her nature represents a "radical undermining of the aesthetic system," the Queen, though beautiful, also embodies what Paul Mattick Jr. calls "the Female Sublime or—from the dominant point of view—the Bad Sublime."[30] Mattick reminds us that one of the most despised figures for Burke was the woman in the violent mob, such as those who helped to bring down Queen Marie Antoinette during the French Revolution. As Mattick notes, such women "inspire Burke with horror by their negation of womanly beauty, but this horror is not one that can lead to delight and the sublime. The women of the mob are [for Burke] by social nature ugly—'swinish' and 'vile.' Their action spells the abolition of the social differentiation both exemplified and symbolized by the male privilege implicated in the category system of sublime and beautiful."[31] In fact, from at least the seventeenth century onward, women were associated with the active threat of social revolt. By the eighteenth century, "married women had lost most of their earlier legal, economic, and political rights," and thus the figure of the wife—a "potentially disorderly woman"—could be used "to figure both the hierarchical order required for social health, and the threat or actual disruption of that order."[32] In this context, then, it is striking that the Queen makes her last stand with a small insurgent mob—four women and an alienated slave—that hardly stands a chance against the Brotherhood's forces.

THE QUEEN'S PARTING SMILE

In the Ingmar Bergman film version of *Die Zauberflöte,* the Queen gazes at her audience with a paradoxical smile just before she succumbs to her abysmal expulsion. It is almost a smirk, and it sends a clear message that she does not consider herself *undone.* Although Bergman misses the mark on many things in his fanciful production, his final shot of the Queen captures perfectly her latent power. She represents a daunting question mark, one that lingers after the curtain falls and that is not so easily dismissed today as in 1791. Has she ever really been silenced? Or has she found, more than two centuries after her creation, a new kingdom? The Queen may have been the "bad lady" of the opera for more than two hundred years, but sympathies are not so fixed today. The critical lens is being focused more clearly on the words and actions of Sarastro and the Initiates: how can we reconcile the misogyny and racial bias of their "tolerance" with current conceptions of civil humanitarianism? Despite the reams of apologias that attempt to explain away these aspects of the opera—not the least of which is the long-held tradition of holding up Pamina's "elevation" as more than adequate compensation for the opera's general tone of *Frauenfeindlichkeit*—it is increasingly difficult in a postfeminist world to accept the fundamental hypocrisy of *Die Zauberflöte.* Sarastro's Brotherhood reduces the "human" to a carefully prescribed social set, implementing a rigid segregation even as they sing anthems to tolerance and enlightenment. A woman may ascend with her elected husband to a certain height, but without him the doors of the temples are closed to her.

All of the women in *Die Zauberflöte* are silenced or ridiculed when questioning or opposing the opinions and mandates of the masculine power structure. When the Queen objected to her husband's decision to leave the Sun-Circle to Sarastro, he ordered her not to meddle in matters beyond her womanly ken. The Three Ladies raise their concerns about Sarastro's Order to Tamino, who answers them—indirectly—with condescending disdain. Again and again the Initiated Ones warn against the intrinsic foolishness and duplicity of the female voice when unguided by a man of their understanding:

A woman does little, chatters much. (Priest to Tamino; 1.15)

A man must guide your hearts, for without him every woman is wont to step outside her sphere of activity. (Sarastro to Pamina; 1.18)

Guard against feminine wiles: that is the first obligation of the Craft. (Priests to Tamino and Papageno; 2.3)

A wise man weighs matters and disregards what the common rabble says . . . prattle repeated by women, but contrived by hypocrites. (Tamino to the Three Ladies and Papageno; 2.5)

Discrimination—rationalized as defense of wisdom, reason, and beauty—is an explicit part of Sarastro's realm, raising obvious questions about who is oppressing whom in the opera. The inconsistency between what Sarastro declares (in, for instance, "In diesen heil'gen Hallen") and what he actually does causes more problems now than perhaps it did for Mozart and his contemporaries, particularly his brother Freemasons at the lodge Zür Wohltätigkeit (Charity).[33] Two centuries after *Die Zauberflöte*'s premiere, Solomon is moved to observe, "Sarastro, true to his practice of ideological hypocrisy (early on, Tamino grasped this when he exclaimed, 'This it is all duplicity!'—'alles Heuchelei!'), explicitly disavows vengeance—'these sacred halls know not vengeance'—but takes it anyway."[34] Volkmar Braunbehrens addresses the issue of racism, in particular Sarastro's treatment of Monostatos. He contends that the "cynicism of a ruler toward his subordinate—in this case one already despised and disadvantaged because of his color—was not introduced without a purpose." He is especially critical of the scene in which Sarastro sentences the Moor to the bastinado; this brutal punishment would seem to discredit Sarastro's claims of universal tolerance in "In diesen heil'gen Hallen." Braunbehrens concludes that, in his famous aria, the leader of the Initiated Ones "is spouting pure ideology, for his behavior does not correspond to his solemn utterances."[35] If this kind of critical reevaluation costs Sarastro some of his long-touted moral superiority, it concomitantly allows the Queen more humanity: she is not merely the face of unreason, unwisdom, and unbeauty, but rather an antiheroine who will not submit to the Brotherhood's rigorously patriarchal regime. This is not slippery maneuvering in the name of political correctness; the libretto and music of the opera allow for it. Even Nagel, a confirmed admirer of the general message of human goodness in *Die Zauberflöte*, is compelled to admit the essential flaw in the Enlightenment's "reasonable" ideas about humanity and, consequently, about tolerance and mercy:

The metaphor of light and darkness answers the favorite riddle of today's enlightened critics who choose to ignore what the Enlightenment was. How does it happen, they ask, that Sarastro preaches pardon, but, as his first action on stage, orders that Monostatos's feet be lashed "seventy-seven times"? If the critics had seen something more in this incident than their chance to display verbal brotherhood with slaves and blacks, they might have added a deeper puzzle: Why is *the* programmatic deed of *Die Zauberflöte*, the pardoning of the Queen in the *Hallen* manifesto, followed nonetheless by her descent to hell? Such lack of logic leads to the heart of the Enlightenment's revolutionary logic. The enemy, black as night, is unreal; therefore he can be whipped, damned, annulled. Humanity is valid only for humans, not for monstrous non-humans—valid, that is, only within one's own party. "Anyone not cheered by these teachings / Does not deserve to be a man."[36]

For many, the Queen's final, eternal punishment is unsettling, especially in the context of a long-beloved opera that pitches enlightened tolerance. Forgiveness, sings Sarastro, makes the enemy a friend, but he also declares that not everyone is considered worthy of being human, and therefore some will be denied the virtues of friendship and pardon. Of course, strong resistance to the Brotherhood's order automatically places one in that *Unmensch* category. This is where the Queen has usually been filed; she and her supporters are simply "taken care of," just before the sun rises on a new day. Oddly enough, Mozart provided a very different denouement in his last opera seria, *La Clemenza di Tito,* which premiered only a few weeks before *Die Zauberflöte*.[37] Both Emperor Titus and Sarastro preach forgiveness, but only one of them chooses to risk offering clemency to an enemy. When Emperor Titus discovers that his beloved friend Sestus and the future empress, Vitellia, have conspired and attempted to assassinate him, he is, naturally, outraged. Long revered for his merciful policies, Titus is put to the extreme test; he fights an internal battle between a wrathful desire for vindication and seemingly impossible pardon. In the end, he pardons both traitors completely and welcomes them back into his care: "I know all, I forgive all, I forget all."[38] Conversely, Sarastro's forgiveness is a null hypothesis. Just before he sings "In diesen heil'gen Hallen," he tells Pamina that after Tamino and she are joined, her mother "must return to her castle in shame."[39] Sarastro already knows that should events go as planned, the Queen will be defeated and cast out from the realm of "humanity," the society of the Sun, by political coup. Pamina does not ask for mercy for her mother, and Sarastro does not offer.

As the daughter ascends to the matrimonial throne, lauded as help-mate and consort of the newly initiated Prince, the mother is cast down, disgraced, into the metaphorical dungeons of the "Bad Sublime." This was her fate from the beginning—it had to happen that way. Her tale calls to mind Eleanor of Aquitaine, another queen imprisoned and closely monitored for rebellious schemes and political maneuvering. In the 1968 film adaptation of James Goldman's superb play *A Lion in Winter,* the figure of Eleanor strikes me as a fleshed-out Queen of the Night. Even in exile she shrewdly opposes her husband, King Henry II, in a potentially lethal battle of wits. It is difficult, if not impossible, for her to win outright, since Henry is king and holds the keys to her free-dom. Hoping to regain power and position, she plots for the ascendancy of her favorite son, Richard, and works hard to keep his allegiance. It is striking, however, that during the entire drama Queen Eleanor never shows to any of her three sons the maternal affection she demonstrates for Alais, the sister of Philip II, king of France. As part of a treaty with Philip's father, the late king Louis VII, Alais was betrothed to young Richard as a little girl and came to live as Eleanor's ward. Now, Alais has replaced Eleanor in Henry's heart and taken her chair at his table. Nevertheless, disembarking from her royal barge to enjoy a short period of liberation, Eleanor approaches Alais and warmly embraces this rival-daughter. When the young woman offers her only a prim curtsey, Eleanor chides her with a smile: "No, greet me as you used to. Fragile I am not: affection is a pressure I can bear."

Later, when Henry has forcefully confined everyone to the castle, Eleanor comes to Alais's chamber. In an earlier scene she had asked the girl, "After all the years of loving care, do you think that I could bring myself to hurt you?" Alais replied coldly, without hesitation, "Eleanor, with both hands tied behind your back." In the role of Eleanor, Katharine Hepburn bows her head and fights back tears at these words, as though acknowledging what is true, though she does not want it to be that way. (Having witnessed this scene, Henry asks, "Is there anyone I could have chosen to love to gall you more?" to which Eleanor replies, "There's no one.") Alone now with Alais in her room, the dishonored queen is not at all surprised by the younger woman's hostility, yet she persists in reaching out to Alais—"the child I raised, but didn't bear"—who is as powerless as she is. Alais observes that al-though Eleanor loves Henry for his power, she loves Henry the man and wants Eleanor to leave him alone. Their dialogue is both appalling and deeply poignant:

> *Alais.* Were you always like this? When I was young and worshiped you, is this what you were like?
>
> *Eleanor.* Most likely. Child, I'm finished and I've come to give him anything he asks for.
>
> *Alais.* Do you know what I should like for Christmas? I should like to see you suffer.
>
> *Eleanor.* Alais . . . just for you.

Their eyes meet, and suddenly Alais collapses, weeping bitterly, in Eleanor's arms. Eleanor moans, "Ah, ma petite," and Alais weeps, "J'ai peur, Maman" ("I am afraid, Mother"). One woman is in favor with the king, the other not, but both are Henry's captives. They are, as Rosenberg pointed out, "on the same side of existence." Soothing this foster daughter, Eleanor begins to sing softly to her. The estranged queen mother and her suffering, conflicted child are united again in a nocturnal embrace, weeping over their loss of one another, relatively defenseless against the schemes of men who determine their fates. Curiously, a distressed Henry walks in on them at this moment, remarking "the sky is pocked with stars." His world has just been turned upside down, for none of his sons has met his expectations. Probably hoping to find comfort from Alais, he instead discovers her cradled in Eleanor's arms, the two women united in a way he will never understand, under a black, star-flaming sky.

We cannot know whether the anarchic Queen of the Night and Pamina—frozen in "the mortuary telos of perfected order"—have their own opportunity for recognition and reconciliation as well. It is difficult to accept, however, that in a contemporary sequel to *Die Zauberflöte* the Queen would remain, quiet and defeated, in her mountain-encased fortress. Although most of the early sequels to *Die Zauberflöte* presented the Queen as the adversary of the heroic Tamino, today she is increasingly assuming a new significance:

> Highly dramatic heroines—from Beethoven's Leonora via Senta and Isolde to Brünnhilde—seem to have been forerunners of women's emancipation. Did the Queen of the Night start the movement? . . . [W]hen she sees that nothing can be of help to her, that the natural order has assigned women their place, then she responds logically, albeit with fanatical vindictiveness, by destroying natural ties—and herself. . . . No wonder the Queen of the Night reacts to this situation with hysterical excitement. It simply shows that the woman is not what she wants to be—a practical politician. But her habitual "wickedness" is not proved by the developments into which her husband, his friend Sarastro, her imagined auxiliary Tamino, and her daughter Pamina gradually force her.[40]

Perhaps this is why the smile of Bergman's Queen seems appropriate. In the latter days of the twentieth century, the Queen's star began to rise as the sun of the Enlightenment began to glow less brightly. It is still rising. She is not always gracious, nor gentle, but she has survived to a time in which, finally, her starlit sublimity can be fully appreciated.

CHAPTER 5

Good Daughter, Good Wife

Pamina

"Are you so glad, then, Kristin, you are going from me so far
and for so long?" asked her mother. Kristin was abashed and
uneasy, and wished her mother had not said this. But she answered as best she could: "No, my dear mother, but I am glad
that I am to go with my father." "Ay, that you are indeed,"
said Ragnfrid, sighing.

Sigred Undset, Kristin Lavransdatter

Mother the car is here / Somebody leave the light on / Black
chariot for the redhead dancing girl / He's gonna change my
name / Maybe you'll leave the light on / Just in case I like the
dancing / I can remember where I come from.

Tori Amos, "Mother"

Human love in its many forms is one of the primary themes of *Die Zauberflöte*. The opera solemnizes Freemasonry's distinctive brand of fraternal attachment, and it comments on familial and conjugal devotion
as well. All of the characters invoke love, but it is Pamina who is most
motivated by—and vulnerable to—love's claims. Committing herself to
Tamino with ingenuous fervor, the daughter of the Queen of the Night
goes mad because of conflicting loves. Both the Queen and Sarastro attempt to annex her affection and her future, allegedly as a sign of caring. Monostatos adores her, too, but she rejects his coercive passion.
Prince Tamino, smitten by her picture, describes his ardor for the
princess in rhapsodic song, yet he also allows her to be used as an unwitting prop in his own initiation, ignoring her tearful pleas for an explanation in order to prove his manly discretion. For Pamina, these ex-

amples are corruptions of "true love" and therefore incomprehensible to her. Her almost simplistic devotion to her love for Tamino is both her strength and her limitation. Tamino happily unites with Pamina, but his initiation is more about proving himself worthy of the Initiated than about becoming Pamina's husband. On the other hand, Pamina's only goal is to be with the prince. Unlike her husband-to-be, she faces baffling circumstances without help or instruction, guided almost exclusively by her own naïve heart. Pamina loves easily and generously, but the opera's social mandate requires that she make a terrible choice: relinquish her ties with her mother or else lose Tamino and paternal favor.[1] She must, in a word, love her father more than her mother. In tacitly forsaking the Queen of the Night, Pamina fully satisfies the requirements of a Brotherhood-friendly femininity, renouncing entirely her maternal origins.

THE QUEEN'S PASSIONATE DAUGHTER

Oddly enough, the opera suggests that Pamina will be a good wife precisely because she has been a good daughter. For much of the first act of the opera, she is defined in terms of the close bond with her nocturnal mother. Following Tamino's exultant admiration of the princess's portrait, the Three Ladies recount to Tamino the Queen's "maternal" response: if the youth is as bold as he is tender, then "her daughter Pamina" is most surely rescued. Later in the first act the Three Slaves discuss Pamina's escape from Monostatos (and Sarastro), the First Slave exclaiming, "how the timid doe must be hurrying with mortal fear to the palace of her loving mother" (1.9). In her first appearance (in No. 6, "Du feines Täubschen"), Pamina declares to a menacing Monostatos, "Death does not make me tremble. I am only sorry for my mother; she will surely die of grief." After Monostatos has been frightened off by the feathered Papageno, Pamina awakes from a swoon, saying, "Mother . . . Mother . . . Mother!" (1.13). Papageno hails her not as "Princess," "Lady," or even "Pamina," but as "daughter of the nocturnal Queen" (1.14). (It is striking that Pamina does not recognize her mother by this designation—the "nightly" Queen—but understands that Papageno is speaking about her mother only when he refers to the "star-blazing Queen.") During this scene with Papageno, Pamina learns that her mother has sent a prince—a prince who *loves* her—to rescue her from Sarastro's captivity.[2] Filled with new and marvelous emotions, she momentarily forgets about her escape. Together with the bird-man, the

young princess sings a paean to marriage, "Bei Männern, welche Liebe
fühlen" (No. 7):

Pam.	Bei Männern, welche Liebe fühlen, Fehlt auch ein gutes Herze nicht.	A man who can feel love does not lack for a good heart.
Pap.	Die süßen Triebe mitzufühlen	To feel with him these sweet urges
	Ist dann der Weiber erste Pflicht.	is a woman's first obligation.
Both.	Wir wollen uns der Liebe freun, Wir leben durch die Lieb' allein.	We wish to enjoy love, we live through love alone.
Pam.	Die Lieb' versüßet jede Plage, Ihr opfert jede Kreatur.	Love sweetens every suffering, every creature makes sacrifices to it.
Pap.	Sie würzet unsre Lebenstage, Sie wirkt im Kreise der Natur.	It seasons our daily lives, it works within the circle of Nature.
Both.	Ihr hoher Zweck zeigt deutlich an: Nichts Edlers sei, als Weib und Mann. Mann und Weib, und Weib und Mann, Reichen an die Gottheit an.	Its higher purpose clearly shows that nothing is nobler than wife and man. Man and wife, and wife and man attain unto godliness.

Mozart sets this piece in the key of E-flat major, the "Masonic" key
and also the primary key of the opera. The unobtrusive chordal pulsing
of the strings and modest woodwind interjections set a serene mood that
is charmingly incongruous with the rescue plan. Pamina's gently con-
toured vocal line—firmly diatonic and laid out in short phrases—takes
its impetus from a consistent dancelike pulse: it is a charming pastorale,
the ideal musical meeting place for earthy Papageno and ingenuous
Pamina. The overall rhetorical effect complements the musical scheme.
When singing alone, Pamina and Papageno offer different perspectives,
feminine and masculine, on the same subject, using parallel open
phrases; harmonic resolution comes with the shared vision of man
and woman united, the beatified "we." They sing together the fundamental message of the duet: we live for love, which aspires to the divin-
ity of marriage. The awesome power of "Mann und Weib" inspires
the hushed reverence and ecstatic longing of the closing section (mm.
33–49), culminating in Pamina's twin cadenzas (mm. 44–47). Given the
platonic relationship between the two singers, the moralizing text, and
uncomplicated musical style and structure, the duet is often categorized

as more spiritual than sensual. Jean-Victor Hocquard describes "Bei Männern" as "a sort of canticle in honor of the couple united in love," with Papageno and Pamina not sharing but rather celebrating a bond that is neither erotic nor merely conjugal.[3] Likewise, Nicholas Till suggests that the duet's "new embodiment of Pamina's pre-social sexual desires" acts as a corrective to the "lascivious advances of Monostatos." Like Hocquard, Till emphasizes the ingenuous quality of Papageno's and Pamina's testimonial, this "simple hymn to the power of love, so childishly naïve, and yet in its innocence resembling the wide-eyed wisdom of a child." Even the "dramatically inapposite moment" when Papageno and Pamina "ought to be fleeing for their lives" reinforces the idea of a "spiritual, and not a romantic (far less erotic), ideal of love"; Till infers that Schikaneder and Mozart clearly wished that "Bei Männern" should occur "when it could be sung by a couple who are not romantically involved."[4]

Admittedly, there is a family-values aspect to "Bei Männern," but the duet also blushes with unaffected sensuality, signaling Pamina's awakening to adulthood. Anticipation warms the solemn declarations; high-minded sincerity does not preclude fervid desire for the beloved. The same sensual artlessness pervades Susanna's "Deh vieni non tardar, o gioia bella" in *Le nozze di Figaro*. Both numbers are pastorales in an andante tempo, characterized by pulsing, predominantly string accompaniment (pizzicato or light staccato), graceful woodwind embellishments, and a lilting, arpeggiated melody. Other comparable examples include Don Giovanni's canzonetta "Deh vieni alla finestra" (2.3.16) and the duet between Countess Almaviva and Susanna, "Che soave zeffiretto" (3.10.20). The spontaneous passion of Pamina's effusive sighs at the end is one of the most winning aspects of the duet, especially given the conduct-book subtext: already we hear about a woman's "duty" *(Pflichte)* to share *(mitzufühlen)* her husband's feelings. Far from being a spiritually elevated but bloodless ode, "Bei Mannern" captures Pamina's innocence and yearning as she dedicates her whole self to this new love.

It is crucial to acknowledge this passionate side of Pamina, for her experience of what we now call romantic love—both its spiritual and sensual qualities—stirs something profound in her: it unleashes her own resolute, (star-)glittering spirit. Even in the face of punishment or possible death, Pamina affirms her attachment to Tamino for which she will suffer greatly. Her boldness is clearly revealed in the finale of act 1 when she and Papageno, attempting to escape, hear the priestly chorus announcing Sarastro's return (1.17). While the bird-man cowers in terror, fretting about what they should say when caught (1.18), Pamina affirms without hesitation, "Die Wahrheit, die Wahrheit, sei sie auch Verbrechen!" ("The truth, the truth, even if it be a crime!"). In the face of Sarastro's judgments, Pamina will conceal neither her actions nor her motives. In the Larghetto that follows she preempts Sarastro's inquiry, falling to her knees and confessing her "crime" with the same serene conviction she expressed in her "Wahrheit" phrase. Nagel remarks that in this passage we appreciate "Ilia's, Constanze's, and now, immeasurably greater, Pamina's decision that predicts and compels mercy from above. The tremulous question in the midst of peril, 'Was werden wir nun sprechen?' (What shall we say now?) is cut short by the brightest turning point in the history of opera, and of the human subject: 'Die Wahrheit, die Wahrheit, sei sie auch Verbrechen.' Thou shalt speak the truth, even if it were a crime—yet *her* truth, Pamina's own truth, is not repentance but self-discovery. It lends the confession and the pardon, which now conventionally ensue, a heretofore-unknown dignity."[5]

Pamina's petition transcends the opera's otherwise shallow discourse on entreaty and mercy. It is the only time that Sarastro fully pardons, though it seems odd that the kidnapped Pamina should be the one asking forgiveness. Mozart set this exchange between captor and captive in a remarkably lyric arioso style, much more expressive than Constanze's similar entreaty in *Die Entführung aus dem Serail*, which is spoken. In fact, this musical dialogue is crucial to the story, clearly defining Pamina's relationship with Sarastro and confirming the mutual enmity between the rulers of day and night:

Pam. Herr, ich bin zwar Verbrecherin!—	Sir, I am truly a criminal!
Ich wollte deiner Macht entfliehn.—	I wanted to escape from your power.
Allein die Schuld ist nicht an mir!	But the blame is not mine alone!
Der böse Mohr verlangte Liebe,	The wicked Moor demanded love,
Darum, o Herr, entfloh ich dir!—	that is why, oh Sir, I ran away from you!
Sar. Steh auf, erheitre dich, o Liebe;	Arise, be cheered, o beloved one;
Denn ohne erst in dich zu dringen,	for without demanding it from you,
Weiß ich von deinem Herzen mehr,	I know more of your heart:
Du liebest einen andern sehr.	you love another very much.
Zur Liebe will ich dich nicht zwingen,	I will not force you to love,

| Doch geb' ich dir die Freiheit nicht. | Yet I will not grant you freedom either. |

Sarastro's prophetic "without demanding it from you, I know more of your heart" is surely meant to amaze the young woman and gain her trust. Perhaps his acuity results from magical powers (or a hidden monitoring system), but Pamina also provides subtle clues about her emotions. When she sings of the harassment by the "evil Moor," for instance, the music seems strangely unsuited to the words. The harmony turns from anxious D minor toward G major as the accompaniment quickens with the pulse of expectation rather than fear. Her languid melody is sweetened with an appoggiatura and a graceful slur on "Liebe": in a single phrase she simultaneously rejects Monostatos and welcomes Tamino into her heart. Sarastro defers to her preference. "You love another very much," he declares, and the solo flute doubling his melody two octaves higher identifies the unnamed suitor (mm. 412–16). Soon he will accept Tamino as a son or, perhaps more accurately, as a surrogate, for Pamina's union with the prince will serve Sarastro's higher aims, if not his personal desires.

There is one love, however, that Sarastro will not tolerate in Pamina: her affection for her mother. When Pamina reminds him that filial duty obliges her to return to her mother, Sarastro gruffly interrupts her, remarking that the Queen lies in his power, his words emphasized by a brusque, intimidating cadential gesture. He then declares that Pamina's own happiness would have been forfeit had he left her with the Queen. His voice rises to the top of the bass range before sinking down a diminished seventh—a prominent melodic formula, as noted above, in the Queen of the Night's aria "Der Hölle Rache." Unswayed, Pamina resumes her loving speech about her mother, whose name is "sweet" to her. Sarastro cuts her off again with a curt cadence: the Queen of the Night is nothing but a "proud woman." More gently, but with a father's authoritative resonance, he then explains that a man must direct the heart of every woman, "for without him every woman would step outside her designated domain." Here Mozart uses a simple but effective harmonic contrast to characterize a woman's two options. Sarastro lauds masculine guidance with a minor-sixth leap up to a sustained D— a relatively high note in his range—over a bright B-flat-major chord (mm. 438–39): the emphasis is specifically on "ihn" or "him." Finally, the patriarch hovers on the rootless dissonance of a diminished-seventh chord (m. 440), stressing the fundamental instability of any woman who chooses to go her own way, overstepping her socially prescribed sphere

EXAMPLE 14. *Die Zauberflöte,* No. 8, Finale (act 1, scene 18)

or "Wirkungskreis" (Ex. 14). This is a decisive moment for Pamina, who, until now, has been motivated by devotion for Tamino *and* her mother. Sarastro is telling her now that these two attachments are in some way incompatible, that her daughterly allegiance must be transferred to a man, either a worthy father figure or husband. Having justified Pamina's abduction by accusing the Queen of being a bad mother, Sarastro now proclaims that, in the end, no woman (apparently even those who are good mothers) is capable of guiding her children to adulthood. The Queen's alleged shortcomings only make more imperative what Sarastro claims to be a universal truth, namely that *every* woman's health and happiness depend on male supervision. Sarastro will not force Pamina to love, but he will educate her to love the right people: the Queen cannot occupy a vital place in Pamina's heart if a proper social order is to prevail. In the end, Sarastro implies, Pamina must choose between her husband/father and her mother.[6]

PAMINA'S CHOICE AND THE BONDS OF NATURE

Pamina's test of allegiance comes early in the second act. She is sleeping, alone, senseless of the approaching Monostatos, who moans with passion for this white woman who has inflamed his heart. He cannot resist kissing her sleeping form, and tells the moon to hide her eyes. (Inexplicably, Sarastro has left Pamina unguarded, though he knows of the Moor's desires.) Suddenly, the moon-Queen herself appears, commanding the slave to move away from her daughter (2.8). Pamina awakens at the sound of her mother's voice and throws herself into the Queen's arms. For the moment she forgets Sarastro's admonishments and even asks her mother to take her away: "Oh let us flee, dear mother! Under your protection I will brave every danger." The girl welcomes the familiar security of her mother's arms in this bewildering place where she has no steady companion, where she has been assaulted by Monostatos and ignored by other men, including Tamino. She looks hopefully to her mother for refuge, but soon learns that the Queen—the widow of a dead monarch who left her under Sarastro's rule—can do little to change either of their circumstances. The conversation between mother and daughter spells out Pamina's dilemma: she cannot return to her mother's home without forsaking Tamino. Then she hears about her deceased father's decree that she and her mother must submit to Sarastro and the Initiates, to whom he bequeathed the mighty Sun-Circle, the emblem of authoritarian rule. This revelation changes everything for Pamina: she accepts without further questioning that Sarastro has claimed what was lawfully entrusted to him by the dead king, including her obedience. "My father," whispers Pamina, and she forgets that only minutes before she had wanted to flee with her mother from Sarastro's domain. "Dear mother, might not I love the youth as tenderly as an Initiated One as I love him now? My father himself was allied with these wise men; he always spoke with delight about them, praised their goodness—their intelligence—their virtue. Sarastro is no less virtuous." One has to wonder why Pamina suddenly remembers her father's chummy association with the Brotherhood. It is surely one of the most contrived moments in the opera—I am reminded of those routine amnesia episodes in soap operas—but it serves to substantiate the primacy of the father, who even from the grave exerts a palpable influence on his daughter. It is only after hearing her father's words—as conveyed by the Queen—that Pamina's thoughts shift from fearful flight to eager advocacy of the Initiates. In that instant Pamina takes the fateful step away from her mother and, whether consciously or not, places her destiny in Sarastro's hands. The manly trinity of father, guardian, and fiancé will guide her heart, in fulfillment of the opera's social doctrine. Heard in its entirety, this dialogue between mother and daughter cuts through Sarastro's "Isis and Osiris" mumbo jumbo and exposes the power politics that are behind the credo of the opera. The Queen of the Night pulls out the "mother's curse" only after she senses Pamina's imminent defection. "Der Hölle Rache" is not the cause of Pamina's separation from the maternal world, but rather a failed attempt to reverse Sarastro's latest victory.

Left alone, Pamina frets over the dagger her mother left her, but she refuses to carry out the assassination. Monostatos reappears, having eavesdropped on the mother-daughter encounter. He threatens to inform Sarastro of the plot, then tries to extort Pamina's affection by threatening her with the Queen's dagger, but she staunchly refuses him. Just as Monostatos raises the knife to strike, Sarastro appears at Pamina's side. He seems to be aware of everything that has taken place, for he is unsurprised when the young woman beseeches him to be merciful to her mother. The patriarch soothes her with words about friendship and forgiveness and manly endeavors (none of which, of course, have much to do with the Queen's ultimate fate). He tells his ward that he will have his vengeance when he sees her happily coupled with a fully initiated Tamino. Sarastro can afford to be gracious: Pamina has proven to him that she is a good daughter and that she will not cause any trouble. Nevertheless, the princess still has much to learn about her role in the fraternal Order. Her ardor for Tamino is virtuous but needs proper conditioning, so her contact with the youth is restricted and closely monitored. Like Tamino, she will endure various trials, but unlike the youth—who has Papageno's company and the Initiated Brothers' guidance throughout his trials—Pamina must pass through the stages of her feminine initiation almost entirely alone and in relative ignorance.

Still unattended (why is Pamina never allowed a female companion?), the young woman is overjoyed to find Tamino again (2.18), but he, too, turns his face from her. Tamino's trial is to show that he is able to withstand her tears and dismay, to keep silent around her, and to make his priorities clear. She may be his betrothed, but his faithfulness to the tenets of manliness must come first:

Pam. You here?—Kind gods! Thank you for leading me this way.—I heard your flute, and so I ran as swift as an arrow after the tone.—But you are sad?—You speak not a syllable to your Pamina?

Tam. (sighs) Ah!
(gestures for her to leave)

Pam. What? Am I to keep away from you? Do you no longer love me?

Tam. (sighs) Ah!
(waves her away again)

Pam. Must I leave without knowing why?—Tamino, sweet youth! Have I offended you?—O
do not injure my heart anymore.—I seek comfort from you—
assistance—and you can wound my loving heart still more?—Do
you no longer love me?
(Tamino sighs)

Pam. Papageno, you will tell me, what is wrong with my friend?
*(Papageno has some food in his mouth, covers the food on the table
with both hands, waves her away)*

Pam. What? You, too?—At least explain to me the reason for your silence.—

Pap. Shh!
(He points for her to go away)

Pam. Oh, this is worse than offense—worse than death! *(pauses)* Beloved, only Tamino!

It is difficult to imagine what this scene might have meant to Mozart, how a Masonic trial of silence fit into his own world, but whatever the case, his sympathies seem divided. Tamino passes his test, but Pamina is the one who sings here, and, in opera, music trumps ideology. The heart-rending aria "Ach ich fühl's" indicts the ideologically sanctioned cruelty of the scene. It also expresses the anguished discovery of the risk that is assumed by all those who love, namely, that their love may be forsaken or unreturned:

Ach ich fühl's, es ist verschwunden!	Ah, I feel it, it has vanished!
ewig hin der Liebe Glück!—	forever gone is love's happiness
Nimmer kommt ihr Wonnestunden	Those blissful hours will never
meinem Herzen mehr zurück!	again return to my heart!
Sieh Tamino! diese Tränen	See Tamino, these tears which
fließen Trauter dir allein,	flow, dearest, for you alone!
fühlst du nicht der Liebe Sehnen,	If you do not feel love's longing,
so wird Ruh' im Tode sein!	then I must find tranquility in death!

This profoundly beautiful expression of grief shifts the dramatic focus away from Tamino and his formalized trials. Brigid Brophy notes the "subversive" effect of the aria, which establishes Pamina as more than a feminine ornament or ideological foil: Mozart does not allow Pamina to "suffer inertly."[7] Moreover, Pamina's G-minor lament reestablishes a bond with her mother.[8] "Ach ich fühl's" has none of the Queen's stylistic extremes, but it is not difficult to hear an "inherited" lyric intensity. Pamina reproaches Tamino's senseless silence with all the elements of musical pathos that her mother used in her own G-minor lament, "Zum Leiden bin ich auserkoren": dissonant appoggiaturas, delicate ornaments, chromatic descents, and Neapolitan harmonies.[9] As early as the sixth bar ("der Liebe Glück") Pamina raises her voice over a flat-sixth chord to high B-flat, the apex of her range. After a sudden and striking harmonic turn toward the relative major, her next phrase—now in B-flat major—again descends from the fifth degree to the tonic. Expressing perfectly the bittersweet blend of remembered delight and present agony, the vocal line balances the graceful melodic fall of "Nimmer kommt ihr Wonnestunden" (mm. 8–10) with the poignant chromatic ascent of "meinem Herzen mehr zurück" (mm. 10–11); the section concludes with a brief melismatic passage (mm. 12–16), fragile and nostalgic, on the word "Herzen."

The vocal line in the second half of the aria (mm. 17–41) milks the plaintive effect of the descending diminished seventh, either as a direct leap, an arpeggio, or a filled-in scale. Such an abundant use of this interval is unusual; Mozart uses it sparingly in his other G-minor opera arias.[10] As we have already seen, however, the Queen of the Night's melody in "Der Hölle Rache" also makes striking use of the descending diminished seventh. In fact, there is a strong dramatic connection between the two arias; both "Der Hölle Rache" and "Ach ich fühl's" rebuke betrayal. But while the Queen's hurt erupts into vituperative wrath and a desire for revenge, Pamina surrenders to sorrow and thoughts of death. Like her mother, however, she employs the descending diminished seventh to underscore a threat. The Queen uses this interval in "Der Hölle Rache" to highlight the moments that are characterized by the most frightening rhetoric: when she describes to Pamina the death and destruction "blazing around her" (mm. 8–10); when she threatens her with the breaking of "nature's bonds" (mm. 81–82); and when, in order to demonstrate her seriousness, she calls the "gods of vengeance" to witness this vow of renunciation (mm. 90–93). In "Ach ich fühl's," the descending diminished seventh initially appears when Pamina speaks directly to Tamino for the first time in the aria: "See Tamino, these tears which flow, dearest, for you alone" (see especially the *sforzandi* of the flute and oboe in measures 17 and 19). Moments later she returns to this interval for her own dreadful vow. Four times she sings the words "fühlst du nicht der Liebe sehnen" ("If you do not feel love's longing"), and each instance she uses some form of the falling diminished seventh. The melodic line lifts briefly when Pamina contemplates the peace that will be her only consolation. She highlights the word "Ruh," first with a breathtaking Neapolitan A-flat in her middle range and then with a heavenly octave leap to a sustained high G.[11] Her closing phase, however, reminds us that the tranquility to which she refers is fatal. The vocal melody collapses one last time over a diminished seventh on the word "Tode" as she makes her final plea: if Tamino cannot love as she does, then she will die and be lost to him forever. Pamina's "revenge" is fundamentally self-destructive, but, like the Queen's vow, it is also a punishment for inconstancy, the threat of eternal separation.

Despite her choice to remain with Tamino and the Initiates, Pamina is, in fact, bound to her mother in rejection and isolation. Perhaps this is why, in the scene of her attempted suicide (2.27), she initially accuses the Queen of bringing her to this misery, which she links to her mother's curse: "Mutter, durch dich leide ich, und dein Fluch verfolget mich!" ("Mother, through you I am suffering, and your curse follows me!"). It is, in one sense, a strangely incongruous accusation. The Queen's "curse" was to abandon her daughter. There was no other malediction, no threat to make Pamina's life wretched. Nevertheless Pamina, dejected and alone, thinks of her mother; she even sings like her. She addresses the dagger's blade as the "bridegroom" that will soon end her grief. Just as her mother sent Tamino to her, she also left the dagger, the male surrogate. Pamina's melody, in C minor, is reminiscent of the Queen's highly disjunct melodic style (mm. 45–49). She then promises herself to the dagger with chilling effect, her lethal vow all the more horrible for being set to a lilting melody. Her gasping, sobbing vocal line is an erratic array of broken syllables, tortured leaps, diminished-seventh falls, and pathetic appoggiaturas, all in the minor mode. Pamina speaks her mother's language here, and she also shows some of the Queen's unwavering resolve. At measure 75 she moves toward G minor, committing herself fully to the death she first contemplated in "Ach ich fühl's": "Better to die by this knife than to perish from love's grief!" Her mother's words come back to haunt her: "The first gleam of day will decide whether he will be given wholly to you or to the Initiated Ones." The vocal line sinks chromatically from G to D ("The cup of my wretchedness is surely full!"), and Pamina bids a final, accusatory farewell to Tamino ("False youth, farewell!"). Still firmly in G minor, she now makes explicit the punitive aspect of her suicide, declaring, "See, Pamina dies because of you, this dagger kills me!" At the beginning of this phrase, the vocal line collapses down a major seventh, then sobs back up through the chromatic scale to C (mm. 89–91). The parallel chromatic slide of first-inversion chords in both the strings and woodwinds clashes against the incessant pulsing G of the second violins, the grating sonority of wrenched reason. At the cadence (m. 92), she thrusts the blade toward its mark.

FATHER KNOWS BEST

Whose name is missing from Pamina's indictment? Curiously, the princess says nothing about Sarastro, though it was he who resolved to separate her from her mother and keeps Tamino at a distance as well. Catherine Clément's remarks on "dead women" in opera come to mind: "there is always this constant: death by a man. Whether they do it themselves, like Butterfly, or are stabbed, like Carmen, the provenance of the knife, or the choking hand, or the fading breath is a man, and the result is fatal."[12] Reinforcing the shaky categories of good and bad in the opera, Pamina blames her absent mother, though it is Sarastro who is in control of her and Tamino's circumstances. In fact, the full scope of Sarastro's authority is revealed in a peculiar scene that comes between "Ach ich fühl's" and Pamina's suicide attempt (2.21). Hooded, Pamina is led into a room where Sarastro waits. Perhaps her veiling indicates that she, too, is being subjected to initiation, but the covering may just as easily represent her status as woman: the Queen and her Ladies also wear veils. After her hood is withdrawn, the young woman immediately inquires about her beloved:

> Pam. Where am I?—What a dreadful silence!—Tell me, where is my young man?—
> Sar. He awaits you in order to say his last farewell.
> Pam. His last farewell!—Oh, where is he?—Lead me to him!—
> Sar. Here!—
> Pam. Tamino!
> Tam. Stay back!

Rebuffed again—and no doubt anxious about Sarastro's ominous reference to a "last farewell"—Pamina does not, however, retreat in tears this time. Love—her claim on Tamino—brings out the nascent rebel in her: bypassing Sarastro, who sets himself between the couple, Pamina addresses the young prince directly in the trio (No. 19) "Soll ich dich Teurer nicht mehr sehn?" ("Shall I never see you again, dearest?").

The trio is not generally considered one of the musical highlights of the opera, but it can be gripping if smartly sung and staged, as it represents the closest thing to a standoff in the context of *Die Zauberflöte's* heavily gendered ideology about love. On one hand, Tamino is being trained to accept a "manly" philosophy that subordinates (female) love to (male) duty: his first loyalty must be to a masculine domain, and no woman should ever be able to exert any predominant influence on him. On the other hand, as Papageno indicated in "Bei Männern," Pamina's primary duty as a woman is devotion to Tamino; she must place their union and his wishes above all else, and she must not have other loyalties that interfere or lead her outside this sphere. Pamina fulfills this first obligation with great zeal, but in doing so she simultaneously complies with and challenges the system. Her attempt to communicate openly with Tamino, and to come between Sarastro and her beloved, infuses what would otherwise be a fairly maudlin goodbye scene with much-needed suspense. It is arguably the princess's bravest moment—far more so than the asinine fire and water trial that comes later—because she refuses to let the Brotherhood mediate her love:

Pam.	Soll ich dich, Teurer, nicht mehr sehn?	Shall I never see you again, dearest?
Sar.	Ihr werdet froh euch wiedersehn!	You will see each other again in joy!
Pam.	Dein warten tödtliche Gefahren!	Mortal dangers await you!
Sar. & Tam.	Die Götter mögen mich bewahren!	May the gods preserve him/me!
Pam.	Du wirst dem Tode nicht entgehen, Mir flüstert dieses bewahren!	I feel this foreboding that you will not escape death.
Sar. & Tam.	Der Götter Wille mag geschehen, Ihr Wink soll ihm/mir Gesetze sein.	Let the will of the gods be done, their sign will be his/my law.
Pam.	O liebtest du, wie ich dich liebe, Du würdest nicht so ruhig sein.	Oh if you loved, as I love you, you would not be so calm.
Sar. & Tam.	Glaub mir, fühlet/fühle gleiche Triebe,	Believe me, he feels / I feel the same urge,

	Wird/Werd' ewig dein Getreuer sein.	he will / I will always be faithful to you.
Sar.	Die Stunde schlägt, nun müßt ihr scheiden!	The hour strikes, you must now depart!
Pam. & Tam.	Wie bitter sind der Trennung Leiden!	How bitter are the sufferings of separation!
Sar.	Tamino muß nun wiederfort!	Tamino must be on his way again.
Tam.	Pamina, ich muß wirklich fort!	Pamina, I really must be on my way!
Pam.	Tamino muß nun wirklich fort?	Tamino must really be on his way?
Sar.	Nun muß er fort!	He must go now.
Tam.	Nun muß ich fort!	I must go now!
Pam.	So muß du fort!	Then you must go!
Tam.	Pamina,	Pamina,
Pam.	Tamino,	Tamino,
Pam. & Tam.	lebe wohl!	farewell!
Sar.	Nun eile fort, Dich ruft dein Wort! Die Stunde schlägt!	Now hurry away! Your vow calls you! The hour strikes! We will see each other again!
Pam. & Tam.	Ach, gold'ne Ruhe, kehre wieder! Lebe wohl!	Ah, golden peace, return again! Farewell!
Sar.	Wir sehn uns wieder!	We will see each other again!

The tug-of-war between Sarastro and Pamina, each pulling for a particular response from Tamino, is cleverly reflected in the music. Though the number begins and ends in B-flat major, both the subdominant key (E-flat) and relative minor (G minor) figure prominently; these keys form a triad of associations, connecting to dramatic themes that are crucial to the scene and the opera. The keys of E-flat major and G minor, for instance, have been connected with two contrasting ideas, love's bloom and sweetness (No. 3, "Dies Bildneß," and No. 7, "Bei Männern," in E-flat major) and the loss of a beloved (No. 4, "Zum Leiden," and No. 17, "Ach ich fühl's," in G minor). There is a hierarchical relationship between these two keys as well, in terms of the overall tonality of the work: the opera's primary key, E-flat major, is used to represent male amorous emotion and matrimonial harmony, while G minor, the "weaker" mediant key, is used to convey feminine suffering and separation. In contrast, B-flat major has been used in numbers emphasizing duty: in this key, the Queen commissioned Tamino to rescue her daughter, the Three Ladies sent him off to the task, and the priests agreed to accept him for initiation (as symbolized in the thrice-stated three chords, No. 9a). Here, too, in the B-flat-major trio, the demands of masculine Duty ultimately take precedence over those of feminine Love.

For most of the first half of the trio, Sarastro and Tamino are studiously—even artificially—united, singing together and providing the only full cadences. Sarastro answers for the youth or responds simultaneously with him; Pamina stubbornly continues to speak only to Tamino. Sensing that the girl's earnestness might unsettle Tamino's masculine resolve, Sarastro hastens to calm her ("You will see each other again in joy!"), but Pamina will not be so easily pacified. Turning toward the subdominant E-flat, she exclaims her fear to Tamino: "Mortal dangers await you!" Tamino responds stoically ("May the gods preserve me"), his melody comparatively restrained. His formulaic reply only increases Pamina's apprehension, and her melody climbs to A-flat, again accentuating E-flat through its dominant seventh. Quick to counter the rhetorical effect of Pamina's appeal, Sarastro bolsters Tamino's efforts at self-restraint. The male voices ascend together in parallel thirds and finish somewhat more confidently on a unison B-flat. Even when Pamina sings of her terrible dread (mm. 13–17), Tamino and Sarastro reply in tandem, valiantly accepting what the gods may will; the young man even adds jaunty ornamentation to his line. Their seemingly cavalier attitude offends Pamina, who reproaches Tamino: "Oh if you loved, as I love you, you would not be so calm." Fittingly, this passage (mm. 21–27) moves to the key of G minor; the diminished-seventh sonority on the word "du" and the sobbing effect of the appoggiaturas (mm. 24–25) recollect her similarly plaintive accusation in "Ach ich fühl's." There is the weight of conviction to her words: for the first time in the trio, in fact, Pamina's melody culminates in a perfect cadence.

Persisting in their now unnatural (and almost comic) oneness, Sarastro and Tamino assure her that the youth feels as she does and "will always be true" to her. The harmony turns abruptly away from Pamina's lugubrious G minor toward E-flat major (mm. 27–33)—the key, as we know, of Tamino's portrait aria and "Bei Männern." Sarastro may be sympathetic to Pamina's distress, but his overriding concern is Tamino's initiation. With characteristic gravity he announces that the hour has arrived for the young man's departure and final trials; his musical line leads the young couple, by way of a descending sequence, back toward obedient B-flat major (mm. 33–39). Pamina's words, however, hit their mark, for now Tamino, unable to repress his emotions any longer, joins her in shared anguish: "How bitter are the sufferings of separation!" Their parallel sixths are graced by the poignant sonority of paired oboes and bassoons in thirds. The master intervenes, forcefully now, to bring his apprentice back into line: "Tamino must be on his way once more." Even when the prince obediently echoes these words, Sarastro presses the point with references to the tonic minor on "wieder fort" (D-flat in m. 41) and "scheiden" (G-flat in m. 44). It is a not-so-subtle warning: Tamino must leave, *now*.

Despite these admonitions, Pamina musically resists the closure that Sarastro demands. The high priest initiates a new section at measure 39, and Tamino imitates his mentor's melody exactly an octave higher. Although Pamina follows the sequence, she shatters the prudent boundaries of Sarastro's line, expanding the initial leap to an octave (to high B-flat) and transforming his restrained stepwise descent of a third into a more demonstrative minor-tenth fall (mm. 41–43). She calls out Tamino's name, but the men insist that the prince must depart (mm. 47–48), with Tamino following Sarastro's melodic lead. Pamina, characteristically, answers in her own way: she questions rather than confirms the need for Tamino to leave her once more, punctuating her phrases with doubtful upward appoggiaturas (mm. 48–51). Though Sarastro himself is silent during Pamina's pathetic exclamations, the cellos and violas counter her weak phrase endings with decisive movements toward the tonic, representing, perhaps, the older man's unspoken bass-register thoughts. Finally, unable to resist, Tamino cries out with his own voice. Disregarding the mandate of silence, he calls to Pamina in the key of his affection, E-flat major, and she answers him with equal ardor (mm. 51–53).

They begin their farewells unconvincingly, singing "Lebe wohl." Sarastro brusquely reminds Tamino that he has a promise to fulfill and drives him toward a final, affirmative cadence (m. 54–58) by settling on a B-flat pedal. Still the couple will not break from one another: "Ah, golden tranquility, return again!" Sarastro's chromatically ascending vocal line conveys his growing impatience with this emotional goodbye, and he begins gradually to "raise" his voice. The dynamics of the trio have changed decisively, as Tamino acknowledges Pamina again and again, offering comfort (if not an explanation) for the hurt that began with "Ach ich fühl's." In this moment, Pamina's love proves stronger than duty. Ultimately, Sarastro sabotages the unhappy pair's intimate cadence in G minor with a high, ringing E-flat and escorts them once more to the tonic by way of the subdominant (m. 64). Assured now of

Tamino's obedience, Sarastro abandons his grave commands and offers the couple an optimistic prediction: "We will see each other again!" Pamina's and Tamino's lines still waver between C minor and G minor (mm. 65–67), but the bass line conducts them back to tonic compliance. The men leave while Pamina, helpless, watches.

Meine Hülfe war zu schwach: the Queen was too weak to do anything when Sarastro took her daughter away. Does Pamina sense the parallel between her own situation and her mother's dilemma? Sarastro will direct love, just as he does power, and Pamina must wait for his will. Knowledge, too, is denied her: she is given hints and allusions but no instructions or guides. In the Brotherhood's world, all women are marginalized to one degree or another. Female friendship, support, tutelage, and authority are either minimized or expunged altogether. Sarastro, for example, seems intent on leaving Pamina alone with her fears, confused by his vague references to final farewells and future reunions. Watching Tamino walk away, Pamina in her own way experiences the Queen of the Night's frustration, powerlessness, and solitude. It is all the more striking, then, that comfort finally comes to her—the *good* future wife and mother—in the form of children. The Three Boys introduce the act 2 finale, echoing Pamina's and Tamino's prayer for peace:

"O holde Ruhe, steig hernieder, Kehr in der Menschen Herzen wieder" ("Oh sweet peace, come down to us, return again to human hearts"): the voices of the Three Boys, fragile and pure, are heralds of the promised utopia, a domesticated and stabilized Day. We first learned of these special children early in act 1, when the Three Ladies introduced them as Tamino's guides to Sarastro's kingdom. They describe the Boys—who are apparently not in the Queen's service—in pleasing terms ("handsome, gentle, and wise"), though they never actually interact with them during the course of the opera. Jacques Chailley suggests that this is because they are "messengers," capable of attaining the perfect knowledge that the women can never possess; because of their nascent masculinity, the Three Boys are allowed entrance into the Brotherhood's halls and gardens. In this manly realm they seem to function as pages, bringing food to Tamino and Papageno during their trials and encouraging them to be "mannlich."

But now they have stolen into the garden, into the woman's space, perhaps at Sarastro's command, perhaps not. They watch the princess from their hiding spot. Recognizing that Pamina is "out of her senses" and "tormented by rejected love," they resolve to console her in Tamino's absence. (In fact, the stage directions at the beginning of scene 27 indicate that Pamina is "halb wahnwitzig," or "half mad.") The Three Boys remind her of the youth's love, of his bravery in the ordeals, and of the sinfulness of suicide. But Pamina sees only the dagger, much as she saw only Tamino in the trio, barely noticing the presence of others. The music heads toward a cadence in G minor, as Pamina prepares to strike herself. Imitating Sarastro's maneuver in "Soll ich dich," the Three Boys prevent the cadence on G minor by imposing a deceptive E-flat and hold back Pamina's knife (mm. 93–94). The magical boys clearly have learned Sarastro's language, but their earnest directness is more closely allied to Pamina than to the impassive Initiates. Ultimately they recapture Pamina's interest not with commands and warnings, but by appealing to her heart: "Should your young man see this, he would die from sorrow, for he loves you alone." They do not explain Tamino's standoffish behavior, but invite the princess to "see with wonder that he has consecrated his heart" to her. Their voices lift higher and higher over the anticipation-laden sound of a dominant pedal (mm. 123–30) as they seek to describe the astonishing revelation that awaits the princess.

Pamina believes them, and she asks to be led to Tamino. Her melody here (mm. 134–45) sounds like a major-mode variation on the opening phrase of "Der Hölle Rache." The playful moral statement—the syllables of "Herzen" are literally separated in Mozart's setting—denounces any force that would try to break love's bonds:

Zwei Herzen, die vor Liebe brennen,	Two hearts, which burn for love,
Kann Menschenohnmacht niemals trennen.	can never be separated by human powerlessness.
Verloren ist der Feinde Müh',	Lost are the enemies' efforts,
Die Götter selbsten schützen sie.	the gods themselves protect them.

Joining in song with the Three Boys, Pamina dismisses the "enemy" against whom she claims divine protection. This is the moment when Pamina herself officially breaks with her mother. Her melody in the closing proverb represents her final answer to the shocking caveat of "Der Hölle Rache." Pamina's ringing B-flat (Ex. 15)—the same climactic note that topped her mother's curse—and her subsequent melodic fall of nearly two octaves from the top note outdoes her mother's powerful cry and diminished-seventh descent (Ex. 16). There is even a phonetic connection between the two passages: Pamina's ecstatic "Gött-er" echoes her mother's "Hört!" and nullifies it at the same time. The *Bande der Natur* unravel completely, because the "powerlessness" of the "enemy" will never be able to challenge the opera's "gods," who speak and act

EXAMPLE 15. *Die Zauberflöte*, No. 21, Finale (act 2, scene 26)

through Sarastro and the Brotherhood. Pamina's trials help her to "reject all memory of her nocturnal origin"; surrounded by guardian cherubs, she forgets the night stars and her mother, moving decisively toward "final solar apotheosis."[13]

EXAMPLE 16. *Die Zauberflöte*, No. 14, "Der Hölle Rache"

MOZART AS FEMINIST?

One of the most popular and abiding themes in the reception of this opera has been the idea of Pamina's successful ascension with Tamino in the Order of the Sun as an indication of Mozart's liberal views on the inclusion of women in fraternal societies such as the Freemasons.[14] Some commentators have gone so far as to describe Pamina's initiation as a feminist triumph. Chailley, for instance, concludes that "*Die Zauberflöte* is an antifeminist work only in appearance," for, in the figure of Pamina, "Woman as such has been officially authorized to undergo initiatory trials."[15] In her discussion of *Die Zauberflöte* in *Mozart the Dramatist,* Brigid Brophy goes so far as to devote a whole section to "How Mozart makes the opera feminist after all," in which she strongly promotes Pamina as a symbol of women's independence:

> Once the ruling has been given that Pamina is worthy to be initiated, the way is open for this thoroughly Mozartian drama utterly to overturn Sarastro's pronouncement about a woman needing a man to guide her. Reunited with Pamina, and about to face the final ordeals, "Here," sings Tamino, "are the gates of terror, where distress and death afflict me"; and Pamina not only replies that she will go with him through it all, and not only has the wit to suggest he use the magic flute to charm their way through, but also and expressly tells him: "I myself lead you; love guides me." It is as though Mozart were expressly telling Sarastro that, if anything, it is the man who goes astray without a woman to guide him, but that in fact both will lose their way unless directed by the presiding deity of all Mozartian dramas, love. (164)

Likewise, in the Cambridge Opera Handbook for *Die Zauberflöte,* Peter Branscombe sees Pamina's initiation as redeeming the opera's generally disparaging view of women:

What of the low opinion in which women are held? To this there are two answers: women were looked upon by Freemasons as unworthy to participate in their activities . . . because they were held to be indiscreet; but in Pamina, Sarastro and the brotherhood identify for the first time a woman with exceptional qualities that command more than mere admiration ("A woman who does not fear night and death / Is worthy, And will be initiated," II, 28). Without the advantage accorded to Tamino and Papageno of knowing about the trials to be undergone, she survives her own trials, and even leads Tamino through the fire and water. She is honoured as no woman has been honoured before—the final stage-direction specifies "Tamino, Pamina, both in priestly raiment."[16]

Mozart may well have intended his heroine as an exception to the stringently antiwoman atmosphere of eighteenth-century Viennese Freemasonry, but her ascent with Tamino at the end of the opera simply does not offer a sufficient remedy for the generally sexist tone of the opera. Pamina's rise with the Sun, paired in opposition with the Queen's fall into darkness, might reasonably be seen as the ultimate antifeminist accomplishment, guaranteed to meet approval with a real-life patriarchal, Masonic culture. Any claim of a protofeminist spin on Mozart's part is undermined by at least two factors: 1) the altogether ancillary nature of Pamina's "initiation," and 2) the forced separation of daughter and mother, or, more broadly, the division between Pamina and the general female community.

Pamina's admittance into the company of Initiates is fundamentally dependent on Tamino; however outstanding her qualities, it is her status as Tamino's chosen helpmate that opens the temple doors to her. Sarastro himself alludes to this subordinate role when he convenes with his fellow priests to gain support for Tamino's candidacy (2.1). He first explains, "This youth will tear from himself the veil of night and look into the sanctuary of greatest light. To watch over this virtuous man, to offer him the hand of friendship, should be one of our most important duties this day." Only after the priests have given their approval to accept Tamino as an initiate does Sarastro mention Pamina's role in the matter: "However, evil prejudice [represented by the Queen] must disappear, and it will disappear as soon as Tamino takes possession of the greatness of our difficult Craft. The gods have intended Pamina, the gentle, virtuous maiden, for the gracious youth; this is the main reason why I took her from her proud mother. . . . Tamino, the sweet youth, will ally himself with us and, as an Initiate, will be the reward of virtue and the punishment of vice."

The final chorus, too, reinforces the hierarchical, gendered division of Pamina's and Tamino's final promotion: "The strong have conquered and been honored with the reward of the eternal crowns of Beauty and Wisdom." Throughout the libretto of *Die Zauberflöte*, only women and the young boys are categorized in terms of beauty[17]—Pamina, especially, is associated with beauty and virtue—but nowhere is a woman directly identified with wisdom, though the word appears with almost tiresome frequency in dialogues pertaining to Sarastro, Tamino, the Initiates, and the manly ordeals.[18] Sarastro, the "godlike Wise one," rules in the Temple of Wisdom, the place where the chorus of "O Isis und Osiris" is sung and the female priests are conspicuously missing. Just before he begins his trials, Tamino explicitly acknowledges the objective of his initiation—with Pamina functioning as prize, not peer—declaring to the Speaker, "May the teachings of wisdom be my victory, Pamina, the sweet maiden, my reward" (2.3).

We may wonder, of course, how the trial of fire and water fits into the picture, for it is the one place where Pamina would appear to assume some control, insisting to Tamino that she will lead him through the perilous ordeal with love as her own guide. Jules Speller, for example, strongly rejects the notion of Pamina as an auxiliary helpmate in Tamino's initiation, arguing that Mozart himself, through his music, highlights Pamina's commanding role in the final trials:

> Not only is . . . Pamina allowed by the Armored Men to go on the final test and also the inauguration to find her dignity . . . but she even assumes the lead: "I myself will lead you // Love guides me," she says, whereby she takes the beloved yet again by the hand. . . .
>
> . . . Mozart adds an acknowledgment. Also with him as composer, Pamina leads, and Tamino follows. As evidence, an example (likewise from II, 8) is given, which is so unique that it even provides a counter-proof [of Pamina's ancillary function]. Not long after Pamina's above-quoted words, the libretto even designates that "Tamino and Pamino" announce together: "We gladly walk by way of the tone's power through death's gloomy night!" and that afterwards "the Armored Men" offer their agreement with modified words. But while the two Armored Men (a beat after Tamino) begin to sing together in parallel thirds, Mozart gave precedence to Pamina in the preceding passage for the love-pair: she opens the singing, and Tamino follows only after a full measure. This procedure of the composer is only too understandable. For Pamina had just made the following statement . . . very much from the heart and full of initiative to her Tamino: "Now come and play the flute, / it leads us on the horrible path." If everything is deceptive, then the daughter of the queen in this scene has the booklet/dagger fixed in the hand![19]

Although Pamina is allowed to undergo the final trial with Tamino, neither her participation nor her demeanor is as revolutionary as Speller imagines. In order to read Pamina's initiation as equal to Tamino's, Speller analyzes the scene independently from the rest of the opera; he also fails to take into account the historical context, specifically the Masonic practices of the time. How can Pamina, who has been strictly excluded from conscious understanding about Tamino's (and even her own) trials, effectively conduct him through this last test? The answer lies in formalized ritual: her leadership is symbolic and tightly regulated by those who have the actual power. Fundamentally, the "couple" trial of *Die Zauberflöte* resembles an actual Masonic ceremony called the "Conjugal Avowal" or "Masonic marriage," which involves an auxiliary female "installation." Chailley explains that this rite is a "white dress" ceremony—that is, open to everyone, even non-Masons—and "has as its object, when a Brother comes to marry, that of acknowledging his wife in the bosom of the fraternity of the Order—without her being really initiated." During the Conjugal Avowal, the "Brothers form a chain broken by a vacant place, that of the husband," who stays near his wife until the Venerable "expresses the wish to see the Brother retake his place and reconstitute the chain, and begs the wife herself to lead him there." In this way, the wife of a Freemason learns that she "always must encourage her husband to fulfill his Masonic obligations regularly."[20]

Discussing the trio of Tamino and the Armored Men and Pamina's subsequent arrival, Chailley remarks that Pamina "merits being one with the Man who is going to behave as a man, *als Mann zu handeln*, and that is why, upon entering, she will fall into his arms and will remain linked to him, hand in hand, through the decisive trials." In the trials of fire and water, Pamina acts as the "complementary element of the Couple," accompanying Tamino "exactly as the Masonic ceremonial of Conjugal Avowal prescribes."[21] It is true that Pamina takes the first step, musically and literally, but she immediately subordinates herself to the most prominent musical force in the scene—the magic flute itself—which, as Pamina explains, was created by her father: in this way, the princess now acts—like her mother before her—as the feminine conduit of a power-exchange between father and (surrogate) son. As the couple and Armored Men all acknowledge, the flute—played by Tamino, *not* Pamina—is the true musical guide of the ordeal.

Far more troubling than Pamina's subordinate role in a quasi-Masonic initiation—the spectacle of which is a little silly in even the most elaborate productions—is her almost complete isolation from other women. This is one of the main reasons why *Die Zauberflöte* is the *least* feminist of Mozart's operas, if indeed such an idea has any is validity at all. In *Die*

Entführung aus dem Serail and the three Da Ponte operas women are devoted to their men, but they also depend on women for friendship. Blondchen advises and comforts Constanze, and Countess Almaviva confides in Susanna. The women of *Don Giovanni* come together to thwart the prolific seducer. The sisters of *Così fan tutte* share their joys and troubles. All of these characters sing together in an ensemble with at least one other female. But, according to the musical score, Pamina never once sings with other women. Many productions have the singer playing this role join the soprano line of the final priests' chorus, but there is no indication in the stage directions or the score for her to sing. These presumably female "priests" are themselves a bit of a mystery since they are present only for public crowd scenes, apparently uninvited to the "closed-chambers" choral numbers like No. 10, "O Isis und Osiris," and No. 18, "O Isis und Osiris, Welche Wonne!"

In fact, these mixed choruses support the kind of distinctions that Chailley makes regarding Masonic practice: women were allowed to attend and even participate in various "open" ceremonies but were restricted from the more esoteric aspects of the Craft. In any case, none of these female Initiates or priests has any interaction with Pamina. The Queen speaks with her daughter, but the opera denies them a shared song. Set apart from the other women in the opera, and principally the Queen of the Night, Pamina forms the positive pole of a familiar duality in dramatic and literary constructions of femininity. Having dedicated herself wholly to loving and obeying her spouse and accepting her father's will, she merits the sunny fortune that Sarastro predicted. The insurgent Queen, on the other hand, denounces patriarchal authority and, as a consequence, comes to a ruinous end. The split reflects a viewpoint that pervades far more than the boundaries of the opera.

As Nicholas Till notes, "*Die Zauberflöte* simply gives structural form to the Enlightenment's consistently dichotomous attitude to women: in the public sphere (as represented by the Queen and her Ladies in the opera) they are feared and denigrated, whilst in the private, domestic, moral and spiritual sphere they are idolized."[22] Clément describes the split between Pamina and the Queen of the Night as the most terrible example of the "crushing symbolics of men over women" in *Die Zauberflöte*. Especially painful to her is how the opera positions mother and daughter, so rarely represented together in opera, as adversaries in order to reinforce masculine power. She relates this story to that of Clytemnestra's murder, which is justified not only by Orestes and Apollo, but also by Athena and, passively, Electra:

The mother, dead, in the long history of a feminine law, will have been the final incarnation of the mythical matriarchy; with her the historic undoing and defeat of femininity begins. The victorious woman, the one who defends the father's power, will, with her vengeance, have betrayed the cause of women. . . . The fight between men and women is even more deadly when a woman makes herself the instrument of men's vengeance against their peers. And it is more permanently deadly when the fight pits a daughter against her mother.[23]

The circumscribed world of *Die Zauberflöte* presents Pamina as greater than a queen, courageous in her constancy, angel-voiced and human-hearted, but, as Clément reasons, her magical story and glorious music cannot be extricated from the opera's oppressive ideology. This is not to say that Pamina is merely an infatuated, pliant beauty whose only achievement is servitude camouflaged as enlightenment, for she demonstrates a genuine strength of will in defending love. Her tenacious call for recognition in the trio with Tamino and Sarastro effectively destabilizes their fraternal unity, impelling Tamino to speak to her, to look her in the eye. But the shining crown carries a high price: as the good daughter of the banished Queen of the Night, she is both the victim and weapon of social intolerance sheltered within the temples of Wisdom and Reason.

EPILOGUE: PAMINA AND BEETHOVEN'S NEPHEW

Der Zauberflöte has been touted as both a manifesto of post-Enlightenment, humanitarian idealism and a naïvely charming musical fairy-tale. One of the latest reception trends, in fact, targets children: *The Magic Flute* is now often performed as a child-friendly introduction to opera.[24] Perhaps more than any of Mozart's stage works, *Die Zauberflöte* has been overprotected by critical tactics of evasion. No one wants to pin it down and make it answer real questions. Instead, the opera is *universal* at its best and *historical* when it comes to the troubling bits. It deals with prejudice, power, and gender relations, but it should not be taken too seriously. As one devotee said to me, "It isn't like the Da Ponte operas: it isn't *real* life. You cannot read it in those terms or take it so seriously."

Yet there was at least one artist—Ludwig van Beethoven—who took *Die Zauberflöte* very seriously, both as a great musical work and as a cultural code to live by. The composer of the utopian Ninth Symphony (who kept a quote of Isis on his writing table and was asked by Goethe to provide music for a sequel to *Die Zauberflöte*) explicitly referred to the opera as a source of inspiration in one of the most disturbing episodes in his life: the custody battle over his young nephew Karl. When his brother, Kaspar Karl, began to succumb to tuberculosis, Beethoven became obsessed with the idea of taking charge of his son and rescuing the boy from the influence of his mother, Johanna, whom Beethoven considered a woman of low morals. Even after his brother exhorted Beethoven in his last will to act as co-guardian with Johanna, Beethoven set about building a legal case to gain sole custody of the nine-year-old. Armed with records concerning Johanna's alleged embezzlement of some of her husband's money, Beethoven successfully appealed to the Imperial Landrecht; Karl left his mother's home in February of 1816. Beethoven considered the rescue complete: "I have fought a battle for the purpose of wresting a poor, unhappy child from the clutches of his unworthy mother, and I have won the day—Te Deum laudamus."[25] Following the Landrecht decision, Johanna was able to see her child only when his legal guardian allowed it; at times, Beethoven insisted that she not see Karl for weeks, or even months, at a time. Far from satisfied with this arrangement, Johanna fought back.

Frau Beethoven's resistance only strengthened Beethoven's vision of himself as the rescuing hero or, as Solomon says, "the conquistador of his innermost fantasies."[26] Apparently, Beethoven found a rich source of inspiration in *The Magic Flute*:

Letters to Karl's schoolmaster, Cajetan Giannatasio del Rio:

> In regard to the Queen of the Night the present arrangements are to stand; and even if K[arl] should be operated on at your school, in which case he will be laid up for a few days and therefore more sensitive and irritable than usual, she is to be admitted even less often, seeing that so far as K[arl] is concerned, all those impressions might easily be renewed; and that we cannot allow. How much we can count on her improvement, you will see from the disgusting scrawl which I am enclosing; the only reason why I am sending it to you is that you may see how right I am to hold fast to the attitude I have adopted towards her once and for all. Meanwhile I have replied to her this time not like a Sarastro, but like a Sultan—[27]

> It is true that Karl costs me great sacrifices; but these I have just mentioned rather on his account. For who knows in what way his mother will some day succeed in influencing him? She is determined to resemble more and more the Queen of the Night; for everywhere she is spreading the news that I have not paid nor am paying anything at all for Karl but that she has done and is doing everything.[28]

Letter to Johann Nepomuk Kanka:

> The trio in question will soon be engraved and published; and this is always preferable to copied music. So you will receive it in engraved form together with several *other naughty children* of mine. Meanwhile please look only at

their fine qualities and forgive these poor innocents any incidental human frailties—By the way, I am full of cares, for am now the real and true [this should be read "bodily" or "natural"] father of my deceased brother's child; and in this connection I too could well have produced the second part of the Zauberflöte, seeing that I also have a Queen of the Night to deal with—[29]

Similar to the libretto of *Die Zauberflöte*, this biographical episode is full of omissions and assumptions. There is no reliable evidence that Johanna was as morally or intellectually insufficient as Beethoven claimed, or that Karl's welfare was in any way threatened under her care. Even the fact that she was found guilty of taking money from her husband says more about the unfairness of early nineteenth-century property laws than any criminal inclinations she might have had. As Solomon points out, Johanna had actually "stolen" her own money; her marriage dowry had been substantial, and she had inherited the house where she and her husband lived, and which they rented, contributing substantially to the family income.[30] Alone and relatively powerless after her husband's death, Johanna came under the hegemony of her brother in-law, who relentlessly molded reality into a form that better met his psychological needs. As he did so, he cited what he felt to be an unimpeachable evidence of his heroic purpose: his favorite Mozart opera, the virtuous, edifying *Zauberflöte*.

Certainly the dynamics of power are similar in the two stories. Beethoven, the surrogate father, took Karl away from his mother, justifying his actions as being in the child's best interests. Johanna, for her part, was "too weak"—to quote the words of the Queen of the Night—to thwart Beethoven's claims to the Landrecht or to protect her own son, even when he ran away from his uncle's home, as he did more than once. One can imagine her echoing on those occasions something like the Queen's words to a frightened Pamina, who begs her mother to take her home, away from Sarastro's realm: "Dear child, your mother can no longer protect you. My power went with your father to the grave." Johanna's social and legal puissance could not hope to match that of a celebrated artist with many influential friends and patrons, including the regional archduke.[31] Beethoven's political associations paid off. The final ruling of the courts was in favor of Beethoven in 1820, after which the case was officially closed.

The repercussions of the case did not end, however, with this final judicial mandate. In the final act of this real-life drama, Karl van Beethoven attempted suicide by shooting himself in the head one July morning in 1826, professedly driven to desperation by his uncle's neurotic domination. No fairy children stayed his hand on the trigger or buoyed him with hope of happiness; his survival may only be attributed to the unreliability of nineteenth-century firearms. For years Beethoven had kept Karl under careful surveillance, and as the boy grew into a man the composer's desire to control his nephew's every move only increased. Even when Karl was under the care of other people, Beethoven asked for reports and demanded that his charge not be allowed to engage in the usual evening diversions of young men his age. After suffering years of custody battles, the rancorous relationship between his uncle and his mother, and Beethoven's oppressive dictates, suicide must have seemed like the only means of attaining a lasting peace: *so wird Ruh' im Tode sein*. It is revelatory that, after having wounded himself, the young man asked to be taken to Johanna's house. Only later did the police remove him to a general hospital. Solomon reasons that the "suicide attempt liberated Karl from his own extreme rejection of his mother—which had taken place, as he thought, on the instructions of Beethoven, and which for several years exceeded Beethoven's own negative attitude in intensity. The pistol shots were a child's cry for help, a way of telling Johanna that her son still needed her and wanted her forgiveness and love."[32]

"Mutter! Mutter! Mutter!" Pamina, too, called to her mother after her encounter with an impassive Tamino. When one looks at her, glowing with nuptial anticipation and joy in the final moments of *Die Zauberflöte*, it might be easy to disregard the compromises she has had to make. But the finale also leaves many questions unanswered. Have the concessions and isolation she had to accept before attaining "Isis' luck" ended? Will she never regret the loss of her "zärtliche" mother? Will she have to endure other unexplained silences from Tamino, as he concentrates on his manly obligations? Will she always be so submissive to Sarastro's seemingly ubiquitous authority? Certainly, the radiant final scene with its glorious chorus tells us that everything will continue "happily ever after" for her. Thinking back to Pamina's own suicide scene, however, I wonder if the Three Boys negotiated no more than a shaky truce between Pamina's warring emotions. Dedicating herself to paternally sanctioned matrimony, she abandons, and perhaps condemns, the first love of her life, her nocturnal origins. Like Karl, she will be dutiful for now, perhaps for years, or even for life, provided that the lonely exclusion and its attendant anxiety are truly things of the past and do not drive her again into that fateful garden, crying out, "Mutter!"

CHAPTER 6

Woman's Identity I: Sacred and Profane

The Three Ladies and Papagena

Near the ancient Lodges / None might come to see;
None might come to listen there / Save a sign gave he,
For the ancient Lodges / As of those today,
Kept the outer, creeping folk / Very far away.

Wilbur D. Nesbit in *A Treasury of Masonic Thought*

With the figures of the Queen of the Night and Pamina, femininity fissions into two extreme poles: the tenebrous Mother cast down in humiliation, forever rebuked for her rebellious pretensions to power, and the yielding Daughter who accompanies her husband up the ranks of brotherly initiation with tender devotion. Between these two representations of womanhood we find the Three Ladies. Inseparable, they occupy a middle ground that does not always conflict with the Kingdom of Light, but is nevertheless prohibited from becoming part of it. Unlike the Queen, the Ladies engage in dialogue with Papageno and Tamino, participate in the musical "morals" of the opera, and even dramatize many of the symbols of initiation. Nonetheless, once they step into the realm of the brotherly Initiates, they meet with utter contempt and condemnation. In their supportive role, they exhibit neither Pamina's high-minded dignity, nor the Queen's majestic audacity, but the Three Ladies illuminate best the "normal" parameters of female participation in the community of the Initiated and may well tell us something about Mozart's and Schikaneder's outlook on women and Masonry.

A close look at the symbolism surrounding the Ladies suggests strongly, and somewhat surprisingly, that they are themselves initiates of a sort. Female Masonry was one of the most pressing issues for Masons in Mozart's time, since the lodges' secret practices and exclusively male membership offered valuable ammunition to anti-Masonic forces, both political and clerical. Even the wives and female relations of the Brothers themselves voiced displeasure about the Brotherhood's rigid segregations. It is not surprising, then, that eighteenth-century Masonry began to allow women limited access through means like the Lodges of Adoption, honorary rites such as the Conjugal Awoval, and, in rare cases, the "mixed" lodge.[1] The nature and extent of female participation was hotly contested among the Brothers throughout continental Europe, and Vienna was no exception. Although it is unclear whether the city actually hosted any Lodges of Adoption, the voices behind such reforms surely were heard in Vienna, and Die Zauberflöte appears to weigh in on the matter at a time when Masonry was undergoing a serious downturn in the Austria.[2]

Mozart and Schikaneder—both Masons—may not have had first-hand experience of such mixed lodges, but they were apparently familiar at some level with the symbolism and rites associated with them. Jacques Chailley points out how "the entire beginning of the libretto bristles with allusions to the feminine ritual of the Lodges of Adoption. The serpent that the Ladies kill, the birds Papageno sells them, the padlock they place upon his mouth—all these figure in that ritual."[3] These symbols are drawn from the biblical account of the Temptation and Fall, with its "authoritative" demonstration of woman's frailty, her envy, and her potentially corruptive effect upon man. To attain the first degree, for instance, "future Sisters must hold the figure of a serpent in their hands," while the trial of the next degree, Companion, requires that they "relive the Edenic scene," tasting the fruit of knowledge, a halved apple, with its "feminine" five-pointed-star at the core.[4] Even the concept of the padlock is featured. To help the Companion overcome the temptation to garrulousness—a vice that Masons traditionally ascribed to women and cited as a sufficient reason for barring them from the Craft—the Inspectress applied the paste of the "seal of discretion" to her mouth. Thus, Freemasonry took the rationalized terms of Enlightenment gender categorization and made them a part of a ritualized initiation. While "participation in the Masonic brotherhood and initiation into its secrets" could develop in male Masons the key virtues of rationality and enlightenment, the "parallel rite" of Adoption implied a gender-specific "cure" to feminine deficiencies.

As Margaret Jacob notes, even the term "adoption" alludes to women's tangential, even "unnatural," relationship to Masonry's core. She explains that the "origin of the term 'adoption' to describe lodges for women is shrouded in mystery," though "some clue may lie in the way the word was used as a verb." She compares Brothers' descriptions of "having been 'made' freemasons, or having been received into the order," with the few available records from Masonic sisters, where they speak of having been "adopted" during their initiations. Jacobs reasons that this term "may have been used purposefully to conjure up the adoption of children into a family where, by nature, they would not normally have been placed."[5] The Lodges of Adoption were not peer lodges, then, but honorary or auxiliary institutions, always under male supervision. Even so, for many Brothers, they represented a disturbing adulteration of the Masonic men-only fraternal ideal. Mary Ann Clawson emphasizes this fundamental essence of European and American fraternal forms of association, which historically have "reached across boundaries, tending to unite men from a relatively wide social, economic, or religious spectrum."[6] At the same time, however, such "fraternalism bases itself on a principle of exclusion, from which it derives much of its power." Whatever political and domestic benefits female or mixed Masonry offered, these concepts also threatened to subvert one of the Craft's strongest attractions and fundamental qualities. Not surprisingly, most reactions toward these feminine rites were uneasy or downright hostile.[7]

For the most part, *Die Zauberflöte* takes a fairly traditional position on the issue. In the opera, wives are allowed a symbolic involvement in rites akin to the Conjugal Avowal, but the sardonic representation of the Three Ladies also reflects the more predominant Masonic ambivalence about women as Initiates. Mozart and Schikaneder may well have been using the Three Ladies to demonstrate how the virtues of women are not strong or constant enough for the Craft, since they eventually succumb to "natural" vices. Accordingly, although the Three Ladies first appear as valiant and serious, they soon reveal a propensity for vanity and infatuation. In the end, the Initiated Ones expose their ignorance and untrustworthiness: a variant of *così fan tutte*. Fundamentally, the Three

Ladies demonstrate woman's failure to meet the requirements of initiation. They also illustrate a perceived threat, identified by Sarastro's
priests and the real-life Masons of Mozart's time: namely, that initiated
women might break away completely and form their own autonomous
Craft.

In their impressive first entrance, the Three Ladies appear as she-war-
rior heroines, emerging from a temple whose doors open and close as if
by magic (1.1). Veiled, with silver javelins in hand, they confront the
giant serpent preying on a defenseless Tamino, piercing the beast into
three pieces. In unison they condemn the menacing beast to death—
"Die, monster, by our power!"—extending Tamino's prepared cadence
in C minor into a preparation for their majestic victory cry in the opera's
keynote, E-flat major: "Triumph, triumph! The heroic deed is done! He
is liberated through our bravery!" After this brave display, however,
their martial musical style softens into simpering lyricism. Sweetly
chromatic violin lines replace the martial horns and drums as the Ladies
begin to sigh over the attractive youth, who has swooned from the terror of the chase (mm. 62–87). Each comments on Tamino's gentle and
fair appearance—"sanft und schön"—and declares that her heart could
only be given in love to this youth. They are completely rapt in their
adoration, until, remembering the pressing interests of their unhappy
Queen, they resolve in a twittering series of staccato chords and breathless, broken syllables to inform her about the handsome stranger.

Whether or not Mozart and Schikaneder intended this as a send-up
of women's initiations, the scene certainly strikes the first satirical blow
against feminine high-mindedness: after the succinct solemnity of the
serpent ritual, they transform the fearless rescuers into a trio of common
girls who fawn over a pretty guy. When the Three Ladies realize that the
object of their desire is not easily shared, they succumb to puerile jealousy, engaging in a mild form of the conventional comic-opera cat fight.
At measure 104 the First Lady disrupts the trio unity and sets off on her
own, changing cheery A-flat major to suspicious F minor. In a moment,
the sisterly "uns" becomes self-seeking "ich":

1 Dam.	So geht und sagt es ihr, Ich bleib' indessen hier.—	So go and tell her; I will stay here in the meantime.
2 Dam.	Nein nein, geht ihr nur hin, Ich wache hier für ihn!	No, no, you go along to her; I will watch over him.
3 Dam.	Nein nein, das kann nicht sein, Ich schütze ihn allein.	No, no, that cannot be: I alone will protect him.
1 Dam.	Ich bleibe,	I will stay,

2 Dam. Ich wache,	I will watch,
3 Dam. Ich schütze,	I will protect,
All. Ich, ich, ich!	I, I, I!

In the G-major Allegretto section that follows (mm. 120–52), the Ladies cease even to address one another directly, expressing their invidious thoughts in asides: "Must I go? Aha, how nice! She would gladly be alone with him: no, no, that cannot be!"[8] Though they yearn to stay with Tamino ("What would I not give to live with this youth. If only I had him all to myself!"), the Ladies consider the Queen's reaction—implied by the sudden return of the horns and timpani (mm. 163–66)—to this self-indulgent deferral of duty: "But no one goes; it cannot be! It is best I leave now." The orchestral *sforzandi,* tremolos, and trills waggishly inflect their imitative chitter-chatter, exaggerating further the depiction of giddy girlishness. Bidding farewell to the sleeping young man, the Three Ladies reunite, using the intimate, broken-syllable musical style used in many of the opera's *sotto voce* moral reflections (mm. 173–77, 187–91). The effect here, however, is not solemn, but mawkish, each phrase punctuated by an oboe's chromatic sigh. Reluctant to leave their idol, the Ladies stretch out the final phrase, "bis ich dich wiederseh'" ("until I see you again"), lingering warmly on the final word (mm. 182–84, 196–98) before returning to the temple and their Queen.

When they return (1.3), the Three Ladies resume their initial dignified manner, summoning Papageno, who has falsely taken credit for killing the serpent. Like the Inspectresses of the Lodges of Adoption, the Ladies discipline the bird-man in the name of the Queen—the Mistress of their Order, as it were. Instead of the wine, cakes, and sweet figs he usually receives for his captured birds, they give him water, a stone, and a golden padlock on the mouth to punish his fibbing.[9] A short time later, in the quintet "Der Arme kann von Strafe sagen" (No. 5), the Three Ladies, again at the Queen's behest, remit Papageno's punishment, but admonish him against future lying. They then join the men in the first of the opera's aphorisms (mm. 54–77): "If only every liar received such a padlock on his mouth; love and brotherhood would endure, instead of hatred, slander, and black gall."

On one hand, this scene would seem to establish the virtue of the Three Ladies. They facilitate the prince's chivalrous introduction to the lovely Pamina via the portrait, instruct Papageno about the deleterious nature of lying, and supply essential magical instruments—including the eponymous magic flute—to the youth and his bird-man companion to protect them during the rescue mission. That they did these things in the service of the Queen of the Night also reflects well on her character and kingdom. Through Papageno, however, Mozart and Schikaneder introduce a note of doubt, weakening the women's authoritative effect. Although he moans about his punishment, Papageno generally responds to the Three Ladies with the merry impishness of an irreverent schoolboy poking fun at his spinster governess. In answer to Tamino's inquiry, "They are presumably very beautiful?" the bird-man says, "I think not! If they were they wouldn't veil their faces." His jibe suggests that the "three schöne Damen" are camouflaging their real ugliness. Despite all the good deeds that the Three Ladies accomplish in these early scenes, it is the incriminating little details—implications of petty jealousy, physical unattractiveness, schoolmarm pedantry, and reflexive infatuation—that carry forward in the story. When Tamino enters Sarastro's temples, the Speaker and other priests dismiss the women and their works as manipulative deceit. For the prince, indoctrination supplants actual experience; in a short time, he will scorn and mistrust the women who were once his defenders. Tamino no longer needs their help: he has new friends to whom he can turn, including the Three Boys who replace the women, both dramatically and musically.

Mozart marks this substitution even before Tamino changes sides. Just before the prince and Papageno leave on their mission, they ask the Three Ladies how they will find Sarastro's castle. A brief but arresting prelude (mm. 214–17) introduces the Ladies' reply. The tempo slows to andante, and the warm, *dolce* long-held tones of the clarinets and bassoons combine with the delicate, fey sonority of pizzicato violins. When the women finally answer, their sotto voce harmonies bring to mind the transparent *voce bianco* sound of choirboys: "Three little boys, young, handsome, gentle, and wise, will hover above you on your journey. They will be your guide; follow their counsel alone." Productions sometimes visually reinforce this striking overlap of character and music, spotlighting the Boys somewhere on stage. In his film version of the opera, Ingmar Bergman makes the replacement explicit, letting the Three Boys sing this passage themselves while the Three Ladies freeze in a pose, each laying a finger over her mouth in a gesture of self-silencing.

Sometimes productions "gender neutralize" the Three Boys into the Three Spirits or Three Genies, but the libretto explicitly identifies them as boys. This is no small point given the opera's preoccupation with the hierarchies, intersections, and boundaries of male and female spheres. The Three Boys represent the most liminal masculinity, but reinforce with Tamino and Papageno the one-way passage from mother's to father's world, a transition based on sociohistorical reality and which has been particularly relevant to fraternal associations and ideals. Since the early modern period, European modern fraternal associations, such as guilds and trade associations, had "publicly affirmed the values of a patriarchal society in which social adulthood, proprietorship, and masculinity were inextricably linked."[10] Even younger males had their fraternal social groups that reinforced this exclusivity:

> Fraternal youth institutions developed early among those groups who could either anticipate an eventual succession to patriarchal authority or assert their moral right to it. Fraternal association was *not* found among servants, casual laborers, or young women, only among journeymen and peasants. They used the cultural materials of patriarchalism—the metaphors of domestic life and assertion of masculine privilege—to create institutions that were detached from the structure of the patriarchal household but grounded in its social assumptions and concerned with its dilemmas.
>
> As servants or apprentices, young men occupied a position in the family roughly similar to that of women—both were subject to the adult male head of household. . . . But although both young women and men were subject to the authority of the head of household, their positions were not equivalent, for young men were only temporarily dependent and subordinate. Fraternal youth institutions can be seen as an attempt to distinguish between young men and young women, to express the fact of eventual male authority.[11]

Together, the Three Boys, Tamino, and Papageno represent this "fact of eventual male authority" at various levels of society. They are invited into the fraternal circle and, in the case of the prince and the bird-man, given access to secrets that no woman, including Pamina, may share. Eighteenth-century Viennese Masonry exemplified this kind of restricted fraternal organization. One leading Freemason in Vienna, Ignaz von Born, sanctioned exclusivity in his *Über die Mysterien der Aegiptier* (Mysteries of the Egyptians), which is recognized as a likely source for Schikaneder's libretto. In this lengthy essay, which appeared in the first issue of the *Journal für Freymaurer* (Freemason Journal) in 1784, Born describes the beliefs and socioreligious structures of ancient Egypt and relates them to then-modern Masonic practice.[12] Explaining how candidates for a special order of priests in the ancient world "had to be free," and that artisans, peasants, and women "were excluded forever from serving the gods," Born establishes the connection between these tenets and Masonic initiation.[13] "To join our brotherhood," he writes, "a candidate must be a free man, too, and artisans and field workers are excluded, because we suspect them not to have the necessary knowledge for our royal art and their character to be lacking the ability for noble action that is made possible only with suitable education."[14] Likewise, Born praises "our wise law-givers" for excluding "the beautiful sex from our secrets" for fear that "the charm of the sisters would interfere with the brothers' work." To show, however, how much more the Brother Masons value their women than did the ancient world, Born goes on to say that "instead of dirtying their hands like the Egyptian women, we ask [our ladies] to tie the ribbons of our ornaments and aprons and reward them with gloves and swear faithfulness and devotion as we advance each level, as befits true knights."[15]

WOMEN, HELL, AND THE CONCEPT OF THE "PROFANE"

The social environment of Die Zauberflöte is slightly more flexible than the one Born proposes, but it follows the same basic tenets. Papageno would fall somewhere in the servant/peasant/artisan category, yet he goes through some of the trials with Tamino, is permitted to stay within the brotherly domain even after he shows little interest in the Mysteries, and gains a little wife for his efforts. As helpmate and noble companion to Tamino, Pamina does more than tie ribbons and aprons, but her abiding devotion to her knight indeed seems to be her main accomplishment. Her participation in the ordeals of fire and water and her final elevation are definitely ancillary to Tamino's progression. The seemingly unattached Three Ladies, however, are shut out of the sacred portals. Although the first act portrays them as benevolent participants in some kind of ritualized "order," the second act designates them only as unworthy women and enemies of the Initiates. Early in act 2, they slip anxiously into the temples, only to discover Tamino and Papageno undergoing the trial of silence. Their bustling music frets and scolds, for they are truly astonished to find Tamino and Papageno "in this frightful place," lamenting that the men "shall never be so fortunate as to escape." The Three Ladies exclaim that the Queen herself is near, moving secretly in the temples. Papageno is amazed by this news, but Tamino says nothing, having renounced any interest or loyalty toward the Queen of the Night.

Now that Sarastro has been reclassified as "good," the actions and words of the Three Ladies demonstrate their corrupting influence, their garrulousness and gullibility, which masculine rationality and resolve must withstand. Tamino has already been prepared for this encounter by the Speaker and Second Priest, who warned him to "beware of

women's treacheries" since this is the "first obligation of the Craft";
they remind him, too, that "many wise men have let themselves be en-
chanted" without knowing it, only to be forsaken and scorned in the
end, with "death and despair" as their reward. In the quintet, Tamino
shows that he has learned the lesson well:

Damen.	Tamino hör! du bist verloren! Gedenke an die Königin! Man zischelt viel sich in die Ohren Von dieser Priester falschem Sinn!	Tamino, listen! You are lost! Think of the Queen! One often hears whispers about the deceitful ways of these priests!
Tam.	*[für sich]* Ein Weiser prüft und achtet nicht, Was der gemeine Pöbel spricht.	*[to himself]* A wise man weighs matters and disregards what the common rabble says.
Damen.	Man sagt, wer ihrem Bunde schwört, Der fährt zur Höll' mit Haut und Haar.	It is said that whoever is sworn into their order goes straight to Hell!
Pap.	Das wär' der Teufel! Unerhört! Sag an, Tamino, ist das wahr?	By the devil, that would be out-rageous! Tell me, Tamino, is that true?
Tam.	Geschwätz von Weibern nachgesagt, Von Heuchlern aber ausgedacht.	Prattle repeated by women, but contrived by hypocrites.
Pap.	Doch sagt es auch die Königin!	But the Queen says so as well!
Tam.	Sie ist ein Weib, hat Weibersinn! Sei still, mein Wort sei dir genug, Denk deiner Pflicht, und handle klug.	She is a woman, has a woman's sense! Be quiet, let my word be enough for you, remember your duty and act prudently.

Even in those moments of the quintet when Tamino does not verbally
express his new attitude toward the women and other "common" people, the music conveys his silent disapproval. The prince's response to
the fussing Ladies can be heard in the accompaniment even when he is
silent; the flute's serene motive reminds us of his stalwart purpose, and
the syncopated leaps in the first violin express his aggravation (mm.
9–11, 13–15, and 45–43). These musical elements alternate with the
Ladies' exclamations—avoiding contact—but occur simultaneously
with Tamino's aphoristic retorts to the women: "A wise man weighs

matters and disregards what the common rabble says" (mm. 57–59) and
"Prattle repeated by women, but contrived by hypocrites" (mm. 76–78).
Finally, the Three Ladies concede that neither of the men will "chatter"
with them. Curiously, before they leave, the Ladies join Tamino and Papageno in professing the moral, which characterizes the women as
empty-headed magpies that tempt men with their gossip:

Damen.	Wir müssen sie mit Scham verlassen,	Shamefully we must leave them,
	Es plaudert keiner sicherlich!	surely no one will chatter.
	Von festem Geiste ist ein Mann,	A man is of firmer spirit,
	Er denket, was er sprechen kann.	he thinks about what he might say.
Tam. & Pap.	Sie müssen uns mit Scham verlassen,	They, in shame, must leave us,
	Es plaudert keiner sicherlich.	surely no one will chatter.
	Von festem Geiste ist ein Mann,	A man is of firmer spirit,
	Er denket, was er sprechen kann.	he thinks about what he might say.

Disheartened, the Ladies neither rant nor weep but rather meekly turn
to withdraw. But this, evidently, is not enough. Suddenly, the sotto voce
G-major cadence is interrupted by a dreadful unison C-minor roar that
echoes from unseen halls: "Profaned is the sacred threshold! Down with
the women to Hell!" exclaim the temple priests (Ex. 17). Thunder and
lightning fill the room with horrible noise and blinding light. The Three
Ladies respond fearfully ("O weh!"), their cries mounting to form a chilling diminished-seventh chord before the women sink from view. Many
critics ignore this passage, evidently unsure of how to explain satisfacto-
rily the priests' fire-and-brimstone outcry in the context of an opera that
sets the Brotherhood in opposition to punitive fanaticism, superstition,
and prejudice. Dent exaggerates the nature of the Three Ladies' intervention, claiming that they "threaten" the men "with the Queen's anger,
and with eternal damnation as well," but in fact the women refer only
vaguely to the priests' "execrations." It is interesting, however, that in the
original libretto the Ladies do not mention hell, though they believe that
anyone associated with the Brotherhood "is cursed from head to toe"
("ist verwünscht mit Haut und Haar"). In the same way, Brigid Brophy,

EXAMPLE 17. *Die Zauberflöte*, No. 12, "Wie? wie? wie?"

whose antipathy for Christian doctrine and reverence for Enlightenment thought explicitly shapes her interpretations of Mozart's operas, ignores the significance of the priests' condemnation by refusing to see it at all. She argues that while *Don Giovanni* is "a thorough-going Catholic opera, whose purpose is to attest to the reality and horror of hell," *Die Zauberflöte*—a "pro-enlightenment" opera—lifts "precisely that fear from mankind by attesting that life must no longer be corrupted by fear of death because there is no hell."[17]

But Brophy got it wrong. Hell is, in fact, a powerful concept in *Die Zauberflöte*, invoked by both sides in the opera's ideological war, and every bit as fearsome as the fiery abyss of *Don Giovanni*. (The Queen's final descent into "eternal night," usually through a trap door on the stage, certainly calls to mind Don Giovanni's similarly theatrical infernal plunge.) In fact, the Initiated Priests anticipate the Queen in wielding hell as a threat; the music with which they anathematize the Three Ladies clearly signals menace. Eric Smith observes that the key of C minor is "nearly always connected with death or the threat of death" in the opera.[18] Also, the shape of the melody—the ascending leap of a minor sixth, stepwise descent to the tonic, and fall to the dominant—is almost an exact precedent of the Queen's melody in "Der Hölle Rache." It is possible that the moment is intended as somewhat ironic, the priests purposely frightening the women away with the kind of apocalyptic language that is most likely to unnerve the unenlightened. Or the condemnation may be just one of the many inconsistent elements of the libretto. One thing is certain: thinking forward to the final plummet of the Queen and her Ladies—a disposal that the Brotherhood will

celebrate—the priest's cry of outrage rings out with the terrifying weight
of a death sentence.

What exactly have the Three Ladies done to merit such strident condemnation? Can we really believe that it boils down to the "crime" of
engaging in gossipy tittle-tattle? In part, yes, but only as a symptom of
what the Brotherhood views as a larger objectionable category: the
"profane." Here, the middling status of the Three Ladies is turned
against them. Once they enter Sarastro's realm they step beyond the
auxiliary position allowed them, and their fidelity to the Queen—
another woman—relegates them inevitably to outsider status. When the
priests denounce the women for having "profaned" ("entweiht") the sacred threshold, they are referring specifically to what Masons understood as a class of uninitiated and, in many cases, unworthy people. According to Jacob, the term was used widely in continental European
Freemasonry during the 1740s; in the 1770s and 1780s, particularly in
France, the tension between the lodge and the profane was "unmistakable."[19] Eighteenth-century Masonic "condemnation of the profane increasingly identified them with the commonality of men and, at least in
theory, all women. Increasingly the profane came to mean 'the vile pop-
ulace,' the superstitious and uneducated, who thwart the fruits of masonic labor."[20] Moreover, Masonic aversion toward those whom they
deemed profane persisted even in locales where there was little or no
anti-Masonic sentiment. Even for lodges frequented by men of import,
sanctioned by the court and clergy, "a profane could be a woman, or a
man, even of noble rank, who was clearly an outsider. In every case,
however, the distance between the safety and sanctity of the lodge and
'the world' was palpable and its bridging unacceptable."[21]

This may explain in part why the Three Ladies are never offered an
opportunity to increase their understanding and reason alongside the
Initiated within the "sacred threshold." Chailley maintains that "what
profanes the Temple is the presence of women as women, not as adversaries." But this is not the whole story: the Three Ladies represent a particular type of woman, the woman who is not, in Sarastro's words, letting herself be properly directed by a man. This type of woman has no
husband, no brother, no father (dead or alive) that figures into the story.
The only women allowed limited access to the temples are, in fact, the
approved mates of male Initiates. Even Papagena, the feminized reflection of the plucky bird-man, will be allowed a place in the new society.
Whether she is actually the old woman who first appears to Papageno
or the lovely, feathered creature who sings with him about future little

Papagenos and Papagenas, Papagena is primarily conceived of as a necessary complement to her husband, his reward for displaying the minimal qualities of character that the Brotherhood deems a prerequisite to marriage. The Three Ladies serve only their Queen, echoing her grievances and vowing loyalty to her leadership. In the most radical sense, the Queen and her Ladies are rogue femininity, cut loose from masculine direction or even sympathy. Unattached women—widow and wallflowers, imperfect and inessential—they band together for community. Their "rebellion" is partly by choice and partly a necessity: regardless of Sarastro's high-minded proclamation in "In diesen heil'gen Hallen," there is no place for these women inside the temples of Reason, Wisdom, and Nature. Even the Lodges of Adoption and other auxiliary or mixed lodges submitted to a male authority. It is probable, of course, that the priests' complaints in *Die Zauberflöte* about hypocrites and superstitious forces reflect a real historical threat during the eighteenth century (particularly the anti-Masonic attitudes of the Jesuits and Empress Maria Theresa), but their protests also strongly reinforce the ideas of fraternal exclusivity and female subjugation. Seen in this light, Pamina's rise is hardly the "frankly revolutionary" proposal that Chailley envisions, and the eradication of the Queen and her Ladies damages the integrity of the Brotherhood (as well as the opera's intended message) more than any dagger could have.

THE SUN DRIVES AWAY THE NIGHT

Restricted fraternalism continues to appeal even today. Though "co-Masonry," Lodges of Adoption, and similar orders allowing women members have proliferated during the last century, mainstream Masonic lodges still generally restrict membership to men. Female relatives of Freemasons may now become members of the Order of the Eastern Star, an organization that is closely associated with Masonry. Dr. Rob Morris, a nineteenth-century American poet laureate of Masonry, developed the concept of the Eastern Star in 1850 and first conferred this auxiliary degree on his wife, daughters, and a few neighbors. Although the Order offered women who were married or related to Masons a chance to participate in the Masonic ideal in a carefully limited way, Dr. Morris's own words attest to the subsidiary status of the Eastern Star and to his strict adherence to the "doctrine of separate spheres." In his *Lights and Shadows of Freemasonry*, Morris declares, "in the very constitution of the sexes, in their different spheres of action . . . there is a history for each, which the other is forbidden to know, and which nothing but an unclean curiosity ever induces the desire to know." In fact, Morris argues that "it is only those viragos who yearn for a beard, and who unsex themselves in their conventions for Woman's Rights," who try to breach this sacrosanct division of knowledge that separates the sexes.[22]

Written during the Victorian age, Morris's words nevertheless illustrate fundamental attitudes that have characterized fraternal associations throughout history: zealous protection of the male-only space, animosity toward "profanes," and scorn for anything that challenges fraternal aims and authority. As Clawson explains in her discussion of Order of the Eastern Star and the Odd Fellows' Degree of Rebekah, these honorary degrees were never "intended to establish separate women's organizations," but "were proposals to initiate women [related to members of the fraternity] into honorary membership."[23] The honorary degrees would have placated many disgruntled Mason's wives, and provided them with an incentive to support their husband's secret society. They were offered an ex officio space in the circle: after all, women are indispensable for producing more Masons. Although these nineteenth-century degrees were superior to earlier honorary initiations—like Pamina's in *Die Zauberflöte*—in that "they allowed the creation of active social bonds among women, bonds that had been created by a largely feminine initiative," the relationships between women that they established still reflected patriarchal controls:

> The legitimacy of those bonds derived from an already-existing relation among men. Membership thus represented an extension of a familial role rather than a form of independent and coequal participation. The men retained their autonomous associations in which they could be free of feminine scrutiny or influence, while their women relations participated in organizations that were practically as well as symbolically subject to masculine authority. In this sense the auxiliaries were little different from the honorary degrees they replaced. If the creation of separate women's networks, activities, and institutions is a potential source of power, then the presence of men within supposed women's organizations presumably acts to inhibit such possibilities.[24]

Today, of course, women in many places in the world (particularly the United States and Europe) organize themselves with comparatively little opposition, creating social associations that recognize shared gender experiences and address a remarkable spectrum of social concerns and issues, yet few of these associations emphasize gender separation or gender exclusion in their membership requirements. Contemporary political women's organizations invite the participation and help of men, no doubt in part because the reins of economic and political power throughout the world are still held primarily by men.[25] The Order of the Eastern Star, for example, has many male members in its chapters.[26] The more inclusive approach of these women's organizations may well derive from their origins, that is, a reaction against exclusion. The history of women's groups—consider, for instance, the development of women's symphonies—has been largely driven by the idea of creating an "auxiliary" or "alternative" to a male institution from which women were barred. Conversely, fraternal organizations such as the Freemasons have historically operated from a hierarchical position of power that permits exclusion, with women operating "in their own sphere," as Sarastro says, through appendant groups such as the Eastern Star and the Order of Amaranth. Presumably there is value in the idea of the fraternal organization, a place where men may congregate in the spirit of "brotherhood." The problem is not so much the single-sex socializing, but male fraternalism's impulse to consolidate power and access to knowledge. In the case of Freemasonry, "the possession of secret signs delineated the righteous, or separated believers from the world. Masonic fraternalism has always been concerned with ethical issues, and among the most fundamental moral imperatives of early modern European society were the rights and duties of the father. Patriarchal authority was taken, certainly by men, to be the basis of all order in society and government. Masonic fraternalism built upon that presumed truth, thereby incorporating gender as absolutely fundamental to determining who might be permitted to join the new fraternity."[27] Modern Freemasonry continues to profess high moral values, but it also guards its secrets, mixing ideals about brotherhood with wary us-and-them rhetoric.

How does *Die Zauberflöte* figure into this cultural landscape centuries after its creation? Very often commentators attach a warning label of sorts on the opera: "Musical-dramatic masterpiece of a bygone era: take as directed, prejudices and all." Many feel that a serious critique of the opera and its social message is both misguided in terms of the opera's nature and fruitless as regards the ordinary opera lover. Branscombe sums up this position: recognizing that *Die Zauberflöte* "has always been a controversial work," he also insists that it is "at root a simple fairy-tale opera with a strong admixture of comic and more profound elements."[28] It is the word *simple* that grates here, for there is nothing straightforward about Mozart's final opera. It is a messy work—as messy as human history—an erratic jumble of proverbs, racial slurs, brotherly love, greed for power, civil war, marriage vows, Egyptian myth, Masonic symbolism, and misogyny. If today's audience is able to observe without uneasiness the racist caricature that is Monostatos and the demonization of the Queen and her followers, then it is not because these problems are no longer relevant, but because of Sarastro-inspired voices that have followed *Die Zauberflöte* into the twenty-first century, assuring spectators with paternal conviction that there is nothing amiss, that this is just a harmless fable. Enjoy the show.

Sisterly Alliances and Sisters Subverted

CHAPTER 7

Sisterhood and Seduction II: Friendship and Class

Countess Almaviva and Susanna

The Countess occupies prime place in our attentions because
of her depth and intensity of feeling, as well as her sacrifices
to her love for the Count.

> Tim Carter, *W. A. Mozart: Le Nozze di Figaro*

Susanna rules over the opera, omnipresent.

> Wolfgang Hildesheimer, *Mozart*

Will the *real* prima donna please stand up? This question seems to be a
starting point for much of the critical discussion regarding the Countess
Almaviva and her maid, Susanna. Social rank is usually the trump card
in opera buffa when all other virtues are more or less equal, but the heroines of *Le nozze di Figaro* pose a special case. For every spectator, inter-
preter, or critic that holds the noble Countess up as the opera's first lady,
there seems to be a strong answering claim in favor of Susanna. If it were
possible to ask the Countess Almaviva and Susanna, I doubt that they
would be able to settle the argument. It is more likely that each would
say that the other was more admirable, and their generosity would not
be rooted in false modesty or dispassionate courtesy, but, astonishingly,
in *friendship*. In a genre that thrives on catfights and romantic rivalries
between women, the Countess and Susanna display a remarkable soli-

darity, more so than any other two female characters in Mozart's operas. *Le nozze di Figaro* turns on this rapport, the strength of which ultimately generates the happy denouement to the *folle journée*. Brigid Brophy claims that the affection of these two women not only "gives the opera its rarity and touchingness," but also makes it "a revolutionary document" arguing for the individuality of servants and women.[1] Quoting Virginia Woolf's *A Room of One's Own*, she remarks on the exceptional nature of this friendship:

> It was and perhaps still is rare for women in works of fiction to be capable of friendship and not to be thrust apart the instant a cause for sexual jealousy appears between them as the Count appears between Susanna and the Countess. Even in 1928 Virginia Woolf found it necessary to point out that "Sometimes women do like women." Drawing from an imaginary novel of the twentieth century the sentence "Chloe liked Olivia," Virginia Woolf commented: "And then it struck me how immense a change was there. In fact, Chloe liked Olivia for perhaps the first time in literature." In fact, it was not the first time. There is no doubt that Susanna and the Countess like one another, and no doubt that Mozart and da Ponte made *Le Nozze di Figaro* a work not only of music but of literature.[2]

Unquestionably, the author of the original Figaro plays, Pierre Augustin Caron de Beaumarchais, deserves no small credit for imagining this remarkable example of "sisterhood." The playwright stressed the unity between all of the female roles and created an explicitly disapproving monologue on the subjugation of women for Marcellina, most of which, sadly, had to be left out of Da Ponte's adaptation. Still, Brophy's point is well taken. Mozart and Da Ponte may have cut the play's most overtly political commentary, but they certainly spotlighted this friendship across the classes. Wye Jamison Allanbrook notes how the relationship between the two women is not only the hub of the drama, but also the very thing that captures and keeps our interest in the outcome:

> Susanna and the Countess are the characters at the opera's center; they step out from behind the masks of comic convention, and in doing so enable some of the other characters, touched by the humanity of the two women, to undergo a similar metamorphosis. The opera concerns the two women's friendship, one based on mutual trust and affection, which has begun before the opera opens. The warmth radiating from this friendship generates in us a real concern for the various couples in their couplings and uncouplings, and raises the plot above the level of mere farce. It moves us to be genuinely happy for Marcellina's transformation, in act IV, from bluestocking harridan to beaming mother, when ordinarily we would have felt mere relief at the fortuitous resolution of a serious complication. And it makes us momentarily disappointed in Figaro, late in the day, when he fails to put his trust in the two women's grace. The opera is about this grace.[3]

This grace is evident from the first time we see the Countess and Susanna together (2.2). Comic convention could easily have stoked their shared mistreatment at the hands of the Count into hostility, the Countess blaming Susanna as much as her husband for his adulterous desire. Even Beaumarchais includes an episode where the Countess doubts—though only for a moment—her maid's fidelity. Instead, Mozart and Da Ponte seem to draw a more absolute distinction between the bitchy dialogue between Susanna and Marcellina, who sling veiled insults at one another while a snickering Bartolo looks on, and the refreshing "women's space" of the Countess's room, where she and Susanna deny foolish jealousy any satisfaction. The Countess welcomes her maid as "dear Susanna," inviting her to tell "the rest of her story" regarding the Count's latest indiscretions. Susanna speaks openly, though she wisely leaves out the mortifying details of the Count's latest attempt at arranging a sexual tryst. When the Countess asks, "So, he wanted to seduce you?" Susanna answers dryly, "Oh, my lord the Count does not give such compliments to women of my station. He came with a money arrangement in mind." As her mistress's closest servant and companion, Susanna is keenly attuned to the Countess's hurt and wants to reassure her. Admittedly, her self-effacing reply also highlights what may be the only genuine limitation of their friendship, at least for an eighteenth-century audience: a difference in social class. Allanbrook observes that Mozart and Da Ponte were not necessarily trying to revolt against social order in their representation of the countess and her servant, though they made it quite special. The opera finds a place for the women's friendship "without violating either character's delicate sense of propriety"; this "meeting ground must be beyond class, and with its own sense of time; it may not be permanent, or even of more than one mad day's duration."[4]

Perhaps this extraordinary "meeting ground" is transient, but we hope not. Listening to the letter duet of act 3, it is hard to believe that the intimacy between the Countess and Susanna is merely an antidote to the Count's debauchery, a fleeting idyll. The customary partition between noblewoman and maidservant bends more than usual with their alliance, because ultimately they both lie so close to the social margin. Before her marriage, the Countess was Rosina, Dr. Bartolo's harassed ward, who possessed just enough nobility of blood to make her a legitimate wife for Count Almaviva. In Bartolo's home, she had no maidservants to help her; like many a maid-mistress in comic opera, she used her wits and powers of deception to escape from the greedy doctor's clutches. Susanna, on the other hand, is educated and polished enough to serve as companion as well as a servant to her mistress: she is a lady's maid, not a lower-rank chamber servant. The two women, distinguished as they are by class boundaries, nevertheless share many qualities, both dramatic and musical, and reflect them back at one another. The Countess's arias are steeped in love-anguish, but she has a playful side, too, and enough spirit to counter the injustices of her husband. For her part, Susanna is not merely plucky or shrewd, but exhibits wisdom, sensitivity, and a moral integrity that does not shift with the scenery. When, in the last act, the two women actually exchange clothes and "become" one another, their demonstrated compatibility raises this moment above the level of stage device, especially for a modern audience, which may or may not understand eighteenth-century class politics, but is likely to appreciate the affinity between two such likable heroines. Their swap is not so unnatural if the clothes are seen to represent character more than class. In a sense, the Countess had borrowed her maid's "wardrobe" long before she became the Countess, and the potential for their friendship was established even before they met. To understand this better, we must look back to the origins of the Countess's story, namely Beaumarchais's play *Le barbier de Séville* (1775) and, subsequently, Giovanni Paisiello's celebrated operatic version, *Il barbiere di Siviglia* (1782).[5]

ROSINA, UNTITLED

In the list of characters for his play, Beaumarchais describes Rosine as "a young person of noble extraction, and ward of Bartholo." Early in the comedy, Rosine's gentility is affirmed when the Comte Almavive tells the barber Figaro what he has learned about the mysterious woman he has trailed from Madrid to Seville: "her name is Rosine, she is of noble blood, an orphan, and the wife of a doctor named Bartholo in this town" (1.4). Figaro corrects the Comte on only one point, that Rosine is Bartholo's ward, not his wife, but says nothing about her family origins. Driving the point home, Beaumarchais again cites Rosine's lineage in the last act, when the Comte, who has successfully wooed the young girl, claims her as his spouse, saying, "The lady is noble and beautiful; I am a man of title, young and wealthy; she is my wife; who means to dispute this title which honors us equally?" (4.8). The Comte's words verify that Rosine is entirely worthy, classwise, of a place at his side, and that no one would find anything improper in their union.

In his concise operatic adaptation of the play, Paisiello uses only Almavive's first reference to Rosine's high birth, but this description would have been enough to advise any audience members who were not already well acquainted with Beaumarchais's celebrated play.[6] As Daniel Heartz explains, "An advantage of treating a play that was so popular and well known" was that the opera libretto could "cut many corners and still remain intelligible"; likewise, the original comedy, "with all its richness of detail and allusion, could serve as a kind of subtext or commentary on the compressed action of the opera."[7] Both play and opera reinforced traditional class structures during a time when many daughters of a burgeoning European merchant class were indeed marrying into the aristocracy. For all its superficially subversive humor, eighteenth-century comic opera almost always supported the necessity of class stratification, so that even those heroines who appear to be of humbler origins are found to be noble before they marry the aristocrat hero.[8]

How is it, then, that so many prominent scholars have mistakenly assumed that Rosine/Rosina hails from the middle class? Mozart biographer Volkmar Braunbehrens, for example, argues, "the countess, who comes from a bourgeois background, makes it increasingly clear that she . . . subscribes to the bourgeois moral concepts of love and fidelity."[9] Wolfgang Hildesheimer takes this idea further, saying that Rosina could "easily have married Figaro, after he proves to be Bartolo's illegitimate son."[10] From a different perspective, Stefan Kunze maintains that the Count's only unconventional act is his marriage to a "bourgeois girl" *(Bürgermädchen)*.[11] The bourgeois Rosina also figures into Mary Hunter's excellent essay on the Countess as a sentimental heroine; comparing the Countess Almaviva and Rousseau's heroine in *La Nouvelle Héloïse,* Hunter explains that on the one hand the "nobly born" Julie Wolmar "married a landed gentleman" but adopted a "bourgeois ideal" in her marriage, while on the other, "the originally non-aristocratic Countess . . . has married into the aristocracy."[12] Likewise, James Webster introduces his analysis of "Porgi amor" by observing that the Countess Almaviva is "a noblewoman of middle-class origins."[13]

The assumption about Rosina's middle-class status is not just an oversight. In the strict sense, she is noble-born, but we meet her in the very middle-class setting where she has spent most of her life. Even the original casting signaled her hybrid nature: the singer who created the role, Anna Davia da Bernucci, was adept enough at comedy to play Serpina in *La serva padrona* in 1781.[14] Indeed, the roots of her character may be found in centuries of clever "innamorata" roles—most of which were not aristocratic—though she also displays contemporary accoutrements of the eighteenth-century sentimental heroine. Many details of the original play—faithfully preserved by Paisiello in his opera—bolster the concept of her as noble of spirit, if not of blood. Even the notion that Rosina could be attracted to a commoner like Figaro is not completely baseless in terms of the story; after all, she initially falls in love not with the Count, but with his alias Lindor, a student without title or fortune and, she is led to believe, a relative of Figaro.[15] The "noble" Rosina herself is sadly bereft of the kind of connections that could protect her from Bartolo's schemes. She has her inheritance, but no power over it, and she enjoys a modest level of social status, but no title. If the Count had actually been a Lindor, very little of the fundamental comedy—a vintage comic formulation where young lovers, helped by clever (servant) allies, thwart a scheming old fogey—would have been lost.

Both context and character have contributed to the idea of a bourgeois Rosina. In Beaumarchais's play and Paisiello's opera, she represents a femininity that is at once lofty and grounded, feisty and hesitant, sensual and demure. She also exhibits a capacity for audaciousness unimagined by her genteel, sentimental peers. As Hunter explains, in the social framework of opera buffa, "the sentimental heroine is essentially passive with regard to the action. She engineers nothing; indeed, it is in large part her sweet passivity that marks her as noble." The sentimental plot archetype depends "on the arousal of sympathy for the heroine," and evokes "a moral world quite foreign to the deceit and the bamboozlement so riotously enjoyed by the 'maid-mistress' and her descendents."[16] Yet Rosina's freshness, and the dramatic tension she manifests so charmingly, stem from the very fact that she is both a noble ingénue and, when necessary, an effective (if reluctant) bamboozler. In the play, Rosine explains that her intrigues are only self-defense: "My unhappiness is my excuse: alone, under lock and key, exposed to the persecution of a man that I hate, is it a crime to try to escape from slavery?" (1.3). She later implies another apology, directed to the audience: "I am far from having those worldly ways that, I am often told, guarantee that a woman will be able to keep her composure whatever happens! But an unjust man would succeed in making innocence itself resort to cunning!" (2.15). She offers this sheepish justification right after one of her nervier displays of craftiness, when she tries to distract the doctor from his suspicions. Lowering her eyes she remarks shyly to him, "If you knew how to please me, ah! how I would love you!" (2.15). Rosine may not exhibit the hard-edged shrewdness of the servant-maid type or the imperturbable artfulness of a courtier, yet she is sufficiently "well read in the romanesque literature of the age" to know how to get a letter to her lover and throw an infatuated old man off course.[17]

Beaumarchais depicts Rosine's mettle brilliantly in several scenes with the overbearing Bartholo. She upbraids the doctor with some of his own nastiness, for instance, when he insinuates that she is up to something with the barber:

> *Rosine.* What? Don't you grant that I have enough princi-
> ple to resist the seduction of Mr. Figaro?
>
> *Bartholo.* Who the devil understands the eccentricities of
> women? And how much have I seen of theoretical
> virtues?
>
> *Rosine (angrily).* But, sir, if we [women] are pleased by anyone who
> is a man, why do I find you so displeasing?
>
> *Bartholo (surprised).* Why? . . . Why? . . . You have not answered my
> question about this barber.
>
> *Rosine (beside herself).* Alright, yes, this man entered my room, I saw him,
> I spoke with him. I will not hide from you that I
> found him very genteel,[18] and I hope that you die
> of spite!
> *(she leaves)* (2.4)

It is a wonderfully satisfying comedic moment, and a nice example of "good-girl" temper. Understandably, Paisiello retained this mordant scene for his opera; the libretto even sharpens the barb a little by changing "genteel" to "good looking."[19]

Of course, there is another work that has greatly contributed to the confusion about the class background of the operatic Rosina. Rossini's ever-popular *Il barbiere di Siviglia* (1816), which has almost completely eclipsed Paisiello's version in the annals of opera history and public favor, features a very different kind of female protagonist. Eighteen years after the French Revolution, Rossini's librettist, Cesare Sterbini, had no trouble throwing out Rosina's claim to nobility and transforming her into a generic heiress whose legacy Dr. Bartolo hopes to control. The Rossini-Sterbini Rosina makes a few gestures toward girlish modesty and trepidation, but they are hardly credible. This version of the character trades in the original ingénue blushes for a mixture of titillation and wariness. When she questions Figaro about the identity of Lindoro's beloved, for example, she begins, "So I am . . . the lucky one," then asks suspiciously, "You are not fooling me?" When she is convinced that Figaro is telling the truth, she adds as an aside, "I already thought so; I knew it before you did." While both Beaumarchais's and Paisiello's heroines trembled fearfully at the idea of Lindoro attempting a visit, Rossini's updated Rosina relishes a rendezvous: "Good, good! Let him come, but cautiously; I am already dying of impatience! But it is so late, what is he doing?" No wonder that Figaro tags her as a "sharp little fox." Her showpiece cavatina, "Una voce poco fa," offers vivid testimony to Rosina's unabashed shrewdness and determination:

> A little while ago a voice resounded here in my heart;
> My heart is already wounded, and it was Lindor who injured it.
> Yes, Lindor will be mine, I swear it, I will win there!
> My guardian will refuse, I will sharpen my wits,
> In the end he will accept it, and I will be happy.
> Yes, Lindor will be mine, I swear it, I will win there!
> I am sweet, I am respectful, I am obedient, beloved sweetness itself,
> I let myself be ruled, I let myself be led.
> But if they strike me where I am weak, I will be a viper
> And will set a hundred traps before I give up.

Indeed, as Michael Zwiebach observes, "Rossini's conception of Rosina's character as a self-possessed young lady, wise beyond her years, is much different from the vivacious but shy person of Beaumarchais' play."[20] Critics have long debated the relative merits of the "ingénue" Rosina (Paisiello) and "coquette" Rosina (Rossini). Even the first major Rossini biographer, Stendhal, weighed in on the matter, scolding Rossini for Rosina's lack of modesty and genuine warmth, which he suggests is due to the composer's "abnormal coldness and indifference" and his "fundamental inability to draw any fine distinction between one woman and another."[21] Certainly the Rossini version seems to have influenced Edward Dent's understanding of the Rosine/Rosina character, which he describes as "a typical young girl of the Latin race, quite ready for an intrigue with a strange man, and knowing instinctively how to arrange all the preliminaries of an elopement."[22] Spike Hughes offers a similar take—primed with the same sense of cultural superiority—when he bemoans how "the Italians are by nature incapable of portraying on the operatic stage the elusive characteristics of what we understand by a Lady," and wonders how the "enchanting, but hardly aristocratic perkiness of Rossini's Rosina" could possibly develop into the "superbly poised figure of The Barber's operatic sequel."[23] Hughes's lapse in chronological logic shows how much Rossini's opera has retroactively influenced the reception of Mozart's Figaro, though it may well be that Hughes would have complained about the "unladylike" behavior of the earlier Rosinas as well.

Rosina's frequent class "demotion" is only one example of the fascinating interplay between the Beaumarchais plays and various relevant operatic settings in the reception history of *Le nozze di Figaro,* one that has affected—and continues to affect—critical response to Mozart's Countess Almaviva and Susanna. Even Rosina's transformation into the Countess Almaviva—first by Beaumarchais and then by Mozart and Da Ponte—reveals two divergent concepts of what Hughes terms a "lady." While the Parisian play allowed for the young woman's imperfections as well as her virtues to be carried forward into the sequel, the operatic Countess became the exemplary and unimpeachably faithful wife that the more straitlaced Viennese audience preferred. With a less drama-savvy composer and librettist, this rarified Countess might have been reduced to the sweet but insipid heroine popular at the time. Happily, Mozart and Da Ponte were careful to tuck a little Rosina-ish scintillation discreetly into the bodice of their character, ensuring her lasting appeal.

CONFLICT AND VIRTUE: THE COMTESSE ALMAVIVE

Even in relatively liberal Paris, Beaumarchais had to fight off accusations of depravity regarding *Le mariage de Figaro.* In a lengthy preface that appeared with the authoritative edition printed in 1785, the playwright defended his comedy, insisting that every major character served a beneficial purpose, conveying some moral lesson to the audience. In particular, he included a vigorous defense of the Comtesse Almavive, whose subterfuge and unclear relationship with her godson, the page Chérubin, had appalled some critics. He contended that if the Comtesse had used deception to blind her philandering but jealous husband

> "with the design of betraying him, she would become guilty herself; she could not bring the Count to his feet without degrading herself in our eyes. Since a wife's vicious intention breaks a respected bond, it would be just to reproach the author for having portrayed blameworthy morals. For our judgments on morals always apply to women; one does not esteem men enough to require much from them on this delicate point. Yet so far is she from this vile project, as is well established in the opening, that she does not wish at all to deceive the Count, but only to keep him from doing the same to all the world.

Heartz remarks that Beaumarchais may have "protested a little too much about the innocence of the Comtesse, particularly since he had already mentioned in the same preface his plans for a third play in the cycle," to be titled *La mère coupable* (The guilty mother).[24] In this melo-dramatic finale to the Figaro trilogy, the Comtesse and Chérubin engage in a very brief affair resulting in a son, Léon. Nevertheless, Beaumar-chais may have "felt justified claiming her innocence, because in succes-sive editions of *Le mariage de Figaro* he toned down some of the more suggestive passages pertaining to the countess, so that in the final ver-sion she is merely ambiguous" in her rapport with the youth.[25] Still, such changes do not negate what was already in the playwright's mind: the occasion when the chaste admiration of a thirteen-year-old boy and the sentimental affection of his godmother—still quite young herself—convert into erotic passion.

How can the Comtesse of *Le mariage* still command respect in view of her future guilt, hinted at in Beaumarchais's darkly clairvoyant pref-ace? First, Beaumarchais believed that a character's intention and cir-cumstances must be considered when weighing his or her fundamental virtue. His description of the Comtesse in the introductory "Characters and Costumes of the Play" of *Le mariage* makes it clear that the play-wright thought integrity and internal struggle could be compatible, for though the Comtesse is "troubled by two conflicting sentiments," she exhibits "nothing above all that degrades her lovable and virtuous char-acter in the eyes of the spectator." In his preface, Beaumarchais identi-fies these "conflicting sentiments":

> Abandoned by a husband she has loved too well, when is [the Comtesse] first presented for our consideration? At the critical moment when her benevolence for a lovable child, her godson, could become a dangerous preference, if she allows the resentment that encourages it to gain too much authority over her. It is to emphasize better her love of duty that the author includes a moment when she must contend with a nascent fondness that battles against it.

The playwright goes on to point out the hypocrisy of the critics, noting that while every queen and princess of serious drama has "fiery passions that they must combat to one degree or another," no one will allow in a comedy that an "ordinary woman should fight against the smallest weakness." But this is exactly what the playwright wants—an ordinary woman whose personal struggle is heroic:

> The sorrow of losing a husband is not what touches us here: such personal grief is far from being a virtue. What pleases us here in the Comtesse is her candid struggle against an incipient fondness that she condemns and a legit-imate resentment. The efforts she makes therefore to recover her unfaithful husband place her two painful sacrifices, of her affection and her anger, in the most favorable light. One had no need to think twice before applauding

her triumph; she is a model of virtue, the exemplar of her own sex, and the love of ours.

Beaumarchais valued the Comtesse's *striving* to be good as much as her righteous suffering. He also valued her initiative and wit. Having finally escaped the oppressive Dr. Bartholo through marriage to the Comte Almavive, the Comtesse finds herself (a mere three years later) imprisoned in a different sense, barely noticed by her philandering husband, except as the victim of his jealous tirades. In many ways she is a conventional *épouse abandonnée,* but she is also the Rosine who used her wits to defend her happiness from Dr. Bartholo's machinations. So, too, the Comtesse Almavive is able to take matters into her own hands after Figaro's letter scheme nearly ends in disaster. This time she creates a purely female alliance, dictating a new plan to Susanna and forbidding her from sharing it with her wily fiancé:

> *Comtesse.* You see, Suzanne, the pretty scene your harebrained fiancé got me into with his letter.
>
> *Suzanne.* Ah! Madame, you should have seen your face when I came out of the dressing room! It turned completely white, but this passed like a cloud, and little by little you became red, red, red!
>
> *Comtesse.* So he jumped from the window then?
>
> *Suzanne.* Without hesitation, the charming boy! Light . . . as a bee!
>
> *Comtesse.* Ah! That fatal gardener! I was so shaken . . . I could not muster two ideas!
>
> *Suzanne.* Ah, Madame, on the contrary: it was then that I saw how moving in high society gives ladies the talent, when necessary, to lie without showing it.
>
> *Comtesse.* Do you think the Count was fooled? And if he should find this child in the castle?
>
> *Suzanne.* I will see to it that he stays well hidden . . .
>
> *Comtesse.* He must leave. After what has just happened, you will certainly understand why I do not want to risk sending him to the garden in your place.
>
> *Suzanne.* I will certainly not be going either. So now my marriage is once again . . .
>
> *Comtesse (rising).* Wait . . . what if, instead of sending you or someone else, I went there myself!
>
> *Suzanne.* You, Madame?
>
> *Comtesse.* No one else would have to be put in danger . . . The Count would not be able to deny it then . . . To have punished his jealousy and proven his infidelity, it would

be . . . Come, we were lucky in our first risk: I am encouraged to take a second. Let him know immediately
that you will be in the garden. But above all, do not tell
anyone . . .

Suzanne. Oh! Figaro.

Comtesse. No, no. He would just want to put in his two cents.

In this intimate scene the Comtesse proves that she is still capable of
giving an unjust man his comeuppance when forced, and, as in *Le barbier*, she immediately expresses regret at having to wield this power.
When Suzanne leaves the room to retrieve something for her mistress,
the Comtesse opens her heart to us in her one soliloquy:

It is quite brazen, my little project. *(She turns.)* Ah, the ribbon! My dear
ribbon! I forgot you! *(She takes it to her wing chair and rolls it up.)* You
will never leave me . . . You shall remind me of the occasion when that unhappy child . . . Ah, my Lord Count, what have you done? And me, what
am I doing in this moment?

Her reflection is brief but dense in meaning. We see the Comtesse's satisfaction with her plan and, simultaneously, her humiliation at having to
put it into place. The more painful conflict here centers around the
"dear little ribbon," the one that Chérubin stole in order to have something of hers near him. Returned to its rightful owner, the ribbon now
seems to inspire the sensual leanings that made Rosine respond so ar-
dently to Lindor's serenades. Indeed, in the first play, Rosine described
herself as "made for love." Sadly, Lindor is no more, replaced by a
Comte who thoughtlessly proffers sexual invitations to every pretty female in his domain, even barely pubescent girls and the Comtesse's own
personal maid. No doubt Chérubin's song, written and performed especially for her, revives bittersweet memories of Lindor's long-ago serenade. The young page charms her, too, with his impetuous, chivalric devotion to anything that has touched her skin. The ribbon acts as both
consolation and temptation for the Comtesse, who has been forsaken
and humiliated by the person she loves most.

Still, the Comtesse does not actually commit adultery in *Le mariage*.
She may lapse into a wistful reverie or fuss about the state of her hair
when Suzanne talks about the impetuous page, and she may even notice
his beauty, but she ultimately rejects an illicit attachment. By the end of
the play, with the Comte Almavive once more at her side, she tosses the
ribbon away as the wedding garter, willingly giving up this particular
folly in a day of follies. Beaumarchais could not resist, however, sneak-

ing in a final note of ambiguity, perhaps as a preparation for the third installment. After Chérubin snatches the ribbon up, declaring, "Who here
wants to fight me for it?" the Comtesse slips back into reverie. She is so
lost in thought that when her husband jokes to her about Figaro having
mistakenly received his punch, she answers, inexplicably and with great
emotion, "Ah, yes, dear Count, for all my life, without distraction, I
promise you." A few moments later, in the final *vaudeville* where each of
the players offers a kind of moral to the story, the Comtesse seems to admonish herself, subtly disparaging her own mysterious pledge to the
Comte:

> The woman who no longer loves her husband
> Is proud and takes care of herself,
> Another, almost unfaithful,
> Swears to love him alone.
> The least foolish, alas, is she
> Who keeps watch over her marriage,
> Without daring to swear anything.

Earlier, in the garden scene (5.7), Beaumarchais offers advice on how
exactly to "watch over her marriage," at least from a man's point of
view. Thinking he is seducing Suzanne, the Comte explains that "three
years of marriage" have made his love for Rosine "so respectable,"
which is to say, dull: "Our wives think that it is enough to love us. Once
they have said it, that they love us, they love us (when they love us!) and
they are so obliging and so consistently compliant, and forever, and
without rest, that one finds satiety where one looked for happiness." He
concludes that if men "pursue elsewhere the pleasure that escapes" them
with their wives, it is because wives "do not study enough the art of
keeping our interest, of renewing love, of reviving, that is to say, the
charm of possession through the allure of variety." Almavive desires
"less monotony, more spiciness of manner, some inexpressible quality
that makes up charm," even "an occasional rebuff." The Comtesse murmurs in an aside that she will not forget this lesson, and even Figaro and
Suzanne second her declaration from their separate hiding places.

However, the "lesson" has no real value for the Almavive household.
It is difficult for the dutiful wife to become the hunter's prize again, particularly if the husband is extremely jealous by nature. When, after their
row over the locked closet, the supplicating Comte addresses his wife by
her Christian name, the Comtesse angrily reproaches him, saying "I am
no longer her, that Rosine who you pursued so much! I am the poor

Comtesse Almavive, the sad, neglected wife, who you no longer love" (2.19). She was referring not only to her own view of herself, but how others—including her husband—see her. She is a married woman, the wife of a titled man, and is expected to live up to the part: to be *respectable*. The hyperinvidious Comte would probably not recognize, much less tolerate, in his wife the provocative qualities he praises in a prospective mistress: any capriciousness or rebuff on her part would be suspect. The fate of Beaumarchais's Comtesse is to be devoted to her husband, but neglected in love since it is impossible for her to become "Rosine" again for him. In fact, she will have to struggle against being that Rosine, sensual and "made for love." When, at the end, she responds reflexively, "Ah, yes, dear Count, and for all my life," pledging herself once more (and simultaneously resisting the attraction of Chérubin's amorous fervor), it is obvious that neither her internal conflicts nor the problems of their marriage have been resolved by an essentially formal reconciliation.

MOZART'S COUNTESS AND THE POWER OF PURE LOVE: FEELING VERSUS DOING

Comparing the Comtesse of *Le mariage* to the "impetuous" Rosine of *Le barbier,* William Howarth remarks that the former "is a character of great dignity, with a controlled sensibility which will come out more clearly in Mozart's treatment."[26] Howarth may also have had Mozart's representation in mind when he assigns to the Countess "a matronly maturity that is difficult to associate with the impetuous young heroine of *Le barbier* a mere three years on." Traditional opera casting has contributed to the aging of the Countess, since the role is often sung by an older (and frequently more *saftig*) singer in contrast to a pert and trim Susanna. As Tim Carter observes, casting a "mature woman instead of a young wife at most in her early twenties" enhances the Countess's status as sympathetic victim—the long-suffering wife, with all the accompanying gravitas. Certainly, Mozart's Countess demonstrates more of "a controlled sensibility" than Beaumarchais's. The composer and his librettist took care to expunge almost every hint of un-godmotherly affection for Cherubino.[27] Gone, too, is her penchant for daydreaming when he is mentioned, her girlish concern about messy hair, and her attachment to the ribbon. *Le nozze di Figaro* re(de)fines the Countess, so that she is understood as completely steadfast in her love for the Count. Her internal conflict, elucidated in two arias, revolves around a single theme: her husband's love as absolutely requisite to her happiness and her very life. Carter believes that the irreproachable virtue of Mozart's noble wife "produces a potential imbalance"; unlike her prototype, this Countess "lacks her 'human' flaw and so remains apart" from the rest of the characters.

As Hunter explains, this imbalance and separateness are essential attributes of the sentimental heroine, signaling to the eighteenth-century audience a distinct type of idealized femininity, one that "emphasizes feeling rather than external action, character rather than plot, 'being' rather than 'doing.'"[28] A comparison of the entrance scenes of the two Countesses demonstrates perfectly this dichotomy. Beaumarchais's Comtesse makes a comparatively discreet entrance into the drama, accompanying Figaro and the peasants into the room where Almavive and Bazile have been harassing Suzanne, unaware of the eavesdropping Chérubin (1.10). She soon moves, however, to the center of the action. When Figaro begs the obstinate Comte to demonstrate formally his renunciation of the *droit de seigneur* by placing the virginal toque on Suzanne's head, the Comtesse supports the couple's plea, reminding her husband that "this ceremony will always be dear to me, since its motive should lie in the charming love you had for me." A few moments later, hearing that Almavive has banished young Chérubin, the Comtesse again intercedes, imploring, "Ah, my Lord, I beg your pardon for him." Dignified and graceful, this Comtesse distinguishes herself from the outset as a woman who will actively protect the interests of those she loves, even as she bears the pain of her husband's indifference. Her resistance to the Comte's injustice is made clear in the next scene, when she pledges to Suzanne, "You will marry Figaro."

In the opera, this poised "doing" is replaced, at least initially, by sentiment-laden "being." We meet Mozart's Countess in the privacy of her bedroom, far away from Figaro's schemes and the Count's salacious advances toward Susanna. The scene stands out from almost everything that has come before it. There is a faint echo of Cherubino's aria "Non so più" (the first aria in the opera to use the key of E-flat major and feature the clarinet), but the Countess's languid, single-minded lovesickness is the exact opposite of the page's breathless, scattershot desire. The musical tempo eases to a leisurely Larghetto, the slowest tempo indication thus far. Time is suspended, and during the fourteen bars of formal orchestral introduction—the longest in the opera, particularly given the tempo—we are encouraged to gaze at the Countess as a physical presence. In the words of Allanbrook, the Countess does not so much make an entrance as she is "discovered."[29] She is, almost literally, as pretty as a picture, and the spectator is transfixed: we study her, preoccupied with her grief, before we finally hear her "private" prayer to Amor:

Porgi, amor, qualche ristoro	Offer, Love, some relief
Al mio duolo, à miei sospir.	To my grief, to my sighs
O mi rendi il mio tesoro,	Either give my treasured one back to me
O mi lascia almen morir.	Or, at least, let me die.

Rejecting the "usual critical language about this aria," which casts the audience more as voyeur than tacitly acknowledged addressee, Hunter argues persuasively that "Porgi amor" presents the sort of performance-within-a-performance favored by sentimental heroines in late-eighteenth-century opera buffa:

> In the context of Viennese *opera buffa*, this sort of performance—a moment of self-absorbed, song-like beauty, used to introduce a character—is overwhelmingly a female moment. Men do sing arias as they walk on stage, but these are not laments or pastorales. Men do plead for the audience's sympathy in touching cantabile pieces, but these are always preceded by engagement in the action. The act of making one's first stage appearance alone singing fully fledged solo music, and engaging the audience's sympathies by doing so, was, by convention, a female act, and in the context of this repertoire, the Countess is making a peculiarly female claim on the audience's attention.[30]

By moving the Countess's entrance to the second act and introducing her alone in her room, Mozart and Da Ponte not only added a special spotlight (and a figurative halo) to Beaumarchais's original character, but drew on a familiar—and effective—dramatic representation of femininity, one that would have signaled immediately to a contemporary audience that they should empathize with her. We are meant to do more than listen in at the Countess's door, for she is appealing to *us* as much as to divine Amor. Her cantabile song communicates a "chaste power" that "appeals to both the moral and the aesthetic sensibilities of the audience," eliciting a special empathy that "not only justifies (in part) her final victory, but also renders the final re-establishment of domestic harmony plausible and moving."[31]

In addition to capturing our attention, the sentimental petition of "Porgi amor" also establishes the Countess as the affective and moral center of the opera and boosts her stature as a lodestar of wifely virtue. Hers is not an ecclesiastical style per se. "Porgi amor" uses a *mezzo-carattere* combination of noble march (in the accompaniment) and

EXAMPLE 18. Missa solemnis in C, K. 337, "Agnus Dei"

EXAMPLE 19. *Le nozze di Figaro*, No. 11, "Porgi amor qualche ristoro"

EXAMPLE 20. "Coronation" Mass in C, K. 317, "Agnus Dei"

EXAMPLE 21. *Le nozze di Figaro*, No. 20, "Dove sono i bei momenti"

amorosa melody: the Countess carries herself like an aristocrat but speaks to us in a softer lyric mode, assisted by the melting harmonies of paired clarinets and bassoons. Still, there is something about the Countess, from this very first scene, that is compatible with a particular ideal of orthodox sanctity. Like most sentimental heroines of the period, in literature and drama as well as opera, she aligns herself with the sacred by "reiterating both the patient suffering and the unswerving constancy of Christ."[32] Mantled with beatific lyricism, the Countess supports—especially in her arias—the ideal of woman's moral power, passively exerted through affective private expression, devotion to others, and self-sacrifice.

Interestingly, the Countess's two arias have a special relationship to Mozart's church music. Heartz points out that the opening melodic motif of the Countess's first aria "may be found set by Mozart to sacred words many times over,"[33] but it is particularly striking that the melodic incipits of both "Porgi amor" and "Dove sono" have precursors in Mozart's Agnus Dei movements from the Missa solemnis in C, K. 337 (in E-flat major) and the "Coronation" Mass in C, K. 317, respectively (Ex. 18–21). Obviously, very few if any spectators from Mozart's time would have known these earlier sacred works well enough to make the connection, but it is curious that the composer twice borrowed music from this particular portion of the Mass, a petition that emphasizes self-sacrifice, forgiveness, and peace. For us, these close borrowings may "color our conception of the countess and of the seriousness of her plight,"[34] not only because of the association between formalized and private prayer, but also through an implied correspondence between a supplicating and compassionate Countess and a self-sacrificing, clement Lamb of God. While the poetry of "Porgi amor" is secular in its allegory, its music is aligned with Mozart's particular sacred language. (Even the Countess's great act of forgiveness is experienced plagally, a striking G-major episode within the D-major finale.) The Countess begs for mercy from Love, and grants mercy to the beloved who abuses her.

A RENEWED SENSE OF PURPOSE (AND CLASS)

This ethos of selflessness no doubt contributes to Carter's belief that "if there is a 'message' in the opera, it seems less the equality of man than the redeeming power of a woman's love": the Countess's love is her credo, and through it she has the power, theoretically, to reform her husband.[35] Her two revelatory arias and final act of forgiveness are frequently understood as forming a psychological arc from introspection to action, as she chooses to exert this special power. Carter, for instance, adduces that for the Countess "the 'folle journée' is a day of intense personal exploration and renewed self-understanding" and that the final two acts of the opera are "concerned less with Figaro and Susanna than with the Countess and her attempts to recover her husband."[36] Describing the implications of "Porgi amor" for the rest of the opera, Hunter proposes that this "profoundly important moment of self-realization mirrors in small her movement from self-pity to self-confidence in the course of the opera," particularly since "Mozart makes palpable the possibility that she might not have moved or changed."[37]

The Countess does in fact gain a renewed sense of purpose between "Porgi amor" and her next aria, "Dove sono i bei momenti," a full-blown two-tempo rondo (3.8.19). She handles herself masterfully in the confrontation with the Count over the locked closet: trembling with fear, she matches his fierce indignation and maintains joint control over the situation almost to the very end. She also devises the plan that will force the Count to face his own hypocrisy. The first step has already been taken before "Dove sono": Susanna, per the Countess's instructions, has pretended to accept the Count's invitation to an intimate encounter. In this context of intrigue, "Dove sono" serves as a development and recapitulation of the Countess's inner conflicts and conveys fresh hope for their resolution:

Dove sono i bei momenti	Where are those lovely moments
Di dolcezza e di piacer,	of sweetness and pleasure,
Dove andaro i giuramenti	Where have they gone,
Di quel labbro menzogner?	those vows made by false lips?
Perchè mai, se in pianti e in pene	Why then, if everything has been changed
Per me tutto si cangiò	For me into tears and pain,
La memoria di quel bene	Has the memory of that happiness
Dal mio sen no trapassò?	Never passed away from my breast?
Ah! Se almen la mia costanza	Ah! If at least my consistency
Nel languire amando ognor	in yearning for him always with my love
Mi portasse una speranza	Could give me a hope
Di cangiar l'ingrato cor.	of changing that ungrateful heart.

In "Porgi amor," even the customary ultimatum of the *donna abbandonata*—give me love or give me death—sounds languid and passive; there is certainly little of the quivering tension, for instance, of Pamina's threat, "If you do not feel love's longing, then I must find tranquility in death," in "Ach ich fühl's." "Dove sono," however, energizes the Countess's contemplative nostalgia with purposeful hope, verifying her dramatic transition from inert "feeling" to heartfelt "doing." Musically, it is also the heftier and more complete of the two numbers—a real prima donna showpiece. The two-tempo rondo exhibits a balanced formal organization that the through-composed "Porgi amor" lacks, suggesting the possibility that for the Countess, "things now seem in a clearer perspective."[38] Analysts have often noted, too, a kind of harmonic "indecision" in the final section of "Porgi amor" that finds its true resolution in "Dove sono." In the earlier aria, the sustained high A-flat on the word "morir" (m. 31)—the high point of the Countess's despondency—yearns for resolution to G; this happens, but obliquely, without conviction.[39] In the final passage of "Dove sono," the Countess convincingly masters the tricky G, not as the insecure third of E-flat major (in "Porgi amor"), but as the dominant tone of C major. Exuberant with new optimism, she easily soars to a thrilling high A, sliding down effortlessly to the dominant tone: "di cangiar," to *change* that ungrateful heart. Two scenes later, the Countess confidently dictates to Susanna the entrapping letter of invitation. When Susanna hesitates, worried, the Countess assures her, "Go on, write, I say; and I will take it all upon myself" (3.10).

The Countess's subterfuge raised another dramatic challenge for Mozart and Da Ponte, for they had to find a way to justify it as compatible with her place as the opera's moral core. Their basic strategy was to downplay the Countess's managing role in the conspiracy until after "Dove sono," which serves to both explain her actions and garner sympathy. This was a striking departure from the stage play, in which the Countess's scheming scene with Susanna in the privacy of her boudoir occupies a crucial structural position in the drama—the final scene of act 2—and in which her actions are not mitigated by a lyric aria. Da Ponte's adaptation cuts the dialogue between the Countess and Susanna into two parts, one before "Dove sono" and one after. He relegates the ladies' first dialogue to a more modest position (3.2), a short recitative tucked discreetly between the Count's bombastic "Vedrò mentre io" and his smarmy duet with Susanna. Da Ponte also made the dialogue seem less devious by moving the two women out in the open; their minimal exchange functions as background counterpoint to the Count's own more spiteful scheming. Whispering upstage from the unseeing lord of the manor, who is planning his own revenge against Figaro, the Countess urges Susanna, "Go, take heart: tell him to wait for you in the garden," adding that Susanna should not tell Figaro anything about it since "I intend to go in your place." When Susanna still hesitates, the Countess pleads, "Remember that my peace is in your hands." Unlike the play, which emphasized how the Countess was helping Susanna—"Madame, your plan is charming . . . and whatever else happens, my marriage is certain now"—this recitative focuses on the Countess's plight, stressing her dependence on Susanna's help. Nowhere in this scene do we see even the impish and subtly retaliatory tone of Beaumarchais's Comtesse: "To have punished his jealousy and proven his infidelity, it would be . . . Come, we were lucky in our first risk: I am encouraged to take a second" (2.24). This is the daring spirit of Rosine, which the Comtesse reveals early in the play. Mozart's Countess, on the other hand, warms to the game much later—"Hold on: it will be easier now to catch him" (3.10)—*after* she has established her virtuous intentions in "Dove sono."

Nevertheless, the Countess of the "Dove sono" *scena* is not absolutely perfect. In the *seria*-style accompanied recitative that precedes the aria, the Countess waits anxiously for Susanna to return with news. She tries to calm herself down, but is aware of the risk she is taking in misleading the jealous Count. The highly charged ending of the recitative, however, highlights a very different concern:

E Susanna non vien! Son ansiosa	And Susanna does not come! I am anxious
Di saper come il Conte	to know how the Count
Accolse la proposta. Alquanto ardito	received her proposal. The plan seems
Il progretto mi par; e ad uno sposo	rather daring to me; and with a husband who is
Sì vivace e geloso . . .	so vigorous and jealous . . .
Ma che mal c'è? Cangiando i miei vestiti	But what harm is there? Changing my clothes
Con quelli di Susanna, e i suoi co' miei . . .	with those of Susanna, and hers with mine . . .
Al favor della notte . . . O cielo! A quale	under cover of night . . . O heavens! to what
Umil stato fatale io son ridotta	humiliating, fatal state I have been reduced
Da un consorte crudel; che, dopo avermi,	by a cruel husband; who after having,
Con un misto inaudito	with an unheard-of mixture
D'infedeltà, di gelosie, di sdegni,	of infidelity, jealousy, and contempt,
Prima amata, indi offesa, e alfin tradita,	first loved, then offended, and finally betrayed me
Fammi or cercar da una mia serva aita!	now makes me seek help from one of my servants!

It is disappointing to think that the height of the Countess's mortification is the insult of having to conspire with her maid, to have to put on servant's clothes. One has to wonder if there is a smidgeon of irony behind the strings' indignant dotted rhythms and the spectacular vocal leap to the summit of the Countess's range, a high A at the words "Fammi or cercar da una mia serva aita!" The effect is made more dramatic (and more humorous?) by the *sforzandi* in the orchestral accompaniment, the melodramatic melodic collapse of a ninth, and the morbid harmonic sequence: a treble-heavy Neapolitan that acquires a hint of augmented-sixth pathos before cadencing on E major as the dominant of A minor

EXAMPLE 22. *Le nozze di Figaro*, No. 20, Recitative, "E Susanna non vien!"

(Ex. 22). She seems to have set herself up for a good cry—or a flash of noble indignation—in A minor, yet the aria itself draws back from the hyperbolic tone of the recitative, slipping discreetly into quiet C-major nostalgia.

Critical attention is naturally directed primarily to the aria proper—which communicates perfectly the Countess's sweetness and dignity—but the recitative is no less relevant in terms of characterization. After the rhetorical build up to a "final straw," the Countess's complaint comes across as a starchy, even silly, anticlimax. There is a disappointing hint of patrician pride, too; it is not the senescent snobbery of a Marcellina, yet it does sound like the kind of complaint that harbingers a vapor spell. For a modern audience, which is certainly not scandalized by women fighting back against abuse and neglect, the Countess's sudden fit of class consciousness—her sense of superiority over Susanna—may be her least attractive moment. This particular "flaw" in the Countess is all the more striking because it is unique to the operatic version of the story. The Beaumarchais play emphasizes a different kind of rift between the two women; his Comtesse succumbs to a fleeting bout of jealousy, believing that Suzanne has come to an arrangement with the Comte in order to secure a dowry for Figaro. In response, Suzanne falls to her knees. The maid's horrified reaction shames her mistress: "You do not know, Madame, how you have hurt Suzanne! After your continuous kindness and the dowry you have already given me!" The Comtesse quickly helps her companion to her feet, kissing Suzanne on the forehead and saying, "I was just being absurd." Reunited in affection, they begin to write the letter.

There is no need for reconciliation between the Countess and Susanna in the opera, since the maid does not hear her mistress's grievance. But we have heard it, and must settle with it. It is impossible to say how Mozart understood this moment; in any case, it serves to remind us that the Countess is mortal after all. She does not wholly rise above the folly that surrounds her; self-pity leavens her "humanity" with snobbery. Indeed, the *scena* of "Dove sono" follows closely upon the notoriously ironic *seria* outburst of the Count's "Vedrò mentre io." The juxtaposition only raises the Countess higher in our eyes. Her somewhat indulgent display of pique does not last long: during the brief pause between recitative and aria she abruptly drops the arch accents of aristocratic indignation and becomes again her natural, more *mezzo-carattere* self. The letter duet, "Che soave zeffiretto" (No. 20), acts as an antidote to the recitative of No. 19, reinforcing the gracious bond between mistress and maid. Voices echo and join together in parallel, so alike and yet so different in circumstance. "Che soave zeffiretto" is the Countess's only duet, and, with its combination of friendship and action, it is also the most liberating of her numbers. She no longer remains apart, for even she has had to overcome a human fault and has come out the better for it.

Her new self-assurance is obvious when she steps out of the grotto in the last-act finale, stupefying her hard-hearted husband, who can do nothing but beg forgiveness in front of his astonished servants. In this final scene, the Countess proves that she has overcome the dejected lethargy of "Porgi amor" and brought to fruition the hopeful promise of "Dove sono." Her love—and her intelligence—forces the Count into unqualified contrition. The music supports the dramatic solution: the Countess's checkmate gesture silences the Count's self-righteous display and hastens the cadence in G major. The move to this key resolves not only the tension of the Count's repeated dominant-key (D) "No!" but also the conflict around G in the Countess's arias. No longer the evasive mediant tone of "Porgi amor" or the expectant dominant in "Dove sono," G becomes the stabilized tonic for this indisputably profound passage, culminating in the joyful triumph of the Countess's and Susanna's unison high G: "Ah, tutti contenti saremo così!" ("In this way everyone will be happy!").

What is missing, of course, is a true uniting of Count and Countess in song. Pardon is asked and given (they may even draw closer together physically as the crowd moves in on their public reconciliation), but there is still separation. It seems clear that the Countess's psychological course is fated to be cyclical, not linear—at least in terms of her relationship with the Count. The Count's memory of his repentance will fade in a month or two, and the Countess will be crying again in her bedroom. Indeed, at the beginning of Beaumarchais's next installment of the Figaro trilogy, twenty years after the Comtesse's single act of infidelity, Almavive is still withholding forgiveness, though his own dalliances have gone unchecked. There is also a sequel of sorts in *Don Giovanni,* in which Mozart returns to the theme of a debauched man and the redeeming power of a woman's love, though with a decidedly more cynical outlook. Donna Elvira, deserted by Don Giovanni, introduces herself and her dilemma in E-flat major using the same orchestration as "Porgi amor." More desperate than the Countess, Elvira strives to rise above her circumstances, but she never fully escapes from her E-flat-major obsession. Composer and librettist play her constancy for tears *and* laughs. In the last finale, her short E-minor phrase—"I will take myself to a retreat [convent] to finish my life"—seems the negative image of the Countess's G-major coup. Elvira dramatizes hope's end and the resulting estrangement from society. The Countess, however, is protected by love and companionship. Both as Rosina and as the wife of Almaviva she foils the selfish plots of men who should be caring for her and is fortunate always to find friendly assistance. In *The Barber of Seville,* aid comes from a suitor and his paid collaborator. In *Figaro,* however, friendship moves beyond convenience or romance and achieves a special significance with two women who share much more with each other than the superficial trappings of class.

SUSANNA: ROSINA'S LADY IN WAITING

If Rosina is mistakenly considered middle class, Susanna is sometimes reduced to a typical soubrette role, lumped into the same class as Zerlina and Despina. Yet in his "Characters and Costumes" descriptions, Beaumarchais explicitly distinguishes Suzanne from the common maidservant type: "Clever young person, lively and given to laughter, but without that almost brazen gaiety of our corrupting soubrettes." He elaborates further in the preface:

> Why does Suzanne, the lively, clever, and laughing chambermaid, also deserve our sympathy? It is because, under attack by a dominating seducer with more than enough advantages to conquer a young woman of her status, she does not hesitate to report the Count's intentions to the two people most interested in watching over her conduct: her mistress and her fiancé. It is because, in this role, which is nearly the longest of the play [in terms of number of lines], there is not a phrase or word that does not breathe mod-

esty, good sense, and a love of duty: the only ruse she permits herself is for
the sake of her mistress, to whom her devotion is precious and whose
wishes are honorable.

In fact, Susanna's duties (in the play and in the opera) indicate that she
is in fact what Daniel Pool calls a "lady's maid." This "most exalted" of
female servants, the lady's maid "was free of the housekeeper's control,
unlike the other maids, and attended the lady of the house, personally
dressing and undressing her, arranging her hair, reading to her if need
be, and using her needlework skills to do repairs on items of personal
dress." He adds that "in all events a lady's maid was supposed to be
youthful and more personable than the housemaids who drudged away
all day long doing the household's heavy manual labor"; moreover, she
"had the privilege of being given her mistress's cast-off clothes."[40]

The role of Suzanne/Susanna seems a perfect example of Pool's description. In the play, the Comtesse even fibs to the Comte that Suzanne
is in the closet "trying on dresses that I gave her as a wedding present."
Susanna enjoys the lady's maid's special access to the noble sphere of society. Frits Noske notes her exceptional social mobility, which he attributes to her being "an intelligent female servant" who, having some access to education in the eighteenth century, has "no great difficulty in
bridging, at least externally, the distance from her mistress. She daily observes the manners of the higher classes and soon succeeds in imitating
them."[41] While emphasizing the essential importance of class difference,
Noske also concludes that both Susanna and the Countess exemplify
Rousseau's philosophies, as the "Countess's *noblesse* of mind exceeds
the nobility of her birth" and Susanna "possesses a singleness of heart
to which her innate refinement and coquetry remain subordinate."[42]

Today, productions often reinforce the difference between the two
roles, not least by casting the maid with a lighter voice, the better to contrast with the more "dramatic" noblewoman, who brings out the big
guns vocally. (This type of casting also strengthens the association between Susanna and Mozart's real soubrettes, Zerlina and Despina, as
singers with similar physical and vocal traits are tapped for all three
roles.) The cast of the opera's premiere performance in 1786 as well as
that of the 1789 Viennese revival, however, demonstrated a much more
complicated dynamic. In 1783, the first Viennese production of Paisiello's *Il barbiere di Siviglia* featured the celebrated English-Italian soprano Nancy Storace—only eighteen years old—in the role of Rosina.
The opera would occupy the Viennese stage again in 1785, with Luisa
Laschi appearing as the noble orphan. With these two productions fresh

in the minds of the Viennese opera public, Mozart wisely brought both sopranos together for the premiere of *Le nozze di Figaro,* with Laschi continuing as Rosina—now the Countess Almaviva—and Storace as the irrepressible Susanna. These casting choices further demonstrate the congruence between the roles of the Countess Almaviva and Susanna, which are, in a sense, two variations on the "theme" of Rosine/Rosina. In *Figaro,* the Countess finds herself under a new Argus: instead of the greedy Bartolo, she faces an unreasonable husband who is both jealous and unfaithful. Susanna's situation also resonates with the younger Rosina. She is happy in love but must resist the advances of the Count, who, as her master and guardian, should be safeguarding her honor and looking after her interests. Susanna also has Rosina's feisty spirit and nobility of character. Nowhere do we see in her Zerlina's fickleness or Despina's treachery: as the playwright himself noted, she is honest and faithful to her husband and mistress, even when it might be easier to go along with the flow and keep silent. Susanna is not afraid of the truth and looks at reality with clear eyes. Candor and loyalty are her best weapons against the Count, who acknowledges the threat she poses early in act 3: "And Susanna? Who knows if she has betrayed my secret . . . oh, if she has talked, I'll make him marry the old woman."

Susanna is, in fact, the opera's hub of interaction: she is the only character involved in every numbered ensemble (excluding choruses No. 8 and No. 21) and sings with all the major characters in an extraordinary collection of six duets, two trios, and a sextet. From the very first act, everyone seems to be looking for her: Marcellina to frighten her into rejecting the Count's offer so that she might profit from his revenge, Cherubino to share his troubles and gain access to the Countess, the Count to harass her once more about a possible "arrangement," and Basilio, allegedly to look for the Count on Figaro's behalf. For her part, Susanna responds by sizing up everyone, even Cherubino, with fearless accuracy. She pegs gossiping Marcellina as unreliable ("What a tongue! Fortunately everyone one knows what it's worth.") and upbraids Basilio as the "vile panderer for another's lasciviousness" (1.7), adding within earshot of the Count, "I have no need for your morals, the Count, or his love." Even Cherubino cannot charm her into foolishness; when the page offers his song to her as payment for the Countess's ribbon he has stolen, she is unaffected, countering brusquely, "And what am I supposed to do with it?" (1.5).

Susanna's forthright speech and intelligence are reminiscent of Blonde in *Die Entführung aus dem Serail,* who also serves her mistress Constanze with good sense and a frank tongue. Captured by a Turkish ruler, the Pasha Selim, Constanze and Blonde both contend with unwanted suitors. Whereas Constanze tries to deter the Pasha through tears and vocally resplendent avowals of unshakable constancy, Blonde cows Osmin, the Pasha's bullying overseer, with impervious self-confidence and the threat of sharp fingernails. She matches Osmin's macho vocal demonstrations punch for punch, declaring, "Girls are not wares to give away! I am an Englishwoman, born to freedom, and defy anyone who will force me to do anything!" Blonde does not mince words with her mistress either, though she only desires her happiness. The maid sees no benefit in pining away since "men truly do not deserve that one grieves oneself to death on their account," so she urges Constanze to cheer up and "be hopeful." When her mistress sighs, "How lucky you are, maiden, to be so composed about your fate! Oh, if only I could be like that," Blonde replies sensibly, "That choice rests only with you."

No doubt Blonde would have been proud of the Countess, who overcomes sadness through hope and action, engineering the very plan that saves the day. She also would have applauded Susanna, who deals handily with her adversaries and also helps to "awaken" Rosina, the strength and spirit that the Countess needs to overcome the melancholy inertia of "Porgi amor." Susanna helps her mistress not only by following her directions and by giving her levelheaded counsel, but also by looking out for her unspoken needs. She tries, for instance, to assuage the pain caused by the Count's faithlessness and diffidence by cheerfully turning the visit with Cherubino into what Allanbrook describes perfectly as an "innocent tableau" of "loveplay," which allows the young page to pay court to the Countess.[43] Susanna urges the page to sing his song for their mistress and then has fun dressing him, allowing the Countess to keep a discreet distance. The gentlewoman mildly scolds them for "such nonsense," but is also diverted from her cares. Susanna's action aria, "Venite inginocchiatevi" moves along at a brisk, get-down-to-business pace ("Come, on your knees, stay still here"), but the first violin's chirpy motive belies her sisterly glee at being able to treat Cherubino like a doll ("Slowly turn: good, that looks fine") and poke fun at his moony glances toward the Countess ("Now turn your face towards me, your eyes on *me*: Madame is not here").

There is a general instance of silence in the accompaniment before the violins and bassoons, in parallel octaves, introduce this last phrase— "Madama quì non è"—with a gently falling gesture. The sparse texture abruptly swells as the other strings enter, accentuating the melodic fall of a ninth with the other tones of the inverted dominant seventh chord (mm. 36–40). It may be that Susanna stops to admire her "innocent tableau" before restoring the bustling momentum with an efficient cadence. The musical parenthesis may also represent Cherubino's natural, irrepressible sensuality, which is obvious to everyone: the little amorous butterfly, as Figaro jokingly called him, cannot help himself. A few measures later, the violins and bassoons return with their lovesick refrain, and Susanna, less indulgent now, jumps in earlier and more emphatically. Still, she purposely calls attention to Cherubino's infatuation: his adolescent crush may be foolishness, but it may also serve as a harmless, flattering balm to a young Countess who has begun to doubt her desirability. Susanna discreetly encourages her mistress to enjoy the admiration of young Eros, for no one can refute his beauty or charm. Gazing at her handiwork, she murmurs to the Countess, "Just look at that little rascal, look at how pretty he is! What a cunning aspect, what charm, what a figure!" Then, when the bassoon and violin melody returns for the last time, the lady's maid adds, "If women love him, they certainly have their reasons."

There is nothing like this phrase in Beaumarchais's play, and it is curious that Da Ponte added it. It is possible that Susanna's whispered comment acts as a subtle hint about the Countess's attraction to the page. More likely, however, is that Mozart and Da Ponte wanted to underscore Cherubino's undeniable erotic appeal without incriminating their Countess. It is safer for Susanna—whom the page calls "sister" and who is fully satisfied with Figaro's love—to engage in childish pranks ("ragazzate") without ensuing scandal. Nor is this the only time in the opera when she stands in for the Countess in relation to Cherubino. When, for example, the Count refuses to forgive the page after he discovers him hiding in the chair, Susanna interjects, "But he is only a child" (1.8), a line that went to the Comtesse in the play. The closeness between Susanna and Cherubino—even her recognition of his beauty and erotic power—is "safe." Given that Mozart and Da Ponte excised almost all signs of the Countess's emerging attraction to her godson, Susanna's teasing remarks and candid awareness of Cherubino's charms bring a discreet but necessary erotic charge to the dress-up scene.

UP THE DOWN STAIRCASE: SUSANNA'S MUSICAL STYLES

Susanna is able to share some of the Countess's dramatic space convincingly because she possesses the same mixture of *buffa* spirit and *mezzo-carattere* grace that Rosina exhibits in *Il barbiere*. Moberly calls

Susanna a born mimic, presumably because she is good at aping the musical mannerisms of others, but there is more to it than that. From her first numbers, the duettinos with Figaro, Susanna the lady's maid shows herself to be fluent in both courtly and comic idioms, utilizing them as appropriate to the situation. In the duet that opens the opera ("Cinque, dieci, venti") she answers Figaro's "military masculinity"—the march topos he uses while measuring the room for their new bed—with "the feminine grace of one of the most *gallant* courtly dances," the gavotte.[44] Allanbrook identifies Figaro's phrase as a bourrée pattern and notes that both the bourrée and gavotte are "dances of *mezzo carattere*," and that the couple's use of them not only fits their station as servants to the Count, but also "leaves open the possibility that the pair possesses a real, and not adopted, distinction."[45] It is their wedding day: Susanna is proud of the hat she has made for herself and calls out to Figaro to admire it. The third-beat accent of her melody unsettles Figaro's deliberate downbeat, creating "ambiguity and delicacy" that are essential to her character.[46] It is clear that *something* interferes with the valet's concentration, for when he takes up his tallying again, he comes in "early," throwing his vocal tallying out of sync with the original accompaniment (mm. 36–44). Susanna quickly fills in the space with a daintily pestering melody, a patter of repeated notes that nudges his musical accent back toward the middle part of the measure and his attention toward her pretty handiwork. Sensing a pause in his calculations, she gives up on subtlety and demands that her beau look at her. It will not be the first time that Figaro fails to take a hint, but in the end he sings his pretty fiancée's tune. They finish the duet as a pair, voices joining in cheerful thirds: "How sweet to your/my bridegroom is this charming hat that Susanna made herself on the morning of our approaching wedding!"

Susanna brings her future husband around to her way of thinking in the next duet, too, though this time by taking over his optimistic material—another bourrée—and revealing to him its disagreeable flipside. When Figaro announces that the Count has given them this very spacious bedroom—which just happens to be in close proximity to his own—Susanna answers tartly, "As far as I'm concerned, it's all yours." Surprised, Figaro asks for a reason, to which his bride—amazed at his obtuseness—taps her head and says, "I have my reasons." At first she is hoping that he will trust in her conviction without further discussion, but the perplexed bridegroom presses the issue: how can she not see the room's advantages? "Because I am Susanna, and you are crazy," she retorts.

Figaro dryly thanks her for her kindness and then proceeds to show her how convenient the room would be. In the next number, No. 2, "Se a caso madama," Figaro's music moves with the same jaunty energy as in the first duet; the two numbers also feature the same orchestration and accompaniment style with busy arpeggios in the second violin under a relatively simple melody. Here, too, Figaro is in constant motion; he always has to be *doing* something. Here, he playacts his argument, marching about and ringing imaginary bells, hoping to change Susanna's mind: "Suppose Madame calls you in the middle of the night? Ding, ding! Why in two steps you would be there! Then when it happens that the Count wants me—dong, dong—in three hops I can be at his service." Rebuffing Figaro's bright B-flat major, Susanna replies in G minor. Her version of his theme is both portentous and sardonic: clear-sighted Susanna will stop "Signor Action" in his tracks. She confronts him with a slightly different sequence of events: "So, if one morning the dear, dear Count—ding, ding—sends you three miles away—dong, dong, *dong, dong.*" Imitating her fiancé's onomatopoeic chimes with ironic zest, Susanna sets up the bitter punch line: "The little devil comes to my door, and in three hops . . . " Instead of doubling the vocal line as it did with Figaro, the first violin breaks away from Susanna's part with an amusing counterpoint; its rapid staccato rhythm on a single note connotes the sneaky tiptoeing of the Count as well as Susanna's underlying agitation. When her vocal line rises up indignantly to a higher tessitura, Figaro tries quickly to shush her, but Susanna does not relent until her beloved is ready to hear the truth about the Count's "generosity."

Another example of how Susanna uses another character's "language" to get her point across is the duet with Marcellina, "Via resti servita" (1.4.5). Just as Rosina threw Bartolo's nasty comments and suspicions back in his face ("But, sir, if we [women] are pleased by anyone who is a man, why do I find you so displeasing?"), Susanna returns the governess's insults with fatally accurate parody. It is an easy victory for Susanna: her conscience and reputation are clearer than Marcellina's. When, for instance, the older lady taunts her with "The Count's pet," Susanna naturally takes umbrage at what is a malicious lie. In contrast, when Susanna replies, "The love of Spain!" Marcellina reddens not only from anger but from shame: her illicit relationship with Bartolo is long past, but her bitterness about this affair has not faded. Susanna then vanquishes her dowdy rival with the "age before beauty" barb. It is not her most gracious moment but is nonetheless hilarious, and, since her raillery is done primarily in self-defense, it does not detract from our appreciation of Susanna's fundamental decency and intelligence.

In her interactions with Figaro and Marcellina, Susanna demonstrates just how well she can adapt the musical idiom of another character. In her duets with Figaro, Susanna cajoles him into joining in with her melody and then knocks him affectionately over the head with his own. Provoked by Marcellina, the lady's maid vanquishes the former governess with her own brand of overstuffed, fake civility. There is one number, however, in which Susanna shares the musical language of another character not as a means of defense, but as an extension of her own natural "voice." In "Che soave zeffiretto," she and the Countess compose a letter in the form of a little song to the Count, confirming the maid's consent to a twilight rendezvous. The pastorale they create together temporarily abates the opera's frenetic pace and dramatic tension: for a few minutes, there is harmonious calm. It is, in fact, the first time in almost three acts that Susanna has had such a quiet moment. She sits and writes down the words of the Countess's "canzonetta":

Countess (dictating).	"Canzonetta sull'aria"	"Song on the Air"
Susanna (writing).	"Sull'aria . . ."	"On the Air . . ."
Countess.	"Che soave zeffiretto . . ."	"What a sweet breeze . . ."
Susanna.	"Zeffiretto . . ."	"Breeze . . ."
Countess.	"Questa sera spirerà . . ."	"Will waft tonight . . ."
Susanna.	"Questa sera spirerà . . ."	"Will waft tonight . . ."
Countess.	"Sotto i pini del boschetto . . ."	"Beneath the pines of the grove . . ."
Susanna (asking).	Sotto i pini?	Beneath the pines?
Countess.	"Sotto i pini del boschetto . . ."	"Beneath the pines of the grove . . ."
Susanna.	"Sotto i pini del boschetto . . ."	"Beneath the pines of the grove . . ."
Countess.	Ei già il resto capirà.	He will already under stand the rest.
Susanna.	Certo, certo il capirà.	Certainly, certainly he will understand.

The women repeat the final phrase together, "He will already understand the rest / Certainly, certainly he will understand," then read the entire letter together.

There is no rivalry, no apprehension, only mutual understanding: they are of one voice. The duet shows the two ladies drawing closer to one another, each adopting the other's inflections in the way that women friends often do in conversation, until it is difficult to distinguish one from the other. The Countess assumes the lead, dictating the letter; Susanna re-

EXAMPLE 23. *Le nozze di Figaro*, No. 21, "Che soave zeffiretto"; mm. 4–10

peats her words with her own melodic lilt. It is not a matter of aping repetition or mimicry, but rather of sharing a common language. For instance, while the Countess's initial phrase, "Che soave zeffiretto . . ."
falls to the lower part of her range, Susanna's murmured, "Zeffiretto
. . ." hovers appealingly like the breeze itself (Ex. 23). The Countess
seems to appreciate what she hears; a few measures later, she will use Susanna's phrase herself ("sotto i pini del bosco," mm. 23–25). Her appropriation of Susanna's music may also be a gesture of reassurance.
When the Countess's reference to the pine grove accentuates the letter's
sensuous connotations with two delicious appoggiaturas, Susanna hesitates, "Under the pines?" She may not have caught her mistress's words,
but it is just as possible that she understood them all too well and is questioning, discreetly, whether the Countess is sure about this. The Countess repeats the words, but to Susanna's melody. The only real melodic

EXAMPLE 24. *Le nozze di Figaro*, No. 21, "Che soave zeffiretto"; mm. 38–44

echoing occurs when the two women nod to one another, knowingly—
the Count "will surely understand" the rest. As they read the letter together, one can easily imagine the Countess sitting down next to Susanna
or perhaps resting her hands on her maid's shoulders as she leans in to
survey their work. Their vocal lines, too, converge; phrases that were
once separated during the dictation of the letter now overlap. Susanna
begins with the Countess's opening melody, and the Countess dovetails
the phrase with what was Susanna's response (Ex. 24). The last seven-
teen measures of the duet illustrate a bond as affecting as any in the
opera. The soprano lines mirror one another and then embrace in par-

allel singing, rising to a heavenly pinnacle third (G–B-flat) before the cadence.

The evanescent pastoral moment, traditionally the shepherd and shepherdess's brief pause before returning to the day's work, is a moment of repose to be enjoyed before it disappears. Yet dramatically "Che soave zeffiretto" is not merely a gorgeous parenthesis—like Cherubino's canzonetta in the Countess's room—for the letter is the key in many respects to bringing about the opera's satisfying denouement. Though productions sometimes pause for applause after this favorite number, the score indicates less than a beat before practical Susanna continues in recitative, "The paper is folded . . . now how do we seal it?" There is, in fact, little time to lose. The letter is quickly sealed and dispatched to its target. Once this is done, Susanna lies low; though she still appears on-stage for the third-act finale, she then disappears until scene 9 of act 4, shortly before her last aria. By that time, the female alliance is basically complete, for Marcellina has joined the Countess and Susanna, warning them that her suspicious son is eavesdropping. It is too late: the trap is set, and there is no way to warn Figaro without jeopardizing everything. Besides, it is the second time in the opera that Figaro's suspicions have wrongly impugned Susanna. "The rogue is playing the watch-guard, so we'll have some fun, too: let's give him a reward for his doubts," she muses (4.10). Knowing that her fiancé can hear her voice (but not see her dressed in the Countess's clothes), she invents her own voluptuous pastorale, "Deh vieni non tardar," introducing it with an ardent accompanied recitative:

Giunse alfin il momento	The moment has finally arrived
Che godrò senza affanno	when I will enjoy myself without worry
In braccio all'idol mio! Timide cure,	in the arms of my idol! Timid scruples,
Uscite dal mio petto,	leave my breast,
A turbar non venite il mio diletto!	Do not disturb my delight!
Oh, come par che all'amoroso foco L'amenità del loco,	Oh, how the loveliness of this place, the earth and heaven,
La terra e il ciel risponda!	seem to respond to my amorous fire!
Come la notte i furti miei seconda!	How the night aids my furtive affairs!

The interplay between the trills and Scottish snaps in the string accompaniment and Susanna's impassioned vocalizing captures perfectly the warmth and humor of the situation: she is, of course, thinking of her bridegroom, not an illicit lover, but Figaro does not know this. Suppressing laughter, Susanna's steeps her "revenge" in affection. Almost every phrase dips down into her sultry lower range: the plush eroticism of her middle-C sigh when she says "Oh how the loveliness of this place, the earth and heaven seem to respond to my amorous fire" is meant to stir up more than Figaro's jealousy. After all, Susanna should be celebrating her wedding night, and her desire for that moment informs both the recitative and the aria that follows. Improvising in a musical language that is quite familiar to her, she borrows a little from both "Voi che sapete" and "Che soave zeffiretto," the other "love songs" of the opera. The opening instrumental interlude combines the paired oboe and bassoon (soon joined by a solo flute) of the Countess's "canzonetta sull'aria" with the pizzicato strings that stand in for guitar accompaniment in "Voi che sapete":

Deh vieni non tardar, o gioia bella,	Come now, do not delay, oh lovely joy,
Vieni ove amore per goder t'appella,	come where love calls you to pleasure
Finché non splende in ciel notturna face	while night's torch shines in the sky,
Finché l'aria è ancor bruna e il mondo tace.	while the air is still dark, and the world is silent.
Qui momora il ruscel, qui scherzo l'aura,	Here the brook murmurs, here the breeze jests,
Che col dolce susurro il cor ristaura;	so that the heart is refreshed by its sweet whispers.
Qui ridono i fioretti, e l'erba è fresca;	Here the flowers laugh, and the grass is cool;
Ai piaceri d'amor qui tutto adesca.	everything entices you to the pleasures of love.
Vieni, ben mio: tra queste piante ascose	Come, my dear: amidst these hidden trees,
Ti vo' la fronte incoronar di rose.	I want to crown your brow with roses.

Susanna's canzonetta borrows something from the Countess's style, with decorously erotic descriptions and provocative appoggiaturas. The first of these—"qui ridono i fioretti, e l'erba è fresca"—strongly recalls the Countess's reference to the pine grove in "Che soave zeffiretto." Both phrases feature melodies in relatively stepwise motion—contrasting with the predominant vocal arpeggios—and conclude with a chromatically raised 2–3 appoggiatura (G-sharp–A) on the tonic chord. Tantalizing the listener further, Susanna calls to her lover—"Vieni, ben mio"—raising the appoggiatura up a third (B-natural–C). The humor of the situation is never lost on the young woman, however, and her amusement seems to rise up with the effervescent, staccato scales of the flute, oboe, and bassoon trio that punctuate her song. She even seems to echo them with her breathless scale on "incoronar" (m. 62), crowning her own song with the graceful leap up to high A. Summoning her lover with her voluptuous pastorale, Susanna enjoys the moment, fully in control of the musical idiom and the situation.

"Deh vieni" is unquestionably one of the most popular arias in the opera, so it is difficult to imagine that it might have been something of a concession on the part of Nancy Storace, who created the role of Susanna. It may well have been in consideration of Storace's status—she was a favorite of the emperor and the Viennese public—that Mozart first thought to compose the garden aria as a full-blown rondo in two tempos, much like the Countess's "Dove sono." Existing sketches show thirty-six measures of this rondo, "Non tardar amato bene" ("Do not delay, dearest beloved"), but, for some reason, Mozart abandoned the piece and settled on the more modest—though arguably more fetching— "Deh vieni." As Heartz explains, there was bound to have been some tension over the decision:

> From [Storace's] point of view, it is easier to understand why she wanted a big dramatic rondo to sing when masquerading as the countess. She may in fact have demanded one, believing that parity of the two roles was at stake. Laschi had sung one in the middle of act 3, and it was the most serious piece in the whole opera, "Dove sono i bei momenti," a piece with which Mozart took infinite pains, as his melodic sketches show. Originally he inscribed it, twice, with the title "Rondo" and it is just as proud an exemplar of the two-tempo rondo in form and style as Donna Anna's "Non mi dir," Fiordiligi's "Per pieta bell' idol mio," or Vitellia's "Non più di fiori." Mozart scratched out, or someone scratched out, the proper appellation *Rondo* on "Dove sono" in the autograph and replaced it, twice, with *Aria*. When Storace lost her rondo in act 4, it was easier to keep the peace in the family if Laschi's rondo were at least not called a rondo. It is just possible that "Non tardar amato bene" was only a feint by Mozart until he brought Storace around to singing what he wanted her to sing all along. . . . To the everlasting credit of Nancy Storace, she settled finally for "Deh vieni non tardar" . . . a marvel of subtle understatement.[47]

If in fact Mozart did a little scheming of his own to protect the integrity of his creative concept, he was lucky to have the versatile and relatively accommodating Storace. Perhaps she understood better than her soprano peers that the strength of Susanna's character was not enhanced by virtuosic display—quite the opposite, in fact. Unfortunately, when *Le nozze di Figaro* returned to the Viennese stage in 1789, the new singers were not so flexible. For this production, Da Ponte's mistress, Adriana Ferrarese del Bene, took over the role of Susanna, paired with Caterina Cavaliere as the Countess. The result was a battle between prima donnas, with both roles undergoing major changes to punch up the amount of coloratura dazzle. For "La Ferrarese"—who would soon premiere the role of Fiordiligi—Mozart composed not one, but two new arias. In place of the action aria "Venite inginocchiatevi," he substituted "Un moto di gioia," a vocal bonbon with none of the energetic humor that vitalized the original aria. Mozart granted Ferrarese del Bene the two-tempo rondo that he had denied Storace as a substitute for "Deh vieni." The new aria, "Al desio di chi t'adora," is a vocal showpiece, made flashier still by the obbligato embellishments of paired bassett horns. The casting of La Ferrarese may suggest that Susanna was considered the prima donna role, but Cavalieri was not likely to have considered herself as second fiddle. She had already created the formidable role of Constanze in Mozart's *Die Entführung aus dem Serail*. Mozart also crafted the new (and enduring) rondo "Mi tradì" for her when she took over the role of Donna Elvira in the 1788 revival of *Don Giovanni*. It is hardly surprising, then, that when the composer revised "Dove sono," he sacrificed it, as he had the role of Constanze, to the "flexible throat" of Cavalieri.[48] However, none of these changes to *Figaro* benefited its main female roles or the opera. History has upheld Mozart's original conception: the 1789 changes are rarely adopted for productions today.

One general modification that Mozart made during the original production further complicates the question of who the "first lady" of the opera really is. Before completing the third and fourth acts, Mozart had already begun to switch the two parts, giving to Susanna what had originally been the Countess's melody. We know this from the changes he made in the autograph and also in the performance parts for act 2. By the time he began composing acts 3 and 4, Mozart consistently assigned the higher part to Susanna. It is not known exactly why Mozart chose to make this exchange. It is possible that Laschi was having vocal problems; Storace did not have a particularly extensive vocal range, so it seems unlikely that Mozart would have changed the parts to suit her better. Moreover, the new voicing introduced at least one dramatic incongruity, namely Susanna's twice-repeated high C when she is supposed to be whispering, avoiding discovery by the furious Count. Whatever the reason for these changes, they are found in almost all of the manuscript and printed scores, and they are reflected in almost all productions today.[49]

Considered together, the cast history, abandoned sketches, alterations, and substitute arias reaffirm what is obvious to every listener today: Susanna is special. Clearly the role was attractive enough to interest two of the most prominent singers of the day. It was also sufficiently adaptable to permit Mozart to enhance it with *seria* oomph for Ferrarese del Bene; it was not unreasonable to make Susanna's musical language even more "noble," to bring her closer to the Countess's sphere. Nevertheless, this may actually have been the greatest drawback of the changes: the ladies became *too* alike. The sketch for "Non tardar amato bene," for instance, exhibits obvious similarities to both "Porgi amor" and Rosina's E-flat aria, "Giusto ciel," from Paisiello's *Il barbiere*. (In fact, Mozart appears to have used "Giusto ciel" as a model for "Porgi amor"; borrowing the earlier aria's key, meter, tempo, and mood, Mozart acknowledged Paisiello's work, then exceeded it.)[50] Susanna and the Countess have compatible personalities and many common virtues, but they are not generically interchangeable. Susanna's fluent spontaneity is unmatched in the opera and has been a key to her charm for more than two centuries now.

SISTERHOOD AND THE SOUND OF FREEDOM

In the 1994 movie *The Shawshank Redemption*, convict Ellis "Red" Redding listens, transfixed, as music begins to play over the prison PA system. His fellow inmate, Andy Dufresne, has locked the guards out of the room and temporarily taken over the system. Andy selects a specific disc from the pile of LPs, and, after he drops the needle, we hear the opening bars of "Che soave zeffiretto." In a voice-over, Red describes the effect the music has on him:

> I have no idea to this day what those two Italian ladies were singing about. Truth is, I don't want to know. Some things are better left unsaid. I'd like to think they were singing about something so beautiful it can't be expressed in words—and makes your heart ache because of it. I tell you those voices soared, higher and farther than anybody in a gray place dares to dream. It was like some beautiful bird flapped into our drab, little cage and made those walls dissolve away. And for the briefest of moments, every last man at Shawshank felt free.[51]

The original Stephen King short story, "Rita Hayworth and Shawshank Redemption," does not include this episode, but it is one of the high-

lights of the film, contrasting the guards' crude language and brutish behavior with the convicts' desire and appreciation of beauty. The transparent texture, pleasing harmonies, and soaring soprano lines of "Che
soave zeffiretto" freshen the prison's dank, hopeless air. As the music
surrounds them, Red and the other inmates experience their own brief
arcadian moment and pause, astounded, in the middle of their hum-
drum tasks.

It is noteworthy that the film associates the women's duet with a sense
of freedom. In the opera, the letter duet marks a turning point—the mis-
treated wife and her beleaguered attendant finally have reason to be optimistic. Their friendship liberates them: together they can hope to make
things right. In all of Mozart's major operas, it is the only duet in which
two women are both united in purpose *and* represented in a favorable
light. There is no duet for Blonde and Constanze. Donna Anna, Donna
Elvira, and Zerlina sing together, but only when joined by at least one
male character. The Queen of the Night and her daughter never join
voices. Sisters Fiordiligi and Dorabella sing two duets, but these serve
only to emphasize their romantic dizziness, first when they pledge undy-
ing love to their lovers' portraits and later when they decide to dally with
two handsome strangers. In fact, the Countess and Susanna are in many
ways more in sympathy with each other than *Così*'s siblings, who drift
apart during the course of the opera. The noble heroine and lady's maid
of *Figaro* are two conventional character types that Mozart makes unconventional through his music, and nowhere more so than in the letter
duet. The composer will never again have the opportunity to create such
a pair, the eighteenth-century opera buffa ancestors to Woolf's imaginary
Chloe and Olivia. Moberly sums it up perfectly, "Mozart, who enjoys
differentiating characters in music, has deliberately gone naïve, by un-
differentiating his two heroines. They are blended. Both are Rosina, enjoying traditional rituals. Both are the Countess, in the new-found confidence of *Dove sono*. Both are the Susanna of *Deh vieni*. It is one of the
big moments in the serious inner meaning of Mozart's opera; a shared
lyrical moment, tending towards the great moments of forgiveness and
general reconciliation at the end of Act Four."[52] Whatever influence social class, aria types, and casting choices may or may not have in determining the superior heroine, "Che soave zeffiretto" renders the question
moot and frees us from having to choose either. That singular moment
of feminine alliance—Rosina "squared"—proves that there is plenty of
room in the opera and our hearts for both women to reign.

CHAPTER 8

Woman's Identity II:
Loss and Legitimacy

Marcellina and Barbarina

I tremble to think, what a sad hazard a poor maiden of little
more than fifteen years of age stands against the temptations
of this world, and a designing young gentleman, if he should
prove so, who has so much *power* to oblige, and has the kind
of *authority* to command, as your master.

Samuel Richardson, Pamela

Well, at least your boy's alive. *He's alive.* That's what matters.

Mrs. Croft to her sister, Mrs. Wilson, in Gosford Park

The premieres of *Le barbier de Seville* (1775) and *Le mariage de Figaro*
(1784) were separated by nine years of royalty disputes, censorship, and
imperial prohibition. Beaumarchais may have completed the sequel to
Le barbier as early as 1776, but it had been revised and cut numerous
times before it was finally staged by the Comédie Française with the
king's permission. Censors prescribed some of the revisions, but Beaumarchais also streamlined the overly long original. Even with these extensive revisions and trimmings, *Le mariage* ran three and a half hours,
which extended to five hours at the first official performance due to the
numerous outbursts of prolonged audience applause. By any standard,
the play was an amazing success, with an exceptional first run of sixty-
eight performances, yet when he published the first edition of the play,
Beaumarchais indicated in the preface that he regretted having cut one

particular passage: Marceline's imposing speech on the injustices and
abuses that men inflict on women of every rank. Beaumarchais ex-
plained that he originally eliminated this episode from the trial scene in
act 3 at the request of the Comédie Française players, who "begged me
to strike it out, fearing that so severe a passage would cloud the gaiety
of the action." In the published version, the playwright was so keen to
establish the importance of Marceline's "candid admission" about her
unhappy past that he quoted the entire passage in his preface, urging the
readers (and particularly critics) to study it:

> *Brid'oison.* It's clear: he [Figaro] will not marry
> her [Marceline].
>
> *Bartholo.* And neither will I.
>
> *Marceline.* Neither will you! And your son? You
> promised me . . .
>
> *Bartholo.* I was insane. If such mementos were
> binding, one would be forced to marry
> the whole world!
>
> *Brid'oison.* A-a-and if one looked at it closely, no
> one would marry anyone.
>
> *Bartholo.* Such notorious faults! A deplorable
> youth!
>
> *Marceline (heating up by degrees).* Deplorable, yes, and more than one
> may believe. I do not intend to deny
> my faults: this day has proven them too
> well! But it is difficult to have to re-
> dress them after thirty years of modest
> living! I myself was born to be judi-
> cious, and I became so when I was per-
> mitted to use my reason. But in the age
> of illusions, of inexperience and needs,
> when seducers assail us, while misery
> cuts us to the quick, how can a child
> oppose so many enemies assembled to-
> gether? Perhaps there are even such
> people right here, men who, judging
> us most severely, have abandoned ten
> unfortunate women in their own
> lifetime!
>
> *Figaro.* The guiltiest are the least generous:
> that is the rule.
>
> *Marceline (loftily).* Most ungrateful men, who condemn
> with scorn the playthings of your pas-
> sions, your victims! It is you who

Figaro (angrily).
Marceline (in a state of exaltation).

should be punished for the errors of our youth; you and your magistrates, so vain about the right to judge us, who, through their blameworthy negligence, take from us any honest way of making a living. Is there one single possibility for unfortunate girls? They have a natural right to all the tasks having to do with women; instead they set up a thousand workers of the opposite sex to do these things.

Figaro (angrily). They even make soldiers do embroidery!

Marceline (in a state of exaltation). In the highest ranks of society, women receive from you only a mocking consideration: enticed by hollow gestures of respect, they are in reality living in servitude; treated like children as regards our possessions, but punished like adults for our errors! Ah! From all aspects, your conduct toward us must inspire horror or pity!

Figaro. She's right!

The Count (aside). Only too right!

Brid'oison. M-my God, she is right!

Beaumarchais goes on to say that if the actors had "had the courage to restore the scene at my request, I think that the public would have been most appreciative." He adds that reinstating the scene would also have answered critics' complaints about being coerced into taking interest in a "woman of low morals." Directing these "critics of the *beau monde*" to this scene, the playwright offers this Marceline-ish response: "No, sirs, I do not speak of it in order to excuse her morals, but to make you blush at your own regarding the issue most destructive to public decency: *the corruption of the young*. And I have reason to say that if you find my piece too ribald, it is because it is often too severe. It depends on how you look at it." Marceline's speech was reinstated in the published version of the play (3.16), but it appears that, despite the author's passionate arguments, the excerpt was not performed on the national French stage for many years following its premiere. The prickliness of the content (a problem with the trial scene in general), along with the length of the play, seemed to have been generally prohibitive.

It is hardly surprising, then, that when Lorenzo da Ponte adapted the play into an opera libretto, he left out most of the trial scene, including

Marceline's speech—which he reduced to a relatively short passage of recitative—and concentrated instead on Marcellina's recognition of Figaro as her son. Subordinating sentiment to comedy, Da Ponte and Mozart shaped the reunion of son and parents into a hilarious sextet (3.5.18). In general they tailored Marceline's character to fit more neatly into the mold of the amusing *vecchia donna,* steering clear of the more mixed tone of Beaumarchais's characterization. In the original play, Marceline wavers between the absurd and the pitiable. Bartholo describes her early on as "bitter and insulting" (1.4), but the same scene also reveals details about her unhappy life.[1] We learn that she and Dr. Bartholo had a child out of wedlock, that she expected the doctor to live up to his duty and marry her, but was snubbed, and that the child was subsequently lost to her in a mysterious fashion. In this context, her wild scheme to force Figaro's hand in marriage as payment of a debt he owes her seems like a desperate grab at the happiness she was denied long ago. When the good doctor snaps at her for dredging up the past, she responds hotly, "Very well. We will not speak of it again. But, if nothing can persuade you to live up to your obligation to marry me, then at least help me to marry another." Goading her former paramour, she praises Figaro affectionately in terms that sharply contrast with the bilious doctor: "never angry, always in a good humor, living in and enjoying the moment, with as little thought to the future as to the past, lively, generous, charming."

CONTEXT, CONNECTIONS, AND THE POSSIBILITY OF CHANGE

Adapting this scene for the opera, Da Ponte focused exclusively on Marcellina's desire to force Figaro into marriage with the doctor's help, and the doctor's vengeful delight at being able to marry off his former housekeeper to Figaro:

> *Bartolo.* And you waited until the day set for the wedding to speak to me about this?
>
> *Marcellina (holding a contract in her hand).* I have not lost heart, my dear Doctor: a pretext alone has been sufficient to break off engagements even more advanced than this one; and he has other obligations with me beside this agreement as I well know. But enough: we must frighten Susanna, we must cleverly induce her to refuse the Count. In revenge, he will take my side, and then Figaro will be my husband.

Bartolo. Good, I will do all that I can: tell me everything,
and no holding back. *(Aside)* I will very much enjoy
giving my old servant away in marriage to the one
who helped steal my sweetheart from me. (1.3)

Nowhere in this dialogue is there mention of Marcellina's past affair
with Bartolo; her secret shame does not come up until act 3, where it is
revealed in a series of almost wholly humorous revelations that serve to
facilitate the happy outcome of the trial. Without the explicit, humanizing backstory of her lost loves, Marcellina's mission to snag Figaro appears callous and perverse; she seems an old spinster trying to mess up
the happiness of a young couple without any clear motive except envy.
Consequently, we are even more inclined to take pleasure in her comeuppance at Susanna's hands in the next scene. Da Ponte shaped Beaumarchais's nasty exchange of poisoned politeness between the two
women into a piquant duet, No. 5, "Via resti servita":

Marcellina (curtsying).	Via resti servita, Madama brillante.	Please, after you, my sparkling lady.
Susanna (curtsying).	Non sono sì ardita, Madama piccante.	I'd not be so bold, my spicy lady.
Marcellina (curtsying).	No, prima a lei tocca.	No, you go first.
Susanna (curtsying).	No, no, tocca a lei.	No, no, you go ahead.
Both (curtsying).	Io so i dover miei, Non fo inciviltà.	I know my duty, I would not be so rude.
Marcellina (curtsying).	La sposa novella!	The bride-to-be!
Susanna (curtsying).	La dama d'onore . . .	The matron of honor . . .
Marcellina (curtsying).	Del Conte la bella . . .	The Count's pet . . .
Susanna (curtsying).	Di Spagna l'amore . . .	The love of all Spain . . .
Marcellina.	I meriti . . .	Your qualities . . .
Susanna.	L'abito . . .	Your dress . . .
Marcellina.	Il posto . . .	Your position . . .
Susanna.	L'età!	Your age!
Marcellina (furious).	Perbacco, precipito, Se ancor resto qua!	By Jove, I will cause a scene if I stay here any longer!
Susanna (making her look like a fool).	Sibilla decrepita! Da rider mi fa!	Decrepit old witch! You make me laugh.

Marcellina is vanquished almost before she starts to sing. She had hoped that her jabs at Susanna's reputation would throw the maid off balance, giving her the upper hand. (In the play Marceline tells Bartholo about "women's little secret," the vital importance of protecting one's reputation above all other concerns.) Regrettably for her, the plan backfires stupendously. Jaded and bitter, poor Marcellina does not recognize her distinct disadvantage in this battle: it is *she* and not Susanna who has the more vulnerable reputation. Susanna's finishing blow—her reference to Marcellina's more advanced years ("L'età!")—is not insinuation, but fact. The inescapable reality of middle age crumples the little composure Marcellina has left, and she detonates with the aggravation. Both the text and the music of the duet declare Susanna the clear winner. The maid emulates Marcellina's studiously courteous melodic phrases for most of the face-off, until her triumphant "Sibilla decrepita!" at measure 36. Her disdainful put-down sounds very much like a trumpet's battle call, an effect heightened by the wind-only accompaniment: after nearly thirty-six measures of nonstop bustle the strings suddenly go silent. Toward the end, Susanna lays melodic claim to the snickering triplets that have peppered the musical repartee from the outset. (The stage directions here, *minchionandola,* indicate that Susanna is consciously mocking Marcellina so as to make her look foolish.) Her suppressed laughter bursts in triplet derision ("da rider mi fa!"; mm. 59, 63).

Nevertheless, "Via resti servita" hints at something that will be positive for Marcellina in the end: a musical affiliation with Figaro. It is Marcellina who introduces the duet's opening bourrée gesture, a favorite of Figaro's. As discussed in the previous chapter, this idiom is familiar to Susanna, for it is also one of Figaro's favorites. Furthermore, the scoring of "Via resti servita"—pairs of flute, oboes, bassoons, horns, and strings—is the same as that of Susanna's earlier duets with her fiancé and also that of her first aria, "Venite inginocchiatevi" (2.3.12), which incorporates the bourrée-influenced phrases, too.[2] The play also links the language and rhetoric of these two roles. With the same "energy and resilience" as her son, Marceline "uses several of Figaro's tricks of logic and repartee—yielding to reproach only to turn it to triumph, simultaneously saying 'yes' and 'no.'"[3] Beaumarchais's valet protagonist hints at a common physiognomy with his newly found mother when he asks a jealous Suzanne, "before you go, take a good look at this dear woman here. . . . How do you find her?" (3.18). These similarities between mother and son may not be as obvious in the opera, but they are definitely there. Figaro and Marcellina both favor related dances *"di mezzo carattere"*—the march, bourrée, and gavotte—and demonstrate a penchant for witty banter, intrigue, and an emotional life that is "of the moment." In both the play and the opera, Figaro and Marcellina reflect and correct each other's virtues and vices. When, for example, Figaro makes his about-face in act 4 from imperturbable lover to the rashly invidious whiner of "Aprite un po' quegl'occhi," Marcellina is moving in contrary motion, from backbiting spinster to the benevolent mother and female advocate of "Riconosci in questo amplesso" and "Il capro e la capretta."

Critics commonly dismiss Marcelline's/Marcellina's reclamation as an unbelievable convenience, serving only to remove a significant obstacle to Figaro's marriage. Discussing the play, J. B. Ratermanis and W. R. Irwin call Marceline an "error":

> In order to get his hero out of his predicament, Beaumarchais resorted to the trick of recognition of consanguinity, a favorite device in comedy and fiction. Within a space of a few speeches his worst enemy becomes a loving mother, Suzanne's protectress, and the strongest advocate of their marriage. Beaumarchais presumably hoped that the reader would experience a similar revolution in his feeling toward Marceline, and he attempted to encourage the change by giving her what amounts to a sermon on woman's servitude to justify her previous conduct. But this transformation demands too much of the reader. Marceline's forwardness in seeking a husband and her maternal affections, introduced almost without preparation, are too diverse to be reconciled even within so comprehensive a term as "love." Insofar as she is a comic personality, Marceline is a mistake, without convincing psychic and emotional motivation. She plays two separate roles. Following the recognition scene she could disappear from the play without serious loss to it, for her effectiveness likewise as an aid and obstacle is dissipated.[4]

Likewise, John Wood knocks the climax of the trial scene as sappy, outdated "nonsense." He considers it one of the many inconsistent elements that undermine Marceline's characterization:

> Marceline's speeches in Act Three which the actors wished to have omitted and Beaumarchais restored in the published version involve an ambivalence of another kind. They are of great interest as expressions of a new attitude to women, but they are dramatically out of place, intrusions from another convention. They threaten to overbalance the play into sentiment and sentimentality. Marceline is indeed a curiously inconsistent piece in characterization. In *The Barber* she is a person known to us only by report. In the early part of *The Marriage of Figaro* she is the comic rival to Suzanne, a farcical duenna. She assumes a new dimension and a quite different personality when she is revealed as the long-lost mother, the victim of Bartholo, and the personification of virtue betrayed. Beaumarchais seems to have

known a great deal more about his characters than he revealed in the plays—there are new revelations to come in *La mère coupable*—but what he tells of Marceline is inadequate. The actors were right; the part is unplayable without cutting and the note given by Beaumarchais in the preface to the published edition, that the actress playing the part should rise to the height of the noble opportunities of the revelation scene, is nonsense. It is, however, a sort of nonsense which was very much of the period and to which Beaumarchais had very strong loyalties.[5]

These excerpts allege two basic problems with Marceline, centering on her miraculous changeover and the speech in act 3. First, there is the issue of motivation, the idea that the *vecchia inammorata* and doting mother are two roles "too diverse to be reconciled." Second, echoing the complaints of the original players, there is the question of balance and relevance. Ratermanis argues that Marceline's act 3 speech threatens the comic equilibrium, while Wood would like to see her disappear altogether after the recognition scene because she has fulfilled her purpose. It may well be that Marceline's reproachful sermon tips the scales too much, at least in the prolonged and melodramatic form that Beaumarchais wrote it. Judicious revising could fix this, and yet the trend, even from the first production, has been to mute Marceline's protest altogether. Ironically, the rebuttal to these detractors can be found in the controversial passage itself. Marceline's confession about her unhappy past, her tale about everything she lost in her youth, explains how the embittered spinster was formed, and, likewise, how the restoration of her stolen/lost motherhood changes her. As for comic balance, the fundamental subject of Marceline's speech is completely in keeping with one of the primary, and not very funny, themes of the play: every woman in the play suffers at the hands of a man, whether by jealous abuse or sexual tyranny. Her metamorphosis into the mother figure does not nullify her relevance to the drama but rather completes the circle of female friendship when she unites with the Comtesse and Suzanne: the "sisters," too, have a protective "mother." In this light, Marceline's confrontation with her son in act 4 makes clearer the line in the sand between "ungrateful men" and the women they accuse. When cocksure Figaro succumbs to the very jealousy he previously denounced, it is Mother Marceline who comforts and advises him. However, she also rebukes her son for his hypocrisy and secretly moves to counter Figaro's suspicious petulance: "Now that I have taken the wind out of his sails, let's go see what Suzanne is up to, or better yet warn her. She is such a pretty thing! Ah, when personal interest does not set us against another, we women are all moved to defend our poor, oppressed sex against these proud, these terrible . . . *(laughing)*, and yet rather block-headed men!" (4.16).

LOST AND FOUND

As Beaumarchais implies in her very first scene, the key to understanding Marceline is to recognize what she really wants: her rightful place as Bartholo's wife and the legitimized mother of their child together. Truth be told, she seems to hold her status as mother even dearer than marriage with Bartholo. The discovery of her long-lost son changes everything, allowing her to view her life and the world with fresh and joyful understanding. Addressing Figaro after Bartholo has once again refused to do his duty and marry her, Marceline exclaims:

> But what do we care, my son, about the rejection of an unjust man? Do not look from whence you came, but instead at where you are going: that is the only thing that matters to anyone. In a few months, your fiancé will be free to decide for herself; she will accept you, I will vouch for that. Live then between tender wife and mother, who will only try to outdo one another in loving you better. Be indulgent towards them, and be happy for yourself, my son; be lively, free, and good to all the world. Your mother desires nothing more. (3.16)

A few moments later, when Suzanne is outraged at finding Figaro in the arms of Marceline, it is the older woman who sets the record straight, appealing to "my pretty Suzanne" to embrace her as well. Ecstatic with her unexpected fortune, the housekeeper moves the imperturbable Figaro to tears with her exaltation, "So unhappy as a girl, I was about to become the most miserable of wives, and now I am the most fortunate of mothers! Embrace me, my two children: in you all my affections are united. I am as happy as I can possibly be. Ah! my children, how I will love you!"

The recognition scene in the opera is less melodramatic than the one in the play, but it is still an affecting episode. Da Ponte and Mozart warmly depicted the "new" maternal Marcellina; they also showed—through clever parallels in the music and libretto—an undeniable consistency to her character.[6] Words that she once spoke with sarcasm return with a genuine smile; she refers to Susanna's modesty before "Via resti servita" and again before "Il capro e la capretta," the first sarcastic and the second sincere. Her shrewd wit becomes an aid rather than a weapon once she finds her "little Rafaello" and makes peace with her past. All the same, Marcellina is a far less provocative character than

Marceline. Her restored maternity—so liberating to Marceline in the play—is hastily yoked to (and subsumed by?) Bartolo's paternity in the sextet "Riconosci in questo amplesso" (3.5.18). The two sing together with Figaro in a trio of generic familial adoration, oblivious to the hilarious patter of Don Curzio's ruling and the Count's conniptions. The musical group hug is used to further comedy, all of the serious content of Beaumarchais's original removed:

Marcellina (embracing Figaro).	Riconosci in questo amplesso Una madre, amato figlio.	Recognize your mother in this embrace, my beloved son.
Figaro (to Bartolo).	Padre mio, fate lo stesso: Non mi fate più arrossir.	My father, do the same: do not make me blush any longer.
Bartolo (embracing Figaro).	Resistenza la coscienza Far non lascia al tuo desir.	My conscience will not let me deny your wish.
Don Curzio (aside).	Ei suo padre, ella sua madre: L'imeneo non può seguir.	He is his father, she is his mother: the marriage cannot take place.
Count (aside).	Son smarrito, son stordito Meglio è assai di qua partir.	I am at a loss and bewildered: better to make a quick exit.
Marcellina.	Figlio amato!	Beloved son!
Bartolo.	Figlio amato!	Beloved son!
Figaro.	Parenti amati!	Beloved parents!
	The Count makes to leave. Susanna enters with a purse in her hand.	
Susanna (stopping the Count).	Alto, alto, signor Conte Mille doppie son qui pronte. A pagar vengo per Figaro, ed a porlo in libertà.	Stop, stop, Lord Count: I've got a thousand double crowns here; I have come to pay for Figaro and to set him free.
Count and Don Curzio.	Non sappiam com'è la cosa: Osservate un poco là.	We don't understand what is happening: Look over there.

Marcellina.	Figlio amato!	Beloved son!
Bartolo.	Figlio amato!	Beloved son!
Figaro.	Parenti amati!	Beloved parents!

At the end of the sextet, the libretto finally reconnects Marcellina with the take-charge Marceline of act 3. When Susanna sees her fiancé gazing fondly at Marcellina, she assumes he has decided to marry the "old woman" and gives him a smack in the face. In her vexation, she aligns herself musically with the Count and the sycophantic Don Curzio. The resulting trio of dotted-eighth-note indignation seems even more frenetic against the slow-moving, chorale-like texture adopted by Figaro and his parents, who have joined together again, this time in appreciation of Susanna: "It is all because of her good heart: what she did was completely out of love." Suddenly, Marcellina steps away from Figaro and Bartolo. She embraces Susanna, unbalancing the neatly divided parties and traversing the musical and physical divide between them. Her musical line, a lilting gavotte, reestablishes the tonic key, F major: "Lo sdegno calmate, mia cara figliuola, sua madre abbracciate, che or vostra sarà" ("Now calm your anger, my dear daughter; embrace his mother, who will now be yours as well"). Love, both discovered and recovered, transforms the former rival into another darling child for Marcellina, completing the family circle she has desired for so long.

Mozart and Da Ponte do not pay particular homage to the mother of Figaro in the sextet, but the ensemble does offer an understated portrayal of the "same, but different" Marcellina. There is even an audible change in her music. The opening melody to the words "Riconosci in questo amplesso," though not unpleasant, is noticeably constricted, a singsong phrase that never extends past a fourth and hovers around A, the third of tonic F major. The residual primness suggests that the former governess-housekeeper is still not completely comfortable with her new role (Ex. 25). Her music at "Now calm your anger, my dear daughter; embrace his mother, who will now be yours as well" is a completely different story, familiar, yet new. It combines elements of both the sextet opening and the catfight duet with Susanna (Ex. 26), with maternal benevolence (and the addition of woodwinds to her standard strings-only accompaniment) warming what was once mincing peevishness. Hugging Susanna, "mia cara figliuola," the housekeeper exhibits a delight that is anything but tentative. She punctuates her gracious invitation to Susanna—"sua madre abbracciate, che or vostra sarà"—with an ebullient phrase that finally has tonic-tone conviction, its rainbow shape

EXAMPLE 25. *Le nozze di Figaro,* No. 19, "Riconosci in questo amplesso";
mm. 1–5

EXAMPLE 26. *Le nozze di Figaro,* No. 5, "Via resti servita, madama brillante"

arching up to high F before descending gracefully to the tonic an octave
below (Ex. 27).

There is another of these "inverted" textual echoes a few scenes later,
when Marcellina watches her son stomp off in jealous anger "to avenge
all husbands" (4.4). Left alone, she immediately resolves to help Susanna. In the recitative preceding her aria, she recalls with tenderness
"that face, that air of modesty," words that hearken back to the taunt
she directed at Figaro's beloved in act 1, "With those modest eyes, with
that pious air, and then . . ." It is interesting to note that in the recitative
supporting Susanna, at the words "And even if she is not [innocent],"
the C-major dominant-seventh chord suddenly swerves away from the
expected F major, touching instead on A major, the key of the catfight
duet. But this harmonic surprise does not signal a return of Marcellina's

EXAMPLE 27. *Le nozze di Figaro*, No. 19, "Riconosci in questo amplesso"; mm. 74–80

acrimony—quite the contrary. The possibility that Susanna might be culpable only makes Marcellina more protective. Paraphrasing Beaumarchais, Marcellina proclaims her dedication to (provisional) sisterhood: "Ah, when the heart is not mobbed by personal interest, every woman is moved to defend her poor sex so wrongly oppressed by these ungrateful men." Following this recitative, Mozart and Da Ponte inserted the aria "Il capro e la capretta" (4.4.25). This aria lacks the truculent force of Marceline's censure of men's abuse and hypocrisy, but it still communicates the basic message in a style that is consistent with the opera's lighter treatment of the character:

Il capro e la capretta	The goat and the nanny goat
Son sempre in amistà;	are always friends;
L'agnello all'agnelletta	the ram never wages war
La guerra mai non fa;	against the ewe;
Le più feroci belve	The most ferocious beasts
Per selve e per compagne	in the forests or the country
Lascian le lor compagne	leave their mates
In pace e libertà	in peace and liberty.

Sol noi, povera femmine,	Only we poor women,
Che tanto amiam questi uomini,	though we love these men so dearly,
Trattate siam dai perfidi	are treated by all of them
Ognor con crudeltà.	with cruelty and treachery.

"Il capro e la capretta" has long been dismissed along with Basilio's "In quegl'anni" (4.5.26) as a formal banality, fulfilling the obligation of eighteenth-century opera to give every significant character an aria. Until fairly recently, both numbers were regularly cut from productions. Spike Hughes, writing in 1940, explains that he only refers to these arias "because although one rarely hears them in the theatre, they are included in most gramophone recordings of the opera";[7] even today, Marcellina's aria is sometimes omitted in performance.[8] This omission is a mistake, both in terms of dramatic structure and of character development. Not only does Marcellina's aria provide a potentially stirring response to Figaro's knee-jerk vow to "avenge all husbands," it is strongly tied to the essential theme of female friendship as comfort and protection against (male) injustice. As Beaumarchais himself indicated with regard to Marceline's speech, the responsibility lies with the performer to make it work. The graceful musical style of the aria—it is marked *Tempo di Menuetto*—may tempt singers and directors to treat the seriousness of the subject with refined reserve. Too frequently in performance, Marcellina's tale comes off as tepid posturing, a kind of *seria* "lite." But it is precisely the inter- and cross-relations between words, text, and subtext that make "Il capro e la capretta" interesting and is crucial to realizing its full dramatic impact. Figaro employed a comparable tactic with "Se vuol ballare," his minuet an ironically genteel bow as he promises to lead his lordship in a dance he will not forget. His mother's aria can—and should—generate the same tension if sung by a true soprano and capable actor.

At first, the number reinforces the *vecchia pedante* side of Marcellina. With her pretensions to scholarliness, Marcellina does not speak directly but instead quotes poetry with a long and special tradition behind it; it is her erudite version of the pastorale.[9] Allanbrook reasons that Mozart did not set it as a traditional $\frac{6}{8}$ pastorale, since parading Marcellina in "panniers and bonnets would be too much of a burlesque for his purposes."[10] Robert Moberly proposes that "Il capro e la capretta" can be "very effective when sung and played as meaningful parody of the music of an older generation," and indeed there is something slightly vintage about Marcellina's moralizing minuet.[11] This is not, however, merely precious affectation. Marcellina's paraphrase of Ariosto[12] and her prim dance rhythms set up a context of civility, decorousness, and temperate behavior, behavior that effectively opposes the Count's, Bartolo's, and even Figaro's ungrateful boorishness.

After the restrained civility of the opening minuet, the Allegro should burn with the same spirit that marks Marceline's speech in act 3. A *sforzando* tremolo in the violins at the repeat of the words "Le più feroci belve / Per selve e per compagne" (mm. 44–48) introduces an ominous tone to Marcellina's "lecture." The harmony turns to the tonic minor at "Lascian le lor compagne / In pace e libertà" (mm. 49–52), with the half cadence lingering on the palpably pathetic augmented-sixth chord. The music anticipates the message of the Allegro: of all the creatures on earth, only women are treated in such a consistently bestial manner by the men they love. These words must be sung with the conviction of a woman who knows from experience this brand of cruelty. Her old-fashioned, Handelian musical style suits her personality and the gravity of her rebuke, very much like Donna Elvira's "Ah fuggi il traditor": opera seria still held a certain dramatic clout, even in Mozart's day. In fact, an opera seria heroine is probably not a bad place for the singer of this number to get her inspiration. With the right mixture of vocal conviction and dramatic staging, a gesture such as Marcellina's repeated ascent to high G at "Le più feroci belve" (mm. 45–47) can keenly evoke horror at a lover's cold indifference—or a husband's raised hand. Marcellina's typical bourrée rhythms return in the Allegro, but this section retains some of the *seria* umbrage, culminating in the coloratura exclamations at "ognor crudeltà": *every one of them treats us with cruelty.* The vocal melody rises to a sustained high B-flat, elevated by the kind of exalted, virtuous pride Beaumarchais wanted to convey in Marceline's speech. To carry it off, however, the singer had better direct those coloratura fulminations at every Count Almaviva and Bartolo in the hall with true opera seria outrage.

"Il capro e la capretta" demonstrates even more clearly than the sextet just how consistent Marcellina's characterization is. The pedantic mode of expression, fusty mannerisms, and sharp tongue that typify her early scenes appear in a new and much more sympathetic context in her aria. She has hardly become the excessively kindhearted and indulgent mother of sentimental drama, for there is still something prickly about her. Her indictment against men rings with a shrill indignation that the Countess would never dare to express so bluntly, and she is quick to place herself in a defensive position when even her son starts acting like

one of the guys. Figaro will thank her later, for it is clear she is now acting in his best interest. This makes all the difference.

HISTORY REPEATS ITSELF: BARBARINA

It should be remembered that Marcellina was quite young when infatuation led her into an amorous affair with a man of higher station. Hers
is a faded beauty, weathered by Bartolo's disavowal and condescending
indifference. However, there is an echo in the opera of the youthful,
naïve Marcellina, namely Barbarina, who seems to be headed for the
same fate. Long before we see her, we hear about the gardener's young
daughter (who is also Susanna's cousin) from Cherubino. He sadly tells
Susanna about how the Count found him alone with the girl and sum-
marily dismissed him from service (1.5). A little while later, the Count
himself confirms the story, offering more details: "Yesterday I found
your cousin's door locked: I knocked, and Barbarina opened it, looking
more fearful than usual. Her expression raised my suspicions. I look
around, searching everywhere, and slowly raising the cloth from the
table, I see the page!" (1.7.7).

In Beaumarchais's play, Comte Almavive is amused by Suzanne's
caustic rejoinder that he "no doubt had business" with her cousin—
named Fanchette—but he casually dismisses the charge, explaining that
he had only been looking for her father, Antonio. Later, however, we
learn that even twelve-year-old Fanchette is not below his lordship's
sexual radar screen.[13] When the Comte threatens to send Chérubin
packing for good, little Fanchette steps in to save her darling, saying,
"Oh, my lord, listen to me. All the times that you come to kiss me, you
know what you always say to me: 'If you will love me, little Fanchette,
I will give you anything you want.'" Da Ponte's libretto retains these
lines (3.12), exposing the repellent reach of the Count's libertine desire.
Barbarina's careless revelation also demonstrates a transition—typical
for fictional servant-class girls—from credulous innocence to self-
protecting guile. Da Ponte pointedly draws attention to the advent of
Barbarina's pubescence, her half-aware participation in adult games.
Her father, Antonio, cheers her on when she turns the tables on her
much-older seducer, saying, "Good girl! You have a good master teaching you your lessons!" In the next act, Figaro grumbles about Barbarina's early skill at courtly intrigue; when the girl lets slip (accidentally
on purpose) about the pin the Count has sent back to Susanna, Figaro

remarks caustically, "At such a tender age, you already know how to do your business as well as you do?"

Though Barbarina's is a small role, she attracts notice precisely because of this child-woman ambiguity. Describing her arietta, "L'ho perduta," which opens act 4, Edward Dent comments, "Her *naïveté* adds by force of contrast to the spirit of sinister intrigue that dominates the last act, perhaps all the more because we can never feel quite sure how far the *naïveté* is genuine."[14] Her hands-on "lessons" with Cherubino *and* the Count have taught her to use her few valued assets—sexual appeal and a willingness to serve—to gain advantages. She is childishly pleased by her master's attentions—and accepts his manipulative kisses-for-favors bargaining at face value—but her first love is the young page, and she takes a number of risks for him during the opera. When we first see her onstage, she is taking Cherubino to her house to disguise him as a girl so that he can remain at the castle until Almaviva's temper cools: "Let's go handsome page: at my house you will find all the prettiest girls in the castle, and you will certainly be the prettiest of them all" (3.7). After the Count catches on to their trick, Barbarina reminds her master about his debt for those kisses: "Master, now give me Cherubino as my husband, and I will love you as much as I love my kitten." She swaps another kiss as payment for food to bring to her fugitive sweetheart after he goes into hiding: "Oh, what nice people! I had trouble getting just one orange, one pear, and a doughnut from them! . . . The master hates him, and I love him! But it cost me a kiss . . . And who cares? Maybe someone will give it back to me" (4.5). It is possible that the kiss she lost to a kitchen worker was only an innocent peck on the cheek, but Barbarina's adolescent yearning for *Cherubino d'amore*—from whom she hopes out loud to get a more pleasurable kiss in return—adds an erotic undercurrent to the monologue.

In one sense, the infatuated girl is like her cousin Susanna, scheming to protect her beloved, even against her master's and her father's orders. The original play makes specific reference to the punishment the child has already endured for her rash affection, when Bazile cautions the page about his dalliance: "Be careful, young man, be careful! Her father is not happy; the girl has had her face slapped. It is not studying that she has been doing with you. Chérubin! Chérubin! You will bring her to grief!" (1.11). The singing master alludes to the exact nature of this "grief" with a twisted proverb, "If a pitcher goes too often to the water . . . it gets filled." Unlike Susanna, Barbarina is ruled more by emotional impulse than good sense. She is too young to understand that her dreams of marrying Cherubino are nonsense, that class considerations alone would keep them apart, not to mention his not-so-secret obsession for his godmother. The gardener's daughter is a sweet diversion for Cherubino, but she will never be Rosina Almaviva.

This status as second- (or even third-) class lover is another link between Barbarina and Marcellina. The older woman was Rosina's governess for many years in Bartolo's home and had to witness her exlover's unsuccessful suit for her beautiful pupil's hand in marriage. Barbarina would do well to study this image of the young Marcellina. Da Ponte cut the references to "pitchers being filled" and paternal smacks; comic opera does not allow much time for considering the suffering or perils of secondary characters. However, Barbarina's little cavatina "L'ho perduta" conveys some of the poignancy of her situation, if only as innuendo. When the curtain opens on act 4, we see Barbarina alone in the garden, anxiously searching for something in the twilight gloom:

L'ho perduta . . . me meschina,	I lost it . . . poor me!
ah chi sà dove sarà?	Oh, who knows where it can be?
Non la trovo . . . E mia cugina . . .	I can't find it . . . And my
e il padron	cousin . . . and the master,
Cosa dirà?	what will he say?

This cavatina (in F minor) is one of only two minor mode numbers in the opera.[15] Barbarina's little piece exhibits the pastoral sweetness and high-pathos musical gestures that characterize the music of the Countess and, to a lesser extent, Cherubino. However, the cavatina also connects with Marcellina's upcoming aria, "Il capro e la capretta."[16] Both numbers are scored for strings only and exploit analogous blends of affectation and sincerity. Moreover, they present a dialogue of sorts. "L'ho perduta," frets the girl, and Marcellina answers by example and song: Barbarina stands to lose much more than a pin. The phrase "L'ho perduta" refers to a feminine object—in this case, the little pin or *spilla*—but there are more ominous possibilities as well: *innocenza, verginità, giovinezza*. Marcellina was dispossessed of these effects— innocence, virginity, youth—long ago. Barbarina, her arms loaded with sweet cakes and fruit bought with a kiss, is rushing down the same path. She represents the very type of vulnerable maiden that Beaumarchais claims to defend when he penned Marceline's confession, pointing to "the true culprits responsible for the licentiousness to which so many lower-class girls with a pretty face are driven."

"Il capro e la capretta" is an indictment of these same "true culprits," but it also emanates from Marcellina's new sense of belonging. Recognizing—and being recognized by—her son, Marcellina finally secures the affection and regard she has long desired, and not just from Figaro. Envy kept her from the friendship of women, but she now takes her place happily in the company of her mistress and her future daughter in-law. She even manages to redeem Bartolo's marriage voucher, though this is probably more about social legitimacy than love. Those who pooh-pooh her transformation as unbelievable and unmotivated cannot have thought much about the importance of being fulfilled after years of deprivation, of being acknowledged as something more than "servant," "old woman," and "decrepit witch." Figaro calls her "Mother" now and turns to her for comfort and advice instead of loans. Susanna embraces and trusts her. Bartolo gives her his hand. The wit and goodwill of Marcellina, now unshackled from resentment, comes to the fore, helping to save the day. Her transformation reverses the allusion to loss in Barbarina's lament: instead, Marcellina seems to say, "L'ho trovata!" *I have found it.*

CHAPTER 9

Sisterhood and Seduction III: Intimacy and Influence

Fiordiligi and Dorabella

Ah, where are those days when those feelings were all hon-
ourable, when I was untroubled by those now causing me
such dreadful turmoil and rendering me powerless to control
them while at the same time making it my duty to do so?

> Madame de Tourvel, in *Les liaisons dangereuses*

The thing I blame myself for most, I'm afraid I've got to tell
you, is that I've got a dreadful feeling I didn't resist him as
much as I could have done. I don't know what happened, I
certainly don't love Monsieur de Valmont, quite the opposite,
yet there were moments when I felt as if I did.

> Cécile Volanges, in *Les liaisons dangereuses*

Two young women, the only pair of biological sisters in Mozart's operas, sit together in the morning sun, each gazing dreamily at their
lover's portrait.[1] In a few moments they will take part in a peculiar type
of school, but—having missed the orientation—they will not realize this
until the class is over. Like Pamina, Fiordiligi and Dorabella are the necessary but unwitting participants in a special tutorial, in which experienced (male) reason will strip idealistic (male) youth of its delusions
about love and reveal the true nature of women: *così fan tutte*. Theoretically, the sisters learn something, too, in the process. The opera's
subtitle, "La scuola degli amanti," is gender ambivalent, neither confirming nor denying that this is primarily a boys' school. Bruce Alan
Brown reminds us that Da Ponte himself always referred to the opera as
La scuola degli amanti in his *Memoirs*; he also reckons that "there was

good reason for his circumscription" since the librettist intended his chronicle "for a public consisting primarily of his own female students of Italian, who no doubt would be scandalized by a phrase such as 'così fan tutte', and by any explanation of its premise."[2]

Brown does not specify why Da Ponte's female students might have been offended, or whether these reasons would hold for women today. Instead, he cites the librettist's preference as a basis for framing the opera's moral in terms of co-ed education, proposing, "If we put aside for a moment the more secondary aspects of philosophy in *Così*, there remains a core of ideas on love, fidelity, and enlightenment for which models can readily be found in the writings of the eighteenth-century *philosophes*." He states that the entire opera "is premised on Rousseau's notion that experience precedes understanding," so that "Alfonso cannot simply tell the soldiers that women are inconstant, or the sisters that they know precious little about love. If they are to truly learn his lessons, they must experience the pain that comes from being undeceived of their initial notions."[3] Brown concludes that "così fan tutti" does not represent the true theme of the opera, which Mozart and Da Ponte expressed instead in the final "generous message of reconciliation": "Happy is he who looks on the bright side of things, and in all cases lets himself be guided by reason. May that which makes others weep be for him a cause to laugh, and amidst the storms of this world he will find perfect calm."[4]

Before determining what it is that the sisters learn, we might consider first whether, as Brown suggests, Don Alfonso intended to teach the sisters anything at all: in other words, how, what, and why are the girls "taught"? Many writers have concluded that Don Alfonso offers, explicitly or implicitly, a complementary and ultimately useful education for the women as well as the men. Mary Hunter concludes, "the original lovers unite because there is, as Don Alfonso implies, a lesson in wisdom to be learned from clear-eyed acceptance of what is given; and pain is an inevitable part of wisdom."[5] Along the same lines, Andrew Steptoe identifies the "underlying purpose of the entire plot" as disproving the "romantic, idealistic convention that lovers are made for each other, and that passion is immutable."[6] William Mann argues that the wager is the result of the keen foresight of Don Alfonso, who predicts the unhappiness that follows couples that are "too hastily married," only to grow apart; he wants to show them that "an infatuation is delightful, but must be fed and nurtured before it ripens into an abiding love."[7] Noting that the opera's main title was a "late afterthought of Mozart," Daniel Heartz explains that "Alfonso's 'School for Lovers' is . . . compulsory for both sexes," since all four young people "need to be cured of their ridiculous notions about love and honor."[8] Dorothea Link observes that while "the lovers are initially shown to have an immature understanding of love," the test challenges the men's idealistic assumptions; their transformation into Albanians initiates "the road to self-discovery for all four lovers."[9]

All of these readings imagine a happy outcome to the men's chicanery, which is kicked off by a wager. The fundamental methodology of Don Alfonso's demonstration that "all women are the same," however, is deception, and he heavily rigs the outcome. Whatever they may or may not *learn*, Fiordiligi and Dorabella are explicitly *taught* only one thing: to conform to the motto of the main title so that the Ferrando and Guglielmo will acknowledge it as truth. Don Alfonso never addresses any instruction to the young women that would jeopardize this aim. Their "education" is merely a function of the men's: the women are told only what they need to believe in order to prove Don Alfonso's point. This is the place to start when judging the ladies' actions and when deciding the kind of wisdom they actually gain. It is also worth looking closely at the nature of their sisterhood, examining how it changes during their time at the "scuola degli amanti."

SEPARATE "TOGETHERNESS" AND SIBLING RIVALRY

The curtain opens on the masculine world of the act 1 *introduzione,* a trio of trios that lay out the conflict between rationalist Don Alfonso and his brash soldier friends, Ferrando and Guglielmo. The three men have gathered at the public coffeehouse, the perfect place for philosophical conversation and gentlemanly wagering. It is clear from the soldiers' angry protests that Don Alfonso has questioned their fiancées' ability to remain faithful. Unruffled, the old man halfheartedly tries to beg off the argument when swords are drawn, but he presses his point in the end, paraphrasing Metastasio to suit his purposes: "The faithfulness of women is like the Arabian phoenix: everyone says that it exists, but no one knows where it is" (1.1.2).[10] Ferrando and Guglielmo each insist that his dearest is the very personification of this elusive phoenix, but their mentor only chuckles and asks them how they can be so sure. The soldiers spout off a list of platitudinous proofs: long acquaintance, noble education, sublime thoughts, compatibility, generosity of spirit, stable character, and the promises and protests of love. "Tears, sighs, caresses, swooning—allow me to laugh a little," jeers their companion, and it is he who then proposes the bet. The soldiers (proto-Taminos?) promise obedience and secrecy, and the test of women's constancy begins.

We are now introduced to the two young ladies, who are sitting in a garden near the Neapolitan seashore. The contrast with the *introduzione* is evident: the sisters sit isolated in an outdoor setting, far from the public bustle and debates of the coffeehouse. Like an eighteenth-century garden, the effect of the scene is both natural and contrived. The sisters' duet, "Ah guarda, sorella" (1.2.4), a blend of heavenly singing and the sophomoric language of infatuation, suits Don Alfonso's plan a little too perfectly. With unintentional but convenient irony, the ladies ask Love to condemn them for the very capriciousness the old man is counting on:

Fiordiligi.	Ah guarda, sorella,	Ah, look, sister,
	Se bocca più bella,	if you could ever find
	Se aspetto più nobile	a more beautiful mouth,
	Si può ritrovar.	a more noble face.
Dorabella.	Osserva tu un poco	Look here for a moment
	Che fuoco ha ne' sguardi!	at the fire in his glance!
	Se fiamma, se dardi	As if it were shooting
	Non sembran scoccar.	flames and arrows.
Fiordiligi.	Si vede un sembiante	One sees the look of a
	Guerriero ed amante.	warrior and lover.
Dorabella.	Si vede una faccia	One sees a face
	Che alletta e minaccia.	both alluring and threatening.
Both.	Io sono felice!	I am so happy!
	Se questo mio core	If ever my heart
	Mai cangia desio,	should change its affection,
	Amore mi faccia	may Love make me
	Vivendo penar	live in misery!

Despite the surface intimacy, the presentation of the ladies is clinically aloof. The two sisters—very likely teenagers or a little older—gush over their lovers' attractive faces without revealing more substantial reasons for their attachment: they do not even call their lovers by name. We are (purposefully?) kept from learning anything that might help us to understand their backgrounds and circumstances. Nicholas Till rightly explains, "in *Così fan tutte* we know nothing. We do not know how Fiordiligi and Dorabella come to be in Naples. They seem to have no parents (which places them metaphorically in the same position as Jane Austen's notoriously badly-parented heroines, but at the same time deprives them of some crucial co-ordinates of identity), and we have no idea of their economic or social status."[11] The "deliberate artifice and lack of external referents" place the characters "in a world of essences, hermetically sealed from the redeeming inconsistencies of the real world."[12] Hunter, too, argues that *Così*'s reference to the conventional household structure—in this case, the sisters and their maid—"actually serves to emphasize the separation from the clearly structured social world represented by most operas in their repertory," and "by negative relationship to that convention, defines its world almost exclusively in terms of the experiment."[13] None of the characters are much developed in terms of their background, but, as we shall see, it is precisely this social void around the women that allows Alfonso (and Despina) to guide their actions without interference. Significantly, Fiordiligi and Dorabella are denied a chief dramatic factor of the other Da Ponte operas and *Die Entführung aus dem Serail*: beneficial female counsel that facilitates a happy ending. They are sisters, of course, but this affiliation seems to be primarily a matter of dramatic expediency—both women can be approached and seduced in the same place—rather than a matter of genuine familial affection.

One word that pops up frequently in the reception literature about these two characters is "interchangeable"—not the kind of profound correspondence that the Countess and Susanna enjoy, but a generic sameness.[14] Till dedicates an entire discussion to the subject, arguing that *Così* was only one of many eighteenth-century works, including the plays of Marivaux, to "use a story of interchangeable lovers to deal with the problem of sexual desire that is not securely individuated." He also reminds us that, while the sisters are customarily cast as soprano and mezzo-soprano today, Mozart made no such distinction, "occasionally forgetting which sister was which when writing their names in the score."[15] The composer may not have been able to keep the names straight, but he certainly did not create Fiordiligi and Dorabella as mirror images, either vocally or dramatically. Singers definitely recognize the differences between the two roles, which are quite distinct in terms of range, technical demands, and affect. Mozart may not have been thinking explicitly in terms of mezzo-soprano and soprano, but he knew he was writing for two very different voices. The original Dorabella, Louise Villeneuve, had a darker timbre and lower tessitura than Adriana Ferrarese del Bene, who played Fiordiligi, yet her part stays within the same basic range as roles like Susanna and Zerlina, both of which are now customarily assigned to voices that fall into the higher, narrower vocal category of "soprano" as we understand it today. For her part, Ferrarese del Bene had a more expansive (if not always beautiful) range, with a formidable chest voice that Mozart showcased in much of Fiordiligi's music.

These distinctions are audible from the sisters' very first scene. Despite the abundant parallel singing, there are no exact melodic echoes in "Ah guarda, sorella"; the overall effect is that the roles are not so much interchangeable as complementary. This emphasis on Fiordiligi's lower range alters the usual soprano/mezzo-soprano dynamic, for regardless of whether Dorabella is sung by a mezzo-soprano or a soprano with a healthy middle range, in the end Fiordiligi is allotted the juiciest passages on both ends of the soprano spectrum, singing both higher *and* lower than her sister.[16] This vocal ascendancy is most noticeable during the closing Allegro, in which the sisters ask Love to stand as their judge for any infidelity (the very section that Brown cites as a "demonstration of [the sisters'] interchangeability"). For the first half of this section, they sing together mostly in thirds. Then Dorabella launches alone into a new idea, a graceful ascending arpeggio to a sustained E on "penar." Fiordiligi answers her with a vigorous and husky counterpoint, sweeping down repeatedly to low A. Hardly drawing breath, she alters Dorabella's arpeggio, raising the sustained note to a more impressive A above the staff. Dorabella gamely echoes her sister's jaunty countermelody, but up a fourth, in a moderate range that is comfortable for sopranos and mezzo-sopranos alike.

Besides the obvious vocal differences, there are dramatic factors that distinguish the women from one another, even at this early stage. Notwithstanding the idyllic setting and intimate tone, the scene of "Ah guarda, sorella" presents a complex dialectic of sisterly sharing and sibling rivalry. On one hand, the scene reinforces the sisters' sameness as "not male." The andante triple meter and A-major tonality diverge noticeably from the energetic duple rhythms and C-major triadic outline (C–G–E–C) of the men's introductory trios, yet the duet also subtly illuminates the space that separates the two women, a gap that will widen significantly in the course of the opera. When Fiordiligi beckons her sister to admire the likeness of Guglielmo—has she ever seen such a lovely mouth and noble face?—Dorabella counters by asking her sister to observe the fiery penetration of Ferrando's eyes. Characterizing her lover, each lady tries to distinguish herself as well.

The exchange reveals a potential competitiveness, particularly on Dorabella's part. In her first phrase, for example, Dorabella follows her sister's lead, balancing exactly Fiordiligi's initial seventeen-measure period and paraphrasing her florid cadence. The overall effect, however, is less transposed echo than intensified emulation. Skipping a transitional modulation, Dorabella begins firmly in the dominant key of E major and stays there. The musical sketch she creates of *her* lover is arguably more exciting than her sister's, with its vigorous staccato oscillations, syncopated rhythms in the strings, and martial patina of the horn pedal. Fiordiligi may have a pretty gentleman, but Dorabella's sweetheart is able to inflame, to penetrate the heart with his eyes alone! For her description of Ferrando's heart-piercing gaze, Dorabella borrows one of Fiordiligi's expressive markers, highlighting the world "dardi" with an exaggerated leap between registers.

Fiordiligi's next phrase continues the delicate game of one-upmanship. The gently swaying violins and slow bass pulse of her first line return, but Fiordiligi now takes up her sister's more virile imagery—"one sees the look of a warrior." At the word "guerriero," the placid string accompaniment abruptly transforms into a *seria* recitative exclamation (mm. 53–54), with dotted rhythms and trumpeting woodwinds. The unexpected style change dramatizes the soldier's commanding appearance, but—ah!—that is not all, dear sister. Sinking down a tenth, Fiordiligi lets out a voluptuous sigh, "a piacere," in her lower range, remembering Guglielmo as a gentle *amante* (mm. 54–55). Dorabella enters more quickly this time with a nearly symmetrical response, but she cannot resist piling on the (melo-)dramatic weight. Imitating Fiordiligi's shift to accompanied recitative, she extends the gesture another four measures and adds developmental tension by slipping into the tonic minor. The alluring melodic chromaticism, fierce dotted rhythms, and sharp contours of the violin line illustrate Ferrando's dual nature, both enticing and frightening. Dorabella's half cadence leaves open the possibility of another round of adulation, but the sisters choose instead to join voices for the first time, united in their love of being in love.

There is nothing in the duet akin to the thoughtful alliance between the Countess Almaviva and Susanna, who, in their first scene together—"Vieni, cara Susanna," beckons the Countess—hold a real conversation, one that recognizes "you" as much as "I." Gushing together over their portraits, Fiordiligi and Dorabella interact superficially with an undercurrent of competition. Neither of the sisters actually acknowledges the other's enthusiasm; they answer each other only by complementing their own beaus. The common circumstances, the parallel singing, and the collective appeal to Amore merely impart the semblance of closeness.

The casualness of the sisters' relationship works all the better for Don Alfonso's demonstration: when the girls go to school they will pay more attention to him and Despina than to each other.

A BAD EDUCATION FOR YOUNG LADIES: PART I

The sisters' schooling begins with a subterfuge, as Don Alfonso, the master thespian, comes staggering into their home with "fatal" news: Ferrando and Guglielmo have been called to battle (1.3.5). In the quintet that follows ("Sento, o Dio, che questo piede"; 1.4.6) the soldiers enter, trembling and faltering, to say their final goodbyes. Don Alfonso's mocking words from the coffeehouse—"tears, sighs, caresses, swooning"—come to life as Fiordiligi and Dorabella express their misery, ordering their darlings to "be brave and plunge your swords into our hearts." They beg Ferrando and Guglielmo not to abandon them. "I would rather tear out my heart!" cries Dorabella. "I would sooner die at your feet," moans Fiordiligi. In the succeeding recitative, each lady imagines what she will do if her beloved is killed on the field. Fiordiligi will slay herself with Guglielmo's sword; Dorabella exclaims that a sword would not even be necessary for her, since she would die from grief alone. A military chorus announces that the soldiers' boat is leaving, but the ladies have not finished saying goodbye. In the quintet "Di scrivermi ogni giorno" (1.5.9), Fiordiligi implores Guglielmo to write to her every day, choking out the words between sobs. The equally weepy Dorabella, not to be outdone, presses Ferrando to write *twice* a day if he can.

While the men soothe their disconsolate fiancées, Don Alfonso stands aside, almost convulsing with contained laughter at the lovers' protracted goodbye. His glee is mean-spirited: he has set this up, after all. Nevertheless, the scene is undeniably caricatural. The sisters' threats of self-violence and pleas for death by the sword come straight from a novel (or an opera seria libretto), mimicking the overwrought language of romantic fiction. In fact, the effect of such literary stimulation on girls' imaginations was a subject of some concern in the eighteenth century. In his didactic work *A Father's Legacy to his Daughters* (1774), John Gregory warned young ladies to "shun as you would do the most fatal poison, all that species of reading and conversation which warms the imagination, which engages and softens the heart, and raises the taste above the common life."[17] In his admonition to young ladies, John Burton is more specific and more damning:

That course of Reading must be unprofitable, which is confined to Novels;
and this, I am apprehensive, is too much the case with your Sex. . . . There
are but few Novels, which have a tendency to give a right turn to the affections; or, at least, are calculated to improve the mind. . . . [I]n most Novels,
there is a similarity in the incidents and characters; and these perhaps are
unnatural, or seldom to be found in real life: so that young Women, who
apply themselves to this sort of Reading, are liable to many errors, both in
conduct and conversation, from the romantic notions they will thence
imbibe.[18]

Maria Edgeworth, herself a novelist, wrote in *Practical Education*
(1798) that "sentimental stories, and books of mere entertainment
. . . should be sparingly used, especially in the education of girls," since
"this species of reading cultivates what is called the heart prematurely,
lowers the tone of mind, and induces indifferences for those common
pleasures and occupations which, however trivial in themselves, consti-
tute by far the greatest portion of our daily happiness."[19] Young women
who become "addicted to common novel-reading are always acting in
imitation of some Jemima or Almeria, who never existed, and they per-
petually mistake plain William and Thomas for 'My Beverly!' They have
another peculiar misfortune; they require continual great emotions to
keep them in tolerable humour with themselves; they must have tears
in their eyes, or they are apprehensive that their hearts are growing
hard."[20]

Abandoning themselves to the *ideas* of grief and death, Fiordiligi and
Dorabella are perfect examples of Edgeworth's prematurely cultivated
heart. Their "bad education" seems to have reinforced the very excesses
that Don Alfonso scorns. Ferrando and Guglielmo prize their lovers' per-
fervid sensibility, identifying it with strong (feminine) attachment, but
Don Alfonso turns it to his advantage. It is he, in fact, who sets the tone
for the sisters' melodramatic farewell. He breaks the news to them about
the soldiers' imminent departure in the stammering allegro agitato aria
"Vorrei dir, e cor non ho," a parody of *seria* wretchedness: "I want to tell
you, but I do not have the heart. My mouth stutters; my voice will not
come out, but remains stuck in my throat. What will you do? What will
I do? Oh, what a terrible blow! It could not be worse: I have pity for you
and for them!" (1.3.5). Not surprisingly, the sisters are alarmed, and, in
the subsequent recitative, they ask if their young men are dead. As Brown
remarks, Don Alfonso is "sadistically slow to allay the women's fears,"
warning that they must summon all their strength.[21] Using an inverted
syntax, he finally answers, "Dead . . . they are not, but little better than
dead." The old man himself plants the dreadful thought in the ladies'

minds, equating the call to battle with the grave: as tragic heroines they will be all the more susceptible to both sentiment and seduction.

Like Sarastro in the act 2 trio in *Die Zauberflöte* ("Soll ich dich Teurer, nicht mehr sehn?"), Don Alfonso mediates the communication between the couples in the ensuing goodbye quintet (No. 6), his bass voice acting as chaperon whenever the lovers sing together. In a sense, everyone is playacting, consciously or unconsciously, taking their cues from books, librettos, and Don Alfonso. (Ferrando cannot even think of anything original when he first speaks to Dorabella, but paraphrases Alfonso's aria, explaining that his trembling lips cannot form a word.) The philosopher is very much in control, promoting the impression of woeful misfortune. He asserts himself as the women's paternal consoler, though earlier they referred to him only as a friend of Ferrando and Guglielmo. He pretends to have sympathy for their tears (announcing, after the first quintet, "Let them get it all out: they have good reason to cry") and, after the men leave, exhorts the "dearest girls" to be brave. He even joins them in their prayer for the soldiers' safe voyage, the trio "Soave sia il vento," a celebrated example of Mozart's zephyr music.[22]

This is not to say that Don Alfonso's cynicism completely dominates these scenes. There are musical moments during the farewell that express genuine emotion, a feminine space over which Don Alfonso does not have full control. In the second farewell quintet, No. 9, "Di scrivermi," the old philosopher's sardonic asides are not sufficient to undermine the pathetic beauty of the lovers' music. In the poignant minor-key-inflected development section beginning with Fiordiligi's "Sii constante a me sol!" ("Be true to me alone!"; mm. 7–23), Don Alfonso is silenced altogether. The quintet becomes a quartet as each of the lovers says goodbye before joining together, chorale-like, at "You are breaking my heart in two, my darling." The exaggerated rhetoric of the first quintet abates, approaching a more natural intimacy and sincere grief. There is no more talk of impalement, just tears and requests for letters and faithfulness. Don Alfonso is forced to play it straight, musically at least, in "Soave sia il vento" as well. This prayerful trio, too, places the women in the foreground. There are no pattering chuckles or jibing asides. Discussing this number, Hunter remarks that most critics, "in their helplessness in the face of Mozart's unbelievably gorgeous music," have generally abandoned "any attempt to make dramatic sense of the gorgeousness," leaving "both the characters and Da Ponte behind." She reasons that despite the exceptional musical qualities of these numbers—their cantabile stillness—"they are an essential part of its dramaturgy" in that they "crystallize the eternally ambiguous relation between sympathy and ridicule that is one of the opera's principal topics." In the end, sensitive listeners cannot help but recognize "the tension between the expressive qualities of these moments in *Così fan tutte* and their dramatic circumstances, or the contradiction between the truth implied by the music and the trick being played in the drama."[23]

The truth versus the trick: in these numbers the music is inextricably linked to the women's emotional world, and to the beauty of feeling itself, which the male lovers cannot completely resist. Are the soldiers starting to feel uncomfortable about this hurtful charade? Are we? Both "Di scrivermi" and "Soave sia il vento" highlight the ethical ambivalence of Don Alfonso's curriculum: is such calculated deceit *funny?* Don Alfonso seems to think so. At the closing cadence of the quintet "Di scrivermi"—having been discreetly silent during the couples' more private quartet section—he pops back just in time to reassure us that everything is all right, that he finds the whole scene uproariously comical. His remark in the recitative after "Soave sia il vento"—"I am not a bad actor after all"—is dissociated from the trio itself, and therefore its "capacity to ironize the beauty" of the number is considerably weakened.[24] But Alfonso is a master at getting the last word. After the ladies leave the stage, he offers a scornful assessment of their behavior, and while it is doubtful that his cynicism can completely nullify the affective power of the trio, his words, at the very least, attempt to restore his place as the opera's authoritative spokesperson:

Quante smorfie!	What grimaces!
Quante buffonerie!	What carrying on!
Tanto meglio per me . . .	All the better for me . . .
Cadran più facilmente:	They'll fall more easily:
Questa razza di gente è la più presta	this kind of person is the quickest
A cangiarsi d'umore. Oh, poverini!	to change mood. Oh, poor boys!
Per femmina giocar cento	Who would bet a hundred sequins
zecchini?	on a woman?

Pressing the point further, he sums up his feelings with an arioso proverb: "Whoever puts his hope in a woman's heart plows the sea, sows the sandy arena, and hopes to catch the wind in his net." Alfonso does not so much ironize as dismiss a woman's potential for the kind of emotional truth connoted by the gorgeous music of "Di scrivermi" and "Soave sia il vento." Alfonso has not yet seen (or heard) any compelling evidence that his theory is off beam: for now, *le femmine* are behaving as expected—and taught.

QUANTE SMORFIE! QUANTE BUFFONERIE!

The next two scenes (1.8–1.9) take us into a sanctuary of the women's world, a pleasing salon where the maid, Despina, is stirring her mistresses' chocolate. Despina complains to herself about life as a servant: she does all of the work and gets none of the rewards. Suddenly, her mistresses enter *disperatamente*, still in their most tragic mode. Once again the quality of their education comes into question. Swept away by emotion, Dorabella throws the entire tray of carefully prepared chocolate to the floor, and both sisters tear off their fine jewelry. "What has happened?" cries Despina, astounded. Fiordiligi responds by asking whether a dagger or some poison may be lying about. More rudely, Dorabella turns on the maid in a splenetic accompanied recitative: "Stand back! Fear the sad effect of a desperate passion! Close the windows! I hate the light, I hate the air that I breathe, I hate myself. Who mocks my pain, who consoles me? Go on, get out of here, for mercy's sake, leave me alone!" She continues her diatribe in the allegro agitato aria, No. 11:

Smanie implacabili	Relentless pains
Che m'agitate,	that agitate
Entro quest'anima	in my soul,
Più non cessate	do not cease
Finché l'angoscia	until I am dead
Mi fa morir!	from anguish!
Esempio misero	I will give to the Furies,
D'amor funesto	if I am still alive,
Darò all'Eumenidi,	a miserable example
Se viva resto,	of fatal love
Col suono orribile	with the horrible sound
De' miei sospir!	of my sighs!

Dorabella's *scena* appropriates idioms from Metastasio, Ariosto, and Mozart's own *Idomeneo*. Heartz notes, for instance, the textual parallels between "Smanie implacabili" and Elettra's final recitative and aria, "D'Oreste, d'Aiace ho in seno i tormenti," with its references to sempiternal wailing, the Eumenides, and death wishes. Elettra's aria also "has a turning figure, repeated incessantly in the strings like a haunting obsession, which probably gave Mozart the idea to do something similar in accompanying the raving Dorabella."[25] One fundamental difference, obviously, is the context: *Così fan tutte* is not an opera seria. Elettra has lost her country to war, her mother, father, and sister to murder (by family members), her brother to exile, and the man she loves to an-

EXAMPLE 28. *Idomeneo*, No. 29, "D'Oreste, d'Aiace"; mm. 55–63

other woman. The combined misfortunes drive her to insanity, and her music reflects her understandably nightmarish perspective. Dorabella only *simulates* this musical language for her paroxysm, and her lack of fluency and spontaneity are apparent.

In Dorabella's amateur hands, the careful balance of repetition and variation found in Elettra's aria crosses the line into excess. For instance, in "D'Oreste, d'Aiace," the tortured turn figure appears exclusively with the first poetic quatrain and its repetition; the churning violins of Dorabella's gasping *smorfie*, on the other hand, persist for almost all of the 102 measures of "Smanie implacabili," stopping only briefly (mm. 89–93) to "accompany Dorabella down to her private hell at the words 'col suono orribile.'"[26] A comparison of the climactic passages of the two arias reveals the same attenuating flaw, Dorabella's limited *seria* vocabulary. Elettra's desperate plea for death ("il dolore in me finirà") occurs just two times in "D"Oreste, d'Aiace," the first of which is set rather simply: an emphatic fourth leap up to a sustained high G, which slides up (painfully?) to A on the same syllable (Ex. 28). When this text

EXAMPLE 29. *Idomeneo*, No. 29, "D'Oreste, d'Aiace"; mm. 109–21

returns (mm. 96–127), Elettra erupts into syncopated and chromatic coloratura; the screaming vocal climb to high C and cackling staccato fall completes her disintegration into madness (Ex. 29). Conversely, Dorabella reaches her expressive peak early—the "suono orribile" of her sighs—then repeats the gesture twice with relatively simple alterations and nothing like the intensification of Elettra's aria. In the first instance, the vocal line rises with an arpeggio followed by an emphatic chromatic slide (G–G-flat–F), with the highest note on the natural accent, "or*ri*bile." The diminished chord on the G-flat is the only disso-

EXAMPLE 30. *Così fan tutte*, No. 11, "Smanie implacabili"; mm. 30–35

nance in what is otherwise a bright major-triad cadential phrase (Ex. 30). The second occurrence reverses the formula: the vocal line leaps to G-flat then presses upward toward G and A (Ex. 31). There is more harmonic angst this time (E-flat minor to F minor by way of a diminished-seventh chord), but the colorizing effect of G-flat is starting to wear thin; only seven measures earlier, Dorabella used the same tone (with a Neapolitan chord) to heighten the implications of "funesto." By the time we arrive at the final "suono orribile" (mm. 88–93), the G-flat has become a cliché. Even with an increasingly tortured harmonic progression, the melodic climax is amusingly predictable. Dorabella's declamation in this instance furthers the ironic effect, with the *sforzando* G-flat overaccentuating the final syllable of "orribile" (Ex. 32). This discordant rhetorical gaffe (which occurred less noticeably in measure 81 as well) stuns the orchestra into near silence. After the fermata, Dorabella corrects herself in a deliberate phrase paralleled in octaves by appropriately gloomy-sounding flutes and clarinets. Once she restores the proper emphasis, the string churning starts up again, propelling her to the end of the aria.

EXAMPLE 31. *Così fan tutte,*, No. 11, "Smanie implacabili"; mm. 70–75

EXAMPLE 32. *Così fan tutte*, No. 11, "Smanie implacabili"; mm. 88–93

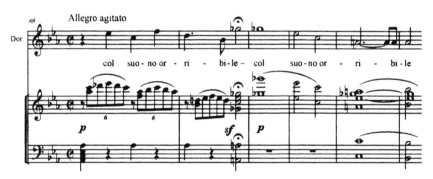

A BAD EDUCATION FOR YOUNG LADIES: PART II

Clearly, in "Smanie implacabili," Mozart treats the *seria* language iron-ically: it is simply too heavy for the circumstances and immaturely exe-cuted. However, as already mentioned, it is not the first *seria* parody in the opera. Just a few scenes before "Smanie implacabili," Don Alfonso effectively modeled overripe *seria* affect for the two sisters in his brief aria "Vorrei dir" (1.3.5).[27] Like "Smanie implacabili," Alfonso's aria is marked "allegro agitato," a rarity in Mozart's later operas; the allegro assai of Elettra's arias and the Queen of the Night's "Der Hölle Rache" is much more common. "Vorrei dir" also features broken speech and a persistent figure in the upper strings, though the effect is less *implacabili* since the number is considerably shorter. In the context of the *scuola degli amanti,* Dorabella's aria might be understood as the first outcome of her training: she has taken a cue from Alfonso's pantomime for her own expression of anguish. Already, then, Dorabella is revealed as someone open to the power of suggestion. As Despina says, "Just mention it, and let the devil do the rest."

In fact, a good deal of *Così fan tutte* relies on putting questionable ideas into the sisters' heads. The result is the breakdown of any honorable notion of fidelity and moral obligation. Both Don Alfonso and Despina direct the sisters' actions by invoking what is allegedly proper "feminine" behavior. In her aria "Una donna a quindici anni," Despina argues that coquetry is not a vice, but rather a natural, feminine quality, a sign of sexual maturity. Don Alfonso plays with a different set of ideas. He does not lecture Fiordiligi and Dorabella but instead skillfully manipulates their "feminine" capacity for pity, persuading them that, under certain circumstances, resistance to desire is unnatural—even cruel—for a woman.[28] With Despina's help, the old philosopher recasts infidelity as a kind of twofold "consolation": deprived of her lover, a lady may offer solace to a worthy suitor and thereby gain some comfort herself. Alone in the sisters' house after the chocolate scene, Alfonso comments on the sad mood: "Poor things, it is really not all their fault. They need to be consoled" (1.10). A short while later, he urges Despina to "console" her mistresses by finding a way to "bring two well-bred gentlemen"— Ferrando and Guglielmo disguised as Albanians—"into their good graces." When Fiordiligi and Dorabella angrily (and loudly) reject the Albanians' professions of love, Dutch uncle Alfonso chides them for the uproar, implying that their umbrage is impolite: "For pity's sake, girls, don't make me look so bad!" He advises them to show "a little sweetness" toward the strangers, who, "after all, are gentlemen and my friends." His admonition carries a subtle message: hard-heartedness is unbecoming. In this way, Alfonso uses the ideals of compassion and courtesy as leverage for seduction.

This tactic is picked up by Despina, who masterminds the poison scene (1.15), the ultimate appeal to pity. After their calamitous first

meeting with the Albanians, the sisters retire to the garden. Alone, Don
Alfonso mutters to himself about their intransigence: "Oh, what a laugh
that would be: with so few faithful women in the world, to have found
two of them here!" He turns to Despina for help in getting "these little
beasts" to give themselves over to temptation. The script that the two of
them concoct with Ferrando and Guglielmo is full of references to pity
and its antonym, cold-heartedness. Approaching the sisters' garden
sanctuary, the faux Albanians exclaim, "Let us die, yes, let us die, if that
is what will satisfy those ungrateful women!" just before they come on
stage, followed by Don Alfonso. They raise two bottles to their mouths
and make a morbid toast—"May the arsenic free me from such cruelty!"—and then toss the now-empty bottles to the ground. Turning to
the horrified sisters, the rejected suitors invite the "barbarous ladies" to
draw nearer so that they might "look upon the sad effect of a desperate
passion and at least take pity."

Don Alfonso reinforces the idea of mercy, singing, "Since these
wretches are close to death, try to at least to show them a little mercy"
("Giacchè morir vicini / Sono quei meschinelli, / Pietade almeno a
quelli / Cercate di mostrar"). His statement is set apart from the Albanian's plea by a conspicuous change of key and mood. Instead of the
pathetic G minor of the poisoning itself—heavy on chromatic colora-
tion, and particularly the gruesome-sounding augmented-sixth chord
at measure 129—Alfonso turns serenely to E-flat major (mm. 138ff.),
beginning with a marchlike, no-nonsense melodic gesture ("Giacchè a
morir") that sweeps up a seventh for dramatic emphasis on "pietade."
The rhythmic pace slows slightly (mm. 143–47) as Don Alfonso lingers
on his main point: "try to show them some mercy." Called to the scene
by the frantic women, Despina, too, pushes the ethical imperative
of pity, saying that it would be "shameful" for the sisters to abandon
the abject men. She urges Don Alfonso to accompany her to the doctor, leaving Fiordiligi and Dorabella alone with the dying foreigners. The sisters draw closer to them, checking for fevers and pulses.
They are gentler now toward the Albanians—Dorabella even remarks
about their "interesting looks"—and pray that help will arrive soon to
save the "poor souls." Ferrando and Guglielmo credit the power of
compassion, muttering in an aside, "in the end, their pity will turn into
love."

Acting out of compassion, the sisters "unwittingly demonstrate . . .
its affinity to the powers of sexual arousal."[29] During their miraculous
recovery, the Albanians try to hasten the conversion of *pietà* to *amore*,

lavishing the girls with gallant praise and kissing their hands. Alfonso and Despina (disguised as the doctor) pipe in as well, encouraging the women to bear with this temporary side effect of the toxin. Though the sisters complain about their threatened honor, their repeated protest—"I can resist no longer"—proves their susceptibility. The men go too far, however, when they ask their idols for a kiss, breaking the mesmeric spell. Despina and Don Alfonso attempt to play the compassion card once again—"Go along with it to show a little kindness"—but they seem to know that the round is lost even before the sisters burst into a new fit of indignation. Don Alfonso's bass line (mm. 500–505) introduces the minor subdominant lead—implying D minor—and carries a distinct edge of intimidation. He is losing patience with the sisters.

Still, Alfonso and Despina are optimistic about the final outcome of all this raging, which they are sure will change into love. Many real-life *philosophes* of the eighteenth century would have agreed with Don Alfonso's premise that woman's natural weakness allows her to feel emotion keenly, but never one emotion for too long.[30] The value of this alleged innate emotional malleability is precisely the theme of Despina's lecture to the sisters at the beginning of act 2. Alone in a room with Fiordiligi and Dorabella, she engages the sisters in some girl talk, trying to persuade them that they are foolishly dismissing good fortune.[31] She calls them "weird girls" and explains what grown-up women are supposed to do: "Treat love like a bagatelle, never miss a pleasant opportunity; be capricious one moment and faithful the next. Play the tease with style; steer clear of the disgrace that is so common to those who trust in men; have your cake and eat it too!"

When the ladies protest, citing their fiancés' distress and the scandal that would arise just for entertaining the men in their house, Despina is ready with a fail-safe plan. The soldiers need never know about it, since the whole affair will be over by the time they return. Moreover, Despina will spread the word that the Albanians are actually coming to visit *her*. She sums up her lesson and her proposal with a colorful aria about the art of charming duplicity that every girl should be capable of by the time she is fifteen: she must know how to be pleasing to all the men she likes without promising herself to any, if that is her will. She finishes up with "E, qual regina / Dall'alto soglio, / Col "posso e voglio" / Farsi ubbidir" ("And such a queen, from her high throne, with "I can and I will" makes them obey"). Despina proffers an appetizing vision of coquetry as harmless, pleasurable, and empowering. Satisfied with the doubt she has created in the sisters' minds, she remarks to herself that they "have a taste for it." She is half right: Dorabella will definitely take to the tutorial, becoming Despina's star pupil.

DORABELLA, OR THE "NATURAL" WOMAN REVISITED

In keeping with the synthetic nature of the story, Dorabella's transformation is expediently prompt. Staged performances usually attempt early on to display her malleable nature though the stage action. On paper, however, Dorabella manages a near about-face in the space of a recitative, just after Despina's "majestic" exit:

> *Fiordiligi.* Sister, what do you say?
>
> *Dorabella.* I am bewildered by the devilish mind of that girl.
>
> *Fiordiligi.* But, believe me: she is crazy. Does it seem right to you to follow her advice?
>
> *Dorabella.* Oh, of course, if you want to flip everything upside down.
>
> *Fiordiligi.* No, I prefer to take it right-side up. Don't you think it is a crime for two girls, already promised in marriage, to do these things?
>
> *Dorabella.* She did not say that we would be doing anything wrong.
>
> *Fiordiligi.* It would be bad enough to stir up gossip about us.
>
> *Dorabella.* When it is rumored that they are coming to visit Despina . . .
>
> *Fiordiligi.* Oh your conscience is too liberal! (2.2)

This pivotal conversation marks a shift in every relationship that the girls have: with the would-be suitors, with their maid "teacher," and, significantly, with each other. As Dorabella answers her sister's questions, she also becomes more and more like the maid, first quoting her, then paraphrasing her, then improvising in her manner. When Fiordiligi asks, "What would our fiancés say?" Dorabella replies confidently, "Nothing: either they will never know about the affair, and it will all be over, or they will hear something about it, and we will say they were coming to see her." Fiordiligi counters with, "What about our feelings?" but Dorabella replies without pause, "They will stay as they are: enjoying yourself a little rather than dying of melancholy does not mean being unfaithful, my sister." Her conviction disarms Fiordiligi, who answers tentatively, "That's true." Twice she defers to Dorabella about what to do, and Dorabella admits that she already has her sights on "the dark one." Her confession initiates another duet between the sisters, who titter and plot about how they are going to tease the Albanians. The faint signs of division between the two women—represented by Fiordiligi's accusation that Dorabella's "conscience is too liberal"—is forgotten with the return of the teasing, amorous mood that invigorated the sisters a few hours earlier in their first scene:

Dorabella.	Prenderò quel brunettino, Che più lepido mi par.	I'll take the dark one, who seems more witty to me.
Fiordiligi.	Ed intanto io col biondino Vo' un po' ridere e burlar.	And in the meantime I will laugh and lark around with the blond one.
Dorabella.	Scherzosetta, ai dolci detti Io di quel risponderò.	Playfully, I will respond to his sweet nothings.
Fiordiligi.	Sospirando, i sospiretti Io dell'altro imiterò.	Sighing, I will imitate the other one's sighs.
Dorabella.	Mi dirà: "Ben mio, mi moro!"	He will say to me: "My love, I die!"
Fiordiligi.	Mi dirà: "Mio bel tesoro!"	He will say to me: "My treasure!"
Both.	Ed intanto, che diletto, Che spassetto io proverò.	And all the while, what fun, What a romp I'll be having!

"Prenderò quel brunettino" turns particularly on Dorabella's readiness, in the end, to "flip everything upside down," to see Despina's logic as more reasonable than "old-fashioned" ideals about decorum and fidelity. As Till explains, reputation is more important than actual moral virtue in the rationalist viewpoint of *Così:* "Dorabella's response to Despina's wily proposals shows how the ground is shifting . . . for she accepts the terms of Despina's rational calculation, and raises a purely pragmatic counter point in which the value of her reputation must be weighed against any possible pleasure that may accrue from pursuing the plan."[32] He draws a parallel with Rousseau's *philosophe* in *Confessions,* who tells a married woman that sexual intercourse "was an act most unimportant in itself; marital fidelity need merely be kept up in appearance, its moral importance being confined to its effect on public opinion; a wife's sole duty was to preserve her husband's peace of mind; ergo, infidelities concealed did not exist for the offending partner, and were non-existent, therefore, to the conscience."[33] This is very close to the reasoning Despina uses to persuade the sisters to enjoy the foreign suitors' attentions. Dorabella's enthusiasm is compelling enough to suppress Fiordiligi's misgivings—at least temporarily. Although Fiordiligi does not express a preference for either of the foreigners, Dorabella has already noted the disguised Guglielmo's more jocular character, begin-

ning perhaps with his waggish appeal in the aria "Non siate ritrosi, occhietti vezzosi" ("Don't be reluctant, charming little eyes"), in which he
invited the sisters to "look, touch, check us out completely," including
their "feathers of love" moustaches (1.11.15). In contrast to "Ah
guarda, sorella," which exhibited Fiordiligi's (vocal) dominance, "Prenderò quel brunettino" highlights Dorabella's sway over her sister as well
as her greater facility in the blithe language of coquetry. This duet inverts the sisters' relationship and also identifies where the rupture between them will take place: over the question of what it means to be
faithful.

There is something forced about Fiordiligi's participation in "Prenderò quel brunettino," a deliberately light musical exercise in fluttering
eyelashes and mock sighs. The naturally more serious Fiordiligi mostly
follows her sister's lead. She echoes Dorabella's melodic phrases, varying them only enough to bring out the textual differences. Only at measures 29–34 does her music exhibit characteristic intensity; after a burst
of coloratura, she comes in early during the musical return, overlapping
with Dorabella. The impression is enigmatic. Fiordiligi's vocal effusive-
ness and precipitous entry might signify a fresh enthusiasm for the
scheme. Then again, her melodic collapse to low A (m. 34) could be read
as an emotional wilting: the moment Fiordiligi begins to speak in her
normal voice she remembers herself *and* her promises. It is a small but
potentially vital detail, depending on how the duet is interpreted. Despite its surface gaiety, the duet subtly forecasts the girls' divergent
courses: Dorabella moving impulsively ahead toward the fulfillment of
the opera's motto, Fiordiligi holding back. It is also the last number they
sing alone together.

Some of Mozart's audience might well have predicted the sisters' divergent views on love, taking a cue from their names, which have precedents in Ariosto's well-known epic poem, *Orlando furioso*. Da Ponte
filled the inventive libretto with allusions to literary works. The names
he selected for the female roles offer hints about their dispositions.
Fiordiligi, for instance, has an exact match in Ariosto's poem: the faithful wife of the warrior Brandimarte, who, learning that her husband has
been killed, "berates herself for not following him into battle." Dorabella, on the other hand, appears to be a clever composite of the fickle
Doralice, who leaves her lover Rodomonte for Mandricardo, and the
virtuous Saracen Isabella, who "escapes [Rodomonte's] embraces by
cleverly contrived suicide."[34] The name "Dorabella" jumbles ideas of fidelity and faithlessness. Her surrender is not preordained, but it only
takes a little push from Despina to tip the balance in favor of Doralice.

By the time Dorabella meets the dark stranger again, fidelity has become a highly flexible concept, bending to the demands of her own pleasure. Opportunity arrives in the form of a lavish party prepared for them by the Albanians. Feigning excitement, Don Alfonso hurries the two young ladies out of the house, exclaiming, "Run to the garden, my dear girls! What merriment! What music! What singing! What a dazzling scene! What magic!" The sisters follow him and are greeted by the gentlemen's serenade (2.4). When the song ends, Fiordiligi and Dorabella turn to Alfonso and ask what the masquerade is all about. Despina prods Ferrando and Guiglielmo to answer, saying "Come on, speak up; be brave! Has the cat got your tongue?" The men fall back on the usual lover's banality—that emotion keeps them from speaking—so Don Alfonso works instead on the ladies, urging them to "Be nice now, and give them some encouragement!" Fiordiligi and Dorabella give the men permission to say what they please, but the rhetorical imaginations of the two Albanians have stalled. Ferrando and Guiglielmo both try to make the other do the talking, but neither of them succeeds in saying anything.

The quartet that follows, No. 22, "La mano a me date movetevi un po," is silly and a little bizarre, effecting a kind of surrogate courtship. The embarrassed pairs remain at a distance from one another, unable to overcome the awkwardness of the situation. Keenly aware that this opportunity may not come again, Alfonso interrupts, exasperated: "Oh, the devil take it! Stop these corny, old-fashioned airs! Despinetta, let's get this over with. You do with that one what I will do with this one." Taking each of the sisters by the hand and leading them toward their suitors, Don Alfonso and Despina carry out the first stage of seduction by proxy. The men manage to repeat a few words of Alfonso's poetic begging-your-pardon speech to the women, but Fiordiligi and Dorabella are silent, responding only with blushes and giggles. Moving in front of the girls, Despina answers for them in a conspicuously lofty recitative, "What's done is done. Let's forget about the past and break that bond which is the sign of servitude." According to the stage directions, Don Alfonso and Despina make the girls break their lovers' garlands and place them on the Albanians. Confident of success, the old man and the ladies' maid hastily exit, leaving the four young people alone.

Ostensibly freed from their previous commitments by this act of ventriloquism and symbolic knot breaking, Fiordiligi and Dorabella arrive at the proverbial moment of truth. They have been told to enjoy themselves, to be "nice" to the foreign swains, to grow up and act like real women. The next scene focuses on Dorabella, the first to show an aptitude for Despina's doctrine (2.5). As Ferrando and Fiordiligi stroll off-stage—the stage directions clearly indicate that she does not take his arm—Dorabella walks arm in arm with Guglielmo, ready to "treat love like a bagatelle." When Guglielmo breaks the awkward silence with yet another round of lovesick moaning—"I feel so badly, so badly, my dear, that I think I will die"—Dorabella reacts coolly. She swears in an aside that "He won't get a single thing" from such antics and answers his complaint with the kind of casual sympathy one might have for a case of indigestion: "It must still be the side effects of the poison you drank." Persevering, Guglielmo gazes into her eyes and declares that he has drunk a more potent toxin from those fiery and cruel volcanoes of love, but Dorabella only teases that "it must be a very hot poison; cool yourself down a little." She warms to the role of coquette, tantalizing her suitor with vague assurances: "Tell me what you want, and you will see." Even Guglielmo is caught off-guard, asking "Is she joking or serious?" Tellingly, Dorabella loses control of the game when Guglielmo presents her with a pretty little heart charm: love *as* a bagatelle. "What a precious gift!" she muses to herself, delighted; she scolds Guglielmo for trying to seduce an "honest heart," but the soldier senses his new advantage, noting "the mountain is starting to rock."

Eventually Dorabella accepts the gift. Like Despina, who displays a weakness for Don Alfonso's gold piece, Dorabella begins to melt when she sees the pretty trinket, though it takes something more powerful to topple her completely. The real seduction begins in earnest with the duet No. 23, "Il core vi dono," as the "brunettino" presses to claim Dorabella's heart as his own:

Guglielmo.	Il core vi dono	I give you my heart,
	Bell'idolo mio.	my beautiful darling.
	Ma il vostro vo' anch'io:	But I want yours as well:
	Via, datelo a me.	Come, give it to me.
Dorabella.	Mel date, lo prendo;	You've given it to me, and I accept it;
	Ma il mio non vi rendo.	but I can not give mine to you in return.
	Invan mel chiedete:	It is useless to ask it of me:
	Più meco ei non è.	it no longer belongs to me.
Guglielmo.	Se teco non l'hai,	If you no longer have it with you,
	Perché batte qui?	why is it beating here?
Dorabella.	Se a me tu lo dai,	If you gave it to me,
	Che mai balza lì?	why does it throb here?

> *Both.* È il mio coricino   It is my little heart
>   Che più non è meco.   that is no longer mine.
>   Ei venne a star teco,   It went to stay with you,
>   Ei batte così.   And is beating like that.

The couple pauses for a moment, listening to and feeling each other's hearts, before Guglielmo moves on to the next part of the duet, during which he officially replaces Ferrando as Dorabella's favorite. He reaches out to the place where she keeps Ferrando's portrait. The libretto states that the portrait hangs from her waist, but some productions place it around her neck; in any case, the contact is intimate.[35] Dorabella resists a little, but Guglielmo is on to her now: "I understand, you sly girl." He turns her face away, *dolcemente* according to the stage directions, so that she cannot see what he is doing, creating a convenient loophole that further relieves her from responsibility. When Guglielmo removes the portrait and substitutes his keepsake, Dorabella exclaims in an aside, "It feels as though Vesuvius resides in my breast." She has caught the Albanian's fever, intoxicated by his touch. Ferrando forgotten, the paramours join together in a standard refrain about love: "Oh, happy exchange of hearts and affections! What new delights, what sweet pain!"

This duet bears obvious similarities to "Là ci darem la mano" and "Vedrai, carino" from *Don Giovanni:* the playful contest of enticement and resistance, the transactions of hands and hearts, the "sentilo battere" convention as the lovers feel each other's heartbeats, and the final maxim about aching pleasures. Listening to Dorabella and Guglielmo it is natural to recall Zerlina and Don Giovanni. As two of the great seduction scenes from Mozart's operas, "Là ci darem" and "Il core vi dono" invite comparison, yet the relationship between the seducer and seduced is quite different in the latter duet. For starters, the players in *Così fan tutte* are of more or less equal social status. There is a less pronounced power differential, determined by gender rather than class. More importantly, both Dorabella and Guglielmo enter the duet with the premeditated aim of pleasure. Dorabella is not the *object* of seduction in the same way as Zerlina in "Là ci darem." Rather, she is a countersubject. The difference between her plan (as expressed in "Prenderò quel brunettino") and Guglielmo's is one of degree: she does not intend for things to go so far.

Dorabella's claim that the Albanian's sly eloquence and his way of handling her are responsible for her surrender allows her to maintain a pretense of helpless virtue. In many ways, however, Dorabella seduces herself, or, in another sense, she has already been seduced by Despina's

ideas. Guglielmo is not an especially gifted smooth talker. In fact, Dorabella has no trouble deflecting and topping his hammy speeches in the
recitative before the seduction duet. His opening melody in the duet itself is not especially lyrical or compelling; it is decorous, but also restrained in phrasing and range. The pause between the words "Il core vi
dono" and "bell'idolo mio" comes across as an awkward "uh . . ." as
the soldier struggles to create a script without Alfonso's help. It is left to
Dorabella to demonstrate the sexy potential of the melody, spinning its
main motive into an ascending sequence that breathes with anticipation,
opening up a full octave. She is playing with her suitor, as she did in
the preceding recitative, answering him like a seasoned coquette. Guglielmo's strength, on the other hand, is his physical magnetism. Only
when he shifts from words to action does he seize the advantage. His
question—"If you no longer have it with you, why is it beating *here*"—
is musically lackluster but strategically brilliant. There are no stage
directions indicated in the score, but obviously he moves to feel
Dorabella's heartbeat—either by touching her bosom or embracing her
tightly against him. Surprised, perhaps, but also pleased, Dorabella
mimics the dark-haired Albanian's words, music, and gestures. The duet
operates in the same manner as paired dancing, playing out a stylized
sexuality, with contact and separation measured out in *grazioso* kines-
thesis. It is not Guglielmo's dialogue that unfastens Dorabella's Vesuvian
desire (and sets off the cuckoldry call of the horns), but the caress with
which he turns her head, *dolcemente,* and finds the locket hanging at
her waist. Guglielmo's "Rimira, rimira, se meglio più andar" ("Look
and see if that doesn't look better") bobs jauntily and repetitively up
and down a fourth, with none of the persuasive heat that energizes
Don Giovanni's final appeal to Zerlina ("Andiam, Andiam!"), but it
does not matter now. Dorabella's response can be felt in the livelier
movement of the first violin part, which thrills and plummets over the
string palpitations.

The Andante grazioso of "Il core vi dono"—so like Zerlina's Andante
music—pulls Dorabella toward a country girl's "naturalness," more
firmly establishing her *mezzo-carattere* standing. Even more than Zerlina, she demonstrates the eighteenth-century view of the feminine body
as a battlefield of conflicting "natural" forces—rampant sexual desire
and modest timidity—that compete for control of the feminine body.
Throughout the century it was generally theorized that nature endowed
women with modesty—rather than reason—in order to control her sexuality. Books on moral conduct directed at young girls reinforced the

idea that women possessed this innate defense.[36] In his lecture "Use of a School of Female Tuition," John Burton asserts, "Modesty is a female Virtue; and it is congenial to your Sex, as Courage to the other. Nature herself gives the alarm at any improper conversation or behaviour."[37] Likewise, Wetenhall Wilkes praises modesty as woman's natural defense against sexual opportunists and wantonness. In his "Letter of Genteel and Moral Advice to a Young Lady" (1740), he claims that, in its true form, "modesty does not prescribe roughness and severity against all who tell you soft things; who unbosom a violent passion for you," but rather "acts evenly, and without formality." He adds that this virtue "will preserve you against insolent attacks and pathetic addresses; and keep your conscience always clear and calm."[38] In theory, modesty fulfills a woman's obligation to courtesy and moderation while simultaneously presenting an impenetrable wall against unchaste behavior: "Chastity is so essential and natural to your sex, that every declination from it is a proportionable receding from womanhood."[39]

Wilkes's oppressive moralism regarding female sexuality appears in *Così fan tutte* only as a ridiculous ideal, which Don Alfonso and Despina endeavor to dispel. The ladies' maid turns Wilkes's principle upside down, declaring that a woman *should* enjoy her instinct for amorous pleasure, as long as she knows how to wield it and keep out of trouble. She is pleased when Dorabella comes to her, gushing about her tryst with Guglielmo, and offers congratulations: "Hell's bells: that is good to hear! We women so rarely have a little enjoyment that we have to snap it up when it comes along!" (2.10). This is not to say that Dorabella experiences liberation in the modern feminist sense through her seduction and the sexual awakening that comes with it. Her affair serves fundamentally as proof of a commonly accepted conviction: woman, enslaved by her body and childish caprice, cannot resist love when it takes an attractive form. "Some call it a vice, and others a habit; to me it seems like a compulsion of their hearts," lectures Don Alfonso. Not only does "Il core vi dono" prove him right in the context of the opera, but it also lampoons the brand of chaste humility that Rousseau, Burton, and Wilkes praised as womanhood's most precious asset. Guglielmo reads Dorabella's mild rebuke about tempting an honest heart as a sure sign of wavering; when she coyly resists the removal of Ferrando's picture—"it can't go *there*"— her new beau winks at her, saying, "I understand you." Modesty is exposed as artifice in Dorabella, who, along with Zerlina and Despina, dramatizes a complex mixture of desire, suspicion, and sympathy that surrounds all of Mozart's "natural" women.

FIORDILIGI: BETWEEN A ROCK AND A HARD PLACE

"I tried to resist," Dorabella tells Despina after her tryst with Guglielmo, "but that little devil . . . could make you fall even if you were made of stone." Da Ponte may have intended Dorabella's reference to stony dispositions as an ironic allusion to Fiordiligi, who likened herself to unassailable rock in the aria, No. 14, "Come scoglio" (1.11) from act 1. Like Dorabella's "Smanie implacabili," this aria is preceded by a high-flown accompanied recitative in the manner of an opera seria *scena*. Incensed at the Albanians' presumptuous flattery, Fiordiligi commands them to leave and sends Despina running for cover, rebuffing the men with a strident caveat, "In vain do you, or anyone else, seek to seduce our souls: the intact faith that we have already given to our beloveds we will keep for them until death, despite the world and fate." She abandons herself completely to classicized high passion à la Metastasio and Ariosto, rebuking the suitors with a violent modesty that no doubt would have appalled the likes of Mr. Wilkes:

Come scoglio immoto resta	Like the immovable rock that stands
Contro i venti e la tempesta	against the winds and storms,
Così ognor quest'alma è forte	so will this heart remain ever strong
Nella fede e nell'amore.	in faith and love.
Con noi nacque quella face	Between us was kindled that flame
Che ci piace e ci consola;	which pleases and consoles us,
E potrà la morte sola	and only death will be able to
Far che cangi affetto il cor.	change the affections of our hearts.
Rispettate, anime ingrate,	Have respect, wretched souls, for
Questo esempio di constanza;	this model of constancy,
E una barbara speranza	and do not let vulgar hope
Non vi renda audaci ancor.	lead you to such impudence again!

In terms of its imagery and vocal virtuosity, Fiordiligi's profession of faithfulness resonates with the same spirit and flashy virtuosity as "Martern aller Arten" from *Die Entführung aus dem Serail*. As in the case of "Smanie implacabili" and "D'Oreste, d'Aiace ho in seno i tormenti," the line between satire and *seria* is drawn by the context. In her bravura aria, kidnapped Constanze declares that "nothing will shake" her faithfulness. She defies the Pasha, crying, "Clamor, rage, storm! Death will free me in the end."[40] She understands that this refusal may cost her her life, and the music convincingly communicates her requisite strength of will and nobility of heart. In contrast, Fiordiligi's repudiation sounds a bit like a teenager's rhapsodic conniption: short on experience in love, she lacks perspective and any sense of moderation.[41] Mozart's musical setting highlights the general impression of exaggeration. The composer exploited Ferrarese del Bene's significant vocal range in creating Fiordiligi's extravagant musical idiom, which is apparent from the opening Andante.[42] Beginning at measure 9 ("against winds and storms"), the wide leaps of her initial melody splinter dramatically at the force of the hurricane-grade tempest she envisions. She manages to fit two leaps of a tenth, one of a twelfth, and one of a fifteenth into the space of three measures; by the end of the six bars of this phrase she has covered more than two octaves with an impetuous melodic disorder that is amusingly at odds with the theme of immovability. The same seismographic angularity—a series of octave-plus shifts—characterizes her vow that only death will alter the feelings of her heart ("far che cangi affetto il cor"; mm. 38–43), and the section closes with a cadential roulade that soars with vertiginous zeal to high C. The return of the first quatrain features another Fiordiligi favorite—the interpolated accompanied recitative passage—before picking up the original melodic material at "così ognor quest'alma è forte." The final Più Allegro section finds her in full *seria* throttle, discharging her imperious disdain in precariously rapid coloratura. Her final warning—"non vi renda audaci ancor"—twice rings the bell on high B-flat. Comedy, however, gets the last word. As the orchestra plays the final cadence Fiordiligi turns with her sister to leave, but the Albanians—seemingly deaf to her threatening tone—preempt her exit. All of her high-flown sentiments are swept aside by Guglielmo's shameless wheedling in "Non siate ritrosi, occhietti vezzosi": "Don't be so reluctant, charming little eyes; flicker two amorous lightning bolts a little our way."

In giving both sisters arias that parody *seria* style, Mozart cast them "of a type," at least superficially. Nevertheless, these two arias also distinguish crucial differences between the roles. While Dorabella maximizes the *feeling* of the moment ("Relentless pains that agitate in my soul, do not cease until I am dead from anguish!"), Fiordiligi is concerned not just with feeling, but with *doing* the right thing. She is the deeper of the two women, serving as both a parallel and a contrast to her sister. Fiordiligi thinks of constancy as a moral obligation and takes her promise to Guglielmo seriously. Her mixture of strong emotion and dutifulness recalls Donna Anna; there is, in fact, a unmistakable musical connection between "Come scoglio" and Donna Anna's "Or sai chi l'onore." The opening melodies of these arias are remarkably similar, displaying a threefold, rising sequential gesture, beginning with a dramatic downward leap of a sixth, that follows the same basic harmonic progression and emphasizes the same tonal steps. It seems probable that Mozart recalled Donna Anna when looking for a model of ardent rectitude, and the association heightens both the comic and serious implications of Fiordiligi's aria. On one hand, "Come scoglio" takes the justifiable, righteous anger of Donna Anna and downgrades it to a more pedestrian moral outrage: Fiordiligi has not suffered ravishment or the murder of her father.[43] Still, the two arias share an ethical root. This aspect of "Come scoglio" continues to develop as the story progresses. Rhetorical piety matures into responsibility and humility; through her trials, Fiordiligi becomes the opera's conscience.

Unlike her sister, who shifts from one beau to another with little discomfort, Fiordiligi experiences a crisis when left alone with the disguised Ferrando. Just as the blissfully happy Dorabella leaves the stage with her new lover after "Il core vi dono," Fiordiligi enters, crying, "I saw an asp, a hydra, a basilisk!" She is running away from Ferrando, who follows her onto the stage, dismayed. In the hidden spaces of the grove, Fiordiligi tried to carry out Despina's advice, to live the blithe duplicity of "Prenderò quel brunettino," but she could not go through with it. Till describes her moral quandary as a clash between the ethical materialism that forms the school for lovers' philosophical basis and an inherent sense of right and wrong. In Don Alfonso's and Despina's school, reason is manipulated to "justify a deed for which the imperatives of feeling have already made their own commitment"; the maid uses slippery rationalizing to convince both sisters that "as long as the happiness of [their] absent lovers is not affected, there can be no moral harm." The theory does not match Fiordiligi's experience. For her, "this denial of responsibility, to which the ethical systems of materialism inevitably led, is impossible; 'infidelities concealed' are not 'non-existent to the conscience' as Rousseau's modern *philosophe* proposed."[44]

Although Fiordiligi's conscience distinguishes her from Dorabella, it does not prevent her from becoming a corroborating statistic in Don Alfonso's demonstration. The ethical sentimentality that protects her vows to Guglielmo also leaves her vulnerable to Ferrando's countermeasures. Ferrando shrewdly directs his strongest appeals to Fiordiligi's sense of decency, to her capacity for pity, to her conscience. When Fiordiligi runs away from him, he tries to lure her back by accusing her of being brutal ("barbara") and cruel ("crudel"). Twice she begs him to leave her alone, countering that he "wants to take away" her peace of mind.[45] But Ferrando refuses to yield; hearing her sighs, he wastes no time in taking advantage of "feminine" frailty. His aria "Ah lo veggio" (No. 24) exploits what Till identifies as the Enlightenment's "easy excuses of a moral skepticism" with its absolute determinism and conflation of sexuality and compassion.[46] Ferrando observes warmly, "Ah, I see now: that sweet soul does not know how to resist my tears; it is not made to rebel against the feelings of kindly pity." He exults in her sighs and sympathetic glances, which he takes as proof that she is responding to his "hot desires," surrendering to his "tender love." Faced with her continued silence, he becomes melancholy once more and rebukes her for her hard-heartedness: "But you flee from me, despising me, without saying a word. Will you hear me languish in vain? Ah, an end to these false hopes: the cruel lady condemns me to die."

The ploy almost works. In the accompanied recitative that follows, Fiordiligi starts to call after Ferrando as he leaves the stage, then checks herself. Recognizing the attraction she felt for him, she condemns herself for it. The list of charges she makes against herself is overwrought, yet poignant because she believes them:

A qual cimento	What distress
Il barbaro mi pose . . . Un premio è questo	this barbarous man is causing me . . . A well-deserved
Ben dovute a mie colpe! In tale istante	reward for my faults! At such a time,
Dovea di nuovo amante	how could I listen to the sighs of
I sospiri ascoltar? l'altrui querele	a new lover? Should I have treated his suit
Dovea volger in gioco? Ah, questo core	more as a game? Ah, you have reason to
A ragione condanni, o giusto amore!	condemn this heart, o just Love!
Io ardo; e l'ardor mio non è più effetto	I burn; and my burning is no longer the effect
D'un amor virtuoso: è smania, affanno,	of a virtuous love: it is frenzy, agony,
Rimorso, pentimento,	remorse, penitence,
Leggerezza, perfidia, e tradimento!	fickleness, perfidy, and betrayal!

This recitative is as dramatic as those that introduce "Smanie implacabili" and "Come scoglio," but its intensity is more legitimately motivated, coming as it does after Ferrando's guilt-inducing reproach. Fiordiligi is truly beginning to understand "smanie" and "rimorso"; she is torn in two directions and thoroughly confused. In the two-tempo rondo that follows (No. 25, "Per pietà, ben mio"), Fiordiligi offers an extended apology to her beloved Guglielmo, remorseful of her weakness:

Per pietà, ben mio, perdona	For pity's sake, my darling, forgive
All'error d'un alma amante:	the error of a loving soul:
Fra quest'ombre e queste piante	let them be forever hidden, o God,
Sempre ascoso, oh, Dio, sarà!	Amidst these groves and shadows!
Svenerà quest'empia voglia	My devotion and my constancy will
L'ardir mio, la mia costanza.	destroy this wicked desire
Perderà la remembranza	and rid me of this memory
Che vergogna e orror mi fa.	that fills me with shame and horror.
A chi mai mancò di fede	To whom has this vain,
Questo vano, ingrato cor!	ungrateful heart been unfaithful?
Si dovea miglior mercede,	Your honest plight, my dearest,
Caro bene, al tuo candor.	deserved a better reward.

As the chief showpiece for Ferrarese del Bene, "Per pietà" endows the impressive register shifts and coloratura flourishes heard in "Come scoglio" with more gravity. The context is serious enough to dull what Hunter refers to as the "double edge" of faux-*seria* referentiality.[47] Ferrando's hot-blooded pathos in "Ah lo veggio" induces Fiordiligi's equally passionate response. Like "Come scoglio," the aria features several examples of word painting, but this time these gestures seem inspired by feeling rather than hackneyed faux-Metastasian imagery. For example, in the melodic fall of a twelfth from high G to middle C at the word "ascose" or "hidden" (mm. 8, 33), Fiordiligi seems to hold up her fault for everyone to see (and hear), before hiding it again, deep in her lower range. She expresses shame and horror ("vergogna" and "orror") with a series of wrenching leaps that increasingly widen, culminating with a plaintive lift of a twelfth to F. Most of the ornamentation is relatively graceful and moderate; her most exultant outbursts are reserved for the word "bene," an affectionate reference to Guiglielmo. This time no one denies the dramatic exit appropriate to a *seria* heroine.

This is not to say that the aria is free from irony, only that the irony is less pervasive and, arguably, less destabilizing than it is in "Come scoglio." The most obvious satiric intrusion in "Per pietà, ben mio" is a stock orchestral pun, specifically the increasingly conspicuous horns—the eighteenth-century's musical sign for the cuckold, or horn-wearing *cornuto*. A comparable allusion occurs in "Il core vi dono," just after Dorabella tacitly allows Guglielmo to replace Ferrando's picture with the heart charm; breaking away from their usual pedal-tone role in the accompaniment, the horns suddenly break into the foreground with a boisterous call. In "Per pietà," the divided horns assume a more melodic role, often joining with the flutes, clarinets, and bassoons in the manner of a wind band. At the repeat of the text "Per pietà, ben mio, perdona," for instance, the horn, bassoons, and clarinets form alternating trios, which respond to Fiordiligi's melodic line with embellished echoes. The preponderance of the winds adds timbral warmth, resulting in a softer Fiordiligi than we heard in "Come scoglio." There can be no doubt, however, that Mozart intentionally pushes the horns into the foreground at important moments, playing with two of the instrument's most familiar eighteenth-century associations: the cuckold and the soldier. The horns enter for the first time (mm. 8–9), in parallel with the flutes, just after Fiordiligi vows that her "error" will remain hidden. The brief horn call adds color to her dramatic cry "sempre ascose" and, at the same time, lets slip the transgression she wishes to hide. The prominent horn fanfares on the word "bene" (mm. 46–48, 76–78)—the only accompaniment to Fiordiligi's sustained note—would certainly have symbolized infidelity for an eighteenth-century audience, but the overall effect is not as straightforward as the brief horn heckle in "Il core vi dono." Brown, for instance, concludes that the horns are primarily significant "as heralds of cuckolding" in "Per pietà," but also points to other possible, undoubtedly concurrent, meanings. He notes that Beethoven used this same aria, horns and all, as a model for one of Leonore's arias, and cites Michael Noiray, who has revealed a tradition in French opera of "using the horn to represent an absent lover . . . perhaps on account of associations of posthorns with distance."[48] The extensive interplay between voice and horn in "Per pietà," even in the final Allegro section, adds to the overall ambiguity. The vigorous horn outbursts that accompany Fiordiligi's wistful remembrances of her darling ("caro bene") may refer to cuckoldry, but they also allow for martial associations, hinting at Guglielmo on the battlefield or Fiordiligi's renewed moral militancy. The hermeneutically charged combination of voice and horn on the word "bene" is much more complex than the obvious punch-line effect in numbers like "Il core vi dono" or Figaro's "Aprite un po' quegl'occhi," where the horn call is strictly set apart from the voice, a wholly unsubtle instrumental wink at the audience. Fiordiligi holds her note while the horn sounds, and the two sounds both complement and compete with one another.

ENTER THE LOVE THIEF

Fiordiligi's resistance in her rondo to the implied significance of the horns—the assumption that she is unfaithful—calls into question the dictates of the "school for lovers." Alone with her Albanian suitor for the first time, Fiordiligi senses that "one cannot play games in these matters, that it may not, after all, be possible to eat the fig and keep the apple, and that it is a mistake to imagine that the indulgence of pleasure necessarily brings happiness."[49] Her resistance to pleasure over principle, and to Despina's definition of womanhood, becomes the focus of the next few scenes, as everyone—even Dorabella—chips away at it. Confessing to her sister about the division in her heart, Fiordiligi is shocked by Dorabella's sunny response: "Seventy thousand kisses for you! You have the blond one; I have the brunette. Look at us: both engaged!" (2.10). On the surface, this dialogue is amusing and only faintly discordant. However, in its own way, the conversation between the two sisters is as grim as the broken bond between mother and daughter in *Die Zauberflöte*. Dorabella now sounds exactly like Despina, dismissing her sister's moral dilemma with a mix of gender determinism and pragmatic self-interest:

Fiordiligi. What are you saying? Haven't you thought about the unhappy pair that left just this morning? Have you forgotten about their tears, their constancy? Where, where did you learn such wicked ideas? How can you be so different from yourself?

Dorabella. Listen to me: are you so certain that our old lovers won't die at war? And then we'll be left empty-handed. There's always a big difference between the bird in the hand and the one in the bush!

Fiordiligi. And then if they come back?

Dorabella. If they come back, tough luck for them! We will both be wives by then, living a thousand miles away.

Fiordiligi. But I don't understand how you can change your heart's feelings so much in a single day.

Dorabella. What a ridiculous question! We're women! And as for that, what have you been doing today?

Fiordiligi. I know how to conquer my impulses.

Despina. You don't know anything.

Fiordiligi. I'll prove that I do.

Dorabella. Believe me, sister, it's better if you just give in.

It is now Dorabella's turn to act like the *signora maestra*. In her aria No. 28, "È amore un ladroncello," she lectures Fiordiligi about love's obstinate ways:

È amore un ladroncello,	Love is a tiny thief,
Un serpentello è amor.	a little serpent is love.
È toglie e dà la pace,	He steals your heart's peace,
Come gli piace, ai cor.	and gives it back as he pleases.

Per gli occhi al seno appena	From the moment he makes an opening
Un varco aprir si fa,	from your eyes to your heart,
Che l'anima incatena	your soul is enchained
E toglie libertà.	and robbed of its freedom.
Porta dolcezza e gusto,	He brings sweetness and pleasure
Se tu lo lasci far;	if you let him do what he wants,
Ma t'empie di disgusto,	but will fill you with disgust
Se tenti di pugnar.	if you try to fight him.
Se nel petto ei siede,	If he has seated himself in your breast,
S'egli ti becca qui,	If he has already pecked you [in your heart],
Fa' tutto quel ch'ei chiede,	Do whatever he asks,
Che anch'io farò così.	for I will do the same myself.

For this aria, Dorabella adopts Despina's musical style—the tripping melody and $\frac{6}{8}$ meter are reminiscent of "Una donna a quindici anni"—as well as her attitudes and earthy language. The piece also connects in various ways with her own seduction experience: Guglielmo inveigled Dorabella with the pretty heart charm, opening a path from eye to heart as it were, then stole Ferrando's picture and sweetheart away. Admittedly, Dorabella enjoyed the vertiginous feelings of seduction and submitted quickly, but she points out that resistance would have been futile regardless. Love can be pleasing, but it is also unrelenting. The musical heartbeats of "Il core vi dono" are replaced here by love's maddening staccato pecking. Even the aria's mini-rondo form reinforces the sense of inevitability: the musical refrain, breezily accompanied by a wind band, reminds us again and again that love will have his way.

The text springs from a commonplace sexual double entendre, referring to the "little snake" who searches for an opening. More interesting is how the poetry exploits the vocabulary of violence in its description of pleasure. Love shackles your soul, steals your peace and freedom, treats you well when it is pleased and punishes you when it is not, and bites and pecks until you do whatever it asks. With this aria, Dorabella reinterprets Fiordiligi's guilty conscience: her sister feels badly not because she is betraying her distant lover, but because she is opposing the demands of *amor*. Dorabella's playful ditty carries a lamentable message: love—even physical love—can never really be denied if the woman feels anything at all for the man. Rousseau uses similar reasoning, in fact, to distinguish between the "natural" necessity of overcoming a woman's resistance to love and "unnatural" rape. He explains to his student Emile that, "Whether the human female shares man's desires or not and wants to satisfy them or not, she repulses them and always defends herself—but not always with the same force or, consequently, with the same success. For the attacker to be victorious, the one who is attacked must permit or arrange it; for she does not have adroit means to force the attacker to use force. The freest and sweetest of all acts does not admit of real violence."[50] He goes on to describe a sexual dynamic that depends on an ambiguous capitulation:

> [T]he stronger [man] appears to be master but actually depends on the weaker [woman]. This is due not to a frivolous practice of gallantry or to the proud generosity of a protector, but to an invariable law of nature which gives woman more facility to excite the desires than man to satisfy them. This causes the latter, whether he likes it or not, to depend on the former's wish and constrains him to seek to please her in turn, so that she will consent to let him be the stronger. Then what is sweetest for man in his victory is the doubt whether it is weakness that yields to strength or the will which surrenders. And the woman's usual ruse is always to leave this doubt between her and him.[51]

Rousseau's "doubt"—the uncertain relationship between physical submission and consent—plays a crucial role in the final seduction scene between Fiordiligi and Ferrando, which follows immediately after "È amore un ladroncello." Dorabella and Despina exit the room together, leaving Fiordiligi alone to consider her situation. She shows more insight and gumption than Don Alfonso would have predicted: "Everything conspires to seduce my heart! But no! I will die before I give in! I made a mistake when I confided in my sister and my servant: they will tell him everything, and he will be bolder than ever, capable of doing anything." She threatens to dismiss any servant who lets "that seducer" into the house but worries that Dorabella might do something behind her back. A rash idea takes shape in Fiordiligi's mind: she will take her sister to the battlefield, where, disguised in soldiers' uniforms, they can be reunited with their proper fiancés. "Be brave," she says to herself, "Ardir!" She tells Despina to bring two of the spare swords, hats, and uniforms from the closet where Ferrando and Guglielmo left them. She even orders six post horses and calls for her sister, hoping aloud that Dorabella will follow her good example ("bell'esempio") and accompany her on the spontaneous journey, the "only way to save our innocence."

On one hand the scheme is laughably drastic, though Fiordiligi's actions are not completely without reason. She is dead right when she says that no one can be trusted, that everyone wants her to give into temp-

tation, and that even the house is not safe. She accurately predicts that
her seducer will be more daring than ever, "capable of anything," and
she fears that she will not be able to resist again. Hearing her mistress's
curious orders, Despina remarks tartly, "That lady seems out of her
mind to me," but, in truth, Fiordiligi is pretty lucid about her circumstances and emotions: she is attracted to the fair Albanian, but she does
not *want* to be. Neither Don Alfonso nor Rousseau makes room for the
possibility that a woman could feel something for a man but say no to
these feelings. Predictably, when the eavesdropping Don Alfonso hears
Fiordiligi's plan, he sees it only as an obstacle to be surmounted, not as
a refusal to be respected. "Ho capito abbastanza," he says to himself, "I
have heard enough." He sends immediately for Ferrando, whose anger
about Dorabella's two-timing (and Guglielmo's boastful swaggering)
adds an edge to his seductive fervor.

Pausing in her preparations, the unsuspecting Fiordiligi initiates what
sounds like a new aria, No. 29, "Fra gli amplessi in pochi istanti," dream-
ing of the moment in which she will once more be in Guglielmo's arms.
She begins in A major (the key of "Ah guarda, sorella"), which is tonally
distant from the B-flat major of Dorabella's love thief, the joking "Prenderò quel brunettino," and Ferrando's "Ah lo veggio." She eases into a
new optimism with the adagio, alla breve introduction, quickening just
a little when she imagines Guglielmo's elation at their reunion:

Fra gli amplessi in pochi istanti	In just a short while I will once more
Giungerò del fido sposo;	be in the arms of my faithful love;
Sconosciuta, a lui davanti	I will come before him disguised
In quest'abito verrò.	in this uniform.
Oh che gioia il suo bel core	Oh, what joy will fill his good heart
Proverà nel ravvisarmi!	When he sees me again!

Her happy reverie is rudely interrupted when Ferrando enters the
room unannounced and makes a ghastly request:

Ferrando.	Ed intanto di dolore,	And meanwhile I, a poor wretch,
	Meschinello, io mi morrò.	will die of pain.
Fiordiligi.	Cosa veggio! Son tradita.	What am I seeing! I have been betrayed!
	Deh, partite!	Please, leave me!
Ferrando.	Ah, no, mia vita!	Ah, no, my life!
	[*Prende la spada dal tavolino, la sfodera*]	[*He takes the sword from the table and unsheathes it.*]

Con quel ferro di tua mano	You will take this steel in your hand
Questo cor tu ferrai;	and wound this heart;
E se forza, oddio, non hai,	And if, by heaven, you lack the strength to do it,
Io la man ti reggerò.	I myself will guide your hand.
Fiordiligi. Taci, ahimè! Son abbastanza Tormentata ed infelice!	Oh please stop talking like that! I am already tormented and unhappy enough!
Both. Ah, che omai la mia/sua constanza, A quei sguardi, a quel che dice, Incomincia a vacillar.	Ah, at these looks, these words my/her fidelity is now beginning to falter.

Ferrando's melodic entrance redirects Fiordiligi's half cadence on E major (m. 15) toward E minor; suddenly, the room itself becomes a battlefield quite different from the one Fiordiligi was imagining. Musically, there is a rupture: her "aria" anticipating a reunion with Guglielmo is forcibly changed into a duet with the man she is trying to flee. Stunned, she turns away from the forbidding key and moves instead to C major (m. 24), begging the desperate man to leave. Her panic jolts the stately pulse of the Adagio introduction into allegro double time (mm. 24–39), and the upper strings quicken into nervous sixteenth-note arpeggios. When Ferrando falls to his knees and demands that she stab him through the heart with his sword, Fiordiligi pleads with him to be silent. The music grows quieter (mm. 39–57), the arpeggios in the upper strings slow to eighth-note oscillations, and the bass line relaxes as well, demonstrating a musical hesitancy. She implores Ferrando to get up, but he refuses, and the harmony shifts again to the minor mode, this time in tonic A. "For pity's sake, what do you want from me?" she beseeches him, her rising anxiety evident in the sharp orchestral *sforzandi* (mm. 61–62). "Your heart or my death," her suitor cries, his voice ringing with horrible determination on a high A. The threat carries the music into D minor, Mozart's key for death and vengeance. Fiordiligi cannot bear it. Ferrando takes her hand, kissing it passionately, and whispers the seducer's incantation: "Cedi, cara" ("Give in, dearest"). Over and over again, he urges her to submission, employing the same verb that Dorabella used when she warned Fiordiligi about the powers of rascally love: "Credi, sorella, è meglio che tu *ceda*" ("Believe me, sister, it's better if you just give in"). At the moment Ferrando begins to kiss her, Fiordiligi cries out, "Ah, non son più forte" ("Ah, I am no longer strong").

Here, too, "Là ci darem la mano" comes to mind, particularly since Zerlina uses the same basic phrase just before she succumbs to Don Giovanni: "Presto, non son più forte." As with "Il core vi dono," however, the parallel underscores difference. Mozart does not repeat himself in setting the "non son più forte" phrase, that musical moment when moral and physical strength fail. In each case, he skillfully reflects Zerlina's and Fiordiligi's distinct experiences of seduction. The mood of "Là ci darem" is generally lighter, with a relatively low level of moral anguish. Zerlina worries briefly about Masetto's feelings, but her reluctance stems primarily from suspicion. She does not want to be fooled by Don Giovanni's gallantry, becoming the one-time remedy for a handsome *cavaliere*'s sexual needs. Nevertheless, his offer of what she could not otherwise have—the life of a gentleman's wife—is what really topples her. Her "Presto, non son più forte" occurs twice in direct response to Don Giovanni's promise to change her fate ("io cangierò tua sorte"). Initially, these words are set to a fluttery, repetitive figure that vacillates nervously in the dominant key (mm. 24–28), seemingly holding back from the return of the tonic and Don Giovanni's repeated proposal (Ex. 33). The second "Presto, non son più forte" (mm. 42–46) begins in the same way, but rather than hovering uncertainly, the melodic phrase eases down gently by thirds with chromatic concupiscence, "falling like a stone" over a minor seventh (Ex. 34). When Don Giovanni urges her one more time to go with him to his house, she answers him languidly, "Andiam."

Fiordiligi's "Ah, non son più forte" is more ambivalent and, from a certain perspective, more troubling. She is not faced with the same social considerations as Zerlina. There is no obvious incommensurability between her two lovers, no clear advantage in leaving Guglielmo for the Albanian. It might be tempting to frame her predicament in terms of a conflict between head and heart, between Guglielmo and the ideals around him—chiefly fidelity—and the Albanian who stirs sensual passion, but this is too simplistic. First, there is every reason to believe that Fiordiligi loves Guglielmo as sincerely as she loves the disguised Ferrando. Her eventual infidelity depends on something more than passion, something weightier than the charming banter and physical titillation that reign in "Il core vi dono." If Dorabella—and Zerlina, for that matter—are both bribed into surrender, Fiordiligi is emotionally blackmailed. Ferrando's dramatic display with the sword takes full advantage of the love/pity pivot that is Fiordiligi's weak spot: he places his life in her hands. Significantly, she sings "Ah, non son più forte" only after Ferrando clearly lays

EXAMPLE 33. *Don Giovanni*, No. 7, "Là ci darem la mano"; mm. 24–29

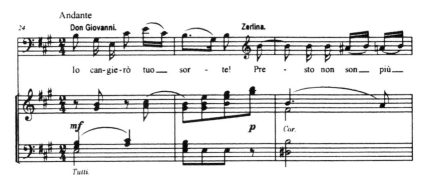

EXAMPLE 34. *Don Giovanni*, No. 7, "Là ci darem la mano"; mm. 42–46

out his shocking terms—her heart or his death. Her swooning melody (mm. 65–69) falls by thirds like Zerlina's, but over a *diminished* seventh (in A minor), the outlines of which Ferrando simultaneously uses for his imploring "Cedi, cara." Suddenly the orchestra erupts with *forte* syncopations on an augmented-sixth chord (m. 73), and Fiordiligi cries out miserably for divine aid, "Dei consiglio!" A question forms in the fermata silence that follows (Ex. 35). Does the orchestral outburst indicate Fiordiligi's agonized indecision or Ferrando's growing forcefulness—his "strength" overcoming her "weakness"—or both? Certainly the interaction between impetuous suitor and reluctant idol in this scene demonstrates the latent violence of Rousseau's description of seduction (though the *philosophe* would no doubt have denied such negative implications). Ferrando's "Cedi, cara" and Fiordiligi's "Non son più forte" lie somewhere between reciprocity and submission; Fiordiligi's conquest is not exactly rape, but it is not wholly consensual either. The expressive weight of Fiordiligi's sustained wail on high A over the orchestra's *sforzando* augmented-sixth chord suggests that we are very close to crossing a line that Rousseau declined to acknowledge: *"the freest and sweetest of all acts does not admit of real violence."*

The section that follows—a $\frac{3}{4}$ Larghetto in Fiordiligi's original key of A major—tips the scale in the other direction. Vigor has had its say and now tenderness takes a turn; this equivocal dynamic helps to insinuate a Rousseauist "doubt" about the nature of Fiordiligi's seduction. Mozart's love thief now approaches Fiordiligi not with the imposing virility of a Don Giovanni or Pasha Selim, but with the gentleness of a Don Ottavio. His words (marked *tenerissimo*) are, in fact, quite close to those of Donna Anna's ever-patient betrothed, who promised to be both husband and father to her. Naturally, Ferrando still continues mildly to press Fiordiligi, always targeting her natural inclination to pity:

Ferrando.	Volgi a me pietoso il ciglio:	Turn, look at me with mercy:
	In me sol trovar tu puoi	in me alone can you find
	Sposo, amante . . . e più,	a husband, lover . . . and more, if
	se vuoi.	you wish.
	Idol mio, più non	My darling, don't wait any
	tarder.	longer.
Fiordiligi.	Giusto ciel! Crudel	Merciful heaven! Cruel man, you
	hai vinto:	have won:
	Fa' di me quel che ti par.	do what you will with me.

Fiordiligi's response—a complicated synthesis of censure, acquiescence, and desire—captures perfectly the uncertainty Rousseau described. Three times she exclaims "Giusto ciel!" The stage directions indicate that she is trembling, her state evoked musically by a return of the quivering sixteenth-note arpeggios in the second violin part. Her gripping octave leap to a sustained high A on the word "crudel" simultaneously preempts and fulfills the upward sequence of Ferrando's line. Spent, she murmurs, "Hai vinto: fa' di me quel che ti par." Her phrase alternates

EXAMPLE 35. *Così fan tutte*, No. 29, "Fra gli amplessi in pochi istanti"

with Ferrando's final ardent plea, "idol mio, più non tarder" (mm. 96–99), but the oboe line connects their melodic fragments into a single line of infinite sweetness. The equivocal language of Fiordiligi's submission—"Cruel man, you have won: do what you will with me"—clashes with the *amabile* rapture of the music. Ferrando holds the overwhelmed woman in his arms, enjoying Rousseau's "sweet" enigma of sexual conquest.

The dreamy Andante that completes Fiordiligi and Ferrando's duet is of the same mold as the final sections of "Là ci darem la mano" and "Il core vi dono." All three numbers speak of the "pain of love," and in each case there is always a double meaning, a suggestion of suffering, reparation, and sexual pleasure. Don Giovanni and Zerlina go off arm in arm "to restore the pangs of love," the verb "ristorare" carrying associations of "refreshment" and also "recompense." Dorabella and Guglielmo celebrate "new pleasures" and "sweet pain." Ferrando and Fiordiligi, too, embrace each other to make amends for hurts already inflicted and suffered: "Let us embrace, my dear love, and may we be comforted for so many pains by languishing in sweet affection, sighing in delight." Their melodious parallel singing—as well as the humorous touch of Don Alfonso holding back an infuriated Guglielmo—obscures the serious side of the oxymoronic language, but the passage nevertheless establishes a residual melancholy that is absent from the other two duets. The formulaic ending does not work very well in "Fra gli amplessi in pochi istanti," partly because we have experienced too much real tension, both dramatically and musically. It attempts to smooth over the complex emotional topography that lies between Ferrando and Fiordiligi, the crags and gaps of their interaction.

Ferrando and Fiordiligi open up possibilities that lie beyond the *buffa* margins. Joseph Kerman alleges, "if ever an operatic lover was sincere, it is Ferrando in the duet with Fiordiligi."[52] We want to believe this, and it may in fact be true, but it is not clear whether this is the truth of a moment or a lifetime. After all, Ferrando admits that he still loves Dorabella, even after this passionate scene. Indeed, he has no trouble revealing himself to Fiordiligi in the final scene and mocking her with affected compliments. Fiordiligi, on the other hand, abandons herself to her new love but must willfully suppress the unhappy intrusions of the past. Sitting with her sister and their Albanian beaus at the prewedding banquet, she raises her glass in a bittersweet toast: "Touch glasses and drink! And in your glass and mine, let every care be drowned, and let no memory of the past remain in our hearts." The main words of her toast are set apart from the initial clinking and drinking of the finale's opening Andante; Fiordiligi drowns her memories in a $\frac{3}{4}$ Larghetto, pointedly recalling the moment of her capitulation. Ferrando joins her, in canon, and the two sing together for several measures before Dorabella enters. For his part, Guglielmo refuses to participate in the canon toast, muttering instead about poisoned drinks. Later, when all the masks come off, one wonders if they will need to repeat the incantation, and what part of the past they will choose to forget.

REPEAT AFTER ME: "COSÌ FAN TUTTE"

Discussing Rousseau's ideas on women's education, Helen Evans Misenheimer identifies a vital difference between the pedagogical ideals of Fénelon and his adherent, Madame de Maintenon, and those of Rousseau, particularly as set forth in *Emile* and *La nouvelle Heloïse*. She asserts that while Fénelon and Maintenon accorded reason the primary role in their education of women, Rousseau fell back on sentiment, yet he "rarely speaks of worthy passions where women are concerned." She notes that with regard to female passions, Rousseau is usually reproachful instead of laudatory, exempting himself from explaining his negative position.[53] In fact, Rousseau places female pupils in a terrible quandary. He posits that since women are incapable of true reason, they must be taught through their passions, but by denying reasoning power to his theoretical woman—such as Emile's bride Sophie—he creates a person who is subjugated to constantly fluctuating emotions. His advice to Emile on the subject of passions and morality—"reason forbids us to want what we cannot obtain, conscience forbids us, not to be tempted, but to yield to temptation"—would be inaccessible to Sophie, who, as Misenheimer points out, is deprived of reason and whose "unexplored and dormant conscience" is "neglected by her education."[54] In most of his writings on the subject, Rousseau asserts that, ultimately, a woman is necessarily reliant on her husband to oversee her passions. Both Sophie and Julie (the heroine of *La nouvelle Heloïse*) are entrusted to men—tutors and husbands—yet each fall into the error of illicit love. And each conveniently dies early, leaving their husbands and lovers behind to learn from the experience.

Rousseau—deriving his educational theories from his understanding of nature—believed that all of a woman's training should be in the service of assisting and pleasing men. Their program of learning is not directed toward freedom or self-reliance; a woman need only be primed for a husband's supervision. And this, in turn, requires that a man be tutored in how to deal with the women in his life. In her concluding remarks on Rousseau's outlook on women, Misenheimer describes an attitude that seems equally applicable to Don Alfonso and, to some extent, to his creator, Da Ponte:

> She is never allowed to possess the innocence even of childhood. From her beginning, he implies, she is coquettish, deceptive and self-serving. She is portrayed as a creature of emotions, no rationality; therefore, he speaks to her in an admonishing and condescending tone. Because he is personally ignorant of women in the true role of wife and mother, his claim to form her is unbelievable and lacking in verisimilitude. Moreover, because of the lack of familial stability in his life, his encounters with women tended to be of only one nature—sexual. . . . It is not difficult then to realize why he was tempted to prepare only one type of women in his educational plan, that of mistress.[55]

In *Così fan tutte,* Don Alfonso concerns himself with a similarly male-centered and demeaning pedagogical aim. He reduces the nature of woman to a single characteristic: capriciousness, in both mood and love. Just before the second-act finale he instructs Ferrando and Guglielmo to marry the girls who have cheated on them, since they are no better—or worse—than other women (2.13).[56] In the recitative that proceeds No. 30, "Tutti accusan le donne," he admonishes the men to take Fiordiligi and Dorabella "as they are," since "Nature cannot make exceptions, to create two women of a different substance, just to privilege your handsome mugs." He stresses that it is necessary to be philosophical about everything and, in his final lecture-aria, he explains his position: "Everyone accuses women, and I excuse them if they change lovers a thousand times. Some call it a vice and others a habit, but to me it appears to be a compulsion of their hearts. The lover who finds he is deluded can blame no one except his own error. Whether they are young, old, beautiful, or ugly—repeat after me—'All women do the same.'"

What Don Alfonso does *not* explore is the difference between the sisters' seductions; he seems unconcerned by how much he and Despina had to interfere in order to make Fiordiligi submit. His explanation of women ignores whatever evidence does not fit his rule, bringing to mind Bertrand Russell's criticism of Aristotle, who, while asserting that women did not have wisdom teeth, had obviously not opened even his own wife's mouth to check.[57] As with the other characters, we are given no history for Don Alfonso, but his language carries a deep disdain for women. Fiordiligi and Dorabella are another "race" (1.7), two crazy "little beasts" (1.8), two "chickens" that he helps to pluck (2.13). At the end of the opera, when the women learn of the trick played on them, Fiordiligi and Dorabella point the finger at "cruel" Alfonso: "Here is the barbarous man who deceived us!" ("Ecco là il barbaro che c'ingannò!"; mm. 527–31). Unflappable, the *philosophe* nullifies their accusation (and their move toward dismal G minor), citing his status as infallible headmaster; he deceived them only to undeceive their lovers, who will now be wiser and "do just what I say." He tells the couples to have a good laugh about the whole thing, just as he has, and to go back to their original pairing and marry. Everyone joins in the final maxim: "Fortunate is the man who looks always at the bright side of life, and lets reason be his guide through trials and tribulations. That which makes others cry will be for him a cause for laughter, and amidst the world's tumults, he will find peace."

Brown proposes that Da Ponte and Mozart intended this as a non-misogynistic and "generous message of reconciliation,"[58] yet productions usually struggle with this moment, settling on solutions with varying levels of skepticism: if nothing else, it is still unclear as to who loves whom and why. The convention of the *lieto fine* demands the participation of the women, but it is not enough to cancel out what has already happened. Moreover, the Rousseauist spirit of the opera precludes unanimous understanding and equal access even in the final moral. Reason, after all, lies outside the experience of woman. Rousseau believed that man had been given a conscience to love what is good, reason to recognize it, and liberty to choose it, but his plan for education denies these things to women, making "the fall of woman . . . inevitable."[59] Likewise, the *scuola degli amanti* in *Così fan tutte* ensures Fiordiligi's failure: she is neither educated nor allowed to become a free and reasonable person. Don Alfonso shackles her and Dorabella to the faults he has established; from him, the sisters learn doubt (of their feelings, judgment, and friends), humiliation, and shame. It is, perhaps, Mozart's music (or our love for his music) that makes us want to imagine that the "school for lovers" has a beneficial lesson for everyone. And yet, as the curtain goes down, a sense of unease remains, even after the most amiable performance. Watching the girls snap back into their original positions at his order, without a single question or hesitation, Don Alfonso chuckles, but his gaze is cold.

CHAPTER 10

Survival Class

Despina

And as for you, you want to remain chaste for your sweetheart, who's making no demands on you; so what you really
want are love's sorrows and none of its pleasures! Splendid!
Keep up that line and you'll end up as a perfect heroine for a
novel. But seriously, how can a girl who's past her fifteenth
birthday be so positively childish?

> The Marquise de Merteuil, in *Les liaisons dangereuses*

The Case was alter'd with me, I had Money in my Pocket,
and had nothing to say to them: I had been trick'd once by
that Cheat call'd LOVE, but the Game was over.

> *Moll Flanders*

In many ways, Despina is the typical maidservant of *buffa* convention:
shrewd, flippant, sensual, and opportunistic. In the context of Mozart's
operas, however, she stands apart from her much-admired predecessors
Susanna and Blonde. Though Despina shares her mistresses' confi-
dences, she never exhibits affection for them; to be fair, the sisters are
not very kind to her either. In the absence of genuine female friendship
and esteem, Despina's cleverness is easily yoked to a man with money in
his pocket. It is not that she schemes *against* Fiordiligi and Dorabella—
she genuinely believes that they will be happier if they focus on easy
pleasure—but her self-professed weakness for gold blinds her to Don
Alfonso's ulterior motives, leading her and the sisters into his net of humiliation. Often, stage and musical directors reduce her to a shallow
conniver whose glib comments on fidelity promote the opera's "così fan

tutte" premise. However, Despina is more complicated than this, as are her attitudes about love. Like Zerlina, she has withstood class and gender inequities; her first aria suggests that she has already braved abuse and deceit before the curtain opens. She has become an expert in evasive maneuvering and is not easily defeated. At the end of the opera, Despina expresses embarrassment at having been fooled by the men, but, in the same breath, she promises to even the score by bamboozling many herself.

Her name, like her character, is provocative and puzzling. If, as with Fiordiligi and Dorabella, Da Ponte was inspired by Ariosto's *Orlando furioso* in naming his dissembling maid, then it seems likely that "Fiordispina"—literally, "thorn flower"—is the source.[1] Ariosto's beautiful Spanish princess, the daughter of Marsilius, is not a major character, but her story is an unforgettable piece of naughty sixteenth-century Italian erotica. The lovely Fiordispina, hunting in the forest, sees a sleeping figure she takes for a knight. She soon learns that the handsome armored slumberer is really a woman, the warrior-maiden Bradamante. Fiordispina's passion does not fade when she discovers the truth, for "Love had thrust in his arrow so deep that it was too late to remedy."[2] The princess invites Bradamante, who has been injured, to stay in her home while she recovers. The two share a bed, with the warrior-maiden sleeping soundly and Fiordispina agonized by dreams of Bradamante as a man. When Bradamante returns home, she tells her family about the unusual experience. Conveniently, she has a twin brother, Ricciardetto, who has often passed for his sister and has always fancied Fiordispina. Taking advantage of the situation, Ricciardetto journeys to the Spanish kingdom dressed as his sister; once there, he describes in private to Fiordispina an outlandish tale of a magical transsexual changeover. The princess, who "saw and touched that which she has so desired,"[3] is gratified without delay by the obliging Ricciardetto.

ACTING LIKE A WOMAN OR PLAYING LIKE THE BOYS?

It is impossible to guess whether Da Ponte was actually making a connection between the voluptuous (and bisexual) Fiordispina and Despina—much less what it might have meant to him—but approaching "Despina" as a trimmed version of the name "Fiordispina" works surprisingly well as a key to the character in general. From this perspective, the "ina" functions not as the usual lower-class diminutive, but as part of a kind of personality-determined sobriquet. She is, in fact, a prickly creation—*"de spina"*— with a tongue as sharp as her wit. She is also missing her *"fior"*: Despina has been "deflowered" both figuratively and, as she strongly implies in her first aria, literally. Left only with the thorns, she approaches work and love with a hardy resolve to take control and pleasure when she can, as evident from her first scene:

> What a cursed life it is to be a servant! From morning to night you work, sweat, and toil, and then after all this labor there is nothing left for us! I have been beating this chocolate for half an hour, and now it is done. Am I only allowed to smell it while my mouth stays dry? Don't I have the same taste as you, dear ladies, who get to have the essence, leaving me only the aroma? By the devil, I am going to try it! How good it is! (1.8)

The chocolate is a fresh, erotically charged detail in what is otherwise a conventional opera buffa servant complaint. On one hand we can understand why she would want to taste the aromatic drink, particularly after working so hard to prepare it. There is a mutinous fire to her sardonic grumbling, which seems more than justified a few moments later when Dorabella flings the tray of chocolate to the ground during her despairing tantrum (1.9)—an obnoxious display unimaginable with the Countess Almaviva, Constanze, or Donna Anna. However, Despina is no Cinderella, either. Envy, like chocolate, can have a bitter aftertaste. Like so many other servant women, she has been jaded prematurely. In fact, nothing in the libretto indicates that she is older than Fiordiligi and Dorabella; the first Despina, soprano Dorothea Bussani, was about the same age as both Adriana Ferrarese del Bene and Louise Villenueve. Despite her youth, she is immeasurably more experienced than her mistresses in almost every possible way, and she shares Don Alfonso's fossilized cynicism about love.

She laughs, in fact, when she hears about the soldiers' departure to the battleground, saying, "So much the better for them: you will see them return covered in medals." Fiordiligi raises the possibility that the men could be killed, but Despina, unmoved, simply inverts the equation, "In that case, then, so much the better for you," since "if you lose those two, there are still plenty of others around." She rolls her eyes at the idea that Ferrando or Guglielmo is special, summing up the ladies' situation with a leveling mixture of contempt and pragmatism:

> All the others have just what they have. You love one man now, you'll love another later: one is as good as the other, since none of them are worth anything. But let's not talk about that: for now they are alive. And they will come back the same. But they are far away, and, rather than wasting time with useless tears, think about enjoying yourself.

This is Despina's philosophy on love, made up of two basic themes: 1) all men are basically cads, and, therefore, 2) a woman should take pleasure where and when she is able. The maid views love as a power dynamic that requires women to offset their socially established disadvantage with cleverness. This philosophy is not the opposite but rather the obverse of Alfonso's. Despina believes that women learn to be unfaithful because men are that way: così fan *tutte* because così fan *tutti*. In her first aria, No. 12, "In uomini! in soldati," the maid elaborates on how fickleness is a woman's means of self-defense and retaliation. Listening to the moony sisters defend the objects of their devotion, she scoffs, "Oh, go on. The time for telling such fairytales to babies is long gone!" The score then indicates "attaca subito l'Aria di Despina," but the beginning of the aria functions as a transition; the versification is typical of recitative, with *settenari* and *endecasillabi* lines; the music, through set in duple meter, moves with a natural, declamatory pace.[4] After the orchestra's brief introductory gesture, Despina asks with dry incredulousness, "In men! ... in *soldiers* ... you expect to find fidelity?" ("In uomini! in soldati / Sperare fedeltà?"). She repeats the question with added skepticism, the orchestra chuckling along with triplet figures, then breaks into laughter herself at the final "fedeltà" (m. 20). This passage also has the expositional function of recitative, posing the question that Despina answers in the main body of the aria. At "Di pasta simile," Despina speaks with an assurance born of experience:

Di pasta simile	They are all made
Son tutti quanti:	of the same stuff:
Le fronde mobili,	fluctuating fronds,
L'aure incostanti	fickle breezes
Han più degli uomini	have more stability
Stabilità.	than men.
Mentite lagrime,	Lying tears,
Fallaci sguardi,	false glances,
Voci ingannevoli,	deceitful voices,
Vezzi bugiardi	charming lies
Son le primarie	are their main
Lor qualità.	qualities.
In noi non amano	They only love us
Che il lor diletto;	for their own delight;
Poi ci dispregiano,	then they disdain us,
Neganci affetto,	depriving us of affection.
Né val da' barbari	It's useless to beg for mercy
Chieder pietà.	from barbarians.

Paghiam, o femmine,	Let's pay back, ladies,
D'ugual moneta	this malignant,
Questa malefica	pushy breed
Razza indiscreta:	with their own coin:
Amiam per comodo,	let's love for our convenience,
Per vanità!	for our vanity!
La ra la, la ra la, la ra la, la!	La ra la, la ra la, la ra la, la!

Despina lays out crime and punishment with the same music, combining bucolic affability with tenacious drive. While the orchestral "bagpipe" drones out the tonic chord in lively $\frac{6}{8}$ time, Despina introduces the dactylic rhythmic idea that propels the number with unremitting, almost aggressive, repetition. The same rhythms persist even when Despina's breezy tune halts on a series of emphatic octave leaps, so that her complaint about how "fluttering fronds are more stable than fickle men" is musically fixed. She lists men's deceitful ploys, mimicking their fake tears and lying glances to the teasing scalar slides of the violins. Only the final phrase of this section (mm. 39–45) breaks from the intransigent rhythmic pattern—"[these] are their main qualities"—with a more lyrical gesture that closes in dominant C major, gently supported by the viola's inner-voice G pedal. Despina hardly takes time for a breath, however, before continuing her offensive. The pedal-tone stability of the first section gives way to developmental instability (mm. 33ff.) and the depiction of a familiar scenario: the devoted woman used and abandoned by her lover. Picking up the rhythmic *moto perpetuo* again, Despina's line moves back sequentially to the tonic (by way of plaintive G minor) as she warns the sisters that men love only for their own gratification. The violin slides are poignant here, underscoring the grim parallel of the text with a whole-step harmonic drop: "il lor diletto . . . neganci affetto" (their delight . . . is to deprive us of their affection"). The vocal line climbs up a sixth to F at the top of the staff ("Nè val da barbari chieder pietà"), a new high point, before breaking into sobs with the repeat of "chieder pietà." Despina lingers pointedly on this idea of mercy denied, her voice soaring to A-flat in the standard augmented-sixth half cadence that is a marker for pathos (Ex. 36). It is an unsettling moment, for we cannot be certain whether Despina is making fun of those pitiful cries or remembering her own—or maybe both. Her solution to this sexual "barbarism," on the other hand, is definite: "Let's pay them back, ladies." She leaves them with the impression of being a dedicated trifler; her blithe la-las seem to linger even after she exits.

EXAMPLE 36. *Così fan tutte,* No. 12, "In uomini! In soldati"

The undertone of sexual experience and the general theme of female mistreatment at the hands of ungrateful men are typical of the *serva/contadina* aria. As Mary Hunter explains, "singers of these arias often take it upon themselves to explain the nature of womanhood to audiences both on and off stage, especially in arias complaining about men; the burden of such pieces is usually that men shouldn't be so cruel to women because women are, after all, entirely agreeable." She notes how complaints about the opposite sex diverge, not surprisingly, according to gender in opera buffa, so that "whereas men spend most of their misogynist diatribes listing female faults, women spend most of their anti-male statements defending themselves rather than attacking men."[5] In the context of these gendered conventions, "In uomini" is notably hermaphroditic, adopting the traditionally male tactic of cataloguing the flaws of the other sex. Moreover, Despina does not bother with a defense based on women's lovability. Instead she proposes a gender-switching strategy, challenging women to play the game like men. Despina's aloofness at the end of the opera counters another convention governing the *serva/con-*

tadina character, who almost always ends up married at the end of the opera to "someone of appropriate status who has either loved them all along but been rebuffed, or who has failed to get the heroine."[6] Not only does Despina remain alone at the finale, she never attaches herself emotionally to anyone during the course of the opera. She rebuffs Alfonso's solicitation—"An old man like you can't do anything for a girl"—until he plainly defines their relationship in terms of business.

Her independence may also be understood as hyperfemale, and even dangerously so. If "In uomini" is to be believed, Despina is fickle by choice, not by nature; the aria is the only explicit rebuttal to Don Alfonso's (and the opera's) determinate assumptions about women and infidelity. This countering aspect of Despina's character basically disappears after she becomes Don Alfonso's partner. When the *philosophe* enlists her help, he reveals only part of the plan—could she help him introduce two fine gentlemen into her mistresses' good graces?—withholding his true purpose. It is a popular misconception that Despina betrays Fiordiligi and Dorabella, knowingly setting them up for humiliation. In truth, she enters the deal with Don Alfonso believing that she is doing the girls a favor. Her advice to them in "In uomini" is offered *gratis;* in Don Alfonso's deal, she sees an opportunity to get paid for the same service.

Despina's basic intention remains the same, but as the story progresses she varies her discourse on love to make it more palatable to the ladies and—unwittingly—winds up supporting Don Alfonso's misogynist theorem. In her second heart-to-heart with Fiordiligi and Dorabella, "Una donna a quindici anni" (No. 19), Despina tweaks the blunt but sincere message of "In uomini"—her belief that women should pay men back with their own false currency—into something she hopes will be more alluring to the sisters: capriciousness as a sign of a woman's maturity and a natural skill that she must refine. In the recitative that proceeds "Una donna a quindici anni," Despina tells the sisters that she is looking out for their own interests and that they should "start acting like women," treating love "like a bagatelle, never miss a pleasant opportunity; be capricious one moment and faithful the next. Play the tease with style; steer clear of the disgrace that is so common to those who trust in men; have your cake and eat it too!" (2.1). She stresses the moral benefits and naturalness of following her example "for the glory of womankind," asking the sisters, "Are you made out of flesh and blood, or what?" The aria itself is a calculated maneuver, a provocative conduct book that is directed to ladies who can "live without love, but not without lovers":

Una donna a quindici anni	Every girl of fifteen
Dèe saper ogni gran moda:	should know the ways of the world:
Dove il diavolo ha la coda,	where the devil keeps his tail,
Cosa è bene e mal cos'è	what is good and what is bad.

Dèe saper le	She should know the naughty little
maliziette	tricks
Che innamorano gli amanti,	That make lovers fall in love:
Finger riso, Finger pianti,	how to fake laughter, fake tears,
Inventar i bei perché	invent good excuses.

Dèe in un momento	She should pay attention to
Dar retta a cento,	a hundred men at the same time,
Colle pupille	speak to another thousand
Parlar con mille,	with her eyes,
Dar speme a tutti	and give hope to all of them,
Sien belli, o brutti,	whether handsome or ugly.
Saper	She should know how to conceal
nascondersi	things,
Senza confondersi,	without losing her head,
Senza arrossire	and how to lie
Saper mentire.	without blushing.
E qual regina	And she should, like a queen
Dall'alto soglio,	on her high throne,
Coll "posso e voglio"	with "I can and I will,"
Farsi ubbidir.	make herself obeyed.
(a parte)	(aside)
(Par ch'abbian	(It appears that they are taking a
gusto	liking
Di tal dottrina,	to this little doctrine:
Viva Despina	long live Despina,
Che sa servir.)	who knows how to serve!)

The first two quatrains are set to an andante tempo. After the orchestra intones tonic G major, Despina enters with a lilting $\frac{6}{8}$ melody, more daintily *grazioso* than would seem suitable to the brazen text.[7] (A preliminary libretto suggests that censors of the time nixed the line about the devil and his naughty "tail," replacing it with the more demure phrase, "that which the heart most desires and praises").[8] This sweet, inoffensive tune, which renders fake tears and equally fake laughter with the same airy motive, captures the coquette's facade of elegant composure. For most of this section, the orchestra supports the voice with simple, even spare, textures; the only noteworthy exception is the shiver of the second violins at the mention of those "maliziette" that drive lovers crazy.

In the contrasting Allegretto section (beginning at m. 21), the orchestra assumes a more active role, anticipating and generally guiding

EXAMPLE 37. *Così fan tutte*, No. 19, "Una donna a quindici anni"

sen - za arros - si - re   sa - per men - ti - re,   sa - per men - ti - re, e qual re-

gi - na dal-l'al - to so - glio col pos-so e vo - glio far-si ub-bi - dir,

the direction of the vocal line. There is a distinctive shift, however, at the phrase "e qual regina dall'alto soglio col 'posso e voglio' farsi ubbidir"; the accompaniment doubles the vocal line at the unison and octave, resulting in a "whitening out" of harmonic color that, along with the *forte-piano* dynamic accents, sets the text in relief (Ex. 37). This statement—the imperative of ruling over men like an indomitable monarch—is the aria's crucial hook; it dazzles the sisters with illusions of their own queenly potential. Incidentally it also introduces the maid's alter ego, *Regina* Despina, whose motto is "I can and I will." Set on earning that gold piece, Despina reinforces her own impression of authority. In the aside that follows ("Par ch'abbian gusto"), she combines the two images she has of herself; she is the queen of love who also knows how to serve. For the return of the "regina" phrase at the end of the aria—transposed to tonic G major and exploiting a slightly higher range—Despina amplifies the imperious tone with a cadential extension, accenting "posso" and "voglio" in melodic octaves. (Bussani was said to have had an impressive chest voice.) In the final *seria*-style dec-

laration, Despina's line rises majestically to high B-flat, as the (masculine) bass line bends to her purpose, adhering closely to her melody, two
octaves below, like a devoted courtier.

A DIALECTIC OF DESPINA

The servant/queen dichotomy captures perfectly the tension between
Despina's limited clout in society at large and the commanding manner
with which she directs her mistresses. "Una donna a quindici anni"
raises the issue of what Hunter calls Despina's "power of action." The
issue of *control* is central to this character; resentful of her subjugation,
Despina seizes every opportunity to be in charge. Critics are divided,
however, as to the stability of Despina's power. Does it in fact increase,
decrease, or stay the same as we pass from the first to the second act?
Hunter argues that during the course of the opera the maid "charts a
progression from efficacy to futility," and claims that the diminishing of
her independence and control is traceable in her arias and in her disguised appearances.[9] She describes "Una donna a quindici anni" as
"more a statement of a predetermined, conventional, and immovable
position than evidence of an inventive and engaged response to a new
situation," observing that Despina's second aria lacks the unique "dia-
logic engagement" between voice and orchestra found in "In uomini."
Hunter concludes that the repetitiveness and vocal compliance in "Una
donna a quindici anni" confirms that "at least in terms of exercising
psychological power over the ladies, Despina has reached her limit."[10]
    To the contrary, Edmund Goehring perceives a more consistent level
of authoritative force in Despina's two arias, which, he argues, manipulate operatic convention in such a way as to elevate Despina and place
her in the role of instructor from the outset. Goehring claims that, in addition to her singular, quasi-recitative start to "In uomini," Despina reinterprets the "infernal" versification Dorabella used for "Smanie implacabili" for her own acerbic "Di pasta simile," in a manner that is both
"ironic and instructive." Goehring contends that "Una donna a quindici
anni" is no less powerful. He points to the "regina" passage—with its
conspicuous succession of "o" vowels and *seria*-style extension at the
repeat—as the "chief point of her exhortation," which, juxtaposed with
her self-congratulatory aside, proves that Despina "does not lose herself
in a role that does not suit her," but displays a rhetorical flexibility that
allows her "to speak the language of her 'superiors' and . . . persuade
them."[11] He adds that whereas neither of the sisters is allowed to make

the traditional *seria* exit after her first aria, Despina leaves the stage after both of hers, and he claims her "ability to exit unchallenged [after her arias] is yet another manifestation of her authority."[12]

Together, these two seemingly incongruent readings help to explain Despina's peculiar relationship to authority. She is simultaneously the victim and victimizer of "In uomini," as well as the sovereign and subject in "Una donna a quindici anni." Both arias paradoxically reinforce Despina's subjection while also displaying the force of her will. She is frankly independent in "In uomini," a tart and audacious manifesto, but the aria itself is a dramatic dead end. The (un)faithfulness of men is not open for discussion in this opera; in fact, the libretto makes the point that betrayed Ferrando and Guglielmo still love their original beloveds. In addition, Despina's harangue fails to convince her mistresses, who flatly refuse to see their departed sweethearts as anything less than perfect. Despina's basic directive in "In uomini"—that the women should be fickle—carries forward to "Una donna a quindici anni," but her personal motive—the retaliatory angle—is left behind. In her second aria, Despina is no longer an independent voice; she has become Don Alfonso's accomplice and, to a degree, his unwitting dupe. Nevertheless, the aria marks the first time that Despina calculatedly and *successfully* persuades her mistresses into crossing a definite moral line: moments after she leaves the room, Fiordiligi and Dorabella select their new paramours. "Una donna a quindici anni" is a consciously tactical, prepared lecture designed to sway girlish minds. It is meant to sound—musically and textually—like conventional wisdom, not an individual opinion. The temperate, agreeable music neutralizes the sour sexual politics of "In uomini," promoting conformity instead of revolution. Even the dramatic tone of "E qual regina" is made to appeal to wannabe opera seria heroines. Despina closes the aria, however, in her natural voice, with a self-congratulating aside: "Long live Despina, who knows how to serve!" The combination of erotic wisdom and regal imagery, of pastoral and seria elements, in "Una donna a quindici anni" generates the energy that drives Dorabella into Guglielmo's arms and pushes Fiordiligi well past her proclaimed boundaries. Far from being the terminus of Despina's psychological influence over the ladies, this aria is perhaps the triumphant demonstration of her leverage that begins with the poison scene in act 1 and extends through the "truce" quartet, No. 22, "La mano a me date."

The importance of Despina's efforts in bringing the two couples together is consistently underplayed in performance and in print. Customarily, Alfonso has been represented as the chief puppeteer of "la bella commedia"; he is the rational sage, almost fatidic in his pronouncements, conjuring up the scheme and forecasting its outcome. The old philosopher assumes a rhetorical superiority via asides and monologues, commenting for the audience's benefit on every other character, including Despina. To her face, he always addresses her as "Despinetta," using a diminutive form that hovers between affection and condescension. Yet relatively early in the opera, Don Alfonso acknowledges that the shrewd maid poses an estimable threat: "I'm a little worried about Despina: that sly girl could recognize them [Ferrando and Guglielmo] and upset the applecart. Let's see . . . maybe a little gift is in order: a gold coin always works like a charm with a chambermaid. But just to be sure, it would be better to let her in on part of the secret . . . an excellent plan" (1.10).

As insurance, Don Alfonso pays for Despina's support in his matchmaking efforts, but Despina does not wait around for his orders. From the outset she lets Don Alfonso know that she is nobody's pet. When Don Alfonso first approaches her, the maid assumes he is making a sexual advance; she answers cheekily that she doesn't need anything from him, adding, "an old-timer can't do anything" for a young woman. Moreover, it soon becomes clear that the maid's cooperation is not just helpful to Don Alfonso's scheme, but essential, much more so than he ever admits. Confident as he is, the "old-timer" is not able to carry out his plan alone, even with the soldiers' complicity. Simply put, he lacks access. To begin with, Fiordiligi and Dorabella never confide in him or seek his advice. His pseudo-paternal posturing cannot rival Despina's feminine advantage, her admission to the sisters' private quarters and intimate thoughts. Nor does he appear to have the flexibility of imagination required to pull off the hoax. Don Alfonso operates on presumptions and is easily frustrated by variables. Having imagined, for instance, that there would be little resistance from the sisters, he is flabbergasted at their initial hostile retreat from the Albanians. Lamenting the "ridiculous" prospect that he might be dealing with two of the last remaining faithful ladies on earth, the philosopher turns again to Despina, who, unconcerned, takes over direction of the whole business:

    Don Alfonso. But in the meantime, those foolish girls . . .

       Despina. Those foolish girls will do whatever we want. It's high time they knew how passionately those two are in love with them.

    Don Alfonso. They know.

> *Despina.* So then they will learn to love them in return. As they say, "Just mention it, and let the devil do the rest."
>
> *Don Alfonso.* But how will you convince those two little beasts of yours to come back now that they have gone, to listen and let themselves give into temptation?
>
> *Despina.* Leave the matter of how to bring it off to me. When Despina cooks up a plot, it always comes off well. I have already led a thousand men by the nose, so I will certainly know how to deal with two women.

It is Despina, not Alfonso, who concocts the make-believe poisoning, brilliantly satisfying three preliminary conditions for the final seductions: stirring the ladies' pity, facilitating physical contact between the couples, and strengthening her image as someone to listen to, the voice of good sense. Her command of the situation is also demonstrated musically. She successfully conducts the sisters' crucial harmonic—and emotional—transition from G-minor tragedy to E-flat-major sympathy, covering up Don Alfonso's blundering attempt to do the same. This process begins when Fiordiligi and Dorabella first see the dying Albanians. They express their horror with Don Alfonso, closing in G minor (mm. 112–36). The old schemer, assuming that the ladies have been sufficiently prepared for the next stage of seduction, hastily abandons his pose of distress. The harmony shifts abruptly to E-flat major as Alfonso tries to coax the women into offering comfort to the poor victims, but his marchlike rhythmic motto (mm. 138–41) is wholly unsuited to the maneuver, inciting the women instead to hysterical cries for help. Initially they take up his musical idea (mm. 146–48), but soon they go their own musical way, darting toward B-flat major as they shout for Despina. At the maid's entrance, Don Alfonso quickly reverts to G minor, reestablishing the plaintive tone: "Furious, desperate, they poisoned themselves. Ah, what singular love!"

Now it is Despina's turn to attempt the transition, transforming the girls from shocked bystanders to caring attendants. She exhibits considerably more finesse than the precipitate *philosophe*, fashioning her own somber variation of Alfonso's march idea, in G minor ("It would be shameful of you to abandon the miserable creatures"), before tightening the snare with a modulation to B-flat major ("They need to be helped"). Her statement hangs in the air like a schoolmistress's disapproval, demanding a response. Obediently, the sisters and Don Alfonso ask what they should do, punctuating their petition with a half cadence on B-flat major. Only now does Despina reintroduce E-flat major as the tonic key, with a simple but unequivocal descending triad: "There is life in them yet" (mm. 184–86). Addressing her mistresses, she advises them via a calming scalar melody to soothe the sick men with their "tender hands." The maid then orders Don Alfonso in no-nonsense patter to help her find a doctor; he follows her without another word. Despina's intervention in the poison scene establishes her capacity for authoritative persuasion even before she puts on the doctor's disguise. She borrows Don Alfonso's basic strategy and musical material but avoids his overly hasty transition from G minor to E-flat major, taking her time instead to establish the new, "love-friendly" tonal center of the section via dominant B-flat major. She pulls the emotional strings so skillfully that the sisters hardly notice the manipulation. By the time she returns disguised as the doctor, the sisters have touched the men and noted with concern their faltering heartbeats and cold foreheads. At the end of the poison scene, Fiordiligi and Dorabella exit in a huff once more, but everyone else agrees that their anger is now rooted in attraction.

It takes only one more small nudge from Despina to bring the lovers together. It is not clear whether she engineers the Albanians' appeasing serenade, but she definitely makes Fiordiligi and Dorabella more receptive to it via "Una donna a quindici anni," her tutorial on the grand and gratifying art of discreet flirtation. Dorabella and Fiordiligi respond with "Prenderò quel brunettino," the first time they seriously entertain the thought of dallying with the handsome foreigners. When Don Alfonso comes with his announcement about the party, he finds Dorabella and Fiordiligi in a favorable mood, yet he must still rely on Despina to guide her mistresses. The Albanians' tongue-tied timidity in front of the women prompts the old man to snap, "Oh, the devil take it! Stop these corny, old-fashioned airs!" He grasps Dorabella's hand and instructs Despina to follow his lead with Fiordiligi in the quartet No. 22, "La mano a me date." Demonstrating proper wooing technique, Don Alfonso addresses the ladies in a charming Allegretto grazioso, as Ferrando and Guglielmo struggle to follow his example. Feebly echoing Alfonso's words, the younger men are more silly than seductive, reducing the ladies to giggles. Thinking quickly, Despina pronounces—in a variation of Alfonso's opening melody—that she will speak for her mistresses, but she wisely forgoes Alfonso's repeat-after-me approach. Drawing herself up with musical dignity, she answers the Albanians in an accompanied recitative style that is pointedly *à la Fiordiligi,* a tacit reminder to the ladies about the magisterial discipline a woman must exert in matters of love. She concludes the ritual by having her mistresses break their garlands and place them on their new suitors. Satisfied, Despina returns to the main musical theme, inviting the men on behalf of the ladies to offer their arms. Her work done, she slips discreetly away with Don Alfonso.

In all three cases—the poison scene, "Una donna a quindici anni," and the reconciliation serenade/quartet No. 22—Despina's competence in "exercising psychological power over the ladies," as Hunter describes it, is not so much a matter of musical originality as it is of implementation. She uses whatever available musical and dramatic resources are necessary to get results. She may borrow material, for example from Don Alfonso or the orchestra, yet she employs it in new and more effective ways. Her influence over the sisters extends to Dorabella's aria "È l'amore un ladroncello," the style of which is clearly derived from "Una donna a quindici anni." Dorabella becomes Despina's disciple and confides in her maid about the tryst with Guglielmo. Fiordiligi, however, never fully converts, and it is in her that we find the real limit of Despina's "power of action." After Fiordiligi runs away from Ferrando, she confronts Despina and Dorabella together and renounces the values of "Una donna a quindici anni," exclaiming, "I've caught the devil, and he can take me, you, her, Don Alfonso, the foreigners, and all the rest of the lunatics in the world!" (2.10). Despina's only substantial remark to this outburst is "You don't know anything." The comment is unintentionally ironic, since Despina herself does not know as much as she would like to think: she is ignorant of Don Alfonso's true designs and has little understanding of the conflict that Fiordiligi feels. Far from showing her superiority, this smug retort equalizes Despina with the other unknowing ladies and points ahead to her own humiliating comeuppance.

This scene is the real turning point for Despina. Fiordiligi has put up a wall against her. Dorabella emulates the maid but also replaces her as pleasure's spokesperson. In her next encounter with Fiordiligi, Despina is silenced almost altogether. Her mistress forbids her so adamantly from talking back that she can only sneak in a petulant aside about "Donna Arroganza." She is back to being the put-upon servant, not realizing that worse is yet to come. Announcing to the Albanians that her mistresses have accepted their marriage proposals, she congratulates herself—"When Despina is involved in a project, she always gets good results"—unaware of the scornful grimace behind the men's smiles. They have already sung the famous "Così fan tutte" slogan with Don Alfonso; Despina is no longer an ally, but just another member of the perfidious feminine throng. No one will be thanking her for her efforts in the final scene. Quite the contrary: when the disguised Ferrando and

Guglielmo reveal their true identities, they mock her right along with the sisters, snidely hailing the "magnetic doctor" who is getting the "respect she deserves." After this revelation, Despina, for the first and only time in the opera, sings *with* her mistresses, the three exclaiming together, "Heavens, what am I seeing? I cannot bear the agony!" The unity is short-lived. Despina does not join Fiordiligi and Dorabella when they blame Don Alfonso, nor does she ask for forgiveness from any of the men. She is alone with her confusion and shame, as she tells us, but she is not ready to concede defeat in the world of sexual power and intrigue.

DESPINA'S LAST WORD

Conflict between the sexes is a common trope in opera buffa, represented mostly in the spirit of "You can't live with them or without them." This is certainly the case with *Le nozze di Figaro,* with its final couplings of all the major characters, including Marcellina with Bartolo and Barbarina with Cherubino. The opera also has an optimistic aspect, represented by Susanna and Figaro. They sustain their love for one another from the opening scene in the bedroom to the final encounter in the garden; it is a genuine affection that survives the Count's intrusions and Figaro's momentary lack of faith. We watch Susanna and Figaro and we believe that they, if no one else, have a real chance at happiness in marriage. In contrast, *Così fan tutte* begins with a negative proposition—that women are incurably inconstant—proves it though demonstration, and then offers everyone cold comfort in the end: a woman's marriage vows mean little, so just laugh and marry her anyway. One could easily imagine an alternative ending in which Don Alfonso ordered the *new* couples to marry, because ultimately the couplings themselves do not matter much. In fact, many productions stage something along these lines. In any case, the final pose of rapprochement cannot dispel the opera's fundamental attitude of antagonism, the rancor that seethes under the surface of Don Alfonso's and Despina's guiding philosophies on love. The old gentleman and the young maidservant adopt similar strategies for protecting themselves and controlling their environment. They work well together as partners in intrigue, but there is nothing approaching genuine respect or sympathy between them. Despina and Don Alfonso represent the *real* battlefield of the opera. Through them, men and women are artificially defined as moral antipodes: Alfonso the Admirable and Despina the Deplorable.

Accordingly, Don Alfonso is able to rationalize his fraud as beneficial, parlaying it into an ongoing hegemony over the men and, as a result, the women: "I deceived you, but the deception was to undeceive your lovers, so that they will be wiser now and will do just what I say." Conversely, his aide, Despina, is marked as a "cunning little vixen" to be used or avoided altogether. She is cast as an incorrigible example of the opera's motto—"women act that way"—and her final words emphasize her skill at treachery: "It's fine if they tricked me, since I will trick plenty of others." Even her participation in the final moral bromide—comic convention superseding all dramatic realism—does not keep her from being a marginalized presence, a woman without a man, a servant resubjugated. So ends *Così fan tutte,* wherein a man schemes to give men proof of woman's inherent fickleness, while a woman schemes to give women the pleasure, autonomy, and command she believes men enjoy and abuse. In this respect, *Così fan tutte* prefigures some of the gender conflicts of *Die Zauberflöte,* which mixes democratic ideals with the same brand of essentializing chauvinism.

The character of Despina forms a crucial point in a thematic bridge in Mozart's late operas, one that stretches from Marcellina (the despised housekeeper, not the sentimental mother of Figaro) and Donna Elvira in act 1 of *Don Giovanni* to the Queen of the Night. These are recalcitrant women who speak out—and act up—against what they see as abuse of power and double standards. These characters challenge us to reconsider inherited definitions of what it means to be a "heroine." Each of them deviates significantly from the feminine ideal of Mozart's time, yet these deviations also illuminate the artificiality and prejudice of such paradigms. Marcellina and Donna Elvira both "convert" to more acceptable representations of eighteenth-century womanhood; the spiteful duenna becomes the loving mother, and the hysterical whistle-blower changes (back?) into the compassionate protector of the man she loves. Of course, such transformations are not a guarantee of happiness. Marcellina is embraced by love, but Elvira is deserted by it. For her part, Despina resists alteration. She is not malleable. In truth, there is little reason for her to expose her "softer" feelings; if anything, her experience with Don Alfonso teaches her to harden herself even more. In the end, *Così* emphasizes her disgrace, obscuring the humanizing "why" that informs the bitterness of "In uomini." Regina Despina is a bit like the Queen of the Night, whose long-alleged transformation really comes down to Tamino's changed perspective, which ultimately defines her as the enemy. The maidservant and the queen call into question the adamantly categorical constructions of goodness and power, nature and reason, that form the foundation of Mozart's two last operas. It is the same shadow that follows Moll Flanders and the Marquise de Merteuil, whose words in the epigraphs at the beginning of this chapter find an echo in *Così fan tutte*. These women call out to us with a single, disorienting revelation that glints through the concentrated beauty of music or prose: *It is not so simple as they say.*

Notes

OVERTURE

1. Carolyn Abbate, *In Search of Opera* (Princeton, 2001), x–xi.

2. Peter Branscombe, *W. A. Mozart: Die Zauberflöte,* Cambridge Opera Handbooks (Cambridge, 1991), 221.

3. Ibid., 216.

4. Ibid., 2.

5. Bruce Alan Brown, *W. A. Mozart: Così fan tutte* (Cambridge, 1995), 181. Italics mine.

6. Richard Taruskin, *Text and Act: Essays on Music and Performance* (New York, 1995), 263–72. The original article, "Why Mozart Has Become an Icon for Today," appeared in the Arts and Leisure supplement of the Sunday *New York Times,* 9 September 1990.

7. Ibid., 267.

8. Ibid.

9. Carolyn Abbate, *Unsung Voices: Opera and Musical Narrative in the Nineteenth Century* (Princeton, 1991), xv.

10. Mary Hunter, "Window to the Work, or Mirror of Our Preconceptions? Peter Sellars's Production of *Così fan tutte," repercussions* 4 (Fall 1995): 42–58. She cites Roman Ingarden, *The Work of Music and the Problem of Its Identity.*

11. Ibid., 50.

12. Ibid., 56.

13. Wye Jamison Allanbrook, Mary Hunter, and Gretchen A. Wheelock, "Staging Mozart's Women," in *Siren Songs,* ed. Mary Ann Smart (Princeton, 2000), 47–66.

14. Catherine Clément, *Opera, or the Undoing of Women,* trans. Betsy Wing, foreword by Susan McClary (Minneapolis, 1988), 17.

15. Ibid., 22–23.

16. Wayne C. Booth, *The Company We Keep: An Ethics of Fiction* (Berkeley, 1988), 11.

17. Ibid., 135.

18. Ibid., 137.

19. Ibid., 43.

20. Ibid., 136.

21. Sydney Janet Kaplan, "Varieties of Feminist Criticism," in *Making a Difference: Feminist Literary Criticism,* ed. Gayle Greene and Coppélia Kahn (New York, 1985), 37–38.

22. William Mann, *The Operas of Mozart* (Oxford, 1977), 478, 509.

23. Frits Noske, *The Signifier and the Signified: Studies in the Operas of Mozart and Verdi* (The Hague, 1977), 85.

24. Ibid., 86.

25. The full original title was *Il dissoluto punito, ossia [or] Il Don Giovanni.* It is striking that this opera, unlike the other two Da Ponte operas—*Le nozze di Figaro* and *Così fan tutte*—has come to us under its secondary title, reflecting, at least in part, the influence of nineteenth- and early twentieth-century reception, which shaped Don Giovanni into a kind of superman.

26. Søren Kierkegaard, *Either/Or,* vol. 1, rev. and with a foreword by Howard A. Johnson, trans. David F. Swenson and Lillian Martin Swenson (Princeton, 1959), 99. Kierkegaard presents *Either/Or* as a publication by an unspecified narrator of the essays allegedly by "Mr. A" and "Mr. B," thereby distancing himself in a technical sense from the commentary on, among other things, the nature of Don Giovanni. Nevertheless, the philosophical positions set forth in Mr. A's "The Immediate Stages of the Erotic, or The Musical Erotic" have influenced numerous writers on the subject, who have taken the remarks as the reasonable, attractive theories of the respected philosopher-author, not just the private musings of a fictionalized character.

CHAPTER I

1. Parenthetical references are to act, scene, and, when appropriate, number (opera) or line (play). All musical examples and original-language texts from the librettos of Mozart's operas will be taken from the relevant volumes of *Wolfgang Amadeus Mozart: Neue Ausgabe sämtlicher Werke,* ed. E. F. Schmid, W. Plath, and W. Rehm, International Stiftung Mozarteum Salzburg (Kassel, 1955–), hereafter abbreviated as *NMA*. Given that Mozart continued to make changes to the libretto after its original printing, the *NMA*, which includes these changes, best represents Mozart's "autograph" version. Where significant differences between the *NMA* text and the original printed libretto occur, the original text will be given in brackets. These original texts are taken from facsimiles published in *The Librettos of Mozart's Operas,* ed. Ernest Warburton (New York, 1992), hereafter abbreviated as *LMO*. I did not always rely on a single original-language source for the major plays that I discuss in this book— Ludovico Ariosto's *Orlando furioso,* Pierre Augustin Caron de Beaumarchais's *Le barbier de Seville* and *Le mariage de Figaro,* Carlo Goldoni's *Don Giovanni Tenorio,* Jean-Baptiste Poquelin de Molière's *Dom Juan ou le festin de Pierre,*

and Tirso de Molina's *El burlador de Sevilla y convidado de piedra*—but I have listed reliable editions in the Works Cited section for the reader's reference. All English translations are mine unless otherwise noted.

2. Day I, lines 5–13. The original source of Tirso's play divides the drama into three acts (designated First, Second, and Third Day) but does not indicate scene numbers, so editors must either suggest scene divisions or use line numbering only.

3. Day I, line 161.

4. Day I, lines 184–86.

5. Day II, lines 516–27.

6. Day III, lines 963–64.

7. Charles C. Russell, *The Don Juan Legend before Mozart, with a Collection of Eighteenth-Century Librettos* (Ann Arbor, 1993), 19–20.

8. It is notable that Da Ponte, though influenced by some aspects of Goldoni's play, created a very different relationship in this case. Goldoni's Anna must rely on Don Alfonso, the king's trusted prime minister, for moral support; he is the one who speaks to her about the nature of noble love, offers paternal consolation after the murder of her father ("If you have lost your father, you will have one in me"—a line that Da Ponte appropriates for Don Ottavio), and acts as prosecutor in her quest for justice against Don Giovanni. Da Ponte's Donna Anna, on the other hand, looks solely to Don Ottavio to fulfill the role of paternal protector and avenger; she also has a number of intimate scenes with him.

9. The text of Bertati's libretto is printed in Stefan Kunze's *Don Giovanni vor Mozart: Die Tradition der Don-Giovanni-Opern im Italienische Buffa-Theater des 18. Jahrhunderts* (Munich, 1972), 159–204. In the early *Extract* from his memoirs (1819), Da Ponte admits that Domenico Guardasoni, the impresario at Prague, invited Mozart himself to compose a new opera on Bertati's libretto in early 1787. Da Ponte wrote disparagingly about Bertati (who was to succeed him as court theater poet at Vienna), but whatever ill opinions he held about his colleague did not stop him from nabbing useful bits from Bertati's libretto.

10. Stefano Castelvecchi, "From *Nina* to *Nina*: Psychodrama, Absorption, and Sentiment in the 1780s," *Cambridge Opera Journal* 8 (July 1996): 102–3.

11. The unstable harmonies reflect Donna Anna's volatile emotional state: E-flat–C-sharp dim7–G-sharp dim7–B-flat augmented sixth chord–A minor. As Anna is overwhelmed by feeling, she moves rhetorically from "blood" to "wound" to "death," and, similarly, from "father" to "dear father" to "beloved father." Castelvecchi describes how "sentimental literature exploits a whole set of devices in order to stress the emotional inadequacy of words: interrupted phrases, broken syntax, repetition, typographical exuberance" (ibid., 103), all of which characterize Anna's music in this scene.

12. Hoffmann's "Don Juan" first appeared in the *Allgemeine Musikalischen Zeitung* in 1813; later, in 1814–15, it was published as part of Hoffmann's collection *Fantasiestücke in Callots Manier.*

13. E. T. A. Hoffmann, *Don Juan*, in *Hoffmanns Werke*, ed. and introduction by Gerhard Schneider, Nationalen Forschungs- und Gedenkstätten der Klassischen Deutschen Literatur in Weimar (Berlin, 1990), 27.

14. Ibid., 28.

15. Edward Dent, *Mozart's Operas: A Critical Study,* 2nd ed., London, 1941, reprint with foreword by Winton Dean (New York, 1991), 158.

16. William Mann, *The Operas of Mozart* (Oxford, 1977), 468; italics mine. Despite its egregious flaws, Mann's book, though now out of print, continues to be a popular choice as a reference and, as recently as 1991, was listed in *Opera News* (in preparation for the Metropolitan Opera's production of *Don Giovanni*) as a good general introduction to the opera.

17. Charles Ford, *Così? Sexual Politics in Mozart's Operas* (Manchester, 1991), 185. Whether it is intentional or not, Ford's rhetorical style is effective in minimizing self-incrimination when presenting "historic" attitudes and stereotypes. Though he begins with the active "we," he moves to the passive voice at a crucial moment. Then, for the most inflammatory statements, he cites a dubiously reconstructed "Enlightenment" or else modern critics like Mann, without, however, offering any qualification or rebuttal.

18. Ibid., 183.

19. Wye Jamison Allanbrook, *Rhythmic Gesture in Mozart:* Le Nozze di Figaro *and* Don Giovanni (Chicago, 1983), 207.

20. Mary Hunter, *The Culture of Opera Buffa in Mozart's Vienna: A Poetics of Entertainment* (Princeton, 1999), 145–46.

21. Russell, *The Don Juan Legend,* 91–92.

22. See, for example, Ivan Nagel's essays in *Autonomy and Mercy: Reflections on Mozart's Operas,* trans. Marion Faber and Ivan Nagel (Cambridge, Mass., 1991).

23. Hunter, *The Culture of Opera Buffa,* 140.

24. I have provided both the original language and an English translation of selections from the operas to facilitate reference to the musical score.

25. Maynard Solomon, *Mozart: A Life* (New York, 1995), 512.

26. Ibid., 513.

27. Leonard Ratner, *Classic Music: Expression, Form, and Style* (New York, 1980), 401–2.

28. Indeed, Ottavio grows fearful that Anna will truly lose her mind viewing the terrible sight of her father's bloodied body; for this reason he immediately asks the servants to remove the dead man.

29. Allanbrook categorizes the alla breve style that Anna utilizes for both of her revenge pieces as a "grand, rather old-fashioned idiom," but also quotes an eighteenth-century source that describes the $\frac{2}{2}$ or cut time as "the most majestic of all meters," to be applied only to "serious, heartfelt passions"; *Rhythmic Gesture,* 19.

30. A similar staccato motive forms part of the second theme group in the Allegro section of the overture (mm. 77ff.), where it is linked with a lively, almost taunting idea (which reminds me, at least in its general affect, of the accompaniment to Don Giovanni's aria "Fin ch'han dal vino"). The two motives provide most of the interesting material for the development section (mm. 121–40, mm. 157–79). The interplay between the two might be heard as the ever-changing dynamic of assailed and assailant manifested in the relationship between Don Giovanni and his victims.

31. Mann labels Vitellia as "the Lady Macbeth of eighteenth-century opera" and goes on to cite Tovey, who called her "the horridest female that ever disgraced a libretto" (*The Operas of Mozart*, 571).

32. Daniel Heartz notes that one of the most impressive elements of the Gazzaniga score is the setting of the Commendatore's death in E-flat minor; see Daniel Heartz, *Mozart's Operas* (Berkeley, 1990), 202.

33. Alfred Einstein, *Mozart: His Character, His Work* (Oxford, 1962), 439.

34. Italics mine.

35. Solomon, *Mozart*, 512.

36. "Rapire" generally means to steal or abduct, but more specifically to rape.

37. Allanbrook, *Rhythmic Gesture*, 228–29.

38. Mary Hunter, "Some representations of *opera seria* in *opera buffa*," *Cambridge Opera Journal* 3 (1991): 107.

39. Ford, *Così?* 183.

40. Hunter, *The Culture of Opera Buffa*, 140.

41. Ford, *Così?* 183.

42. Though Ottavio's melody might appear to recall the first theme of the overture in the context of a performance of the opera, Mozart actually wrote the sextet before the overture, as was common practice.

43. "Sola morte, o mio tesoro, / il mio pianto può finir." The facsimile in the *LMO* reads "Sol la morte," which is the form often adopted in modern performances and recordings.

44. The collapsing trajectory from D minor to C minor in Anna's musical response serves well to depict Anna's unsteady emotional state. As noted above, Elettra's aria "Tutte nel cor vi sento" displays the same harmonic incongruity with a C minor return in a D-minor aria.

45. Allanbrook, *Rhythmic Gesture*, 253.

46. This is also true of Zerlina's affectionate aria "Vedrai carino," which uses the same orchestration as "Non mi dir"; both Zerlina's earlier aria, "Batti, batti," and the duet "Là ci darem la mano" feature oboes instead of clarinets. It is interesting that Mozart introduced clarinets only in the arias in which Zerlina and Donna Anna, each in her own way, intimately express affection.

47. Dent, *Mozart's Operas*, 171.

48. Allanbrook, *Rhythmic Gesture*, 229.

49. Ibid.

CHAPTER 2

1. Lawrence Lipking, "Donna Abbandonata," in *The* Don Giovanni *Book: Myths of Seduction and Betrayal*, ed. Jonathan Miller (London, 1990), 42.

2. Edward Dent, *Mozart's Operas: A Critical Study*, 2nd ed., London, 1941, reprint with foreword by Winton Dean (New York, 1991), 157.

3. It is interesting to note that Molière, not Da Ponte, first used the idea of a character speaking as if out of a book; ironically, in the French play, Dom Juan is the one who merits the description. Following Dom Juan's lengthy speech on the merits of his lifestyle (1.2), his servant, Sganarelle (played on the stage by

Molière himself), remarks, "My goodness, how you talk! It seems like you learned that by heart, and you talk just like a book." Among other things, Molière's Elvire is spared the insinuations of ridiculousness that Elvira has to bear; Sganarelle is far more consistent than Leporello in his expressions of sympathy for the wronged woman and in his distaste for his master.

4. Hermann Abert, *Mozart's Don Giovanni,* trans. Peter Gellhorn (London, 1976), 80.

5. Wye Jamison Allanbrook, *Rhythmic Gesture in Mozart:* Le Nozze di Figaro *and* Don Giovanni (Chicago, 1983), 233–34. It should also be noted that the aria structure itself is unusual for Mozart's later operas in that it features a true orchestral ritornello, the material of which is not thematically related to the vocal line.

6. Dent, *Mozart's Operas,* 159–60.

7. Andrew Steptoe, *The Mozart Da Ponte Operas: The Cultural and Musical Background to* Le Nozze di Figaro, Don Giovanni, *and* Così fan tutte (Oxford, 1988), 201. Italics mine.

8. Allanbrook, *Rhythmic Gesture,* 237–38.

9. Lipking, "Donna Abbandonata," 42–43.

10. Although it serves the requirements of musical form, the repetition of this motive is dramatically unconvincing. Its banality—which worked well for Don Giovanni's and Leporello's furtive discussion about what to do with Donna Elvira—is too dull for Elvira, who, even when deliberating, usually expresses herself more colorfully.

11. This kind of quotation is a rare occurrence in opera of the time. It also tells us a great deal about the consistency of Giovanni's seductive "lines," as he adeptly changes target without significantly changing his tune.

12. Lipking, "Donna Abbandonata," 42, 44.

13. Ibid., 41–42. Of course, Kierkegaard's vision of Elvira with her nun's veil is his own invention, drawn perhaps more directly from Molière's play than Mozart's opera. Though there are many similarities between Elvire and Elvira, Da Ponte never gives explicit evidence (either in descriptions of her costume or in her words) of the latter having been taken from a convent. In her first entrance in the opera she is dressed in "traveling clothes." In any case, it is unlikely that she would come to the balcony in blasphemed holy garb or something approaching intimate apparel.

14. Daniel Heartz, *Mozart's Operas* (Berkeley, 1990), 214–15. Heartz offers an excellent—and eloquent—analysis of this sextet.

15. Allanbrook, *Rhythmic Gesture,* 240.

16. Ibid., 251–52.

17. Ibid., 253. Italics mine.

18. Charles Ford, Così? *Sexual Politics in Mozart's Operas* (Manchester, 1991), 154.

19. Dent, *Mozart's Operas,* 159.

20. Ibid., 165.

21. Spike Hughes, *Famous Mozart Operas: An Analytical Guide for the opera-goer and armchair listener* (New York, 1972), 114.

22. Julian Rushton, *W. A. Mozart: Don Giovanni* (Cambridge, 1981), 101.

23. Don Giovanni's vocal line twice holds the third at the tonic cadence, before sliding in a teasing manner to the fifth (mm. 330–32, 336).

24. Listed in the *NMA* as scene 10d of act 2. Mozart composed the role of Constanze in *Die Entführung aus dem Serail* and that of Madame Silberklang in *Der Schauspieldirektor* for Cavalieri, whose substantial range and skill at passage work (especially bravura-style coloratura) were shown to full advantage in both vocal roles. For a comprehensive study of Catarina Cavalieri, see Patricia Lewy Gidwitz, "Vocal Profiles of Four Mozart Sopranos," Ph.D. diss., University of California, Berkeley, 1991.

25. Rushton, *W. A. Mozart: Don Giovanni*, 101.

26. Jane Miller, *Seductions: Studies in Reading and Culture* (Cambridge, Mass., 1991), 37.

27. Ibid., 28–29.

CHAPTER 3

1. Joachim Kaiser, *Who's Who in Mozart's Operas: From Alfonso to Zerlina*, trans. Charles Kessler (New York, 1987), 191.

2. It is curious that the original text omitted Aminta from the list of characters.

3. It seems that the wedding has already taken place by the time Don Juan fools Batricio with his story, for he mentions that Aminta had captured his heart "for several days" (3.2). Later, Aminta complains to her maid Belisa that the nobleman has driven Batricio from his house and their bed (3.4). Nevertheless, it is implied in the subsequent encounter between Aminta and Don Juan that the marriage had not yet been consummated and could therefore be annulled (3.8).

4. We might reasonably suspect that Tirso's Don Juan fully believes in his own illusions; in the case of Aminta, for example, he make his comments about her hands in an aside to his servant Catalinón, not directly to Aminta herself.

5. Another peasant girl, Maturine, appears briefly in Molière's play. In her one scene she engages with Charlotte in a catfight that Dom Juan slyly engineers (as a diversion) via deceitful asides to each woman (2.4).

6. The *LMO* places a question mark here.

7. The complementary scene in the Bertati-Gazzaniga work is comparatively dull, with Maturina singing an aria in response to Don Giovanni's proposition. The seduction itself is very brief and composed solely of recitative.

8. Wye Jamison Allanbrook, *Rhythmic Gesture in Mozart: Le Nozze di Figaro and Don Giovanni* (Chicago, 1983), 269.

9. Hermann Abert, *Mozart's Don Giovanni*, trans. Peter Gellhorn (London, 1976), 76.

10. Charles Ford asserts that Zerlina's arias "are the only places in the Da Ponte comedies that may make men feel uneasy"; the vacillation between sexual liberty and sexual dependency in these numbers makes Zerlina the "incarnation of male desire. *Così? Sexual Politics in Mozart's Operas* (Manchester, 1991), 172.

11. Abert, *Mozart's Don Giovanni*, 88.

12. Joseph Kerman, "Reading *Don Giovanni*," in *The Don Giovanni Book: Myths of Betrayal and Seduction*, ed. Jonathan Miller (London, 1990), 111.

13. "[È] un certo antidoto"; *LMO*, 166. "Balsamo" evokes a more sensuous meaning, a soothing liquid balm.

14. Maynard Solomon, *Mozart: A Life* (New York, 1995), 509, 517, 516.

15. Kaiser, *Who's Who in Mozart's Operas*, 190.

16. Mary Hunter, *The Culture of Opera Buffa in Mozart's Vienna: A Poetics of Entertainment* (Princeton, 1999), 136–37.

17. Allanbrook, *Rhythmic Gesture*, 274.

18. Mozart inserted four scenes (2.10a–d) between Don Ottavio's aria "Il mio tesoro" (2.10) and the cemetery scene (2.11) for the Vienna production.

CHAPTER 4

1. Jacques Chailley, The Magic Flute *Unveiled: Esoteric Symbolism in Mozart's Masonic Opera*, trans. Herbert Weinstock (Rochester, NY, 1992), 102.

2. For an excellent summary of the most important sources, see Peter Branscombe, *W. A. Mozart: Die Zauberflöte* (Cambridge, 1991), 4–34.

3. Chailley, The Magic Flute *Unveiled*, 92–93.

4. Ibid., 194–95.

5. Robert Moberly, *Three Mozart Operas*: Figaro, Don Giovanni, Magic Flute (New York, 1968), 223.

6. Anthony Besch, "A Director's Approach," in *W. A. Mozart*: Die Zauberflöte, ed. Peter Branscombe (Cambridge, 1991), 199. Besch was responsible for productions of *Die Zauberflöte* for the English National Opera (1975) and the National Arts Centre in Ottawa, Canada (1975).

7. Carolyn Abbate, *In Search of Opera* (Princeton, 2001), 68.

8. Ibid.

9. Ibid., 86.

10. W. H. Auden and Charles Kallman, *The Complete Works of W. H. Auden: Libretti and Other Dramatic Writings, 1939–1973,* Edward Mendelson, ed. (Princeton, 1993), 152–56. Auden inserted the "Metalogue" between the two acts of his and Kallman's English version of the libretto for *Die Zauberflöte;* the stage directions indicate that the "Metalogue" is to be read by the singer playing Sarastro.

11. Alfons Rosenberg, *Die Zauberflöte* (Munich, 1964), 207.

12. Ibid., 206–7.

13. Nicholas Till reminds us of the extreme prescription of the Marquis de Sade, who held that "in the modern republican state all forms of maternal and familial love should be replaced by love of the fatherland, and that maternal love that threatens the state should be punished and overthrown by rape and murder of the mother"; Till, *Mozart and the Enlightenment: Truth, Virtue and Beauty in Mozart's Operas* (New York, 1993), 183.

14. Rose Subotnik, *Deconstructive Variations: Music and Reason in Western Society* (Minneapolis, 1996), 15–16.

15. Ivan Nagel, too, would have us believe that "despite our dubious experiences over the last two centuries," the figure of good in *Die Zauberflöte* "is

never blotted out." He admits, however, that "almost every scene mixes tolerance with the annihilation of the enemy, the idea of equality with misogyny, wisdom with ignorant rumors"; *Autonomy and Mercy: Reflections on Mozart's
Operas,* trans. Marion Faber and Ivan Nagel (Cambridge, Mass., 1991), 23.

16. Ignaz von Seyfried reported in a letter to Georg Friedrich Treitschke,
"On the evening of 4 December M. lay delirious, imagining he was attending
Die Zauberflöte in the Theater auf der Wieden; almost his last words, which he
whispered to his wife, were, 'Quiet, quiet! Hofer is just taking her top F;—now
my sister-in-law is singing her second aria, "Der Hölle Rache"; how strongly she
strikes and holds the B-flat: "Hört! hört! hört! der Mutter Schwur!"'— "; letter
from Seyfried to Treitschke, Vienna, 1840 (?), in Otto Deutsch, *Mozart: A Documentary Biography,* trans. Eric Blom, Peter Branscombe, and Jeremy Noble
(Stanford, 1966), 556.

17. Solomon, *Mozart: A Life* (New York, 1995), 516.

18. Abbate, *In Search of Opera,* 88.

19. The original printed libretto reads "dies tief betrübte Mutterherz."

20. Abbate, *In Search of Opera,* 88. See also chapter 5 of this book.

21. See, for instance, Oberon's aria (1.7.7) in Paul Wranitsky's singspiel of
1789 entitled *Oberon, König der Elfen* (vol. 4: 1–2 of *Die Oper,* eds. Christoph-
Hellmut Mahling and Joachim Veit [Munich, 1992]), which Schikaneder commissioned for his theater. Wranitsky wrote the role of Oberon for Josepha
Hofer, Mozart's sister-in-law, who would also be the first Queen of the Night.
The different natures of these two roles—Oberon is benevolent and helpful to
the story's young hero—testifies to the dramatic flexibility of the more extravagant coloratura style: contrary to what many writers have argued, the choice of
musical style was as much related to a particular singer as to any dramatic sig-
nification. In fact, Wranitsky also exploited the outstanding range of bass singer
Herr Gerl—the future Sarastro—in the role of Almansor, who rants like an
Osmin about the vengeance he will inflict on the young lady who refuses him.

22. Though not as high in range as the Queen of the Night arias, "Martern
aller Arten" calls for a vocalist of great power and finesse; one passage, for example, calls for the singer to hold a high C for one measure, rest for three beats,
and return directly to the perilous note for another three bars accompanied only
by a solo string/wind quartet. All of these elements showed off the skills of Catarina Cavalieri, who originated the role. Likewise, Mozart tailored the Queen of
the Night's two spectacular arias to the formidable vocal abilities of Josepha
Hofer. Carl Ditters von Dittersdorf exceeded the formidable range and en-
durance required by the Queen of the Night's arias with a number from his *Die
Liebe in Narrenhaus* (No. 3, "O wie wollt' ich Dich belohnen"). One coloratura
passage in this aria extends over fourteen measures and exceeds the daunting
range of the Queen of the Night's arias by a whole tone. Mozart satirized the
popular trend toward extreme vocal flashiness in his one-act singspiel *Die
Schauspieldirektor,* in which the sopranos Madame Silberklang and Madame
Herz engage in a duel of vocal gymnastics.

23. Probably the most famous textual reference to "Tod und Verzweiflung"
occurs in the duet No. 11, "Bewahret euch vor Weibertücken," wherein the two
priests warn Initiates and candidates against succumbing to female wiles, for the

man who forgets this primary duty will be rewarded with "death and despair" (2.3). Though the First Priest's melodic setting of these words does not resemble the motive at measures 8–10 in "Der Hölle Rache," it does bear some rhythmic and melodic similarity to measures 5–6, the Queen's first mention of "Tod und Verweiflung." Curiously, Mozart quoted the First Priest's phrase—"Tod und Verzweiflung war sein Lohn"—in a letter (11 June 1791) to his wife Constanze, but seemingly as a playful inside joke in what is an unexceptional, though sweet, letter: "Wonderful to relate, I have got back my watch—but—as I have no key, I have unfortunately not been able to wind it. What a nuisance! Schlumbla! That is a word to ponder on. Well, I wound *our big clock* instead. Adieu—my love! I am lunching today with Puchberg. I kiss you a thousand times and say with you in thought: 'Death and despair were his reward!' Ever your loving husband, W. A. Mozart"; Emily Anderson, ed. and trans., *The Letters of Mozart and His Family* (New York, 1989), no. 599, 953–54.

24. In his film version of the opera (1974), Ingmar Bergman expanded the Queen's forces with many extras.

25. Edmund Burke, *The Philosophical Enquiry into the Origin of Our Ideas on the Sublime and Beautiful*, ed. Adam Phillips (Oxford, 1998), 103.

26. Immanuel Kant, *Observations on the Feeling of the Beautiful and Sublime*, trans. John T. Goldthwait (Berkeley, 2003), 48, 51.

27. Kant stresses the general importance of these categories to gender identity, advising that "all judgements of the two sexes must refer to these criteria, those that praise as well as those that blame; all education and instruction must have these before its eyes" (ibid., 76–77).

28. Ibid., 47.

29. Abbate, *In Search of Opera*, 93–94.

30. Paul Mattick, *Art in Its Time: Theory and Practices of Modern Aesthetics* (London, 2003), 65.

31. Ibid.

32. Ibid., 60–61.

33. Mozart become an Apprentice Mason of this lodge on 14 December 1784, and achieved the highest degree, Master Mason, in 1785.

34. Solomon, *Mozart: A Life*, 514.

35. Volkmar Braunbehrens, *Mozart in Vienna, 1781–1791*, trans. Timothy Bell (New York, 1989), 259.

36. Nagel, *Autonomy and Mercy*, 71. Nagel goes on to describe how this revolutionary logic functioned in the *Terreur*, when those who broke with the party, "that heir to the Order of Light," were consequently expelled "into nothingness." In this way, "death on the guillotine was not the consequence but the verification of an annulment that virtually had already been carried out by the apostate victims themselves."

37. Daniel Heartz discusses the numerous dramatic and musical correspondences between these two works and, more specifically, between the two male protagonists, Emperor Titus and Sarastro, in his chapter "La Clemenza di Sarastro: Masonic Beneficence in the Last Operas," in *Mozart's Operas* (Berkeley, 1990), 255–75. Heartz, too, describes the paradox of Sarastro, who is a "spiritual" ruler yet "reigns over his flock with at least as much temporal might as the

prince-archbishop of Salzburg, whose absolute power Mozart experienced personally, to his great dismay" (271–72).

38. Act 2, scene 3. Titus's statement appears in the last scene of act 3 in Metastasio's original libretto (*La Clemenza di Tito,* 1734).

39. Act 2, scene 12.

40. Joachim Kaiser, *Who's Who in Mozart's Operas: From Alfonso to Zerlina,* trans. Charles Kessler (New York, 1987), 152–53.

CHAPTER 5

1. Tamino's mother is not even mentioned in the opera; his contact with the Queen is too brief to involve any deep feeling or loyalty.

2. Sarastro states that the gods have decreed that Pamina and Tamino shall be joined in marriage, and he suggests that the Queen would not have allowed the pair to be united, but, of course, it is the Queen herself who first promises Pamina to Tamino.

3. Jean-Victor Hocquard, *Les Opéras de Mozart* (Paris, 1995), 718–19.

4. Nicholas Till, *Mozart and the Enlightenment: Truth, Virtue, and Beauty in Mozart's Operas* (New York, 1993), 285–86.

5. Ivan Nagel, *Autonomy and Mercy: Reflections on Mozart's Operas,* trans. Marion Faber and Ivan Nagel (Cambridge, Mass., 1991), 19–20.

6. The mother figure is, in fact, a rare presence in fairy tales and comic opera in general. Many books from the eighteenth century—such as Samuel Richardson's *Pamela* and *Clarissa*—also emphasize the preeminence of the father in determining a daughter's fortune.

7. Brigid Brophy, *Mozart the Dramatist: The Value of His Operas to Him, to His Age, and to Us* (New York, 1988), 162–63.

8. See chapter 4 of this book.

9. Gretchen Wheelock has investigated the association between the minor mode and femininity, particularly in Mozart operas, in which nearly all of the minor-key arias are written for female characters. The key of G minor seems to have been Mozart's "grief" key, as he used it on several occasions to express sentiments related to grieving, separation, and death; see Wheelock, " '*Schwarze Gredel*' in Mozart's Operas: Tonal Hierarchy and the Engendered Minor Mode," in *Musicology and Difference,* ed. Ruth Solie (Berkeley, 1993). As already discussed in the previous chapter, "Ach ich fühl's" shows the "acoustic genealogy" that binds mother and daughter.

10. Both Ilia's "Padre, germani, addio! and Constanze's "Traurigkeit Ward mir zum Lose"—much longer pieces than "Ach ich fühl's"—have only one melodic descending diminished seventh. Nor is this melodic interval particularly common in Mozart's arias in D minor; neither Anna's and Ottavio's duet, "Che giuramento, oh Dei" from *Don Giovanni,* nor Elettra's aria "Tutto nel cor vi sento" from *Idomeneo* use it.

11. Mozart uses a similar melodic gesture at the end of Constanze's "Traurigkeit" in *Die Entführung aus dem Serail.*

12. Catherine Clément, *Opera, or the Undoing of Women,* trans. Betsy Wing (Minneapolis, 1988), 47.

13. Jacques Chailley, The Magic Flute *Unveiled: Esoteric Symbolism in Mozart's Masonic Opera,* trans. Herbert Weinstock (Rochester, 1992), 103–4.

14. Evidence suggests that Masons in eighteenth-century Vienna were largely skeptical about the idea of women participating in the Craft. Paul Nettl, for example, cites Christoph Wieland—whose collection of stories, *Dschinnistan,* may have been a source for *Die Zauberflöte*—who wrote in 1785 that "as far as women were concerned, Freemasons were willing to open their hearts but not their lodges"; *Mozart and Masonry* (New York, 1957), 78–79.

15. Chailley, The Magic Flute *Unveiled,* 152–53.

16. Peter Branscombe, *W. A. Mozart: Die Zauberflöte* (Cambridge, 1991), 217.

17. The Three Boys—embodying the transition between treble femininity and latent manhood—are described as both *"schön"* ("beautiful" or "handsome") and *"weise"* ("wise"). Likewise, Tamino is characterized (by the Three Ladies) as *"schön,"* but this is only while he is still in the Queen's land and before he really becomes "ein Mann." Pamina never calls Tamino *"schön."*

18. In "O Isis und Osiris" the priests refer to the spirit of wisdom being given to the "new pair," but this refers to Tamino and Papageno, not Pamina. Just before the choral prayer, Sarastro specifically tells the Speaker to teach "them" by his wisdom. The Speaker goes directly to Tamino and Papageno; in the course of the opera, he has no contact with Pamina.

19. Jules Speller, *Mozarts Zauberflöte: Eine kritische Auseinandersetzung um ihre Deutung* (Oldenburg, 1998), 64.

20. Chailley, The Magic Flute *Unveiled,* 151–52.

21. Ibid., 153.

22. Till, *Mozart and the Enlightenment,* 288.

23. Clément, *Opera, or the Undoing of Women,* 76–77.

24. In addition to Bergman's film, which focuses on the little girl in the audience, translated stage productions and *Die Zauberflöte* merchandise directed at young people and their families have become very popular. The front flap of Anne Gatti's picture book *The Magic Flute,* with lovely illustrations by Peter Malone, advertises that youngsters "will thrill as Prince Tamino rescues Princess Pamina from the Wicked Queen of the Night." One of the "Classical Kids" CD series, "Mozart's Magic Fantasy" (Children's Group, No. 84237, 2005), combines story ideas and music from *Die Zauberflöte* with an imaginary episode from Mozart's life (focusing on Mozart's relationship to his son, Karl) and the adventure of a young girl who is transported through magic into a production of the opera.

25. All translations of Beethoven's letters have been taken from Emily Anderson, ed., *The Letters of Beethoven,* 3 vols. (London, 1961). This particular extract comes from a letter to Antonie Brentano dated 6 February 1816; Anderson, II, no. 607.

26. Maynard Solomon, *Mozart: A Life* (New York, 1995), 235.

27. Anderson, ed., *The Letters of Beethoven* II, no. 644 (28 July 1816).

28. Ibid., no. 835 (1 November 1817).

29. Ibid., no. 654 (6 September 1816).

30. Solomon, *Mozart: A Life,* 233.

31. Beethoven's own claims to nobility were unquestioned until 1818, yet even when this pretense was exposed, he appealed successfully for a testimonial from Archduke Rudolph.

32. Solomon, *Mozart: A Life,* 372.

CHAPTER 6

1. Noteworthy examples include the Loge de Juste, founded in The Hague in 1751 by the Grand Master of the Netherlands, Juste Gerard, baron von Wassernaer; the Order of Mopses; and the Egyptian Freemasonry lodges set up in France by the adventurer Cagliostro.

2. Members of the mixed Loge de Juste appear to have turned up in Vienna and had close relations with city officials in the 1750s and 1760s; see Margaret C. Jacob, *Living the Enlightenment: Freemasonry and Politics in Eighteenth-Century Europe* (New York, 1991), 135. H. C. Robbins Landon states that there were no women's lodges in Vienna, and that Masonry itself ceased to exist in Austria by 1794; see *1791: Mozart's Last Year* (New York, 1988), 127, 136. Jacob, however, leaves the question open, specifically citing the content of *Die Zauberflöte* as a reaction to such lodges, whether they existed in Vienna itself or only in other Masonic communities throughout Europe.

3. Jacques Chailley, The Magic Flute *Unveiled: Esoteric Symbolism in Mozart's Masonic Opera,* trans. (Rochester, NY, 1992), 110.

4. Ibid., 111.

5. Jacob, *Living the Enlightenment,* 127.

6. Mary Ann Clawson, *Constructing Brotherhood: Class, Gender, and Fraternalism* (Princeton, 1989), 11.

7. Jacob remarks, for instance, that "the lodges of adoption proved so controversial that in one hostile fantasy brothers first queried 'profanes' on their attitude toward these mixed lodges, as part of the process for admission to a lodge"; *Living the Enlightenment,* 140.

8. The *LMO* facsimile prints the first phrase as a question ("Ich sollte fort?"), which makes more rhetorical sense. Though the *NMA* generally offers the most definitive representation of the opera's text, the punctuation is often notably different from the facsimile and, to my mind, sometimes muddles the dramatic and rhetorical effect.

9. Chailley points out that although silver is the traditional "feminine" metal, the padlock that the Ladies use is made of "masculine" gold, which is nevertheless wielded by the Queen and her Ladies.

10. Clawson, *Constructing Brotherhood,* 46.

11. Ibid., 47–48.

12. A celebrated scientist, author, and civil servant, and a member of the Order of the Illuminati, Born was elected Master of the Viennese lodge Zur wahren Eintracht (True Harmony) in 1782. Haydn was among the lodge's illustrious members. For more information on the relationship between Born's essay and the libretto for *Die Zauberflöte,* see Peter Branscombe, *W. A. Mozart: Die Zauberflöte* (Cambridge, 1991), 20–25.

13. Judith A. Eckelmeyer, *The Cultural Context of Mozart's* Magic Flute: *Social, Aesthetic, Philosophical,* trans. Renata Cinti, vol. 2 (Lewiston, NY, 1991), 309.

14. Ibid., 389.

15. Ibid., 394–95.

16. The original printed libretto reads "verworfne Pöbel," or "rejected rabble."

17. Brigid Brophy, *Mozart the Dramatist: The Value of His Operas to Him, to His Age, and to Us* (New York, 1988), 203.

18. Erik Smith, "The Music," in W. A. *Mozart: Die Zauberflöte,* ed. Peter Branscombe (Cambridge, 1991), 130.

19. Jacob, *Living the Enlightenment,* 121–22.

20. Ibid., 123.

21. Ibid., 124.

22. Quoted in Clawson, *Constructing Brotherhood,* 191.

23. Ibid., 193.

24. Ibid., 207.

25. I noted with interest, for example, the name change in 2003 of the Ms. Foundation's "Take Our Daughters to Work Day" to "Take our Daughters and Sons to Work Day." The web site for this program explains that the Ms. Foundation wanted "to broaden the discussion about the competing challenges of work and family. For girls to achieve their full potential, whether it is in the home, workplace, or community, boys also must be encouraged to reach their potential by participating fully in family, work, and community" (http://www.daughtersandsonstowork.org/wmspage.cfm?parm1 = 443#different).

26. Membership to the Order of the Eastern Star continues to be restricted, however, to women with specific relationships (related by blood or by marriage) to Masons and to Masons themselves.

27. Jacob, *Living the Enlightenment,* 123.

28. Peter Branscombe, *W. A. Mozart: Die Zauberflöte* (Cambridge, 1991), 2.

CHAPTER 7

1. Brigid Brophy, *Mozart the Dramatist: The Value of His Operas to Him, to His Age, and to Us* (New York, 1988), 113.

2. Ibid.

3. Wye Jamison Allanbrook, *Rhythmic Gesture in Mozart:* Le Nozze di Figaro *and* Don Giovanni (Chicago, 1983), 74.

4. Ibid., 74–75.

5. Beaumarchais originally crafted *Le barbier de Séville* as a comic opera in 1772, but the Opéra comique refused to produce it. The first version of the play—in five acts—was presented on 23 February 1775, but was coolly received; three days later, the playwright offered a revised version in four acts, which enjoyed great success.

6. In the opera's list of *personaggi* she is described only as "Orphan, Ward of Bartolo, Lover of Lindoro."

7. Daniel Heartz, *Mozart's Operas* (Berkeley, 1990), 111.

8. Opera tended to be much more conservative in this regard than the literary sphere, and especially more than English literature. Samuel Richardson's title character in *Pamela,* for instance, was not a noble when she married Mr. B—this was plainly one of the main points of the novel—but Goldoni made her so in his operatic adaptation. Richardson's moral concentrates on Mr. B's heightened sensitivity, which allows him to recognize Pamela's "noble" virtue: after his bad behavior, he comes to embrace her undeniable good (thus the subtitle, "Virtue rewarded"). Goldoni changed the ending chiefly for political reasons—Venice had a strict law against nobles marrying commoners—but his opera was certainly not alone in reinforcing social stratification.

9. Volkmar Braunbehrens, *Mozart in Vienna, 1781–1791,* trans. Timothy Bell (New York, 1989), 280.

10. Wolfgang Hildesheimer, *Mozart,* trans. Marion Faber (New York, 1982), 185.

11. Stefan Kunze, *Mozarts Opern* (Stuttgart, 1984), 245.

12. Hunter, "Rousseau, the Countess, and the Female Domain," in *Mozart Studies 2* (Oxford, 1997), 2–3.

13. James Webster, "The Analysis of Mozart's Arias," in *Mozart Studies* (Oxford, 1991), 152.

14. Michael Zwiebach, "Marriage of Wits: Comic Archetypes and the Staging of Ideas in Five Comic Operas of Giovanni Paisiello," Ph.D. diss., University of California, 2000, 130.

15. The dialogue between Rosina and Figaro in this scene brings to mind a similar one in *Die Zauberflöte* between Pamina and Papageno: an agent comes to the young woman as romantic intermediary and coconspirator in her rescue, telling the young woman about the man who loves her and describing her with a list of pleasing attributes.

16. Mary Hunter, The *Culture of Opera Buffa in Mozart's Vienna: A Poetics of Entertainment* (Princeton, 1999), 84–85.

17. William D. Howarth, *Beaumarchais and the Theatre* (London, 1995), 145.

18. The word that Beaumarchais uses here is *aimable,* which is often translated as "kind" or "likeable," but which has a more particular meaning here, suggesting the elegance and fashionableness of a courtier.

19. This exchange is found in act 1, scene 9 of the opera.

20. Zwiebach, "Marriage of Wits," 129.

21. He elaborates, "In the duet 'Dunque io son . . . tu non m'inganni?' we are offered the portrait, not of a girl of eighteen, but rather of some good-looking woman, perhaps twenty-six years of age, ardent in temperament and more than a little inclined to flirtation, debating with a confidant upon the ways and means to grant an assignation to a man who has caught her fancy. I refuse to believe that . . . the love of such a creature as Rosina should be so utterly devoid of the slightest suggestion of melancholy, or even, I might dare to add, of certain finer shades of fastidiousness and hesitation. . . . [E]ven the most passionate of loves cannot thrive without a touch of modesty, and to strip it of this essential element is to fall into the vulgar error, common to sensual and unre-

fined persons in every land, of thinking all women alike." Stendhal [Henry Beyle], *Life of Rossini,* trans. Richard N. Coe (New York, 1957), 183–84.

22. Edward Dent, *Mozart's Operas: A Critical Study,* 2nd ed. (New York, 1991), 99.

23. Spike Hughes, *Famous Mozart Operas: An Analytical Guide for the opera-goer and armchair listener* (New York, 1972), 58.

24. Heartz, *Mozart's Operas,* 112.

25. Ibid.

26. Howarth, *Beaumarchais and the Theatre,* 165.

27. There is an aural affinity between the Countess and the pageboy, but it is quite subtle; despite their very different moods, Cherubino's "Non so più" and the Countess's "Porgi amor" use the same orchestration and are both in E-flat major. Tim Carter's quotations are from *W. A. Mozart: Le nozze di Figaro* (Cambridge, 1987), 46–47.

28. Hunter, "Rousseau," 15.

29. Allanbrook, *Rhythmic Gesture in Mozart,* 100.

30. Hunter, "Rousseau," 21.

31. Ibid., 15. Hunter notes the success of this strategy—having the Countess appeal to the audience before "intensify[ing] her emotional position in the imbroglio"—depends on the eighteenth-century ideal of a woman's special domain of influence. In "Porgi amor," the Countess realizes Rousseau's formulation for proper womanhood, which "consists in a sort of conscious artifice, in a constant awareness of the opposite sex, and in behavior calculated to manipulate the feelings of others without their recognizing the nature of the manipulation; in other words, as a perpetual performance to an ever-present audience" (19).

32. Ibid., 11.

33. Heartz, *Mozart's Operas,* 120.

34. Ibid., 120.

35. Tim Carter, *W. A. Mozart,* 48.

36. Ibid., 47.

37. Hunter, "Rousseau," 20–21.

38. Carter, *W. A. Mozart,* 112.

39. Playing with the erotic connotations of the aria, Webster goes so far as to say that most of the aria "is 'about' the Countess's need for and eventual achievement of [high G], which she avoids." Later, he contrasts the Countess's "difficulty" with what appears to be a musically multiorgasmic Cherubino, who "repeatedly attains his structural high point" of G above the staff (*Analysis of Mozart's Arias,* 166, 175).

40. Daniel Pool, *What Jane Austin Ate and Charles Dickens Knew* (New York, 1993), 227.

41. Frits Noske, *The Signifier and the Signified: Studies in the Operas of Mozart and Verdi* (The Hague, 1977), 21.

42. Ibid., 25.

43. Allanbrook, *Rhythmic Gesture in Mozart,* 104.

44. Heartz, *Mozart's Operas,* 147.

45. Allanbrook, *Rhythmic Gesture in Mozart,* 76–77.

46. Ibid., 146.

47. Heartz, *Mozart's Operas*, 152.

48. Letter from Mozart to his father (26 September 1781), in Emily Anderson, ed. and trans., *The Letters of Mozart and his Family*, no. 426 (New York, 1989), 769.

49. For an excellent summary of the manuscript copies, printed scores, and the autograph score for this number, see Alan Tyson, *Mozart: Studies of the Autograph Scores* (Cambridge, Mass., 1987).

50. Heartz notes the parallels between the discarded rondo (set in E-flat major) and Rosina's "Giusto ciel," suggesting that these similarities may have also played a part in Mozart's ultimate decision to discard the rondo; *Mozart's Operas*, 151–52.

51. *The Shawshank Redemption*, DVD (Turner Home Entertainment, 1999), ASIN: B00000399WI.

52. Robert Moberly, *Three Mozart Operas:* Figaro, Don Giovanni, Magic Flute (New York, 1968), 118.

CHAPTER 8

1. In the preceding scene Beaumarchais even offers a hint of a possible reconciliation when Figaro, quoting Voltaire, slyly asks Marceline, "If one does not love, does it mean one must hate?"

2. Wye Jamison Allanbrook, *Rhythmic Gesture in Mozart:* Le Nozze di Figaro *and* Don Giovanni (Chicago, 1983), 113–14.

3. J. B. Ratermanis and W. R. Irwin, *The Comic Style of Beaumarchais* (Seattle, 1961), 54.

4. Ibid., 79–80.

5. Pierre-Augustin Caron de Beaumarchais, *The Barber of Seville / The Marriage of Figaro*, trans. John Wood (London, 1964), 31–32.

6. Francine Levy, *Le Mariage de Figaro: essai d'interprétation*, vol. 173 of *Studies on Voltaire and the Eighteenth Century*, ed. Haydn Mason (Oxford, 1978), 61.

7. Spike Hughes, *Famous Mozart Operas: An Analytical Guide for the opera-goer and armchair listener* (New York, 1972), 73.

8. Allanbrook, *Rhythmic Gesture in Mozart*, 160. Noting that "rigid parallelism is rarely a feature of Classical 'symmetry,' because it weakens a sense of period," Allanbrook argues for the retention of both arias, since unlike the ensembles that "function as secondary climaxes," the succession of solo arias in act 4 "has the advantage of throwing the weight of the final act on the finale itself; the resolution of the imbroglio has the more impact for not following close on the dazzle of a full-blown ensemble." She also points to "hard evidence" of the aria's dramatic significance, asserting that Marcellina's aria (along with Basilio's) forms "an important preface to Figaro's angry soliloquy 'Aprite un po' quegl'occhi.'"

9. Ibid., 163. As Allanbrook explains, Marcellina's quoting pastoral poetry places her in company with Cherubino, who with his schoolboy quoting from Dante and pastoral poetry in acts 1 and 2 introduced the image of the circle of *donne* into the opera. Marcellina's conversion ensures our comprehension of the

importance of this image; when Figaro defects she is delightedly engaged in coming over, and in this aria she gives the pastoral her bluestocking blessing.

10. Ibid.

11. Robert Moberly, *Three Mozart Operas:* Figaro, Don Giovanni, Magic Flute (New York, 1968), 127.

12. The aria's text paraphrases canto 5, stanza 1, from *Orlando furioso.*

13. Both Fanchette and Barbarina were originally played by young girls; for the premiere of *Le nozze di Figaro,* twelve-year-old Anna Gottlieb sang the role of Barbarina.

14. Edward Dent, *Mozart's Operas: A Critical Study* (New York, 1991), 112.

15. The first part of the duet between the Count and Susanna in act 3, "Crudel, perchè finora farmi languir così?" is in A minor, highlighting the Count's "languishing" for the pretty maidservant.

16. Allanbrook notes the pastoral rhythm (a recurrent element in the opera) and points out a few similarities between "L'ho perduto" and the Countess's "Dove sono," including the augmented-sixth half cadence at the end of the number. She remarks that the girl probably learned this cadential formula "from the Countess, who moves into 'Dove sono' from the previous *recitativo accompagnato* by one very much like it" (158). But Marcellina's "Il capro e la capretta" offers an arguably closer match to Barbarina's plaintive half cadence. The Countess unleashes her wretchedness in a highly dramatic cascading melody that exploits the affective weight of a 6–5 appoggiatura (C–B) and an augmented second (D-sharp–C) over an "Italian" augmented-sixth chord; Marcellina and Barbarina use far more modest—and almost identical—formulas: a tritone leap downward resolving up a half step. The small differences between these two complementary cadences (the notes sustained for possible improvised ornamentation and the voicing of the supporting augmented-sixth chord) no doubt reflect the relative abilities of the two singers.

CHAPTER 9

1. Some of Mozart's operas—mostly early works—include siblings, but none of these feature two sisters. Brother and sister pairings include Fracasso and Rosina *(La finta semplice)*, Lucio Silla and Celia *(Lucio Silla)*, and Sesto and Servilia *(La Clemenza di Tito).* In *Mitridate, Rè di Ponto,* Sifare and Farnace are both sons of King Mitridate.

2. Bruce Alan Brown, *W. A. Mozart: Così fan tutte* (Cambridge, 1995), 3.

3. Ibid., 85.

4. Ibid., 56.

5. Mary Hunter, *The Culture of Opera Buffa in Mozart's Vienna: A Poetics of Entertainment* (Princeton, 1999), 296.

6. Andrew Steptoe, *The Mozart Da Ponte Operas: The Cultural and Musical Background to* Le Nozze di Figaro, Don Giovanni, *and* Così fan tutte (Oxford, 1988), 229.

7. William Mann, *The Operas of Mozart* (New York, 1977), 563.

8. Daniel Heartz, *Mozart's Operas* (Berkeley, 1990), 217, 222. Of course, the fact that Mozart chose the main title rather late in the process does not lessen

its predominance, particularly since he gives the motto "così fan tutte" a distinct musical identity that appears in both the overture and the act 2 trio, "Tutti accusan le donne."

9. Link in Stanley Sadie, *Wolfgang Amadè Mozart: Essays on His Life and His Music* (Oxford, 1996), 371–72.

10. Metastasio's original quote comes from *Demetrio* (1.8) and has a more egalitarian slant: "And the faith of lovers is like the Arabian phoenix. That it exists, everyone agrees; where it is, no one knows."

11. Nicholas Till, *Mozart and the Enlightenment: Truth, Virtue, and Beauty in Mozart's Operas* (New York, 1993), 237.

12. Ibid.

13. Hunter, *Culture of Opera Buffa*, 283.

14. Heartz remarks that, like their male counterparts, Fiordiligi and Dorabella begin the opera as nearly identical (*Mozart's Operas*, 222). Likewise, Brown reads the final section of the duet where the sisters switch parts ("Amore mi faccia penar") as an "implicit demonstration of their interchangeability" (*W. A. Mozart*, 29). In a John Eliot Gardiner production of *Così* (DVD: Archiv Production, 2002), the sopranos singing the roles of Fiordiligi and Dorabella actually take over short excerpts of each other's arias.

15. Till, *Mozart and the Enlightenment*, 254.

16. For an excellent introduction to Ferrarese del Bene, see Patricia Lewy Gidwitz, "Mozart's Fiordiligi: Adriana Ferrarese del Bene," *Cambridge Opera Journal* 8 (November 1996): 199–214.

17. John Gregory, *A Father's Legacy to his Daughters*, quoted in Vivien Jones, ed., *Women in the Eighteenth Century: Constructions of Femininity* (London, 1990), 53.

18. J. [John] Burton, *Lectures on Female Education and Manners*, vol. 1 (London, 1793; reprint, New York, 1970), 188.

19. Mary and R. L. Edgeworth, *Practical Education*, vol. 2 (London, 1801; reprint, New York, 1996), 105.

20. Ibid., 51.

21. Brown, *W. A. Mozart*, 29.

22. For an analysis of the connections between this trio and other zephyr music of the *buffa* stage, see Heartz, *Mozart's Operas*, 230–31.

23. Hunter, *Culture of Opera Buffa*, 287–88.

24. Ibid., 293.

25. Heartz, *Mozart's Operas*, 247–48.

26. Ibid., 248.

27. Brown explains that Alfonso's aria was derived from other "stammering" arias in *Il barbiere di Siviglia* and *Una cosa rara*, noting that its "well-known precedents" would have helped audiences understand it as "rehearsed" (*W. A. Mozart*, 137, 139).

28. Pity was generally regarded in the eighteenth century as something natural to women. The encyclopedist Le Roi, for instance, commented that "women's stronger inclination to self-love and pleasure-seeking" were "balanced . . . by their more deeply felt pity." Terry Smiley Dock, *Woman in the Encyclopédie: A Compendium* (Madrid, 1983), 74.

29. Till, *Mozart and the Enlightenment*, 244.

30. Dock quotes the anonymous author of the *Encyclopédie*'s article on maternity, who concludes that "Everything indicates that woman is more delicate than man, and consequently, more sensitive; that is why she is more susceptible to the strongest passions, but she does not retain them as long as man does." Relating this changeable nature to women and education, Deshamis, in his article "Woman," deduces that "Women have scarcely any but mixed, intermediary, or variable characters, either because education alters their nature more than ours, or because the delicacy of their constitution makes their soul a mirror that receives all objects, reflects them sharply, and does not retain a one of them" (Dock, *Woman in the* Encyclopédie, 74, 101).

31. For a more detailed analysis of this scene, see chapter 10.

32. Till, *Mozart and the Enlightenment*, 247.

33. Ibid. Rousseau himself considered a wife's reputation to be an essential counterpart of, not a substitute for, actual virtue. In *Emile* he writes that "it is not enough that they be estimable; they must be esteemed," for women's "honor is not only in their conduct but in their reputation" (Jean-Jacques Rousseau, *Emile, or On Education*, trans. Allan Bloom [New York, 1979], 264). He then asserts that "when a man acts well, he depends only on himself and can brave public opinion; but when a woman acts well, she had accomplished only half of her task, and what is thought of her is no less important to her than what she actually is." Rousseau also charges that a wife's infidelity is much worse than a husband's since she "in giving the man children which are not his, she betrays both," but he does not explore, of course, the possible relationship between the two types of infidelity (ibid., 261).

34. Brown, in *W. A. Mozart*, referring to Elizabeth M. Dunstan's unpublished manuscript "Da Ponte and Arioso." He also points out Fiordiligi's connection with another example of constancy, Bradamante, who gives a speech that clearly inspired Da Ponte's text for "Come scoglio" (ibid., 64–65).

35. The libretto states in act 1, scene 2 that Fiordiligi and Dorabella "gaze at a portrait that hangs at their side" ("che guardano un ritratto che lor pende al fianco").

36. Rousseau, *Emile*, 359.

37. Burton, *Lectures on Female Education*, 212.

38. Quoted in Jones, *Women in the Eighteenth Century*, 29–30.

39. Ibid., 30.

40. Heartz also sees a connection between "Come scoglio" and Idamante's "Non ho colpo" from *Idomeneo*. The two arias open with a similar melodic gesture, and both are set in the key of B-flat major, move from an opening maestoso tempo to an allegro section, and employ nearly identical orchestration.

41. The age of the women is not indicated in the libretto, but one can guess from the way in which the other characters speak about them that they are not very old.

42. Brown suggests that "Mozart undermines [Fiordiligi's] utterances by expanding her vocal leaps to the point of parody—of Ferrarese herself (who was known for her wide range), and of a recent opera by Salieri in which she had displayed this gift" (*W. A. Mozart*, 35).

43. The relationship between the two arias may challenge notions about what makes "Come scoglio" ironic. Brown, for instance, categorizes the repeated notes on the words "scoglio" and "resta" as satirical as they "demand to be sung as prosodic appoggiaturas, according to late eighteenth-century practice" (129). But this same repeated-note phrase ending appears in both "Or sai chi l'onore" and Idamantes' purely *seria* "Non ho colpa"; moreover, as with all such repeated-note endings, the singer would have had the prerogative to sing them as appoggiaturas.

44. Till, *Mozart and the Enlightenment*, 249.

45. Both Heartz and Brown point out that Fiordiligi's "Tu vuoi tormi la pace" ("You want to steal my peace") is set to the same music as the words "intatto fede" ("intact faith") from the recitative preceding "Come scoglio."

46. Till, *Mozart and the Enlightenment*, 250.

47. Hunter, *Culture of Opera Buffa*, 282.

48. Brown, *W. A. Mozart*, 46.

49. Till, *Mozart and the Enlightenment*, 250.

50. Rousseau, *Emile*, 359.

51. Ibid., 360.

52. Joseph Kerman, *Opera as Drama* (Berkeley, 1988), 97.

53. Helen Evans Misenheimer, *Rousseau on the Education of Women* (Washington, D.C., 1981), 74.

54. Ibid.

55. Ibid., 82. Da Ponte's mistress at the time of the opera's premiere was the original Fiordiligi herself, Adriana Ferrarese del Bene; he did not marry himself until 1792, when he was already forty-three years old. His *Memoires* are full of accounts of his rakish exploits; indeed, when he did marry, he kept it secret from his friend Casanova for some time.

56. Brown finds a precedent for Alfonso's reasoning in *Orlando furioso*, where "Iocondo and Astolfo, after suffering untold torments on account of their wives' infidelities, rationally decided that since 'both are as virtuous as the best, / Let us return and live with them at rest' " (*W. A. Mozart*, 56).

57. Russell made his remarks about Aristotle's erroneous presumption in an article, "Science as a Product of Western Europe," published in *The Listener*, vol. 39 (1948), 865–66. I came across this reference in a fascinating book, Alison Gopnik, Andrew N. Meltzoff, and Patricia K. Kuhl, *The Scientist in the Crib: What Early Learning Tells Us About the Mind* (New York, 1999), 14.

58. Brown, *W. A. Mozart*, 85.

59. Misenheimer, *Rousseau on the Education of Women*, 84.

CHAPTER 10

1. Bruce Alan Brown suggests the Ariostan origins of Despina's name (*W. A. Mozart: Così fan tutte* [Cambridge, 1995], 65).

2. Canto 25: 32.

3. Canto 25: 67.

4. The original libretto inserted the indentation for the aria proper at "Di pasta simile."

5. Mary Hunter, *The Culture of Opera Buffa in Mozart's Vienna: A Poetics of Entertainment* (Princeton, 1999), 127.

6. Ibid.

7. A similar mixture of *grazioso* delicacy and sexual innuendo can be found in Zerlina's "Vedrai carino."

8. Brown, W. A. *Mozart*, 22–23.

9. Hunter, *Culture of Opera Buffa*, 277.

10. Ibid.

11. Edmund J. Goehring, "Despina, Cupid, and the Pastoral Mode of *Così fan tutte*," *Cambridge Opera Journal* 7 (1995): 119–20.

12. Ibid., 120, n. 36.

Works Cited

Abbate, Carolyn. *In Search of Opera*. Princeton Studies in Opera. Princeton, NJ: Princeton University Press, 2001.

———. *Unsung Voices: Opera and Musical Narrative in the Nineteenth Century*. Princeton, NJ: Princeton University Press, 1991.

Abert, Hermann. *Mozart's Don Giovanni*. Translated by Peter Gellhorn. London: Eulenburg Books, 1976.

Allanbrook, Wye Jamison. *Rhythmic Gesture in Mozart:* Le Nozze di Figaro *and* Don Giovanni. Chicago: Chicago University Press, 1983.

Allanbrook, Wye Jamison, Mary Hunter, and Gretchen A. Wheelock. "Staging Mozart's Women." In *Siren Songs,* edited by Mary Ann Smart. Princeton, NJ: Princeton University Press, 2000.Anderson, Emily, trans. *The Letters of Beethoven*. 3 vols. London: Macmillan, 1961.

Anderson, Emily, trans. *The Letters of Mozart and His Family*. New York: W. W. Norton, 1989.

Ariosto, Ludovico. *Orlando furioso*. Edited by Emilio Bigi. Milan: Rusconi, 1982.

Auden, W. H., and Charles Kallman. *The Complete Works of W. H. Auden: Libretti and Other Dramatic Writings, 1939–1973*. Edward Mendelson, ed. Princeton: Princeton University Press, 1993.

Beaumarchais, Pierre-Augustin Caron de. *The Barber of Seville / The Marriage of Figaro*. Introduction and translation by John Wood. London: Penguin Group, 1964.

———. *Le mariage de Figaro: Édition critique de la version scénique originale*. Edited by Gérard Kahn. Oxford: Voltaire Foundation, 2002.

Besch, Anthony. "A Director's Approach." In *W. A. Mozart: Die Zauberflöte*, edited by Peter Branscombe. Cambridge Opera Handbooks. Cambridge: Cambridge University Press, 1991.

Booth, Wayne C. *The Company We Keep: An Ethics of Fiction.* Berkeley: University of California Press, 1988.

Branscombe, Peter. *W. A. Mozart: Die Zauberflöte.* Cambridge Opera Handbooks. Cambridge: Cambridge University Press, 1991.

Braunbehrens, Volkmar. *Mozart in Vienna, 1781–1791.* Translated by Timothy Bell. New York: Grove Weidenfeld, 1989.

Brophy, Brigid. *Mozart the Dramatist: The Value of His Operas to Him, to His Age, and to Us.* 1964. Reprint, New York: Da Capo Paperbacks, 1988.

Brown, Bruce Alan. *W. A. Mozart: Così fan tutte.* Cambridge Opera Handbooks. Cambridge: Cambridge University Press, 1995.

Burke, Edmund. *The Philosophical Inquiry into the Origin of Our Ideas on the Sublime and Beautiful.* Edited with introduction and notes by Adam Philips. Oxford: Oxford University Press, 1998.

Burton, J. [John]. *Lectures on Female Education and Manners.* 2 vols. 1793. Reprint, New York: Source Press Books, 1970.

Carter, Tim. *W. A. Mozart: Le nozze di Figaro.* Cambridge Opera Handbooks. Cambridge: Cambridge University Press, 1987.

Castelvecchi, Stefano. "From *Nina* to *Nina*: Psychodrama, Absorption, and Sentiment in the 1780s." *Cambridge Opera Journal* 8 (July 1996): 91–112.

Chailley, Jacques. The Magic Flute *Unveiled: Esoteric Symbolism in Mozart's Masonic Opera.* Translated by Herbert Weinstock. Rochester, NY: Inner Traditions International, 1992.

Clawson, Mary Ann. *Constructing Brotherhood: Class, Gender, and Fraternalism.* Princeton, NJ: Princeton University Press, 1989.

Clément, Catherine. *Opera, or the Undoing of Women.* Translated by Betsy Wing, foreword by Susan McClary. Minneapolis: University of Minnesota Press, 1988.

Dent, Edward. *Mozart's Operas: A Critical Study.* 2nd edition, London, 1941. Reprint with foreword by Winton Dean, New York: Oxford University Press, 1991.

Deutsch, Otto Erich. *Mozart: A Documentary Biography.* Translated by Eric Blom, Peter Branscombe, and Jeremy Noble. Stanford: Stanford University Press, 1966.

Dock, Terry Smiley. *Woman in the* Encyclopédie: *A Compendium.* Madrid: J. Porrúa Turanzas, 1983.

Eckelmeyer, Judith A. *The Cultural Context of Mozart's* Magic Flute: *Social, Aesthetic, Philosophical.* 2 vols. Translated by Renata Cinti. Lewiston, NY: E. Mellon Press, 1991.

Edgeworth, Mary, and R. L. Edgeworth. *Practical Education.* 3 vols. Original published 2nd edition. London: J. Crowder, 1801. Reprint, 3 vols., New York: Woodstock Books, 1996.

Einstein, Alfred. *Mozart: His Character, His Work.* Oxford: Oxford University Press, 1962.

Ford, Charles. *Così? Sexual Politics in Mozart's Operas.* Manchester: Manchester University Press, 1991.

Gatti, Anne. *The Magic Flute,* illustrated by Peter Malone. San Francisco: Chronicle Books, 1997.

Gidwitz, Patricia Lewy. "Mozart's Fiordiligi: Adriana Ferrarese del Bene." *Cambridge Opera Journal* 8 (November 1996): 199–214.

———. "Vocal Profiles of Four Mozart Sopranos." Ph.D. diss., University of California, Berkeley, 1991.

Goerhring, Edmund J. "Despina, Cupid, and the Pastoral Mode of *Così fan tutte.*" *Cambridge Opera Journal* 7 (1995): 107–33.

Goldoni, Carlo. *Tutte le opere di Carlo Goldoni.* Edited by Giuseppe Ortolani. 14 vols. Milan: Arnold Mondadori Editore, 1935–56.

Gopnick, Alison, Andrew N. Meltzoff, and Patricia K. Kuhl. *The Scientist in the Crib: What Early Learning Tells Us About the Mind.* New York: William Morrow & Co., 1999).

Heartz, Daniel. *Mozart's Operas.* Berkeley: University of California Press, 1990.

Hildesheimer, Wolfgang. *Mozart.* Translated by Marion Faber. New York: Farrar Straus Giroux, 1982.

Hocquard, Jean-Victor. *Les Opéras de Mozart.* Paris: Les Belles Lettres, 1995.

Hoffmann, E. T. A. *Don Juan.* In *Hoffmanns Werke,* edited and introduction by Gerhard Schneider. Nationalen Forschungs- und Gedenkstätten der Klassischen Deutschen Literatur in Weimar. 3 vols. Berlin: Aufbau-Verlag, 1990.

Howarth, William D. *Beaumarchais and the Theatre.* London: Routledge, 1995.

Hughes, Spike. *Famous Mozart Operas: An Analytical Guide for the operagoer and armchair listener.* 1957. Reprint, New York: Dover Publications, 1972.

Hunter, Mary. *The Culture of Opera Buffa in Mozart's Vienna: A Poetics of Entertainment.* Princeton: Princeton University Press, 1999.

———. "Rousseau, the Countess, and the Female Domain." In *Mozart Studies* 2. Oxford: Clarendon Press, 1997.

———. "Some Representations of *Opera Seria* in *Opera Buffa.*" *Cambridge Opera Journal* 3 (July 1991): 89–108.

———. "Window to the Work, or Mirror of Our Preconceptions? Peter Sellars's Production of *Così fan tutte.*"*repercussions* 4 (Fall 1995): 42–58.

Jacob, Margaret C. *Living the Enlightenment: Freemasonry and Politics in Eighteenth-Century Europe.* New York: Oxford University Press, 1991.

Jones, Vivien, ed. *Women in the Eighteenth Century: Constructions of Femininity.* London: Routledge, 1990.

Kaiser, Joachim. *Who's Who in Mozart's Operas: From Alfonso to Zerlina.* Translated by Charles Kessler. New York: Schirmer Books, 1987.

Kant, Immanuel. *Observations on the Feeling of the Beautiful and Sublime.* Translated by John T. Goldthwait. 2nd paperback edition. Berkeley: University of California Press, 2003.

Kaplan, Sydney Janet. "Varieties of Feminist Criticism." In *Making a Difference: Feminist Literary Criticism,* edited by Gayle Greene and Coppélia Kahn. New York: Methuen & Co., 1985.

Kerman, Joseph. *Opera as Drama.* Revised edition with preface. Berkeley: University of California Press, 1988.

————. "Reading *Don Giovanni*." In *The* Don Giovanni *Book: Myths of Betrayal and Seduction,* edited by Jonathan Miller. London: Faber and Faber, 1990.

Kierkegaard, Søren. *Either/Or: A Fragment of Life.* 2 vols. Revised and with a foreword by Howard A. Johnson. Translated by David F. Swenson and Lillian Martin Swenson. Reprint. Princeton, NJ: Princeton University Press, 1959.

Kunze, Stefan. *Don Giovanni vor Mozart: Die Tradition der Don-Giovanni-Opern im Italienische Buffa-Theater des 18. Jahrhunderts.* Munich: Wilhelm Fink Verlag, 1972.

————. *Mozarts Opern.* Stuttgart: Reclam, 1984.

Landon, H. C. Robbins. *1791: Mozart's Last Year.* New York: Schirmer Books, 1988.

Levy, Francine. *Le Mariage de Figaro: essai d'interprétation. Studies on Voltaire and the Eighteenth Century.* Vol. 173. Edited by Haydn Mason. Oxford: Voltaire Foundation at the Taylor Institution, 1978.

Lipking, Lawrence. "Donna Abbandonata." In *The* Don Giovanni *Book: Myths of Seduction and Betrayal,* edited by Jonathan Miller. London: Faber and Faber, 1990.

Mann, William. *The Operas of Mozart.* New York: Oxford University Press, 1977.

Mattick, Paul. *Art in Its Time: Theory and Practices of Modern Aesthetics.* London: Routledge, 2003.

Miller, Jane. *Seductions: Studies in Reading and Culture.* Cambridge, Mass.: Harvard University Press, 1991.

Misenheimer, Helen Evans. *Rousseau on the Education of Women.* Washington, D.C.: University Press of America, 1981.

Moberly, Robert. *Three Mozart Operas:* Figaro, Don Giovanni, Magic Flute. New York: Dodd, Mead & Co., 1968.

Molière, Jean-Baptiste Poquelin de. *Œuvres Complètes.* Edited and with a commentary by Jean Meyer. 9 vols. Paris: Maurice Gonon, 1968.

Molina, Tirso de. *Obras.* Edited by Américo Castro. Vol. 2 of Clàsicos Castellanos. Madrid: Ediciones de "La Lectura," 1910.

Nagel, Ivan. *Autonomy and Mercy: Reflections on Mozart's Operas.* Translated by Marion Faber and Ivan Nagel. Cambridge, Mass.: Harvard University Press, 1991.

Nettl, Paul. *Mozart and Masonry.* New York: Dorset Press, 1957.

Noske, Frits. *The Signifier and the Signified: Studies in the Operas of Mozart and Verdi.* The Hague: Martinus Nijhoff, 1977.

Pool, Daniel. *What Jane Austin Ate and Charles Dickens Knew.* New York: Simon and Schuster, 1993.

Ratermanis, J. B., and W. R. Irwin. *The Comic Style of Beaumarchais.* Seattle: University of Washington Press, 1961.

Ratner, Leonard. *Classic Music: Expression, Form, and Style.* New York: Schirmer Books, 1980.

Rosenberg, Alfons. *Die Zauberflöte.* Munich: Prestel, 1964.

Rousseau, Jean-Jacques. *Emile, or On Education*. Introduction, translation, and notes by Allan Bloom. New York: Basic Books, 1979.

Rushton, Julian. *W. A. Mozart: Don Giovanni*. Cambridge Opera Handbooks. Cambridge: Cambridge University Press, 1981.

Russell, Charles M. *The Don Juan Legend before Mozart, with a Collection of Eighteenth-Century Librettos*. Ann Arbor: University of Michigan Press, 1993.

Sadie, Stanley. *Wolfgang Amadè Mozart: Essays on His Life and His Music*. Oxford: Clarendon Press, 1996.

Smith Erik. "The Music." In *W. A. Mozart: Die Zauberflöte*, edited by Peter Branscombe. Cambridge Opera Handbooks. Cambridge: Cambridge University Press, 1991.

Solomon, Maynard. *Mozart: A Life*. New York: Harper Collins, 1995.

Speller, Jules. *Mozarts* Zauberflöte: *Eine kritische Auseinandersetzung um ihre Deutung*. Oldenburg: Igel Verlag, 1998.

Stendhal, [Henry Beyle]. *Life of Rossini*. Translated by Richard N. Coe. New York: Criterion Books, 1957.

Steptoe, Andrew. *The Mozart Da Ponte Operas: The Cultural and Musical Background to* Le Nozze di Figaro, Don Giovanni, *and* Così fan tutte. Oxford: Clarendon Press, 1988.

Subotnik, Rose. *Deconstructive Variations: Music and Reason in Western Society*. Minneapolis: University of Minnesota Press, 1996.

Taruskin, Richard. *Text and Act: Essays on Music and Performance*. New York: Oxford University Press, 1995.

Till, Nicholas. *Mozart and the Enlightenment: Truth, Virtue, and Beauty in Mozart's Operas*. New York: W. W. Norton & Company, 1993.

Tyson, Alan. *Mozart: Studies of the Autograph Scores*. Cambridge, Mass.: Harvard University Press: 1987.

Warburton, Ernest, ed. *The Librettos of Mozart's Operas*. 7 vols. New York: Garland Press, 1992.

Webster, James. "The Analysis of Mozart's Arias." In *Mozart Studies*. Oxford: Clarendon Press, 1991.

Wheelock, Gretchen. " 'Schwarze Gredel' in Mozart's Operas: Tonal Hierarchy and the Engendered Minor Mode." In *Musicology and Difference*, edited by Ruth Solie. Berkeley: University of California Press, 1993.

Wolfgang Amadeus Mozart: Neue Ausgabe sämtlicher Werke. Edited by the Internationale Stiftung Mozarteum Salzburg. Kassel: Bärenreiter, 1955. Opera volumes (series 2, work group 5):
Idomeneo, vol. 2: 1–2. Edited by Dan Heartz. 1972
Die Entführung aus dem Serail, vol. 12. Edited by Gerhard Croll. 1982.
Le nozze di Figaro, vol. 16: 1–2. Edited by Ludwig Finscher. 1973.
Don Giovanni, vol. 17. Edited by Wolfgang Plath and Wolfgang Rehm. 1968.
Così fan tutte, vol. 18. Edited by Faye Ferguson and Wolfgang Rehm. 1991.
Die Zauberflöte, vol. 19. Edited by Gernot Gruber and Alfred Orel. 1970.
La clemenza di Tito, vol. 20. Edited by Franz Giegling. 1970.

Wranitsky, Paul. *Oberon, König der Elfen.* Vol. 4: 1–2 of *Die Oper.* Edited by
    Christoph-Hellmut Mahling and Joachim Veit. Munich: Henle, 1992.
Zaslaw, Neal. *Mozart's Symphonies: Context, Performance, Practice, Recep-
    tion.* Reprint. New York: Oxford University Press, 2001.
Zwiebach, Michael. "Marriage of Wits: Comic Archetypes and the Staging of
    Ideas in Five Comic Operas of Giovanni Paisiello." Ph.D. diss., University of
    California, Berkeley, 2000.

Index